Creative Home Economics Instruction

Third Edition

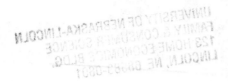

Contributing Authors

Ruth Browning, Ph.D.
Chairperson, Home Economics Education Department
College of Human Ecology and Health Sciences
Indiana University of Pennsylvania
Indiana, Pennsylvania

Merrilyn Cummings, Ph.D.
Professor and Director of Home Economics Teacher
Education
College of Agriculture and Home Economics
New Mexico State University
Las Cruces, New Mexico

Martha B. Frost, Ed.D.
Associate Professor
Center for Human Resources
State University of New York at Plattsburgh
Plattsburgh, New York

Patsy J. Hallman, Ph.D.
Professor, Department of Home Economics
School of Education
Stephen F. Austin State University
Nacogdoches, Texas

Joan M. Kelly, Ed.D.
Former Associate Professor
College of Home Economics
Texas Tech University
Lubbock, Texas

Mary Helen Mays, Ph.D., R.D.
Chair, Coordinate Program in Dietetics
Division of Health and Related Professions
The University of Texas — Pan American
Edinburg, Texas

Susan D. McLaughlin, M.P.A.
Director
Youth Service Bureau
Wallingford, Connecticut

Creative Home Economics Instruction

Third Edition

Valerie M. Chamberlain, Ph.D.
Professor
Home Economics Program and Home Economics Education
University of Vermont

GLENCOE

Macmillan/McGraw-Hill

Lake Forest, Illinois   Columbus, Ohio   Mission Hills, California   Peoria, Illinois

ABOUT THE AUTHOR

Valerie M. Chamberlain, Ph.D. and C.H.E., is a Professor of Home Economics Education at the University of Vermont and formerly held that rank at Texas Tech University. She has also been a faculty member at the Florida State University, the University of Hawaii, and junior and senior high schools in Vermont and Florida.

Dr. Chamberlain has received teaching awards at both the College and University levels. She received the distinguished faculty award given by the Vocational Home Economics Teachers Association of Texas. In 1990, she was presented a Leader Award given by the American Home Economics Association. In 1985, she was recognized by this organization as an outstanding author.

Dr. Chamberlain has authored over 100 articles in juried journals and other professional publications, conducted in-service workshops and seminars in 16 states, and given almost 100 presentations at state and national professional meetings. She has been involved in numerous funded research projects and graduate students' thesis and dissertation research.

Dr. Chamberlain is author of *Teen Guide* and the Teacher's Resource Guide that complements *Homes with Character.* She co-authored *Personal Skills for Home, School, and Work* and its accompanying Teacher's Resource Guide with Dr. Eddye Eubanks. Dr. Chamberlain also co-authored *Survival: A Guide to Living on Your Own* and its guide with Dr. Joan Kelly.

The author wishes to express appreciation to:

Dr. Camille Bell for her original research related to teaching skills.

Dr. Lyndon B. Carew, Dr. Roberta W. Walsh, and Professor Lynn M. Wilson for their ideas about cultural diversity related to food and nutrition, consumer studies and housing, and clothing and textiles, respectively.

Peggy Clark for the computer–generated graphics to illustrate family patterns.

Bobby Dennis for the sample discipline plan.

Dr. Carolyn Douglas Henderson for the Student Assumption of Responsibility Scale.

Dr. Susan Krals for case studies.

Dun-Donnelley Publishing Corporation for "Four of a Kind" by Valerie M. Chamberlain and Joan Kelly. Reproduced by special permission from *What's New in Home Economics.*

The University of Vermont for a sabbatical leave that provided time for the author to work on this third edition.

Send all inquiries to:
GLENCOE DIVISION
Macmillan/McGraw-Hill
3008 W. Willow Knolls Drive
Peoria, Illinois 61614

ISBN 0-02-676684-1

Printed in the United States of America

1 2 3 4 5 6 7 8 9   99 98 97 96 95 94 93 92 91

Contents

PART 1

Introduction to Instructional Strategies

Building the Home Economics Curriculum - A Continual Process

Chapter 1

Merrilyn Cummings, Ph.D.
Professor and Director of Home Economics
 Teacher Education
New Mexico State University

THE WHOLE ART OF TEACHING
IS ... THE ART OF AWAKENING
THE NATURAL CURIOSITY OF ... MINDS

Anatole France

Welcome to the world of home economics educators! The very fact that you have this book in front of you indicates that you are committed to helping others change their behaviors so that they will become more highly productive individuals and family members in a fast-paced, constantly changing world. You are obviously concerned that individuals reach their potentials,

and you are interested in doing that as a professional teacher. Your "teaching" will take place in many different settings. During the span of your professional career you will teach individuals, large groups, and small groups in a variety of locations from classrooms to offices to outdoor settings. Your teaching will take you across the life span as you work with children, adolescents, adults, and elders. You are limited only by your imagination and creativity as you enter the exciting world in which you will be facilitating learning. There is so much that home economics educators have to impart to others that will make this world a better place.

Cultivating teaching competence takes time and practice. For some of you, teaching is a brand new role; others of you have had opportunities to teach. Together we can share and grow. So let's get to work!

No matter what the setting or the age group, effective teaching is systematic and organized and begins with planning. This planning process will come alive and be more meaningful if you think of yourself in your teaching role as a constant decision maker, hypothesis tester, and experimenter. Teaching is a continual learning process for you, the teacher, as you experiment and then shape your future teaching based on past results. Last year's, week's, or hour's successes and shortcomings as a teacher will inspire new experiments which will yield future wisdom and continually make you a better educator. Good planning can enhance your strengths as a teacher and help you make appropriate decisions, test hypotheses positively, and experiment with new approaches and strategies successfully.

The Curriculum Development Process

We must remember that planning and curriculum development encompass much more than what is written on paper. The curriculum planning process is the sum total of all processes that are thought through, written down, implemented, and evaluated so as to achieve desired ends with a given audience. Curriculum development is an on-going, continual process. The diagram on page 9 depicts this process.

THE CURRICULUM DEVELOPMENT PROCESS

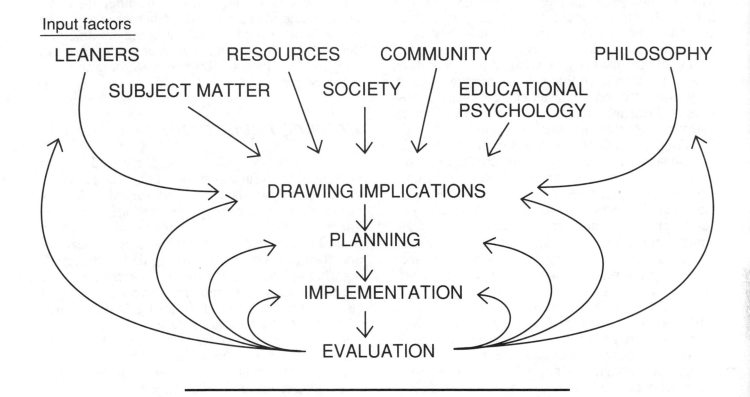

Input factors

LEANERS   RESOURCES   COMMUNITY   PHILOSOPHY

SUBJECT MATTER   SOCIETY   EDUCATIONAL PSYCHOLOGY

DRAWING IMPLICATIONS

↓

PLANNING

↓

IMPLEMENTATION

↓

EVALUATION

Gathering Input Data

So where do you begin? As a home economics educator, you are faced with an enormous responsibility in deciding what to teach and how to teach it. The learners sitting in front of you have so many needs, and you have so much to share with them. As in any good decision-making process, the first step is to gather input data on which to base teaching decisions regarding subject matter content, learner objectives, learning experiences, resources, and evaluation. Teaching decisions based on a solid foundation of accurate, current information will insure relevance in your teaching which, in turn, will generate interest among and motivate your learners.

An effective educator, therefore, starts out by gathering data for a set of input factors. The question then becomes "What do I need to know to make the best teaching decisions?" A good data base will consist, at a minimum, of information on the learners, the latest developments in the subject matter area(s), available resources, societal trends, community characteristics, basic principles of educational psychology, and identification of philosophies of individuals with whom you interact and for whom you work.

As teachers seek to know their audiences, they need to know the learners' demographics and backgrounds as well as their needs, interests, and goals. If teachers are challenged to expand the curiosity of their learners' minds, they must identify "which buttons to push." To accomplish this, teachers need to understand where learners have been and where they want to go. Information on family and life experiences, previous contacts with the subject matter, and future plans of the learners need to be assessed. You will also want to know the ability level, gender, age, socioeconomic, ethnic, and size characteristics of your audience. Gathering these data on your learners allows you to increase the relevance of your curriculum and the efficiency of your planning.

Effective home economics educators constantly keep themselves apprised of the latest developments in the many facets of the discipline. This is in and of itself a challenge as we try to stay on top of new developments in nutrition, textiles, family theory, child development, consumer education, housing, appliances, food science, management, clothing, and hospitality.

As teachers assess resources, they must look at the personal resources they bring to the teaching situation as well as the physical, material, financial, and other human resources available to them in the particular settings in which they work. Teachers today need to be creative in making limited resources go as far as possible. Tight budgets which result in limited supplies are a reality. Start to scan your environments, save all those odds and ends, and recycle. You will provide a role model for your learners while extending your resources. Assess your own personal energy levels and plan your days, weeks, and months so that you balance the demands on yourself and conserve your energy whenever possible. And remember to use all the unharnessed energy in the form of "student power" that is in front of you.

Trends in society, from the individual community to national and international scenes, need to be considered as teachers prepare learners for future interactions that will be impacted by events in all these arenas. Keeping abreast of political, social, cultural, and economic developments is a must for today's educator. In addition, community and state policies, mandates, standards, and attitudes affect teaching decisions. These must be continually assessed by teachers for potential impacts on the curriculum.

Much research has been conducted that shows certain behaviors on the part of teachers are more likely to facilitate learning. As educators we need to constantly reflect on the principles of educational psychology and analyze our teaching to insure their inclusion. Some examples of basic principles of educational psychology follow:
- Active learner involvement increases retention.
- Persons learn best that which is relevant to their immediate lives and future goals.
- Positive reinforcement speeds learning.
- Learning takes place best in a non-threatening, accepting environment.
- Learning that can be generalized is more readily used.
And the list goes on. Planning which is based on a review of and adherence to such principles will foster success.

The first philosophy that needs to be analyzed and integrated into your data base is your own personal philosophy of teaching and learning. You will want to stop and reflect on questions such as:
- What is the role of a teacher?
- What is learning?
- What is home economics?
Teachers need to gather information about the philosophies of others in their situations who impact their teaching decisions. Depending on the educational setting, some of these individuals may include administrators, co-workers, parents, and the learners themselves. The philosophies of these individuals may not always match yours, but an understanding of these differing points of view will make you a more effective decision maker as you build curriculum.

Gathering these data or pieces of input information can take place through a variety of means including talking with or interviewing people, observing, reading, surveying, and listening. Keep in mind that the information gathered to serve as the data base at any point in time is never fixed or final. Gathering new information and updating the information base is a continual, on-going daily process. This makes teaching an exciting challenge!

Drawing Implications

Once you have gathered a set of information about your situation, the next step is to reflect on and carefully analyze this information. This is the step which is identified in the diagram on page 9 as drawing implications. The teacher must look at and analyze what has been learned about the teaching environment and learners and start to make some teaching decisions regarding what this information means for teaching in the specific situation. In this process, the teacher is using an "If . . . . . , then . . . . ." mode of thinking. Some examples that illustrate this approach follow:
- *If* I know that the majority of the learners I am working with are from economically disadvantaged homes, *then* I need to limit the expectations I have for them regarding resources for class projects.
- *If* the teenage pregnancy rate is skyrocketing in my community, *then* I need to try to integrate teen pregnancy prevention information into as many of my courses and FHA/HERO projects as possible.
- *If* the school board does not want sex education – included in the curriculum, *then* my first task needs to be to convince them of the need for this type of education in the home economics curriculum.

The process of drawing implications is continual and ongoing. For each piece of information you collect, you start to draw implications in your mind. Much of this is a mental thinking process. As you gather a variety of input data, your implication drawing process will start to pull various pieces of information together, and you will start to draw implications that are a synthesis of your reflections on various pieces of information.

Planning

The next step in this process of curriculum development is the actual planning process. Your plans are your road maps. They assist you in moving your learners forward toward important goals that will improve the quality of their lives. Your ability to facilitate learning is directly related to how carefully you have used a solid base of input data and drawn implications. Sadly, some teachers try to start at this planning point in the curriculum development process. It should be very evident how shallow and out of touch a person's curriculum is likely to be if the teacher just sits down to plan and never takes time to gather input data and draw implications.

Planning will involve many different types of processes. Block plans for a whole year may be made so that you allocate appropriate amounts of time to various topics, then unit plans may be developed for the individual topics, and, finally, you will be making daily lesson plans. Sometimes instead of starting from scratch, you will be selecting portions of other curricula and personalizing them to fit your needs. We are all too busy to be reinventing the wheel. The resourceful teacher carefully picks and chooses portions of available curricula, adds new material, reworks portions, and shapes a new, up-to-date curriculum appropriate for the current situation.

Most plans consist of some basic components known as concepts, generalizations, objectives, learning experiences, resources, and evaluation techniques. Each of these components is addressed in depth in an appropriate part of this book.

Implementation

Once written plans are in place, you are ready to carry out or to implement these plans. In other words, you are ready to teach. As will be emphasized throughout this book, variety and learner involvement are critical for effective implementation. The implementation step consists of carrying out learning experiences and teaching methods through the use of a number of specific teaching skills.

Evaluation

Next comes the evaluation component in which you gather information from a variety of sources to determine your success, the success of your learners, and the success of your curriculum plan. This evaluation process will involve an honest appraisal of both the strengths and weaknesses of your program, your processes as an educator, and your product — the learner.

Some evaluative feedback will result from testing procedures, however, a tremendous amount of feedback will come from non-testing or informal means of evaluation. Dialogue with and/or written input from advisory council members, parents, administrators, former students, current learners, employers, business leaders, other teachers, and counselors will provide valuable information to help you redesign your curriculum for future use.

Using Feedback

But you are not done! The curriculum process has only just begun. Once you know what went well and what needs improvement, you are ready to feed that information back into the curriculum development process, where appropriate. A teacher may realize that data gathered as input were incomplete or inaccurate, or that the implications drawn were not on target, or that the plans were not as complete as they might have been, or that a skill was not as polished or a method as well orchestrated as possible. All this is simply the reality of teaching. No teacher is perfect; however, a growing, changing teacher continually strives to improve. This is possible when you put feedback to work. You make new decisions, try new experiments, and test new hypotheses the next time you teach. Imagine how stagnant and boring teaching would become if you neglected to follow the arrows at the bottom of the diagram on page 9 and use what you learned from the evaluation process. You would continually repeat your weaknesses instead of using them as stepping stones for growth, revision, and revitalization. You would be "stuck in a rut"!

Teaching is a process of constant, continual change. The dynamic, growing, exciting educator is one who follows this process and continually modifies, changes, and grows so that "each time around" is richer and more rewarding both for the teacher and the learners.

Concepts and Generalizations

Chapter 2

tions drawn will be used to help prioritize the subject matter. You will need to sift out the most important and relevant concepts for your audience. These concepts must then be organized into a meaningful structure.

One of the primary goals of home economics educators is to help students analyze and verbalize relationships among concepts. When students are helped in these processes, they are prepared to formulate their own generalizations that tie together various concepts. Having pulled together their own generalizations, students are ready to apply these ideas to daily problems and decisions in their lives. Learning becomes the development of a series of connections among concepts which hold real meaning and relevance for the learner.

Concepts

A concept is a key idea, topic, or main thought. It is what an individual thinks about a particular subject or topic. A concept consists of a core of abstract meanings the individual attaches to something. As depicted in the diagram on page 13, this core of meanings is enmeshed in feelings and emotions that an individual associates with it. Finally, words or symbols are used to communicate ideas or concepts.

Because background experiences are different, each student will attach different meanings to a particular idea or concept. Thus, each learner in front of you may have a different concept or core of meanings for any given idea. The meanings attached to a concept may be simple or complex depending on the numbers and types of experiences each learner has had. For example, when the question "What do you think of when I say food?" is asked of five-year-old children, the response may be: hot dogs, ice cream, cookies, lunch, eat. Foods that are particularly liked and simple concepts for which the children have a frame of reference will be identified. If secondary students are asked to do the same thing, the response may also include well-liked foods such as pizza and hamburgers. However, because older students' concepts of food are broader and more complex, they may identify nutrition, basic food groups, health, calories, diet, fun, party, and the like. On the other hand, if a dietitian were to talk about food, specific nutrients, dietary allowances, and quality control might be dis-

Planning curriculum is analogous to going on a guided tour. You have several options about how to get to your destination, but by planning your itinerary in advance, much time and confusion may be eliminated. Planning, though, does not preclude the possibility of making a side trip along the way, stopping somewhere while in route, using another means of transportation at the last minute, or being detained because something has happened over which you have no control. It is easiest to reach your goals if you plan how you will attain them and keep in mind that you need to be flexible as you work to achieve them.

Having laid the critical ground work through a thorough analysis of input data, you are ready to forge into the first step of planning which involves selecting and structuring the subject matter you will teach. The biggest frustration home economics educators face at this point is realizing there is much more content to be taught than the time frame usually allows. It is at this point that your analysis of input data and the implica-

cussed. The individuals described think of food differently because their cumulative experiences relating to it have been vastly different.

One of your first goals as a teacher needs to be to assess where your audience members are in terms of their concepts about the topics to be covered. You need to acknowledge that all persons will not enter nor will all exit your learning environment with identical concepts. You cannot teach someone your concept. Your goal is to build upon, embellish, and expand the core of meanings that arrives in the mind of each learner through a series of well-orchestrated learning experiences. In addition, you need to help learners clarify the feelings they attach to their concepts. There is no way to truly separate the cognitive and affective components of concepts. All experiences that have shaped the core of meanings for individuals have also surrounded those meanings with affect.

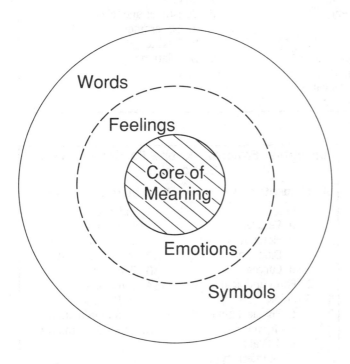

A Depiction of a Concept

In addition to recognizing that concepts vary from one individual to another, you need to remember that these ideas are constantly changing because of additional experiences that may be gained both inside and outside your learning environment. Concepts are never fixed or final. Concepts usually develop slowly because they build cumulatively through a variety of experiences in a variety of situations. Your classroom is one of these vital experiences.

Concepts change and grow not only for an individual, but also within a society. Therefore, an analysis of societal trends needs to precede concept selection for a curriculum. For example, at one time, the American family was thought of as a husband, a wife, and children. Today, families are recognized in many other contexts: one-parent families, couples without children, families without marriage, or people living in groups. For many, the concept of marriage has also changed.

When using the conceptual approach to teaching, skillful teachers will take advantage of opportunities to clarify and reinforce relevant and recurring concepts. For example, safety is a concept pertinent to home economics and might be included in such areas of study as child development, housing, food preparation, consumer education, clothing, and family living. Management, decision making, human relationships, art, and design are other examples of concepts that recur in a wide variety of home economics curricula. Concepts are clarified in a variety of contexts through successive experiences.

Developing a Conceptual Framework

As was noted in Chapter 1, a primary step in curriculum planning is to analyze the needs of the learners in a particular class, course, or program. This process will assist you in identifying the concepts to be included in your planning. Other student-related factors that you need to consider in selecting concepts are the family, socioeconomic, cultural, and academic backgrounds of the learners, as well as their interests, abilities, motivation levels, values, and goals. These factors are combined with input related to resources, philosophies, educational psychology, community and societal trends, and subject matter developments. Based on the implications drawn from your input data, you will prioritize, select, cluster, and sequence the concepts for your curriculum. A conceptual framework is the product that results from the organization of selected concepts into a logical system.

A conceptual framework may be developed for an entire curriculum, for a specific course, for a unit of study, or for one lesson. The major, main, or key concepts are identified first. Then the subconcepts under the major concepts are delineated. Scope is the term used to denote what concepts or subject matter topics are to be covered. These concepts are organized in a sequence corresponding to the order in which they will be included in the curriculum. Concepts are generally organized from known to unknown, from simple to complex, and from concrete to more abstract.

Conceptual Framework for Three Courses

A. Consumer Education I
1. Values
   a. How acquired
      1. Family
      2. Friends
      3. Community
      4. School
      5. Religious group
      6. Mass media
   b. Identification
   c. Changes
   d. Effects on consumer decisions
2. Goals
   a. Short-term
   b. Long-term
   c. Changes
   d. Effects on consumer decisions
3. Needs and wants
4. Managing resources
   a. Money
   b. Time
   c. Energy

B. Consumer Education II
1. Sources of consumer information
2. Buying guidelines
   a. Clothing
   b. Food
3. Labels
   a. Care
   b. Use
   c. Nutrition
   d. Unit price
   e. Open and pull dates
4. Warranties and guarantees
5. Types of marketplaces
6. Checking accounts
7. Credit
   a. Open-end
      1. Charge accounts
      2. Credit cards
   b. Closed-end loans
      1. Installment
      2. Passbook
8. Advertising
9. Fraudulent practices
   a. Referral schemes
   b. Fake gift certificates
   c. Bait-and-switch

C. Consumer Education III
1. Economics systems
2. Types of income
3. Buying
   a. Appliances
   b. Furnishings
   c. Housing
   d. Transportation
   e. Insurance
4. Renting
   a. Housing
   b. Equipment
5. Spending plans
6. Savings and lending institutions
   a. Commercial banks
   b. Savings and loan associations
   c. Credit unions
   d. U.S. government
7. Taxes
8. Consumer agencies
   a. Government
   b. Private
9. Legislation
10. Careers

The conceptual framework should provide enough detail for any person familiar with the subject matter to know what is to be covered. Concepts should be clearly and concisely stated. Nouns are the primary part of speech used in writing concepts; verbs and articles are not needed.

Conceptual frameworks show, at a glance, the development of concepts throughout an entire curriculum. The example of a conceptual framework, shown above, demonstrates one way in which concepts relating to consumer education could evolve throughout three courses.

The conceptual framework for a portion of a course, shown to the right, could be used in teaching art as it relates to housing or clothing for a senior high class. The major concepts are the elements of art and the principles of design. The elements are covered first because a basic understanding of them is necessary before the principles can be applied. Line is the first element to be studied because it is the easiest to comprehend and an understanding of it is necessary before form and shape can be explained. It would be difficult to cover the effects of colors or harmonies without having studied hue, value, and intensity first. There is a logical reason for the order, or sequence, of each of the concepts and subconcepts included.

Conceptual Framework for a Portion of a Course
Senior High

A. Elements of art
1. Line
   a. Vertical
   b. Horizontal
   c. Diagonal
   d. Curved
2. Form and shape
3. Color
   a. Physical qualities
      1. Hue
      2. Value
      3. Intensity
   b. Psychological and emotional effects
   c. Schemes or harmonies
      1. Monochromatic
      2. Complementary
      3. Analogous
      4. Triad
      5. Accented neutral
4. Texture
   a. Visual
   b. Tactile

B. Principles of design
1. Balance
   a. Formal
   b. Informal
2. Proportion and scale
3. Rhythm
4. Emphasis
   a. Dominance
   b. Subordination
5. Unity or harmony

The length of time that it would take to cover this conceptual framework could vary from several days to several weeks, depending on the background experiences, interests, and needs of the students. For some groups it would be feasible to cover each subconcept in depth and, perhaps, to add others; for other students whose needs are more immediate, it might be meaningless to do more than touch on the main points.

The scope of a conceptual framework will vary with the learners. For example, the lack of relevance for 7th graders of much of the senior high conceptual framework should be evident. The following modification might be more appropriate for students at this level. While the scope has been altered, appropriate sequencing has been maintained.

Conceptual Framework for a Portion of a Course 7th Grade

A. Elements of art
1. Line
   a. Types
   b. Effects
2. Shapes created by lines and space
3. Color
   a. Creation
   b. Color wheel
   c. Pleasant combinations
4. Texture
   a. Types
   b. Effects

B. Principles of design
1. Balance
   a. Types
   b. Uses
2. Scale
3. Centers of interest
   a. Importance
   b. Examples
4. Harmony
   a. Importance
   b. Examples

Developing Block Plans or Scope-and-Sequence Plans

Once you have outlined the topics to be covered in courses or portions of courses, you are ready to block out the conceptual framework by weeks and/or days to show which concepts will be covered in specific periods of time. When you put the concepts from your conceptual framework into designated time frames you are building what is known as a block plan or a scope-and-sequence plan.

Many teachers start by taking a calendar format, blocking out the number of weeks they have to teach the course, and writing down the major topic areas to be covered each week on this block. For instance, in an eighteen-week comprehensive course the teacher might block out three weeks for family living, two weeks for child development, five weeks for food and nutrition, three weeks for clothing, one week for housing, two weeks for career skills, and two weeks for consumer education. The teacher would write in these major content areas by weeks on the block or scope-and-sequence plan for the course. Then the teacher would go back and fill in the concepts within each major topic area that would be covered each day. For example, the teacher would take the three weeks for the family living section of the course and distribute the concepts included in the conceptual framework for family living across the fifteen days allocated to this content area. This process would be repeated for each subsequent major topic area.

A block or scope-and-sequence plan may be simple or complex, depending on whether just major concepts or both major concepts and subconcepts are included. A teacher's plan book is often used for making a simple

---

Block Plan or Scope-and-Sequence Plan for a Senior High Class

MONDAY
A. Elements of art
   1. Line
      a. Vertical
      b. Horizontal
      c. Diagonal
      d. Curved
   2. Form and shape

TUESDAY
   3. Color
      a. Physical qualities
         1. Hue
         2. Value
         3. Intensity
      b. Psychological and emotional effects

WEDNESDAY
   3. Color (cont'd)
      c. Schemes
         1. Monochromatic
         2. Complementary
         3. Analogous

THURSDAY
   3. Color (cont'd)
      c. Schemes
         4. Triad
         5. Accented neutral
   4. Texture
      a. Visual
      b. Tactile

FRIDAY
B. Principles of Design
   1. Balance
      a. Formal
      b. Informal
   2. Proportion and scale

MONDAY
   3. Rhythm
   4. Emphasis
      a. Dominance
      b. Subordination
   5. Unity or harmony

block plan. The block or scope-and-sequence plan on page 15 shows one way in which the art concepts previously identified in the conceptual framework for the senior high course could be covered in six days. In this case, major and subconcepts are included in the block or scope-and-sequence plan.

Once you have blocked out the concepts from the conceptual framework into a block or scope-and-sequence plan, you are ready to add additional components such as more subconcepts, behavioral objectives, learning experiences, resources, and key generalizations to this skeletal plan. When these additional components are added to the block or scope-and-sequence plan to give it more detail, the result is known as a unit plan. On pages 48-49 in Chapter 6 you will find an example of a unit plan with additional components included.

Lesson plans will be more detailed and include even more information such as daily objectives, content notes needed by the teacher when presenting the material, key questions to be discussed in class, student activities, and assignments. See Chapter 6, pages 50-52, for an example showing how a lesson plan can be developed from a unit plan.

Generalizations

A generalization is a statement that expresses a complete thought and underlying truth and also has an element of universality. This means that a generalization can be applied in a wide number of situations worldwide. Generalizations are the basic principles and understandings that describe or explain phenomena. They unify various aspects of a subject by showing the relationships among concepts.

There are three levels of generalizations. The first level may be a simple statement of fact, definition, description, analogy, identification, or classification. A second-level generalization shows relationships among ideas or makes comparisons. It may include more ideas than a first-level generalization and involves greater depth and scope of subject matter. A third-level generalization explains, justifies, interprets, or predicts. It may be more remote in time and space than a first- or second-level generalization. Examples of generalizations at the three levels follow:

Level 1: Milk is a food.
Level 2: Your health is affected by the foods you eat.
Level 3: Your body size is partially determined by the kind and quantity of food you consume.

The first example is a simple statement expressing a universal truth. The second shows that there is a relationship between health and food intake. The third example makes a subtle prediction by pointing out that the foods people consume affect their growth and physical maturation.

The level of generalization that students can be expected to formulate depends upon their previous personal and educational experiences, their innate intelligence, and the learning activities in which they engage. Some students may seldom go beyond the first level, while others find little difficulty in formulating third-level generalizations. On the other hand, students may reach only the first level in some subject-matter areas and the third level in others, depending upon their own background experiences, their familiarity with the subject matter, and the depth with which the content is treated in the educational setting. When planning lessons, however, it is generally advisable for teachers to try to help students form generalizations above the first level. At the first level, generalizations often become shallow statements of fact such as "Milk is nutritious." Such facts may be forgotten or become irrelevant in students' lives outside the classroom.

Formulating Generalizations

Usually, twenty to twenty-two words is the maximum number that can be used to formulate a generalization without making it too complex to have real meaning. A generalization expresses only one idea; therefore, it is inappropriate to use a colon or semicolons in writing one. Value judgments are also inappropriate. Consequently, words and phrases like these are *not* used: it is *vital* that ...; it is *important* to remember ...; one *must* ...; a person *should* ...; and, this *ought* to be done so that ...

The following phrases may be helpful in writing generalizations because they minimize the likelihood of making value judgments and facilitate making statements that show relationships:

is affected by	is subject to
is dependent on	may be associated with
is limited by	may be developed by
is promoted by	may be enhanced by
is related to	may be identified by
is the result of	may be necessary for
is an integral part of	may be modified by
is a product of	constitutes a pattern for
is influenced by	contributes to

Students should not be given generalizations but should be led to formulate their own. When students are given generalizations, they are denied the challenge and opportunity to think for themselves and to use higher-level thought processes. Teachers can guide students in developing appropriate generalizations more effectively when teachers themselves have written generalizations in advance. This preplanning necessitates that teachers clarify where they intend to lead their students. It is the teacher's responsibility to plan learning experiences and activities that help students arrive at generalizations that are meaningful to them and that are stated in their own words. Most students will not state generalizations as their teachers would, but through the skillful use of appropriate and probing questions, teachers can encourage students to formulate, clarify, and refine their own generalizations. Initially, students may be helped to generalize by being asked to answer questions such as the following:

• What have you learned from the lesson today?
• How can our discussion be summarized in a few sentences?
• What are the main ideas we have been talking about?
• How are the main ideas we have discussed related?
• How does today's discussion relate to what we studied yesterday?
• How can these ideas be applied to new or different situations?

Answering questions like these not only helps students summarize the material that has been covered, but also aids instructors in evaluating the effectiveness of their teaching. Since most of the disconnected facts that are "learned" by individuals are forgotten in a short time, students must be helped to formulate generalizations that can be used as guidelines in the future as well as the present. When students are able to develop generalizations showing the interrelationships among concepts, they are better prepared to transfer learning from one situation to another.

After the concepts to be included in the curriculum have been identified and developed into a conceptual framework that reflects appropriate scope and sequence and after generalizations have been formulated that link the major concepts and show the interrelatedness among them, the next step in curriculum planning is to develop the behavioral objectives the students will be expected to achieve. Learning experiences are then planned which enable students to meet these established objectives. Resources that are available and needed to accomplish the learning experiences must be planned concurrently with the learning experiences. Evaluating student achievement of the objectives is usually an ongoing and continuous process throughout the unit of study that may culminate at the end of the term in a final assessment or project. Each of these processes is discussed in the next few chapters.

Behavioral Objectives

Chapter 3

The terms *behavioral*, *performance*, and *instructional objectives* are often used synonymously. Behavior can be measured objectively because there is concrete evidence of achievement. In other words, the objectives describe or define what the learners have to do to demonstrate their attainment of the objectives. Since the anticipated results of instruction are clear, there is measurable evidence of the outcome of the educational process. Behavioral objectives are applicable to learners of all ages and backgrounds in a wide variety of situations: classroom students, on-the-job trainees, 4-H members, athletes, student pilots, management trainees, or anyone else for whom there is an expected level of performance.

Domains of Learning

Objectives are divided into three categories of learning called the cognitive, affective, and psychomotor domains. The cognitive domain is concerned with rational learning — knowing and thinking. Knowledge, use of the mind, and intellectual abilities are emphasized. The affective domain deals with emotional learning — caring and feeling. Attitudes, appreciations, interests, values, and adjustments are considered. The psychomotor domain relates to physical learning — doing and manipulating. Speed, accuracy, and dexterity are concerns in developing physical skills in this domain.

No subject-matter area of home economics pertains exclusively to one domain. Each area involves all three domains to some degree, although the study of nutrition and textiles is most closely associated with cognitive learning, family relationships and human development with the affective domain, and food preparation and clothing construction with psychomotor development. Remembering, understanding, relating, analyzing, synthesizing, and assessing nutritional knowledge are not enough. Students also need to develop an interest in, appreciation for, and positive attitude toward using their knowledge. In addition, students have to be able to prepare food so that it is nutritious. Certainly, one of the major purposes of teaching clothing construction is to help students develop skills. However, students also have to develop a desire to per-

In the past, educators formulated their goals in broad, general terms with lots of loopholes. For example, all home economics teachers wanted their students to "gain a greater appreciation of homemaking." However, "appreciation" is a difficult factor to measure objectively. Furthermore, if students are to be graded on their "greater appreciation of homemaking," surely many are astute enough to bluff and to give at least lip service to their "appreciation." How, then, can teachers appraise and assess the students' sincerity? What and how much constitutes a "greater appreciation"? The preceding does not mean that all home economics teachers should not work constantly and diligently to help students develop positive attitudes toward their subject matter and toward the roles of men and women as family members, as managers of their resources, and as homemakers. Instead, the illustration is used to show the inherent weakness in nebulous and vaguely stated objectives.

Recent trends in education emphasize objectives that specify the ultimate behavior expected of students.

form these skills carefully and accurately. Few garments can be made without a basic knowledge of grainlines, pattern symbols, and alteration techniques. All three domains must be considered when planning strategies for teaching each home economics subject-matter area, although for each content area one domain may be emphasized more than others.

Each domain is divided into a hierarchy of levels — from the simplest to the most complex. Most students have to achieve objectives at lower levels before they can accomplish those at higher levels. To attain objectives at each of the specified levels, students generally have had to master the skills of the preceding levels in consecutive order. It is unusual for students to skip levels by intuitively grasping the subject matter. Therefore, behavioral objectives relating to one concept are planned and written to conform to the hierarchies of the domains, and rarely is more than one level omitted in the sequence. Plans may call for student achievement below the highest possible level; in fact, objectives formulated for some content areas may specify achievement that reaches only the first, second, or third step in the hierarchy.

This is not meant to imply that younger students or those of lower ability cannot use higher thinking processes. Students in the primary grades analyze, synthesize, and evaluate in relation to simple concepts. Low-ability students may need to be encouraged to use higher thought processes. Teachers select less complicated content for them to study than that presented to other students. The levels of learning are applicable to all students regardless of age, innate intelligence, or environmental background.

Cognitive Domain

In all three domains of learning, concrete, objective, and measurable evidence is needed for proof of the students' achievement. In the cognitive domain, teachers can gather this evidence by having students identify facts, give examples, apply principles, analyze situations, plan solutions to problems, and evaluate results. According to Bloom in the *Taxonomy of Educational Objectives, Handbook I: Cognitive Domain*, there are six levels of learning in the cognitive domain.

■ *Knowledge: Recalling, Remembering, and Recognizing*

This level emphasizes facts, information, and specifics. It serves as the foundation, or base, upon which the others are built. It involves remembering material in a form very close to that in which it was originally encountered. It depends on memorizing or identifying facts. It may be thought of as the student's "file" of information that can be recalled or brought to mind later. Examples of activity at this level include reiterating the names of color harmonies that have been studied, stating rules for furniture arrangement that have been given previously, and matching cooking terms with their definitions.

Objectives at the knowledge level include the ability to:

cite	label	recite
define	list	reproduce
identify	name	state

■ *Comprehension: Understanding and Explaining*

This level is concerned with grasping the meaning and intent of material. It deals with content and involves the ability to understand what is being communicated. A reading-comprehension test, in which students read a section and then explain what it means, is an example.

Objectives at the comprehension level include the ability to:

convert	give examples	paraphrase
describe	illustrate	summarize
explain	interpret	tell in one's own words

■ *Application: Using Ideas*

Application involves using what is remembered and comprehended. It applies learning to life in new or concrete situations. It includes the ability to use knowledge and learned material in meaningful ways. It may involve applying principles and rules, choosing appropriate procedures, or selecting solutions to problems that are similar to those presented previously. The role of application in the cognitive domain is not to be confused with that of developing manipulative and purely physical skills in the psychomotor domain.

Objectives at the application level include the ability to:

apply	estimate	show
compute	prepare	solve
construct	relate	use
demonstrate		

■ *Analysis: Reasoning*

Analyzing involves breaking material into its constituent parts and determining the relationship of these parts to each other and to the whole. It may include identifying components, analyzing relationships among them, and looking at the principles involved in organization. It is taking one step, portion, or piece at a time to clarify the overall idea. Analyzing includes separating relevant material from trivia, distinguishing facts from hypotheses, and differentiating between objective data and value judgments. An example may include analyzing a floor plan for features such as possible furniture arrangements and groupings, traffic flow, placement of rooms to minimize noise and assure maximum privacy, and building costs.

Objectives at the analysis level include the ability to:

analyze	differentiate	outline
associate	discriminate	point out
determine	distinguish	

■ Synthesis: Creating

Synthesis is the ability to put parts and elements together into new forms. Ideas are organized into new patterns, and materials are put together in a structure that was not there before. Creativity and originality are emphasized. For example, in planning a unit of study for kindergarten-age children, it is necessary to consider everything that has been learned about child development, the subject matter to be taught, methods of teaching, media and materials, and ways of getting young children interested and motivated. Similarly, in designing a new toy it is necessary to synthesize knowledge concerning developmental levels of children, materials that might be used in making toys, and marketing techniques and procedures in order to create a toy that has never been produced before.

Objectives at the synthesis level include the ability to:

combine	devise	rearrange
compile	integrate	reorganize
compose	modify	revise
create	organize	rewrite
design	plan	write
develop	propose	

■ Evaluation: Making a Judgment

Evaluation is concerned with learners' abilities to judge the value of ideas, methods, materials, procedures, and solutions by developing or using appropriate criteria. The criteria are the yardsticks used in making a judgment. Examples include comparing and contrasting theories of child rearing, assessing the facilities and services offered in a home for senior citizens, and weighing the advantages and disadvantages, in given situations, of buying clothes versus making them.

It should be noted that there is some disagreement among educators about whether evaluation actually involves the most complex level of cognitive thinking. Some put it just below synthesis, making the latter the highest step in the cognitive domain. In either case, teachers should strive to include in their teaching strategies learning experiences that necessitate some student synthesizing and evaluating.

Objectives at the evaluation level include the ability to:

appraise	conclude	judge
assess	contrast	weigh
compare	evaluate	

Unfortunately, too often only the knowledge level in the cognitive domain is emphasized and evaluated. Students are taught facts and specifics and are then asked to repeat them in various ways. What purpose does this information serve if students do not understand it and cannot use it? Facts, per se, will be forgotten within a short time. Therefore, it is the obligation of every teacher to work toward higher levels of thinking and to build on the knowledge students attain.

Knowing certain facts is essential, but it is not enough. To illustrate, students need to acquire a basic knowledge and understanding of facts relating to nutrition before they can apply them in planning nutritious meals.

■ Cautions for Writing Cognitive Objectives

It is recognized that a behavioral verb suggested here to specify a certain level of learning can be used in a different context to indicate another learning level. If an objective states, "Compile a list of ... ," this activity may be at the synthesis level or the knowledge level, depending upon the way in which the rest of the behavioral objective is worded and how the subject matter is presented in class. "State in your own words ..." denotes the comprehension level because it involves explaining, which students can do only if they understand the material. However, "state" is more frequently used at the knowledge level in the sense of reiterating information or naming factors, such as "State the principal rule of storage." "Identify the solution ..." implies solving an application problem, even though the word "identify" is generally associated with the knowledge level. These examples illustrate that the behavioral words indicated for each level in the cognitive domain should serve as guidelines only. An objective can be at a level different from that which the lead verb suggests.

■ Sample Objectives in the Cognitive Domain

The following behavioral objectives relating to types of housing provide examples at the sequential levels in the cognitive domain.

KNOWLEDGE: *List* types of housing available in the local area.

COMPREHENSION: *Explain* the characteristics, advantages, and disadvantages of various types of housing available in the local area.

APPLICATION: *Compute* the cost of living in various types of housing in the local area.

ANALYSIS: *Analyze* given situations to determine types of housing desirable for meeting the needs and lifestyles of various individuals, families, and groups.

SYNTHESIS: *Plan* various types of housing to meet the needs of different people and kinds of families.

EVALUATION: *Evaluate* housing available in the local area for the various types of individuals, families, and groups that predominate in the community.

Obviously, students have to identify the different types of housing, such as mobile homes, duplexes, town houses, apartments, and condominiums, before they can describe the homes' characteristics or summarize their advantages and disadvantages. Likewise, students must understand the provisions of living in various types of housing before they can estimate costs and savings related to maintenance, utilities, insurance, and income tax deductions. Similarly, these factors need to be applied when determining types of housing that best meet certain peoples' needs. Each succeeding level is dependent upon satisfactory achievement of the lower level. Occasionally a level can be bypassed, but this should be done with caution. In the preceding example, students could evaluate available housing without having designed any. Plans for teaching do not necessarily have to include behavioral objectives that proceed to the highest level. In this instance, it is conceivable that in a comprehensive survey course, it would be feasible to include only the first two levels of objectives related to types of housing. In a course in which housing is studied in depth, all six levels would probably be included, with several objectives at some of the levels, particularly the lower ones.

Affective Domain

It is much easier to formulate objectives and evaluate accomplishments in the cognitive and psychomotor domains than in the affective domain. A student's interest, attitude, or appreciation can only be measured through observable action. This action, or evidence of learning, needs to be clearly specified, as it is in this behavioral objective: "Show interest in child development by voluntarily participating in a community-service project planned for children, by relating baby-sitting experiences, or by doing extra readings in this area."

According to the *Taxonomy of Educational Objectives*, five levels of the affective domain deal with emotional learning. These range from being aware of a particular phenomenon to developing a total philosophy.

■ Receiving: Attending and Becoming Aware

At this level, learners merely become aware of a situation, idea, or process. They notice and are willing to receive certain stimuli. Awareness is developed through the sensory organs. This level includes perceiving factors with discrimination and developing sensitivity, tolerance, and alertness. Teachers are concerned with getting, holding, and directing students' attention so that students will be willing to try certain behaviors.

Some behavioral tasks associated with receiving are to:

accept	show awareness
acknowledge	notice
be alert	pay attention
show alertness	perceive
be aware	tolerate

■ Responding: Doing Something About the Phenomenon

In addition to perceiving a particular situation, idea, or process in responding, the learners do something with or about it. Students may make the first overt responses in order to comply, but later make them willingly and with satisfaction. Responding involves developing a low level of commitment. At this level, students follow through with directions, select their own problems, and respond voluntarily when given alternatives. They are actively involved in the learning process.

Some words and phrases used to indicate responding are:

accept responsibility	consent
agree to	contribute
answer freely	cooperate
assist	follow
be interested	obey
show interest	participate willingly
be willing	read voluntarily
care for	respond
communicate	visit
comply	volunteer
conform	

■ Valuing: Developing Attitudes

Valuing means that learners accept the worth of an object, idea, belief, or behavior and also show a preference for it. They are consistent in responses concerning a particular issue and express opinions about it with conviction. In fact, they may give opinions publicly, whether they meet with approval or not. There is individual commitment to an underlying value that guides behavior. In other words, the person begins to prize and cherish the position chosen in relation to certain ideas and issues. In addition, at this level, behavior is consistent and stable enough to make students' values identifiable to others.

Because valuing relates to developing attitudes, some of the following words can be used to formulate objectives at this level:

adopt	express
assume responsibility	initiate
behave according to	prefer
choose	seek
commit	show concern
desire	show continuing
exhibit loyalty	desire to
	use resources to

■ Organization: Arranging Values Systematically

This level includes organizing values, determining interrelationships among them, and establishing a hierarchy of the dominant ones. Learners adapt their behavior to the value system they have selected. They also analyze evidence and form judgments about social responsibilities. Students may relate personal ethical standards to those expressed in biographies and fiction.

Since organization is arranging values in priority order, according to a system, some words that can be used to establish behavioral objectives at this level are:

adapt	classify	group
adjust	conceptualize	rank
arrange	disclose	reveal

■ Characterization: Internalizing a Set of Values

At the highest level of achievement in the affective domain, beliefs, ideas, and attitudes are integrated into a total philosophy of life, or world view. Characterization may be expressed as devotion to a cause. Values are internalized to such a degree that there are persistent and consistent responses in similar situations.

It is extremely difficult to measure achievement objectively at this level. However, some behaviors that may be associated with characterization follow:

act upon	influence
advocate	justify behavior
defend	maintain
display	serve
devote	support
exemplify	show consistent
exhibit	devotion to
expose	

■ Cautions for Writing Affective Objectives

If measures of attainment and evidences of achievement have not been preestablished and clearly specified, evaluation of objectives in the affective domain may become highly subjective. Evidence of achievement in the affective domain is sometimes measured by cognitive behavior. Some examples follow:

- Show interest in children's clothing by *pointing out* self-help features.
- Express concern about the depletion of energy resources by *writing* an article or *preparing* an oral report about how to get better gas mileage when driving a car.
- Exhibit loyalty to the school chapter of FHA/HERO by *organizing* a social for new members, by *writing* a code of ethics for officers, or by *proposing* a new installation service.

These affective objectives show that there may be alternative ways designated for measuring affective achievement. When attendance at a certain event is compulsory, when an assignment is required, or participation in an activity is mandatory, there is no behavioral evidence of affective achievement, change, or growth.

Affective objectives at the *receiving* and *responding* levels very often are indistinguishable from learning experiences. Learning experiences are the actual tasks and activities that enable students to achieve planned objectives. It is difficult to differentiate between the following as behavioral objectives or learning experiences:

- to *pay attention* to a demonstration
- to *care for* the plants in the department
- to *contribute* to a class discussion

Objectives at the knowledge and comprehension levels in the cognitive domain are often more appropriate than objectives at the receiving and responding levels in the affective domain. This is true because the intent of objectives at the receiving and responding levels is usually cognitive in nature. For example, in actuality, students pay attention to a filmstrip in order to cite, identify, or list certain facts or to repeat some cognitive information. When voluntarily answering questions, students are often giving examples, explaining, or summarizing in their own words. Therefore, cognitive objectives at the knowledge and comprehension levels might precede objectives at the valuing level more appropriately than would affective objectives at the receiving and responding levels.

■ *Sample Objectives in the Affective Domain*

There are two primary reasons for the difficulty in measuring achievement in the affective domain: the variables are intangible and evidences of attainment need to be predetermined. These evidences may be specified by using phrases such as these:

by volunteering to	by going to
as shown by	by listing
when participating in	by giving examples
as proved through	when doing
by deciding to	

The following examples of objectives relating to the guidance of children are appropriate for students enrolled in an occupational course in child-care services and illustrate the hierarchies in the affective domain:

RECEIVING: *Show* awareness of positive verbal-guidance techniques by noting examples shown in an appropriate film or videotape.

RESPONDING: *Follow* the guidelines established for positive verbal guidance when working with children under supervision in the school child-care laboratory.

VALUING: *Choose* positive rather than negative verbal guidance techniques when working independently with children in a child-care center.

ORGANIZATION: *Adapt* behavior, in a wide variety of situations, to reveal values congruent with positive and established principles of child development.

CHARACTERIZATION: *Exemplify* a philosophy of child development that consistently reflects devotion to causes contributing to the welfare and improvement of community conditions affecting all children.

These examples illustrate the increased complexity of objectives as higher levels are achieved. At the lower levels the teacher does more structuring than at the higher levels, where students become more self-directive.

Psychomotor Domain

Psychomotor learning is concerned with developing physical skills. Proficiency is sought in performing motor tasks. Speed, accuracy, manual dexterity, and economy of effort are important. Simpson, in the "Clas-sification of Educational Objectives, Psychomotor Domain," has identified five levels in this domain.

■ *Perception: Recognizing and Detecting Sensory Cues*

At this level, learners become aware, through the five senses, of objects, qualities, and procedures. In other words, sensory stimulation provides the basis for becoming aware of the action to be performed. Students observe so that they can recognize appropriate behavior and will be able to act accordingly. For example, the teacher may demonstrate kneading bread dough so that students can see and understand how it is done.

Some words that describe behaviors at this level are:

detect	perceive	taste
feel	recognize	view
hear	see	watch
listen	sense	
observe	smell	

■ *Set: Becoming Ready to Act*

Set is a mental, physical, or emotional readiness for a particular kind of action or experience and the willingness to respond to it. Being physically set involves assuming a body stance appropriate for doing a particular task. In learning how to pick up a heavy object, for example, students bend their knees and keep their backs straight to achieve the correct body posture to perform the act.

Some words that describe behavior at this level are:

achieve a posture	position the body
assume a body stance	sit
establish a body position	stand
place hands, arms, feet	station

■ *Guided Response: Imitating and Practicing*

This involves practicing the action under supervision through imitation or trial and error. Learners repeat one phase of a complex skill by doing it as it was demonstrated. In child development, the learner may repeat a finger-play exercise as illustrated. In food preparation, the student may practice making accurate measurements.

Some words that describe behavior at this level are:

copy	operate under
duplicate	supervision
imitate	practice
manipulate with	repeat
guidance	try

■ Mechanism: Increasing Efficiency

At this level, a learned response becomes habitual and is performed with some degree of skill and confidence. There is improved efficiency in performing the act. A student in a wage-earning program in home services may make a bed quickly, smoothly, and with a minimum expenditure of time and energy, using the "once- around" method.

Behavioral tasks include the ability to:

complete with confidence	increase speed
conduct	make
demonstrate	pace
execute	produce
improve efficiency	show dexterity

■ Complex Overt Response: Performing Automatically

Learners perform more complicated acts automatically, without hesitation, efficiently, and with a high degree of skill and self-sufficiency. They proceed with assurance, ease, and muscular control. Students may prepare and serve several meals, managing their resources effectively and using a variety of food-preparation techniques skillfully.

Some terms that describe behavior at this level are:

act habitually	manage
advance with assurance	master
control	organize
direct	perfect
excel	perform automatically
guide	proceed
maintain efficiency	

■ Cautions for Writing Psychomotor Objectives

Sometimes the application level in the cognitive domain is confused with psychomotor learning. Making a chart to show the characteristics of natural and synthetic fibers and their primary uses is a cognitive activity because it involves remembering, understanding, and applying information. The *only* physical skill involved is in drawing straight lines for the chart.

Psychomotor objectives at the *perception* level are often indistinguishable from learning experiences. For example, classroom learning experiences may consist of activities such as *feeling* the textures of different fabrics, *tasting* milk and cheese in a variety of forms, and *viewing* a film showing prenatal development. This situation is similar to the one that exists in attempting to write objectives at the receiving and responding levels

in the affective domain. Low-level cognitive objectives appropriately precede *set* in the psychomotor domain so that *perception*-level objectives are not needed.

■ Sample Objectives in the Psychomotor Domain

The following examples pertaining to clothing construction serve to illustrate progression through the levels of learning in the psychomotor domain.

PERCEPTION: *Detect* errors in the threading of a sewing machine after having watched a demonstration showing the correct procedure.

SET: *Assume* a body position at the sewing machine that minimizes fatigue.

GUIDED RESPONSE: *Practice* inserting a lapped zipper, using the step-by-step directions provided on the zipper folder.

MECHANISM: *Demonstrate* how to insert a lapped zipper quickly and efficiently without needing either written instructions or the teacher's help.

COMPLEX OVERT RESPONSE: *Proceed* skillfully through the steps in making a garment with a minimum amount of guidance and help from other people.

The words and phrases suggested for establishing behavioral objectives in all the domains are intended to serve only as guidelines. The context in which a verb is used can change the meanings and intents so that in actuality another level is indicated. For example, at the mechanism level, students could make a convenience-food product with skill, efficiency, and confidence, whereas at the complex overt-response level they might use a complicated recipe to make a quality food product, using appropriate procedures and efficient management techniques with assurance.

The context in which a behavioral term is used may indicate a domain that is different from that with which it is usually associated. To illustrate this, students could use rules in the cognitive sense of applying them, or they could use their resources to initiate policies in which they believe strongly and to which they are committed, or they could use acquired physical skills to perform a specified task.

Guidelines For Writing Behavioral Objectives

Although some teachers encourage their students to write objectives beginning with "The student should be able to...," the author of this book believes that such wording is contradictory to the basic premise of using the behavioral approach. How do teachers know if students are able to, unless they actually do? Consequently, it is more logical to begin objectives this way:

The students will:

> Name . . .
>
> Describe . . .
>
> Apply . . .

By using this format there is no need to precede every objective with "The students (or club members, or participants) will …" Instead, each objective can be worded concisely, beginning immediately with a behavioral verb that indicates exactly what the students are expected to do.

Behavioral objectives are written to include only one verb and only one idea or variable. It is better to write separate statements for each objective than to include too much in one. If an objective is stated "Identify and analyze …," students may be able to do the first part but not the second. Consequently, use only one verb in stating each objective and *never* use behavioral terms indicating different levels in formulating one objective.

An example of a *very poorly* written objective is: "Develop menus for nine consecutive days for children attending a camp for diabetics and for their nondiabetic counselors who need to lose at least ten pounds." There are two ideas expressed here, so there should be two objectives. One objective should pertain to diabetic diets and the other to weight-reduction diets. In addition, behavioral objectives are written without qualifying numbers. In this case, the number of days and the number of pounds should be omitted. Instead, this type of specificity may be included in the learning experiences that are planned to enable students to meet particular objectives. Improved behavioral objectives might be stated: "Plan appropriate menus for diabetic children" *and* "Develop a dietary plan for losing weight." Menu planning for diabetics should not be limited to camp situations, and there is no reason to restrict dietary planning for losing weight to camp counselors. Behavioral objectives are written in broader and more general terms.

When planning a unit or course of study, higher-level objectives are used. In the cognitive domain, these are usually at the analysis level or higher; however, occasionally a unit objective at the application level is used. These higher-level objectives may be called broad, overall, or terminal objectives. Objectives for lessons or small units of subject matter are called specific, daily, or enabling objectives. Their levels lead sequentially to the level of the broad, overall objective. For example, the broad unit objective, which relates to the major concept, may be at the synthesis level. Daily objectives or those relating to the subconcepts may be at the knowledge, comprehension, application, and analysis levels. Occasionally the concluding daily objective is at the same level as the broad objective. This is most likely to happen the last day of a unit. A specific objective, however, does not exceed the level of the broad objective. If it did, the broad objective would be inappropriate. Daily objectives planned for the beginning of a unit may stop several levels below the level of the broad objective. In the example of the menu-planning unit, the broad objective is at the synthesis level. The seven specific objectives for the first day of the unit might be developed so that there are three at the knowledge level, two at the comprehension level, and two at the application level.

Verbs to Avoid

Objectives beginning with "to discuss" are extremely difficult to measure objectively unless teachers have previously established the exact criteria by which the discussion will be evaluated. Even when this has been done, students often bring up valid points teachers have not anticipated. When this happens and students do not include factors expected in the answers, teachers are faced with the problem of measuring responses fairly.

The following terms are sometimes used erroneously in formulating behavioral objectives. *These are not measurable behaviors unless they are qualified.*

Avoid using:

appreciate	have faith in
appreciate fully	know
ascribe to	learn
become familiar with	realize
believe in	recall
believe truly	recognize
develop a feeling for	recognize the
discuss	importance of
enjoy	see the need for
enthuse	understand
grasp the significance of	value
have an awareness of	

Sharing Objectives with Students

There are advantages in stating behavioral objectives for students. Objectives provide guidance for studying. When it is time to review for a test or to prepare an assignment, students know what is expected of them. Some teachers write the objectives for the day on the board or give students duplicated copies of both broad, overall and specific, daily objectives. In some classes, students help plan the objectives. These may not be expressed in exact, pedagogic terms, but the students are participating in the teaching-learning process. Their contributions should be very worthwhile since they often have accurate and strong feelings about what they need to learn and know.

Evaluation is facilitated when behavioral objectives have been formulated carefully in advance because they predict the type of evaluation that is appropriate and the level at which achievement should be measured. Behavioral objectives also serve as the bases for selecting and planning meaningful learning experiences. Learning experiences are the tasks students perform and the activities in which they participate to enable them to achieve planned objectives.

Competency-based Education

The competency-based approach to education emerged in the late 1960s because of the growing emphasis in many sectors of society on *accountability*. Dissatisfaction with the educational system increased as it became evident that many students were leaving school while lacking the basic skills needed to function effectively in society. Since expenditures for education consume such a large proportion of the public tax dollar, concern also increased for the quality of teacher-education programs and the professional abilities of college graduates planning to teach. *Accountability* as it relates to teachers, then, encompasses relevancy, adequacy, effectiveness, and efficiency.

For students, competency-based education(CBE) can be thought of as criterion-referenced education in which the desired outcomes relating to knowledge, attitudes, and behavior are stated as behavioral objectives. Students understand that certain specified competencies, or measurable and observable behaviors, are expected of them and that they must demonstrate attainment of the required competencies in order to pass. This system takes the use of behavioral objectives beyond their usual application. That is, competencies are ordinarily a measure of *how well* a student has mastered the material, not just *whether* the student has mastered it.

The similarities between the use of behavioral objectives and competency-based education are illustrated by examining the characteristics of competency-based education.

1. Competencies to be demonstrated, or objectives, are stated in behavioral terms and sequenced according to the needs and abilities of the students.
2. Student achievement is measured by determining if preestablished levels of competence, or performance, have been met.

3. Students are informed of the levels of competence, or objectives they are expected to achieve, as well as how they will be evaluated. The criteria for evaluation are also shared.
4. The instructional program provides a variety of learning experiences that use different teaching methods and media to enable students to reach the specified competency levels, or to achieve the stated objectives.
5. Since attainment of specified competencies, or achievement of objectives, is the purpose of the educational program, time is not a factor. Some students may need little time to reach specified competency levels, while other students need much more time.
6. Student assessment of competency performance, or achievement of objectives, is the primary source of evidence used in the evaluation process. A large amount of responsibility, therefore, must be assumed by the student for meeting these preestablished levels of performance. Accountability is thus shared responsibility of the student and teacher.

Terminal Performance Objectives

A terminal performance objective (TPO) represents a broad general area of a competency that serves as a major criterion for evaluating performance related to that component. A TPO is similar to a higher-level, broad, overall behavioral objective that relates to a major concept. The student will have to achieve several interim or enabling objectives before being expected to perform the terminal objective.

Enabling Objectives

A TPO can be divided into a series of enabling objectives. An enabling objective (EO) is similar to a lower-level or specific behavioral objective. Attainment of enabling objectives contributes to the achievement of a TPO as attainment of specific, lower-level behavioral objectives contributes to the achievement of a broad, higher-level objective.

Application in Vocational/ Technical Programs

If you were to visit a CBE program in vocational/ technical education, you might find that some students have just entered the program while others have been there for some time; some will be teenagers while others are adults. Because students work at their own pace on a highly individualized basis, the program may appear to have little structure. The teacher probably will not be "teaching" in the usual, conventional, or formal sense of the word. Emphasis is on students developing and demonstrating specified occupational competencies and being evaluated individually against preestablished criteria, rather than against group norms.

Competency-based instruction places emphasis on the ability to perform, as well as on understanding the how and why. Content for CBE instruction in a vocational/technical program is based on the tasks performed in the occupation for which the student is preparing. In CBE, competence is evaluated by doing. Assessment does not end with cognitive pencil-and-paper tests — unless, of course, the skill needed is a pencil-and-paper skill such as copy editing.

For example, to build a winning football team a coach would not have players only watch pro games on TV, memorize the play book, read stories about football greats' lives, and trace the evolution of football in the United States and then test them on this material. Players might be involved in some of these activities, but they certainly would also practice and play "real" football.

Likewise, a chef's competence is not evaluated by the individual only being asked how to prepare light and flaky pie crusts. Competence is measured by doing it. A student can't be asked to read about how to clean teeth, take a written test on the material, and then be called a competent dental hygienist.

■ *Vocabulary*

Competency-based education in vocational/technical programs may also be called performance-based instruction, mastery learning, criterion-based instruction, and proficiency-based education. Much of the vocabulary used in CBE may be new to you. As you read the terminology that follows, the purposes and strategies in CBE will become clearer to you.

ASSESSMENT: A judgment of the worth or quality of an individual's performance; judgment of a learner's knowledge, skills, and/or attitudes.

CAREER LADDER: A graphic description of the sequence of jobs making up a particular occupation, beginning at the bottom with the job requiring the least amount of experience and training and proceeding up the ladder to the job requiring the greatest number of skills, the most complex skills, and the highest degree of responsibility.

CAREER PREPARATION MAP: A record-keeping form to keep track of a student's competencies and tasks in a specific occupational area. It also may be called a Competency Profile.

COMPETENCY: The ability (including knowledge, skills, and/or attitudes) to perform a specific set of related tasks successfully to meet a specified standard.

CRITERION: A performance standard or specified statement on which a judgment or decision is based.

CRITERION-REFERENCE TEST (CRT): A test constructed to yield measurements that are directly interpretable in terms of specific performance standards. An individual's performance is compared to a criterion; the criterion being the work or performance standard. Thus, the score on a CRT is based on absolute standards, such as job competency, rather than on relative standards, such as class standing.

ENTRY-LEVEL SKILLS: The set of competencies required of a beginning worker in an occupation for immediate productivity upon entering that occupation.

INDIVIDUALIZED INSTRUCTION: Learner-centered instruction in which the materials and activities are tailored to meet the needs of the individual student; includes individual placement and selection of goals, self-pacing, individual monitoring of progress, and adaptation to individual learning style.

INTERIM PERFORMANCE OBJECTIVE: A statement of knowledge, skills, and/or attitudes that learners must have if they are to be proficient in given tasks. A series of interim objectives developed through a task analysis leads a student step-by-step to mastery of a Terminal Performance Objective or competency.

MASTERY: A specified level of performance; meeting all of the specified minimum requirements for completion of a task or competency.

OCCUPATIONAL ANALYSIS: A listing of all the duties and tasks that make up a particular job and are necessary for at least entry-level proficiency. Information may be gathered from observations, interviews, and questionnaires.

OCCUPATIONAL CLUSTER: A group or listing of occupations within a program area that share common experiences, knowledge, and skill requirements, such as food service occupations, human service occupations, and health care occupations.

OPEN-ENTRY/OPEN-EXIT: A scheduling approach that allows students to enter, leave, and reenter a vocational program at any time. Completion of a program of study is possible whenever the student is able to demonstrate competency of selected objectives.

PERFORMANCE TEST: A type of measuring device in which a task is specified and the students are required to actually perform the task using materials and equipment.

STANDARD: That part of a performance objective which describes how well or to what proficiency level a task must be performed.

TASK: A discrete unit of work performed by an individual in the completion of an assigned job competency. It is a measurable element of work from a larger occupational/job activity, usually performed by a single worker in a relatively short span of time.

■ Critical Elements in Competency-based Education

According to the American Association for Vocational Instructional Materials (AAVIM), there are five critical elements in CBE:

1. Competencies are rigorously identified and verified.
2. Assessment criteria and conditions are explicitly stated in advance.
3. Instruction provides for the individual development and evaluation of each competency.
4. Students progress at their own best rate.
5. Final assessment of competency achievement requires actual task performance.

■ Developing a Task List

It is essential to identify the specific tasks performed by workers in the occupations for which students are being trained before an instructional program can be implemented. People are not paid for only knowing something. A chef is paid for preparing food that tastes good, looks appealing, and is nutritious. A chef is not paid for knowing the Dietary Guidelines for Americans or for knowing principles of food safety. Knowledge is an enabler — an essential element for performing job tasks correctly.

Consequently, in developing a task list, it is necessary to focus on what the worker actually *does* in that occupation — what the employee gets paid for. The chef gets paid for producing a product and providing a service. There are specific activities that can be observed. For example, chefs wash their hands before handling food, they place foods that spoil easily in the refrigerator as quickly as possible, and they wash any utensil that falls on the floor in soapy water.

■ Characteristics of CBE Instruction

Instruction in CBE is characterized by the following:
- Instructional materials used are keyed to the competencies to be achieved.

- Environments that duplicate or simulate the work place are available to students during competency development.
- Basic knowledge or background theory is learned as it is needed to support competency development.
- Students are informed about the traits and attitudes important to workers in the occupation and are periodically evaluated regarding their attainment.
- Each student is given continual and detailed feedback on competency development.
- A variety of learning styles and teaching strategies are provided.
- Students with appropriate prerequisite skills and knowledge may bypass instruction on competencies already attained.

■ Benefits of Competency-based Education

The AAVIM has indicated that the benefits of CBE are:

For students
- Learners achieve competencies needed for employment.
- A wide range of abilities is accommodated within a program.
- Learners build self-confidence by succeeding.
- More learning options are available to students.
- Learners are presented with transcripts showing the competencies they have achieved.

For Teachers/Instructors
- Time is used more efficiently and effectively as a leader or manager of the learning process rather than as a "giver of information."
- Less time is required to prepare lectures.
- Less time is required to develop and grade paper-and-pencil tests.
- More time is spent evaluating students' abilities to perform essential occupational skills.
- More time is spent working with students individually and in small groups.

For Administrators
- Instructional staff is used more effectively.
- Building and instructional equipment is used more efficiently.
- Placement of graduates in jobs is easier.
- Students with a wide range of entry-level skills, including the disabled, are accepted.
- Articulating secondary, postsecondary, and part-time adult instructional programs is easier.

- Satisfaction is gained in seeing students achieve their goals.
- There is greater support of training programs by business, labor, and industry.

For Businesses
- There is optimum involvement in the identification of competencies to be learned by students.
- There is more substantive involvement of business experts in establishing performance criteria and other expectations.
- More potential employees trained in the skills required on the job are available.

References

Bloom, Benjamin S., et al. *Taxonomy of Educational Objectives, Handbook I: Cognitive Domain*, New York: David McKay Company, Inc., 1956.

"Prepare to Install Competency-based Education," Module LT-B-4. American Association for Vocational Instructional Materials, The National Center for Research in Vocational Education, The Ohio State University, Columbus, OH, 1985.

"Prepare Yourself for CBE," Module K-1. American Association for Vocational Instructional Materials, The National Center for Research in Vocational Education, The Ohio State University, Columbus, OH, 1986.

Simpson, Elizabeth J. "Classification of Educational Objectives, Psychomotor Domain." *Illinois Teacher*, Winter 1966-1967.

Developing Critical Thinking Skills

Chapter 4

Critical Thinking

During the 1970s and early 1980s, American youth lagged far behind their counterparts in other industrial nations in thinking skills — problem solving, reasoning, creativity, and evaluation. Americans consistently ranked in the lowest 20 percent of all the world's industrial nations. For this reason and others, in the later half of the 1980s the development of critical thinking skills received much attention in the literature. It is, however, a very old approach to teaching dating back to Socrates and his method of questioning to determine "truth." John Dewey's approach of "learning by doing" was built, to a large degree, on the application and analysis levels of thinking.

Teaching students to think is to make learning applicable to real life. It is developing skills needed for living — solving problems and making decisions. As young people have more responsibilities and face life decisions at earlier ages, they need to develop thinking skills that help them make appropriate personal decisions. Thinking skills give individuals the ability and strength to stand up for what they believe in. Students at all ability levels need opportunities to develop higher order thinking skills because students at all ability levels face similar personal choices.

$$15,873 \times 1 = 15,873 \qquad 15,873 \times 7 = 111,111$$
$$15,873 \times 2 = 31,746 \qquad 31,746 \times 7 = 222,222$$
$$15,873 \times 3 = 47,619 \qquad 47,619 \times 7 = 333,333$$
$$15,873 \times 4 = 63,492 \qquad 63,492 \times 7 = 444,444$$
$$15,873 \times 5 = 79,365 \qquad 79,365 \times 7 = 555,555$$
$$15,873 \times 6 = 95,238 \qquad 95,238 \times 7 = 666,666$$
$$15,873 \times 7 = 111,111 \qquad 111,111 \times 7 = 777,777$$
$$15,873 \times 8 = 126,984 \qquad 126,984 \times 7 = 888,888$$
$$15,873 \times 9 = 142,857 \qquad 142,857 \times 7 = 999,999$$

Are you able to figure out the pattern in the math exercise above? If so, you are using the analysis level of thinking. To analyze this sequence of numbers, you need to incorporate lower levels of thinking as well. Obviously, you need to compute or multiply numbers. This is application. In this situation, you need to apply before you analyze. This is the premise on which Bloom et al. have built the *Taxonomy of Educational Objectives*. There are other ideas about thinking skills, too. Some of the approaches espoused by well known home economists are discussed in this chapter.

Definitions

One of the best known definitions of critical thinking has come from Brown and Paolucci who wrote:

Critical thinking is a critical spirit or attitude … the disposition to compare claims or arguments against another, weigh evidence and form conclusions based on sound reasons rather than authority, expediency, whimsy, tradition, or irrational compulsions.

Siegel described a critical thinker as:

… one who recognizes the importance, and convicting force, of reasons. When assessing claims, evaluating procedures, or making judgments, the critical thinker seeks reasons on which to base his or her assessment, evaluation, or judgment. Moreover, to see reasons is to recognize and commit oneself to principles governing such activity. Critical thinking is thus, principled thinking.

Criteria

Although there are no precise prescriptions for teaching critical thinking, Hamer has cited the following teaching environments as those that foster the development of critical thinking:
- Open, accepting atmosphere.
- Teacher as a facilitator — not an information giver.
- Writing as a precursor to thinking.
- Less emphasis on covering content.
- Questioning.
- Flexible time table.

Hamer also noted that, upon examination of these criteria, you may see that a great deal of the success of these strategies will depend on the teacher's attitude. Teachers need to be willing to risk opening the class to controversy and to the acceptance of student thinking. Teachers may no longer see themselves as "in control." Students will not feel free to explore ideas if the ideas are rejected or demeaned.

Barriers

Have you heard teachers make comments such as these that inhibit critical and creative thinking?
- Do it that way because I *said* so.
- This is how you do it in *my* class.
- Now let *me* see you did it *this* way.
- No, that's not it. How could that possibly be it?
- You must not be thinking.

Responses such as these give the impression that there is only one way to do things — the teacher's way. The students are likely to feel they have to think as the teacher thinks because that alone is the right way to think. How might the following teacher's comments be changed to stimulate independent and critical thinking by students?
- I tried that once. It didn't work for me.
- I suppose you might be able to do it that way, but this method is better.
- Don't do it that way. I always do it this way.
- We don't have time to think about that.
- Make up your mind quickly about how you'll tackle that project.

Teachers can take away students' opportunities to make decisions and solve problems by doing this for them. Don't take away your students' chances to grow and mature by doing their thinking for them.

Higher Levels in the Taxonomy of Educational Objectives

If a teacher were to begin a housing unit by asking students to design a floor plan for a given family, this would be a waste of time. Students would not know where to begin. They need to begin at the knowledge level by identifying symbols used in drawing floor plans, such as different types of doors, windows, electrical outlets, and bathroom fixtures. Students need to understand (or comprehend) building features that minimize costs and contribute to satisfying living, such as adjacent placement of plumbing centers, few outside wall angles, and closets placed to serve as noise buffers. At the application level, students might draw architectural symbols in rooms that they lay out. At the analysis level, floor plans can be studied to determine traffic patterns and architectural features that facilitate furniture arrangements. Only after these and other activities are completed would students be expected to design floor plans for families in given income ranges, of varying sizes and ages, and with different lifestyles.

As educators, it is essential to provide students with learning experiences that progress up the levels of learning logically so students have sufficient background to achieve successfully at the higher levels. Too often teaching stops at the knowledge level with imparting facts. At best, students may be expected to understand what the facts mean. Some educators consider higher levels of thinking in the Taxonomy of Educational Objectives as application and above. More often, higher order thinking is considered to be analyzing, synthesizing, and evaluating.

Assuming that appropriate objectives and learning experiences have been identified and implemented to incorporate the higher levels of thinking, study or test questions at corresponding levels should be used. Some examples to illustrate questions at the application level and higher follow.

■ Application

Food Costs

Write **1** by the food in each group that would cost the *most*. Write **3** by the food that would cost the *least*. Write **2** by the food that would be priced between the other two. Assume that all the foods in one group are the same quantity as sold or as reconstituted, if appropriate.

_____ Fruit in season		_____ Cut-up fryers
_____ Dried fruit		_____ Whole fryers
_____ Frozen fruit		_____ Chicken breasts

_____ Sweetened condensed milk
_____ Non-fat dry milk
_____ Evaporated milk

_____ Hen turkey
_____ Tom turkey
_____ Tom turkey, prestuffed

Calorie Count

Write **1** by the activity in each group that burns up the most calories. Write **3** by the activity in each group that burns up the fewest calories. Write **2** by the activity that is between the other two in the number of calories used up.

_____ Watching TV
_____ Playing tennis
_____ Bowling

_____ Skiing
_____ Reading
_____ Working quickly

_____ Dancing
_____ Sewing
_____ Swimming

_____ Doing heavy house cleaning
_____ Playing basketball
_____ Cooking

Menu Substitutions

Make substitutions in the two menus below. For each underlined food suggest another food to take its place that would lower the calories contained in the meal. Use different foods or cooking methods for the underlined words in each of the menus. Refer to an RDA table if you need help.

```
+-----------------------------------------+
|           Fried Trout                   |
| Peas and Carrots   French-fried Potatoes|
|    Tossed Salad with Dressing           |
|         Chocolate Cake                  |
|            Whole Milk                   |
+-----------------------------------------+
```

```
+-----------------------------------------+
|           Sausage Patty                 |
|   Potato Salad    Baked Beans           |
|         Canned Peaches                  |
|            Cola Drink                   |
+-----------------------------------------+
```

■ *Analysis*

Analogies

Circle the letter corresponding to the word that best completes the sentence.

• Warmth is to wool, as drapability is to:
  a. cotton.
  b. linen
  c. silk.
  d. spandex.

• Uncles are to extended families, as stepchildren are to:
  a. nuclear families.
  b. single-parent families.
  c. cooperative families.
  d. blended families.

Most Inclusive Items

Circle the letter corresponding to the most *inclusive* item in each group. In other words, select the item that includes all the others in that group.

  a. Drop-leaf table
  b. Pembroke table
  c. Butterfly table
  d. Gateleg table

  a. Studio couch
  b. Hide-a-bed
  c. Sofa bed
  d. Jack-knife sofa

Most Dissimilar Items

Circle the letter corresponding to the one item in each group that is *not* associated with the others.

  a. Walnut
  b. Mahogany
  c. Oak
  d. Pine
  e. Cherry

  a. Cantaloupe
  b. Apricot
  c. Peach
  d. Apple
  e. Watermelon

■ *Synthesis*

Rewriting Menus

Modify the following menus to conform to the guidelines for planning aesthetically pleasing meals.

```
+-----------------------------------------+
|            Baked Perch                  |
|   Mashed Potatoes    Cauliflower        |
|        Canned Pear Halves               |
|          Angel Food Cake                |
|               Milk                      |
+-----------------------------------------+
```

```
+-----------------------------------------+
|       Creamed Tuna on Noodles           |
|    Stewed Tomatoes    Applesauce        |
|         Chocolate Pudding               |
|          Chocolate Milk                 |
+-----------------------------------------+
```

Fitness Plans

Develop an overall fitness plan for one of the following individuals:
  a. A 40-year-old woman who is a single parent

and works full-time as a secretary. She has three children in elementary school. She has 20 percent body fat.
  b. A 60-year-old widower who lives alone and is healthy other than being 35 pounds overweight.
  c. A teenage girl who has 40 percent body fat and spends most of her time out of school watching TV.
  d. A teenage male who is underweight and spends much of his time working in his wood-work shop.

■ Evaluation

Judging 4-H Events

Judge 4-H family projects using established criteria.

Appraising Job Applicants

Assess the strengths and limitations of job applicants by viewing tapes of interviews, by studying their letters of application and resumes, and by comparing and contrasting their letters of recommendation.

Problem Solving

We all have problems. A problem arises when we want or need something that is not understandable or available immediately. You have a problem when you have to plan a teaching unit for concepts about which you know very little. A big part of the problem is deciding what to teach. You have a problem when you decide on a major for your graduate studies. You have a problem when you select where you will live. You have to decide in which part of the town, city, or country to live; whether to choose an apartment, condo, duplex, or other unit; and if you will live with another person. Decision-making, then, is part of problem solving.

The word "problem" suggests a negative situation, but there are many positive problems to solve in life. Solving any kind of problem presents a challenge. Where should I go to college? Which VCR should I buy? How can I make this relationship work?

Laster has pointed out that research findings show that problem solving is a complex, cognitive, thinking process — not only a searching process but also an understanding process. Knowledge is needed, but it is not enough. Knowledge *and* higher-level cognitive skills are needed to solve problems.

Types of Problems

Laster has described two types of problems: well-structured problems and ill-structured or fuzzy problems. Most questions or problems encountered in academic situations are well-structured problems. Math, science, and technical problems are examples. Information about the problem, the procedure to follow to solve the problem, and the criteria for judging the appropriateness of the solution are often provided.

Ill-structured problems, on the other hand, are the type encountered in everyday life. Everyday problems lack clear procedures for how to go about solving them, and there are no "correct" answers. Criteria for deciding if a problem has been solved must be identified by the problem solver. Individuals and families face unstructured problems everyday. Home economics classes, therefore, provide unparalleled opportunities for students to work to solve real-life problems.

■ Problem Solving Instruction

Laster has indicated that to solve home and family problems students need to:
• Think about problems and problem solving.
• Develop processes for solving different types of problems.
• Solve hypothetical, simulated, and real everyday practical problems.

To meet these needs, Laster proposed these five guidelines for teachers:
1. Help students understand the characteristics of problems and what is needed to solve different types of problems.
2. Help students become critically aware of their world and cultural reality so they can identify problems, the first and most important dimension of problem solving.
3. Pose and help students identify and solve a range of home and family problems: well-structured, structured but requiring productive thinking, and ill-structured. Through experience in problem solving, students develop the knowledge base and cognitive skills needed for solving present and future problems of these types as they work to reach immediate goals.
4. Help students develop an extensive, accessible knowledge base for solving home and family problems:
  • Facts, principles, and concepts;
  • Patterns of action which require other action; and
  • Procedural knowledge for solving different types of problems and different home and family problems.

Because students need knowledge to solve the problems, they need help in developing that knowledge so it will be accessible for use in the future.

5. Help students develop critical cognitive processes needed for solving problems, especially unstructured problems, so the processes become skills that are used automatically. Self-monitoring, self-management processes should lead to checking these problem- solving processes:
    - What is the *real* problem?
    - What should I do first?
    - What information do I need to solve this problem?
    - Where can I go wrong?
    - What are my alternatives?
    - What will be the consequences of doing this?
    - Will the consequences be good for me? my family?
    - Have I forgotten anything important?
    - Do I need to think about this for a while — let this incubate?

Perception processes needed to acquire the informal, tacit knowledge that must be learned outside of school for successfully solving everyday problems include:
- Identifying non-verbal cues.
- Listening and observing for feelings.
- Identifying and verbalizing feelings.
- Inferring from limited information.
- Accurately empathizing with others.
- Questioning; information interviewing.
- Recognizing patterns — visual, verbal, and action patterns.

Practical Reasoning

In home economics there are theoretical problems and technical or how-to problems, but emphasis is on solving *practical* problems. Practical problems focus on what to do or what action to take. Home economists' primary concern is to help individuals and families solve practical, everyday problems encountered in real life. It would seem, then, that the home economics curriculum should be structured to develop practical reasoning ability — the thinking process needed to solve the "what to do" questions encountered throughout a student's lifetime.

It is often taken for granted that people have an innate ability to solve practical problems, but many individuals do not reason well enough to solve the routine everyday or unexpected problems encountered throughout life. Adolescents, particularly, are influenced by peer pressure. Often the consequences of compulsive behavior are not given serious consideration. Tradition may limit the goals an individual sets in life and the satisfaction achieved because some seemingly small problem was handled with limiting results.

Practical, everyday problems are ill-structured, lacking a clear procedure to follow for solution and/or criteria for evaluating the solution. Aren't most interpersonal individual and family problems like this? Practical reasoning involves using higher level thinking processes that are based on adequate and reliable information — or knowledge. Home economics concepts provide the knowledge base for solving everyday, practical, real-life problems of home and family life. This knowledge relates to making healthy food choices, balancing family and work responsibilities, nurturing children, managing resources, selecting appropriate clothing and textiles, weighing housing alternatives to make satisfying decisions, creating aesthetically pleasing environments, and all other home economics curriculum components. Home economics enables family members to gather reliable information to use as the basis for practical reasoning.

Processes such as goal setting; decision making; and managing time, energy, and money are cognitive skills that are part of the home economics curriculum. Incorporating practical reasoning into the program strengthens the base for solving everyday problems that often have life-long ramifications. After all, a major conclusion is based on many previous decisions and conclusions.

■ Instructional Strategies for Developing Practical Reasoning

Laster had indicated that the following standards need to be met to effectively enhance practical reasoning ability:
1. Expectations for developing practical reasoning are clear to students.
2. Learning conditions for a complex skill are provided.
3. There are careful supervision of coping efforts so dangers are minimized, constructive demonstrations and suggestions for ways to handle problems, and enough reality to transfer coping skills to real situations in the future.
4. The realities of everyday home and family problem solving are reflected in the learning environment.
5. Individual learning styles and developmental needs are accommodated.

Reflective Thinking

Dewey emphasized the concept of reflective thinking and described it as "… being or as including critical thinking, problem solving, inquiry, and reflective judgment." He stated that it begins with a real-life problem and ends with a judgment that provides one solution to the problem. The judgment has to be substantiated through an inquiry process that includes sound reasoning and information confirmed by evidence. Reflective thinking, as well as thinking processes described by Bloom and Laster, requires the use of facts or knowledge. The critical point is not to stop there.

Dewey explained that facts form the basis for interpreting, explaining, accounting for something, and deliberating. Ideas come from the mind. Facts or knowledge *and* ideas come from present and past observations and inferences. Inferences refer to possibilities, not actualities. Reflective thinking focuses on the future by continuing through these processes: anticipation, supposition, conjecture, imagination, foresight, prediction, planning, theorizing, and speculation. Every step anticipates the future, and the solution focuses on the future. Reflection involves the past by building on past knowledge and experiences.

Bobbitt has provided an illustration of sequential stages of reflective thinking based on a modification of Dewey's phases. The concept area is maternal and infancy nutrition and health.

Stage 1 believes that women should avoid pregnancy after age 40, due to concern for potential health risks to baby and mother.

Stage 2 views that it is wrong to potentially jeopardize the health of the baby by giving birth after age 40.

Stage 3 realizes that professionals with expertise in maternal and infant health disagree on potential level of risk of pregnancy after 40.

Stage 4 views that individuals vary in their nutrition and health status which may be one of influential factions related to degree of potential childbirth risks after age 40.

Stage 5 considers that knowledgeability of the mother about personal health care and nutrition during pregnancy, along with her willingness to make a commitment to proper nutrition and health care, will enhance the potential maternal and infant health status.

Stage 6 sees relationship between potential health of baby and the present and past nutritional and health status of the mother.

Stage 7 assumes responsibility for learning about proper nutrition and health during one's lifespan.

Bobbitt has indicated that one of the reasons educators fail to teach reflective thinking is because they seldom provide students with the opportunity to judge their products or creations. The educator judges what the student has produced. Students are not taught how to distinguish between acceptable and unacceptable products. They are not taught how to develop their reflective thinking ability.

Practice in reflective thinking promotes creativity. Through practice, students learn to identify more alternatives and to draw better inferences from known facts. It provides practice in testing alternatives and hypotheses and finding the best solution. Each of these experiences helps develop creative thinking.

The FHA/HERO Planning Process

The FHA/HERO Planning Process provides an excellent vehicle for helping students develop higher level thinking skills:

 Identify concerns. Brainstorm to determine concerns or problems the chapter might tackle such as child abuse, latch-key children, landfill use, water pollution, and food safety. Narrow the list down to a workable project that interests most members.

 Set your goal. Determine the chapter goal such as educating other youth about parenting responsibilities or promoting optimal prenatal nutrition. Be sure the goal is realistic and can be evaluated. Consider the resources available to achieve the goal.

 Form a plan. Decide what needs to be done. Determine the who, what, when, where, and how of the project. List the knowledge, abilities, and skills required to complete the project. Identify other available resources such as publications, people, and places. Make a realistic time schedule. Suggest alternative plans in case barriers surface. Decide on ways to recognize achievements along the way.

 Act. Carry out the plan. Call on other home economics teachers, health professionals, public agencies, and community organizations as needed.

 Follow up. Decide if your goal was met. Decide what would be done differently if the project were to be repeated. Share and publicize the results.

There is much educational research that shows that students learn best when they are actively involved in the teaching-learning processes — as they are when using the FHA/HERO Planning Process. Students have to track down information, test theories, and tinker with results. Under this approach, the teacher spends more time facilitating and guiding instruction and less time reiterating facts.

Green has written that the important concept is to teach critical thinking, and not to stop at the lowest levels of cognitive development. This presents learners with an inaccurate picture of the kinds of decisions and levels of thinking needed throughout their lives. Green has stated that one of the most important functions of school is to instill in students a love of learning and a commitment to life-long learning.

References

Bloom, Benjamin S., et al. *Taxonomy of Educational Objectives, Handbook I: Cognitive Domain*. New York: David McKay Company, Inc., 1956.

Bobbitt, N. "Reflective Thinking: Meaning and Implications for Teaching," *Higher Order Thinking: Definition, Meaning and Instructional Approaches*. Washington, DC: Home Economics Education Association, 1987, pages 62-68.

Brown, M. and Paolucci, B. *Home Economics a Definition*. Washington, DC: American Home Economics Association, 1979.

Dewey, J. *Logic: The Theory of Inquiry*. New York: Holt, Rinehart, and Winston, 1938.

Green, K.B. "Teaching Critical Thinking in Home Economics." *Illinois Teacher*, March/April 1988, pages 182-183.

Hamer, B. "Critical Thinking Skills," *Home Economics Instruction*. Lubbock, TX: Home Economics Curriculum Center, Texas Tech University, 1989, pages 121-123.

Laster, J. "Instructional Strategies for Teaching Practical Reasoning in Consumer Homemaking Classrooms," *Higher Order Thinking: Definition, Meaning and Instructional Approaches*. Washington, DC: Home Economics Education Association, 1987, pages 44-61.

____."Problem Solving: Definition Meaning," *Higher Order Thinking: Definition, Meaning and Instructional Approaches*. Washington, DC: Home Economics Education Association, 1987, pages 35-43.

Siegel, H. *The Educational Forum*, Kappa Delta Pi, November 1980.

Designing Learning Experiences

Chapter 5

Various methods of teaching are the vehicles used for implementing learning experiences. Skits, role-plays, sociodramas, discussions, debates, and field trips are a few of the teaching methods available for planning activities. The method selected indicates *how* the subject content will be presented. Transparencies, flip charts, and flannel boards are visual media. Audio cassette tapes utilize sound. Many educational media such as films, video tapes, filmstrips, and computer software utilize both the sense of seeing and that of hearing. Other media, especially in home economics, use the senses of touch, taste, and smell.

Considerations in Designing Learning Experiences

Learning experiences may be carried out by individuals, by a few students working together, or by an entire class. They may be part of the classroom work, an extended learning experience program, or activities of a Future Homemakers of America/Home Economics Related Occupation (FHA/HERO) chapter. Many variables affect the learning experiences, teaching methods, and media used. However, the most important are the concepts to be covered and the objectives that have been established. Other variables to consider when developing learning experiences are discussed below.

Variety

In designing a learning experience for a given situation, you must first ask, "What is the best way to help my students clarify these concepts and reach these objectives?" It is important to select a variety of teaching methods and media, both from one day to the next and within the same class period. Nothing can be less motivating for students than doing the same old thing every day. Ideally, you will seek to have approximately three different types of learning experiences within each class period. Naturally, this does not apply to laboratory lessons. Nor will you change pace just because it is in

After the concepts to be covered have been identified, after the generalizations that students will be guided to make have been determined, and after the behavioral objectives have been formulated, the next step in planning is to select and develop learning experiences. These are the activities in which students participate at school, at home, and in the community to help them clarify concepts, arrive at generalizations, and achieve established objectives. Developing learning experiences involves designing the experience itself, choosing the appropriate teaching method, and deciding what media are to be used. Learning activities may be primarily physical, as in using various types of commercial cleaning equipment; social, as in having an open house in the department; emotional, as in portraying roles in a sociodrama; or mental, as in working a crossword puzzle or computing interest charges. Learning activities need to be planned that will help students meet objectives in all three domains: cognitive, affective, and psychomotor.

the plans to do so. If students are highly stimulated by a particular learning experience, you may capitalize on the teachable moment and continue while interest is keen. There would be little purpose in beginning another activity when the students are still highly engrossed in what they are doing. However, it does not pay, in educational value, to continue or repeat activities simply because students enjoy them.

The Students

The length of the students' attention span will affect the number of different learning experiences planned. Their preferences for certain types of activities need to be considered. The makeup, or personality, of the class also influences the selection of learning experiences. If students are especially active, experiences that involve considerable physical participation may be appropriate. The ways in which students learn best must be determined. Whether they seem to get more from reading, from visual stimuli, from discussion, or from individual and group study projects is a very important consideration.

It is essential that all students become involved in the teaching-learning process. For some students, participation may be passive, whereas for others it may be active. Some students might be engaged in pencil-and-paper types of activities while others are doing something physical. The vehicle for participation can reflect individual preferences; the important thing is that each student be involved in some way appropriate for the individual.

Number of Senses Involved

Generally, there is a greater retention of subject matter when students use several senses in carrying out a learning activity. Whenever feasible, the students should not only hear about the topic under consideration but also see pertinent materials relating to it. Seeing may include reading or viewing appropriate visuals. Home economics teachers have a distinct advantage because it is possible to include the senses of touch, taste, and smell in many of the areas of subject matter studied. For example, in studying various types of fabrics, students can handle samples to determine the tactile effects of fiber content, weave, and various finishes. Tasting and smelling various types of cheese or forms of milk, such as skim, evaporated, and condensed, will leave a more lasting impression than only hearing or reading about their characteristics and qualities.

For the school population as a whole, retention of subject matter is about the same when students are told

How People Learn — Sensory Modes	
TASTE	1 %
TOUCH	1.5 %
SMELL	3.5 %
HEARING	11.0 %
SIGHT	83.0 %

Learner's Ability to Retain Information Studied

10% OF WHAT IS READ
20% OF WHAT IS HEARD
30% OF WHAT IS SEEN
50% OF WHAT IS SEEN *AND* HEARD
70% OF WHAT THE LEARNER SAYS AS HE/SHE TALKS
90% OF WHAT THE LEARNER SAYS AS HE/SHE DEMONSTRATES

Learner's Ability to Retain Information Over Time

	3 HOURS	3 DAYS
TELLING ALONE (LECTURE)	70%	10%
SHOWING ALONE (VISUAL AID)	72%	20%
COMBINATION OF SHOWING & TELLING	85%	65%
TEACHING OTHERS	90%	85%

about or read about the material. However, if both senses — hearing and seeing — are involved, retention after a time lapse of several days is more than four times greater. Consequently, you should make every effort to involve as many senses as possible in a learning experience without becoming repetitious, boring, or insulting to the students. Repeating material exactly as it was covered previously can be interpreted as talking down to students.

In a classic study conducted by the Sacony Oil Company in its management training program with adults, it was found that retention improved significantly when the trainees both heard and read about the subject matter. The most impressive finding is shown in the chart above where recall was 65 percent after three days without intervention when both lecture and reading were used. This is compared to 10 percent and 20 percent respectively when lecture and reading were each used alone.

Time of Day and Year

Classes that meet early in the morning, just after lunch, or at the end of the school day often react to the same learning experiences very differently. The time of year must also be considered. In early fall or late spring the weather may be too warm to make some activities feasible. Furthermore, there are learning experiences that would not be well accepted at the beginning of the school year because the students and teacher are not yet sufficiently acquainted or at ease with one another. For example, students may be reluctant to discuss male-female relationships before rapport has been established within the class. Near the end of the school term, students may be restless. Special efforts often have to be taken to plan activities that are especially stimulating and interesting then.

Physical Facilities

The physical facilities, including the amount and availability of space and equipment, affect the learning activities that can be planned and carried out. For example, it is difficult to have a party for children or an activity for elders in a small or crowded classroom. Sometimes rooms can be borrowed or exchanged for special events, but this possibility is less likely in a crowded school. If it is impossible to darken a room, films will lose their effectiveness, and if the necessary equipment is unavailable, some types of audiovisual media cannot be used. Whether a school is in a rural or urban area will influence the number and types of field trips that can be arranged, and guest speakers who can be expected to come.

Administrators' Attitudes

The attitude and philosophy of the school's administrators has a bearing on the methods of teaching you select. If your school is very traditional or slow to accept new ideas, this will influence the learning experiences you use. On the other hand, if you teach in a school where most of the teachers have creative and interesting teaching strategies, it will be easier for you to be innovative, too.

The Teacher

Naturally, you will favor some methods of teaching and types of learning experiences more than others because you feel comfortable and secure using them. When something has worked well in the past, it is only logical and practical to try it again. However, there is no reason to use only those activities that have proved successful. Students may suggest other ideas that are just as good and some that may be better than ones you have been using. Every teaching method or learning experience that is at all feasible should be given a chance so that you can see if it will work well for you. If you do

not think it has been successful after trying it several times, there are always alternatives from which to choose. Unless you try a method, you have no way of knowing how successfully you can use it.

Basing Learning Experiences on Behavioral Objectives

Sometimes all of the students in a class complete the same learning experiences and sometimes the students are offered choices. Some students may be able to achieve an objective after participating in only one activity, whereas other students may need to complete several learning experiences before they can achieve the same objective.

A learning experience must come up to the level of learning indicated by the corresponding behavioral objective but should not exceed that level. Although a learning experience often begins with components at a lower level of learning than that of the objective, ultimately it should reach and match the objective level to enable students to attain the objective. The following example illustrates an objective at the comprehension level and an accompanying learning experience that begins at the knowledge level and proceeds to the comprehension level:

BEHAVIORAL OBJECTIVE

Summarize the characteristics of different wall finishes. (Comprehension)

LEARNING EXPERIENCE

Read the chapter in the text on wall finishes. List advantages and disadvantages of various wall finishes discussed in the text.

Examine samples of wall finishes. Describe to the rest of the class the characteristics of one sample wall finish. Take turns until all the characteristics of each sample have been explained.

Although an objective at the knowledge level, such as "List various types of wall finishes," might have been used here, it is not necessary. If it were included, the learning experience would be restated in two parts. Every stated objective has at least one separate and parallel learning experience planned to enable students to achieve it. Sometimes more than one learning experience is used to help students achieve an objective because different students learn in different ways. Learning experiences need to be planned for different learning styles. Some students learn best by reading, some by discussing the material, and some by working alone to complete activity worksheets. See pages 43-44 for more about learning styles.

The following examples illustrate how learning experiences can be planned to help students attain behavioral objectives from the lowest to the highest level in the cognitive domain. Although every cognitive level is used here for illustrative purposes, a level is sometimes omitted if it appears that students can continue up the hierarchy without it. The valuing objective is included at a point corresponding to its parallel position in the affective domain. The concepts to be clarified are the types of maturity: chronological, physical, mental, emotional, social, and philosophical.

BEHAVIORAL OBJECTIVES	LEARNING EXPERIENCES
List the different types of maturity. (Knowledge)	Read about types of maturity in a selected textbook.
	Match the names of the types of maturity written on a chalkboard, poster, flip chart, or transparency with each definition, as it is given.
Give examples to illustrate the various types of maturity. (Comprehension)	Divide into groups of three to five students. Role-play situations depicting as a class the ways in which mature and immature behavior are illustrated by the characters in the dramatizations and/or
	draw cartoons illustrating various types of maturity and/or
	describe persons (anonymously) who are mature in some respects and immature in others.
Demonstrate the possible effects of mature and immature behavior. (Application)	Make up and present miniskits showing mature and immature behavior. Show how the situations could be handled differently to obtain more positive reactions from others.
Show a continuing desire to learn more about maturity by completing an extra-credit project. (Valuing)	Give a short oral report relating a situation from literature in which immature behavior had detrimental effects. Tell about an instance in which a literary character showed greater maturity than expected from a person that age. Discuss the effect this had on others or
	read a biography or autobiography about a person having many mature characteristics. Prepare a short written or oral report showing how this person expressed his or her maturity.
Analyze given situations to determine types and levels of maturity. (Analysis)	Read case studies. Point out various types and level of maturity depicted by the people in the stories and/or
	watch a television soap opera or part of a movie in which the characters demonstrate various types and levels of maturity. Project the future consequences of the mature and immature behaviors shown by completing the story.
Propose ways to cope with immature behavior. (Synthesis)	Formulate answers to the letters in personal-advice newspaper columns that reveal immature behavior.
	Develop a set of guidelines for those who work with preschool-age children to use in directing the children's immature behavior into more mature actions.
Evaluate one's own level of maturity. (Evaluation)	Judge one's own maturity, using a scorecard, checklist, rating scale, or questionnaire that has been provided.
	Evaluate progress, after making a plan for self-improvement.

Learning experiences describe what learners have to do and how they are to do it. Like objectives, when written, they begin with behavioral verbs. Often they are written so that the verb indicates what the students, rather than the teacher, will be doing. Either approach is acceptable, but consistency is important to avoid confusion about who is to do what. Learning experiences that are planned for an entire unit of study may be described in general terms, whereas learning experiences that are part of a daily lesson plan are usually given in some detail.

Extended Learning Experiences

The extended learning experience program is a strategy for remediation, reinforcement, in-depth study, or enrichment. An extended experience should provide opportunities for applying home economics subject matter in the real world and contribute to the students' growth. Extended experiences capitalize on individual students' needs and interests. Ideally, projects are selected, planned, and evaluated by the student with support and guidance from the school and home. Some schools and states require extended learning experience projects; others handle them on an informal basis. The teacher who is new to a school system will want to check to find out if there is an established policy in regard to this.

Implementation of an Extended Learning Experience Program

The program will be a valuable educational experience only if it receives ongoing effort throughout the term. Teachers who present out-of-school extended learning experiences in an enthusiastic manner, who have ideas related to each unit of study, and who are knowledgeable about their students' backgrounds will be better able to guide students toward satisfactory selection of their extended experiences and achievement in meeting their goals.

There are a variety of ways to stimulate students' thoughts about possible extended experiences. The teacher might suggest a few interesting ideas initially and then, through a discussion, solicit additional student ideas. Another way to obtain suggestions from a group is to conduct a brainstorming session that would provide a variety of ideas to be refined or clarified later. The teacher might promote a problem-solving situation in which some information is given about a hypotheti-

cal student's plight in identifying an extended learning experience. Students can then be led to ask significant questions and offer possible solutions for the problem. An additional idea would be to invite students and/or graduates who have successfully completed extended experiences to share their observations in planning, implementing, and evaluating projects. It is important that graduates include some of the problem they faced. If former students are not available to share their experiences with others in person, a video or audiotape correlated with slides showing a variety of projects could be used to create interest. Pictures illustrating different extended experiences that were completed during previous school terms could be used to make a thought-provoking bulletin board. Include the name of the student who did the project.

An explanation of the extended experience program should be provided for the students' families before individual class members become involved in extensive planning. An open house in the home economics department, telephone conversations, home visits, or letters written by either the teacher or students may serve to foster closer cooperation between the home and the school.

Early implementation of the program each semester and consistent supervision by the teacher with the student and parent/guardian are very important. Some school districts set a minimum time period that students should spend on extended learning experiences in order to encourage progressive and significant learning. Several smaller extended experiences that would be comparable to the quality and time involvement of a larger single activity may be preferable for some students.

Selecting Extended Learning Experiences

The experiences selected by students should be realistic ones related to their needs and interests and to those of their families. Individual differences and capabilities need to be considered. Caution should be exercised when a student selects a project that is not related to material that has been or will be covered in class. The advantages and disadvantages of working on a project when the subject matter will not be presented in school should be discussed with the student. The additional time needed to obtain sufficient background information in order to proceed with the project needs to be considered. If students choose such projects, it may be necessary for them to plan independent study in order to gain competence in the areas selected.

There is also the problem of how and by what criteria to evaluate an extended learning experience when the student has not studied the subject matter in school.

Plan for Extended Learning Experience Project

Name _____ Class _____ Period _____

1. Brief description of my extended experience project:

2. Date I plan to finish my project:

3. My goals and objectives (What I want to learn):

4. What I plan to do to accomplish these goals and objectives:

5. Information or knowledge I will need:

   Knowledge needed   Source(s)

6. I will evaluate this project by:

(Reverse Side)

Evaluation

1. These are the things that I actually accomplished by doing this project:

2. These are the *new* things I learned by doing this project:

3. The following is a report of my work (How many times it was done, how many were made, how much money was spent, how long it took, etc.):

4. This is how I could have improved my project:

Family member comments:

Teacher comments:

If a student makes a garment before a unit in clothing construction has been covered in class, and has not straightened the fabric nor understitched the facings, it may very well be that the student had no way of knowing that these steps should have been taken. If, on the other hand, clothing construction had been covered, the teacher would recognize that the student should have known these techniques. However, it may also be that making a particular garment meets an immediate and pressing need for the student. Each teacher will have to decide whether the extended experience for a given term must relate to the subject matter covered during that time. Perhaps this could be the general guideline with exceptions made on an individual basis only after a student-teacher conference.

In guiding students in the selection of projects, you also want to keep in mind that the community's impressions of your program are influenced by the extended learning experiences students work on. These projects are highly visible because they are done in the community, not in school. When a student makes a garment or prepares meals, a stereotyped image of home economics is perpetuated. It is recognized, however, that a project in a traditional area of home economics may best meet the need of an individual student or family at a given time. It is advisable to guide students toward more contemporary program areas when these meet individual and family needs equally well. A tangible product is easily shown, while an activity in the affective area is more difficult to report. You can help students plan from the beginning how they will provide evidence of having achieved their objectives.

Planning and Evaluating Extended Learning Experiences

Students should begin planning their extended experiences as soon as their needs have been identified at the beginning of the term. Planning the extended experience is one of the most crucial elements of the activity. Carelessly-made plans often produce poor results and can affect a student's attitude toward the other aspects of the home economics program. It is essential that students understand the importance of the planning stage. The plans do not have to be elaborate, but they should include the objectives, the proposed steps to be taken, the resources available, the approximate costs, and provisions for record keeping and evaluation. A simple extended learning experience report form providing for the planning and evaluation phases is found on page 42. It simplifies paperwork for you and the students if the statements relating to planning appear on the front side of the page and the evaluation statements are located on the reverse side.

Learning Styles

The possible variations in learning styles are almost as great as the individual differences among students. Some students learn best by listening to you, some by working on group projects, and others by trial-and-error in experiential learning situations. Learning styles, then, describe the circumstances under which students learn best. When we say students differ in learning styles we mean that certain teaching strategies such as visual media, auditory approaches, or tactile experiences are more effective with some students than others. Learning styles include not only these preferred ways of learning but also descriptions of personality characteristics that relate to learning such as flexibility, cooperation, and introversion.

Kolb has identified two dimensions of how people learn. His work has been described by Gephart, Strother, and Duckett in "Practical Applications of Research." Kolb determined that learners perceive material along a continuum from concrete to abstract. Some students, those who tend to be concrete learners, sense and feel their way. They become involved in the learning experience. These students jump in to see if something will work. They learn best by doing.

Abstract learners, on the other hand, examine the learning situation from the outside. They think about it. They process information by observing and reflecting. The two methods are equally "good." They just represent what learners do first.

When the concrete and abstract dimensions are juxtaposed, four learning styles emerge:
1. Type One learners perceive *concretely* with their senses and feelings, and process *reflectively* by watching. They are reflective sensor-feelers.
2. Type Two learners perceive with their *intellect* and process *reflectively*, by watching. They are reflective thinkers.
3. Type Three learners perceive with their *intellect* and process by *doing*. They are thinking doers.
4. Type Four learners perceive *concretely* with their senses and feelings, and process actively by *doing*. They are doing sensor-feelers.

Gregorc's model is similar. Like Kolb, he uses the *concrete* and *abstract* dimension, but he crosses it with a different processing dimension which he has labeled *random/sequential*, giving these four types of learner styles:
1. *Concrete sequential learners* are characterized by a tendency to assimilate information through direct and hands-on experiences. They like order and logical sequence. They prefer touchable, concrete materials. They look for directions to follow, like clearly ordered presentations, and prefer a quiet atmosphere.

2. *Concrete random learners* have an experimental attitude and make intuitive leaps in exploring unstructured problem-solving experiences. They learn by trial-and-error, working well by themselves or in small groups. They do not react favorably to teacher intervention in their independent efforts.

3. *Abstract sequential learners* have excellent decoding abilities with written, verbal, and image symbols. They have a wealth of conceptual "pictures" in their minds against which they match what they read, hear, and see in graphic and pictorial form. These learners prefer substantive, rational, and sequential presentations. They learn effectively from authorities and like vicarious experiences.

4. *Abstract random learners* are attuned to nuances of atmosphere and mood. They associate media with messages and tie speakers' manners, deliveries, and personalities to the messages being conveyed. They evaluate learning experiences as a whole. Abstract random learners prefer to receive information in unstructured manners and prefer activities which involve multisensory experiences and lively environments. They like freedom from rules and guidelines. Abstract mode learners seem to gather information and delay reaction. They organize material through reflection to get what they want.

Gregorc found that everyone exhibits all four patterns to some degree, but most learners show definite preference for one or two of these modes.

McCarthy has combined research on learning styles with right brain/left brain processing research. The two halves of the brain, the right and the left sides, process information differently. The left hemisphere deals with intellectual, analytical, verbal, logical, and sequential processing, while the right mode involves intuitive, visuo-spatial, subjective, unstructured, and random processing. Research indicates that both kinds of processing are equally valuable. However, education concentrates heavily on the left brain, while minimizing the development of the right.

You, as a teacher, not only have to be sensitive to your students' learning styles, but you also have to decide how much to adapt to them. If you believe individual students' learning styles are constant and unchanging, you may want to match them. On the other hand, you may want to alter students' learning styles by using greater variety in media, materials, and methods. In working with visual learners, you have to decide whether to use only visual strategies because that is efficient, or whether to use other approaches as well because that broadens the learners' scope. Sometimes it is appropriate to offer students alternatives. Just be sure that all the options enable students to achieve the unit or lesson objectives equally well.

Teaching Styles

The learning experiences and media chosen by teachers should be related to the personal characteristics of their students. Concrete/sequential-oriented learners like to use workbooks and manuals, to view demonstration teaching, to use programmed instruction, to be involved in hands-on materials, and to participate in well-organized field trips. The abstract/random-oriented learner prefers films, group discussions, short lectures accompanied by questions and answers, and videos. The abstract/sequential learner prefers extensive reading assignments, substantive lectures, audio tapes, and analytical "think-tank-sessions." Concrete/random learners like games, simulations, independent study projects, problem-solving activities, and optional reading assignments.

It is important to recognize that teachers' efforts seem to be most effective when their own personal learning styles and teaching styles are in sync. For this reason, you will want to identify your own dominant learning style and how it may affect your teaching and your selection of learning experiences.

You will want to plan your learning experiences to include a variety of teaching methods and media that involve as many senses as possible. The interests, likes, abilities, and learning styles of the students need to be considered, as well as the time of day and year, the equipment and materials available, and the general philosophy of the school system in which you teach.

References

Gephart, William F., Deborah B. Strother, and William R. Duckett. "Practical Applications of Research." Newsletter of Phi Delta Kappa's Center on Evaluation, Development, and Research, Vol. 3, No. 2, 1980, pages 43-46.

Gregorc, Anthony F. "Learning Teaching Style Student Learning Styles: Diagnosing and Prescribing Programs." Reston, VA: National Association of Secondary School Principals, 1979, pages 19-26.

Kolb, David A. "Learning Style Inventory Teacher Manual." Boston: McBer and Co., 1976, rev. 1978.

McCarthy, Bernice F. "The 4 Mat System: Teaching Learning Styles with Right/Left Mode Techniques." Arlington Heights, IL: Mark Anderson and Associates, 1981.

Planning

Chapter 6

A plan for teaching is like a map or tour guide. It shows your destination and allows for adaptability and creativity in reaching your ultimate goal. If you are driving to a distant place for the first time, you have need to plan your trip in considerable detail and map out your route carefully in advance. If you have traveled to this location many times before, you may only have to refresh your memory about the route. In either case, you are free to detour, spend more time at an intermediate point than planned, or take an alternative road for part of the way. Likewise, when teaching you need to be open to student suggestions for changes in plans, sensitive to how they are reacting, alert to innovative ways of covering subject matter, and flexible enough to take advantage of your own second thoughts.

Planning Units

A unit is planned for the number of days or weeks you anticipate spending on one major concept within the curriculum. Unit plans provide the scope or what will be taught *and* the sequence or schedule telling when various concepts and subconcepts will be covered. A unit plan is broad in scope and lacks the details that are an inherent part of a daily lesson plan. Lesson plans evolve from the unit plan which includes the following basics:

- *Conceptual framework or structure* that provides a topical outline of the subject matter to be covered.
- *Broad, overall, or terminal objectives* at the higher levels of learning. It may take several days to reach one broad objective, although occasionally attainment of more than one higher-level objective is anticipated in a single class period. Chapter 3 discusses broad objectives appropriate for use in planning units.
- *Major learning experiences or student activities and evaluation*. Only the most important activities, involving the higher levels of learning, are included in a teaching unit. Learning experiences used for evaluation purposes and other plans for evaluating student achievement are usually included.
- *Resources* such as teacher reference materials and media. Occasionally student resources are suggested.

In addition, unit plans may include a description of the school and community situation such as the kind and degree of support for the home economics program and availability of material and intangible resources. General observations about the interests, needs, and ability levels of student groups in each class are helpful. As you write notes about students, however, keep in mind the possible legal implications of your assessments. Plans for teaching the unit are derived from the data pertaining to the students, school, and community. If a justification is provided, it tells why the chosen concepts are appropriate for inclusion in the unit. If generalizations are included in a unit plan, they should be second- and third-level and should link the major concepts. First-level generalizations are inappropriate for unit plans because they are too narrow in scope.

Unit plans in block form are easy to use because they provide a daily overview of the teacher's broad and general plans for the coming weeks. By planning in advance, media can be requested or developed ahead of time, arrangements can be made for field trips and resource people, and pertinent references can be gathered and studied.

Note that in the sample unit plan on pages 48 and 49, more than one day is devoted to each of the four major concepts. This is often true, but sometimes only one day is planned for a concept. In the sample, the terminal objectives (TO) are at the analysis, synthesis, and evaluation levels; sometimes more than one objective is planned for a day. Only major learning experiences (LE) have been suggested. These enable students to meet the objectives and correspond to them in levels of learning. Labeling objectives in both unit and lesson plans with the following symbols, to indicate domains and levels of learning, facilitates the planning of learning experiences at appropriate levels:

COGNITIVE (C)
Knowledge (C-K)
Comprehension (C-C)
Application (C-Ap)
Analysis (C-An)
Synthesis (C-S)
Evaluation (C-E)

AFFECTIVE (A)
Receiving (A-Rec)
Responding (A-Res)
Valuing (A-V)
Organization (A-O)
Characterization (A-C)

PSYCHOMOTOR (P)
Perception (P-P)
Set (P-Set)
Guided response (P-GR)
Mechanism (P-M)
Complex overt response (P-COR)

Lesson Plans

The extent to which you plan daily lessons varies greatly depending upon your teaching experience, knowledge of the subject matter to be covered, and the types of lessons being planned. For the experienced teacher, this planning may be done primarily in the mind, with only a few key ideas written on paper. The beginning teacher usually has to plan more extensively in order to feel secure and confident when teaching. The student teacher is generally expected to plan lessons in detail. It is recognized that full-time, in-service teachers may not have the time or the need to plan as extensively as they once did. However, lesson plans should contain enough information to permit a substitute teacher

with a background in home economics subject matter to use any given plan when a minimal amount of time is available to prepare for class.

Although you may not choose to write a justification for every lesson, you should ask yourself these questions: Why teach this lesson? How pertinent is this topic to contemporary life for these students? Some subject matter that has been a traditional part of the typical home economics curriculum for many years can be questioned today as to its relevance to changing family life styles. Justifying your lesson plan, at least mentally, will help you to keep your material interesting and fresh while retaining content of proven value. On the other hand, an idea need not be discarded just because it is traditional.

The unit plan provides the broad base from which lesson plans evolve. The sample lesson plan on pages 50-52 is based on the second Friday of the sample unit plan. If the component parts of the lesson plan are capitalized or underlined, the plan is easier to use. To save time, some teachers make multiple copies of the lesson-plan format. Then they fill in the component parts as individual lessons are planned. A substitute teacher would find it helpful to know both the course and the unit for which the lesson is planned because this gives some indication of the type of students that may be in the class and their subject-matter background. Because the times at which class periods begin and end vary in different schools, it is essential that a substitute teacher have this information. The major concept(s) and broad terminal objective(s) are taken directly from the unit plan.

Introduction/Establishing Set/ Anticipatory Set/Motivator

Whether you use the term establishing set, anticipatory set, or motivator, the introduction should be appropriate for the age and ability level of the students, get the attention of the class, be related to the topic, stimulate thinking about it, and provide for a smooth transition into the body of the lesson. For these reasons, the introduction is usually more effective when it is planned carefully than when it is haphazard. Of course, sometimes you will get a better idea at the last moment than the one you had planned to use. You can usually change your approach, but it may be impossible to think at the last minute of a stimulating way to begin.

Having a carefully planned introduction contributes to your security and allows you to think about the students rather than about what you will say and do. See pages 54 and 55 for the discussion about establishing set, or rapport with students.

Specific Objectives

Specific or daily objectives lead up to the level of learning of the terminal or broad objective but do not exceed this level. Since it sometimes takes several days to achieve a broad objective, the specific objectives for some days may fall several levels below that of the terminal objective. There may be several objectives at the same level that relate to different subconcepts.

It is also possible occasionally to skip a level of learning. As the content or a subconcept changes, the specific objectives may revert to lower levels of learning again. Hence, daily objectives could go in this order: C-K, C-K, C-C, C-An, C-E, C-K, C-C, C-An, C-An, and C-E.

In the sample lesson plan, the first three objectives are at the C-K level, then there are three at the C-C level. One of these C-C objectives relates to premiums, one to manufacturers' and store coupons, and one to shopping lists. The C-Ap level was skipped. The last daily objective may or may not reach the level of the terminal objective. In the sample, the last specific objective is at the analysis level, while the terminal objective is at the synthesis level.

Because the three domains of learning interrelate, specific objectives may shift from one domain to another. An objective from one domain may be used to complete the sequential order of objectives in another domain such as C-K, C-C, A-V, and C-An. Because a level is occasionally skipped, a sequence such as this is also possible:
C-K, C-C, P-GR, P-M, and C-E.

Learning Experiences

Learning experiences are the activities in which students take part so that they are able to achieve the specified behavioral objectives. Every objective has at least one learning experience indicating what the students will *do*. Sometimes two activities are planned to provide for attainment of one objective. Sometimes alternative learning experiences are suggested from which students may choose.

Learning experiences in the sample lesson plan on pages 50-52 are written beginning with a verb telling what the students will do. This helps teachers think about activities from the students' point of view, but learning experiences can be written beginning with verbs telling what the teacher will do to involve students. Either form is acceptable; just be sure to be consistent.

Remember that learning experiences correlate with their behavioral objectives in levels of learning, although they may begin with components that are at lower levels of learning.

It is very important that the specific objectives, learning experiences, and content notes interrelate. The three-column format illustrates this interdependence, but you may prefer another lesson-plan form in which the specific objectives, learning experiences, and content notes are written vertically and in sequence.

The following example is a variation in format adapted from the sample lesson provided on pages 50-52:

Specific objectives: List sources of ads consumers use to make food purchasing decisions. (C-K)
> Learning experience: Name sources of ads that influence consumer decisions relating to food purchasing. (2-3 minutes)
> Content notes: Sources of Ads:
> - Newspapers
> - Magazines
> - Radio
> - TV
> - Flyers and circulars
> - Window display posters

Specific objective: Cite ways to identify specials. (C-K)
> Learning experience: View ads on posters showing ways specials are emphasized. (1-2 minutes)
> Content notes: Ways to identify specials in newspaper ads:
> - Bold print
> - Large type
> - Different colors
> - Coupons

When listing learning experiences, it is helpful to include the specific media and teaching methods that will be used. Obviously, some learning experiences will require more planning than others. Sometimes an idea that is better than those that have been planned will come to the teacher or to a student spontaneously. In such a case, it may be wise to depart from the lesson plan, at least in part. Teachers who are secure in their knowledge of the subject matter are able to be flexible about how it will be presented. Teachers who are insecure about their knowledge of the subject matter or their teaching ability are more likely to be rigid and afraid of what will happen if they depart from previously made plans.

Sample Unit Plan

Week 1. Monday	Tuesday	Wednesday

I. SIGNIFICANCE OF FOOD ———————————————————→
 	
   A. Food habits
   B. Cultural patterns
   C. Social values
   D. Psychological
      satisfactions
 	
 TO: Analyze factors that affect the significance food has for individuals and families (C-An)
 	
 LE: Read and discuss case studies and own situations to determine factors influencing significance of food.
	E. Fads and fallacies
	
	 LE: Share examples of food fads and fallacies and discuss how they relate to the significance one attaches to food.
		II. MEAL PLANNING ————————
		
		   A. Nutritional needs
		
		 TO: Plan meals considering nutritional needs, available resources, values, and lifestyles. (C-S) —————
		
		 TO: Evaluate meals for nutritional content, utilization of resources, and characteristics of lifestyles. (C-E) ———
		
		 LE: Judge given menus and special diets for nutritional adequacy, efficient management of resources, and compatibility with values and lifestyles.

Week 2 ———————————————→
 	
 ———————————————————→
 	
 ———————————————————→
 	
 ———————————————————→
 	
 LE: Exchange menus written on Friday. Work in small groups to evaluate menus for nutrition, use of resources, and appropriateness to lifestyles.
	III. FACTORS AFFECTING FOOD PURCHASES ——————————————→
	
	   A. Income
	   B. Family composition and lifestyles ————————————
	   C. Technology
	   D. Trends in processing and
	      commercial marketing
	
	 TO: Determine factors that affect food purchases. (C-An)
	
	 LE: Listen to guest speaker from university discuss relationship between food purchases and various other factors.
	
	 LE: Work in small groups to plan and present some of the following: (Con't. Wed.)
		1. Handout or news article of suggestions of ways in which proportion of income spent for food can be lowered.
		 2. Role-plays showing how family composition and lifestyles affect food purchases.
		 3. Visuals on technology affecting food purchases.
		 4. Skits showing trends in food processing and commercial marketing.

(Continued on next page)

Thursday	Friday	Resources
B. Resources 1. Money 5. Abilities 2. Time 6. Available foods 3. Energy 4. Equipment	C. Lifestyle D. Values E. Daily food patterns	*Modern Meals* Ch.1, pp. 16-29 *Teen Guide* Ch. 48, pp. 382-391 National Dairy Council "You — A Guide to Food, Exercise, and Nutrition" *Teen Guide* Ch. 49, pp. 392-399 USDA "Dietary Guidelines and Your Diet" Learning Seed Computer Program "What Did You Eat Yesterday?"
LE: View pictures showing situations in which meals are being served that reflect use of resources. Point out ways in which resources seem to have been used to advantage. Suggest changes.	LE: Use RDA charts to plan meals that are nutritionally adequate for special groups such as vegetarians, athletes, and non-breakfast eaters.	

IV. PLANNING FOOD PURCHASES
 	
   A. Food grades
   B. Food states and forms
	C. Using ads and specials
	D. Manufacturers' and store coupons
	E. Shopping list
		Modern Meals
		See Index: Grading, p. 629
		
		Food for Today
		Ch. 8, pp. 106-121
		Ch. 11, pp. 161-176
		
		Creative Living
		Ch. 41, pp. 378-383

TO: Compare food grades, states, and forms in making food purchasing decisions. (C-E) LE: Take field trip to supermarket. Listen to guide explain grades, states, and forms of food. Use worksheet to compare various grades, states, and forms observed.	TO: Develop guidelines that utilize effective management of food purchasing skills. (C-S) LE: Present skit about going grocery shopping and analyze factors the characters do and do not consider in planning food purchases.	

Course and Unit: Consumer Education (Consumer Buying-Food)
Class Period and Time: First, 8:35 a.m.-9:20 a.m.
Day and Date: Friday, September 13, 19XX

A. Major concept(s) from unit block plan:

Planning food purchases

- Using ads and specials
- Trading stamps and premiums
- Shopping lists

B. Terminal objective(s) from unit block plan

Develop guidelines that utilize the effective management of food purchasing skills (C-S).

C. Introduction/establishing set/anticipatory set

Ask students to unscramble the eight words written on a poster, all of which relate to shopping. Each word represents a factor to consider for a step to take before making food purchases. Students who finish quickly can be asked to write a sentence showing how each of the unscrambled words can relate to effective food shopping. The letter found between the two vertical lines in each word is in its correct position and forms the word SHOPPING. (8-10 minutes)

```
        D  A | S |
           H  H | L  T  A  E
     S  E  R | O  T  S
     N  O  S | P  O  U  C
              I | P  A  L  S  S  E  C
              T | I  L  S
     G  N  N | N  I  L  P  A
              G | S  R  D  A  E
```

(Note: To save time, students could work in pairs on a single word. If this takes too much time, give students hints, so that establishing set does not take too long.)

D. Lesson body

SPECIFIC OBJECTIVES	LEARNING EXPERIENCES	CONTENT NOTES
	* Can also be used for evaluation.	
1. List sources of ads consumers use to make food purchasing decisions. (C-K)	*1. Name sources of ads that influence consumer decisions relating to food purchasing. (2-3 minutes)	1. <u>Sources of ads</u>: • Newspapers • Magazines • Radio • T.V. • Flyers and circulars • Window display posters
2. Cite ways to identify specials. (C-K)	2. View ads on posters showing ways specials are emphasized. (1-2 minutes)	2., 3. <u>Ways to identify specials in newspaper ads</u>: • Bold print • Large type • Different colors • Coupons
3. Identify specials in given ads. (C-K)	*3. View double-page newspaper ad held up by teacher and name the featured specials. (1-2 minutes)	

(Continued on next page)

Sample Lesson Plan (continued)

SPECIFIC OBJECTIVES	LEARNING EXPERIENCES	CONTENT NOTES
4. Give examples of premiums that influence shoppers to make food purchases. (C-C)	4. Describe premiums that have influenced people in your family and and other individuals when they have been planning food purchases. (3-4 minutes)	4. Premiums that influence shoppers: • Coupons • Games like bingo • Products sold at discount such as dishes, flatware, encyclopedias, children's books • Food samples in stores
5. Summarize advantages and disadvantages of using manufacturers' and store coupons. (C-C)	5. Share results of interview done for homework in which at least one person was asked, "Do you use manufacturers' and store coupons when shopping for groceries? Why or why not?" Discuss advantages and disadvantages of using coupons. (8-10 minutes)	5. Explain the difference between manufacturers' cents-off coupons and store coupons. Show examples of each. Advantages of using coupons: • Saves money if product would be purchased anyway • Provides considerable saving when coupons are triple-off or double-off and coupons of 50¢ to $1.00 are used • Gives encouragement to try new products you might like Disadvantages of using coupons: • May buy products you do not really need • May overspend • Might find store brand still costs less • Takes time to cut coupons out and keep organized • Increases overall prices to consumers because of store costs involved in handling and lower business profits Tips for using coupons: • Use manufacturers' coupons to buy store specials for greatest savings • Use coupons on smaller sizes of products because the proportion of money saved is greater than on larger sizes • Catalog coupons by types of products for use later • Keep coupons handy that have expiration dates in the near future
6. Explain the advantages of preparing a shopping list. (C-C)	6. View pantomime done by one or two classmates of a consumer shopping for food without a list. * Discuss the advantages of using a list when shopping for food. (7-8 minutes)	6. Advantages of shopping list: • Lessens impulse buying • Saves time • Promotes advance meal planning • Serves as a reminder • Helps capitalize on ads, specials, and premiums

(Continued on next page)

51

SPECIFIC OBJECTIVES	LEARNING EXPERIENCES	CONTENT NOTES
7. Point out factors contributing to consumer skill in planning food purchases. (C-An)	7. View skit, "Kim and Pat Go Shopping." (Skit attached.) Compile a list of factors the characters do and do not consider in planning food purchases. (12-15 minutes)	7. <u>Factors contributing to consumer skill in planning food purchases (skit analysis):</u> Kim and Pat considered: • Coupons • Premiums • Prices • Store location • Ads • Specials Kim and Pat did not consider: • Planning very far ahead for purchases • Being hungry leading to impulse buying • Having a shopping list

E. Summary/closure

Have a student interview another student on a mock T.V. talk show. (5-6 minutes)

Questions for interviewer:
1. Why should you as a consumer pay attention to ads and specials?
2. What benefits might manufacturers' and store coupons offer to consumers?
3. When might coupons be a disadvantage to consumers?
4. Why should a consumer develop a shopping list?

Generalization: Consumer skills in planning for food purchases are enhanced when consideration is given to the use of ads, specials, manufacturers' and store coupons, premiums, and shopping lists.

F. Teaching materials

- Poster showing ways to identify specials
- Double-page newspaper ad
- Skit script "Kim and Pat Go Shopping"

SKIT — "Kim and Pat Go Shopping"

KIM: We'd better go shopping for food for dinner tonight.
PAT: Yes, I'm starving!
KIM: Got something special in mind for dinner?
PAT: No, anything that looks good. Where shall we go shopping?
KIM: Supertown Market gives you a free glass with a ten dollar order.
PAT: Aren't prices higher there?
KIM: Maybe. Where do you think we should go?
PAT: Let's try that new place, the Super Savings Store. It's nearer than Supertown Market, too.
KIM: Oh, yeah. They've advertised they're giving double-off on coupons this week. I'll take the coupons we have. Are you ready?
PAT: Let's go. Maybe we can buy enough food for tomorrow too.

G. Evaluation

See starred learning experiences and summary/closure.

H. Assignment

For today: Interview at least one person and ask the question: "Do you shop for food in stores which offer coupons? Why, or why not?" Write the answer on a paper to be turned in.
For next class period: None

Content Notes

The content notes provide the basic subject matter of the lesson. The content notes include the points you want to be sure are covered. Notes are *written* so no content is overlooked and omitted. It is easier to make note of key points and examples before class than it is to think of them while teaching. There are many forms for making content notes. Usually key points can be used for reference more easily than complete sentences in paragraph form. Sometimes it is appropriate to formulate key questions and to jot down points you want to be sure are brought out in the responses. At other times you might want to make reference to an attached handout or other materials by noting, "See attached leaflet" or whatever is appropriate.

Content notes relate directly to each subconcept that is suggested in each specific objective and, of course, to the parallel learning experience. Occasionally one component of content notes pertains to the subconcepts included in two specific objectives. In the sample lesson plan, the content notes labeled *2* and *3* cover points related to specials *and* ads. These subconcepts are referred to in two objectives. You need no additional content notes for subjects previously covered.

Some sources for content notes include textbooks, professional journals, popular magazines, newspapers, and commercial teaching materials. Your own notes from college courses may also be a valuable source if the content is still up-to-date and valid.

Summary/Closure

The summary or closure ties the lesson together by helping students formulate generalizations about the content that has been covered. See pages 52 for the discussion about closure.

Teaching Materials and Resources

Listing the teaching materials needed for a lesson helps you to organize your thinking and plan ahead. A substitute teacher would find it extremely helpful to have a list of the media such as posters, filmstrips, and case studies to be used in the lesson.

Resources include student or teacher references such as texts, curriculum guides, and written materials distributed by commercial concerns. It is helpful to include resources and references so that, if the lesson plan is to be used again at a later date, the subject matter can be reviewed quickly and easily.

Evaluation

Some learning experiences serve to evaluate student achievement. It is helpful to indicate, perhaps with an asterisk as in the sample lesson plan, the activities that serve this purpose. By doing this, it is easy to note the objectives that remain to be evaluated. The objectives that have been formulated will, in turn, influence the methods and levels of evaluation used.

Assignment

The daily lesson plan may or may not include a student assignment to be done during class time or outside class. It could be a project, small-group assignment, survey, experiment, observation, or almost any other form of learning activity. Assignments to be used as a basis for evaluating student achievement should be directly related to the behavioral objectives that have been established.

Teaching Skills

Chapter 7

Teaching skills are specific and identifiable techniques and tools that teachers use to derive maximum value from the lessons they have planned. Only the most important teaching skills are described in this chapter. They include:

- Establishing set
- Using appropriate frames of reference
- Illustrating with examples
- Reinforcing subject matter
- Reinforcing behavior
- Questioning that includes
   Using higher-level questions
   Using probing questions
   Using student-initiated questions
   Balancing student participation
   Timing
- Using silence
- Pacing
- Recognizing and obtaining attending behavior

- Eliciting feedback
- Achieving closure

If you develop expertise in using these teaching skills, the others should be easy for you. Effective questioning skills are so important in the teaching process that Chapter 9 has been devoted to questioning.

Establishing Set

In education, *establishing set* refers to introducing a lesson, but it encompasses more than that. It entails developing rapport with students as a lesson or class period begins. Set may be enhanced by establishing direct eye contact with students and by talking with them as they enter the room, by making sincere comments that reflect your concern for them, and by asking questions that show your interest. There is a direct correlation between effectiveness in establishing set and the effectiveness of a total lesson. When you succeed in creating a positive attitude at the beginning of the lesson, students are more likely to be involved and interested throughout. Similarly, when students are involved in a lesson from the beginning, they are likely to participate willingly throughout the class period.

Reaction to a lesson is likely to be negative when a teacher begins by saying, "Today *I'm* going to tell you *all* about ..." This gives students the impression the lesson is going to be boring and very teacher-oriented. Students want to feel included from the beginning. In a teacher-dominated classroom you hear lots of words and phrases like *I want you to, tell me,* and *my.* In a student-oriented classroom you are more likely to hear *let's, we,* and *our.*

When teachers dominate lessons at the beginning by doing all the talking, students are often reluctant to participate and feel awkward and self-conscious when asked a question 20 or 30 minutes after class has begun. Students realize that when they have not talked for some time, their voices may sound shaky and hesitant when they do speak.

The term *anticipatory set* refers to creating interest in the lesson as you begin. You do not need an elaborate introduction that takes a long time to prepare. It may consist of a thought-provoking rhetorical question you ask while looking right at the students to show your interest in their reactions. You might use an analogy to show the relationship between the topic for the day and some current or historical event, or you might refer to a bulletin board, display, or exhibit. You can stimulate interest by having materials relating to the main concept of the lesson in a paper bag or on a tray that is covered with a towel to create an element of surprise. If you are going to use a poster, turn it toward the wall until you need it in the lesson.

In a lesson on grooming or health, you could pretend to be taking the students' picture with a camera. As the students sit up straight, you might say, "We would all feel so much better if we always looked as we do when we're having our picture taken." In a lesson on the significance of food, you might begin by serving a small snack and then leading into a discussion of the many reasons people eat what they do. For a lesson on personal characteristics for employability, you might drop an effervescent headache remedy into a clear glass containing water. Relate the bubbling action to friendliness, enthusiasm, and good health required for success on the job. You could also use this idea to introduce a lesson on nutrition, energy conservation, or patterns of physical activity and fatigue. Occasionally you can scramble one word denoting the main topic of the lesson on the board to create interest. You need to plan for establishing set, but you do not need to have an elaborate and time-consuming activity.

Using Appropriate Frames of Reference

Frames of reference provide several different points of view through which students gain an understanding of content. Because a subject is better understood when it is presented from different points of view, such a procedure is more effective than using only one. For example, fashion merchandising becomes more meaningful to students when it is seen from the points of view of the garment designer, fabric manufacturer, assembly-line production staff, wholesale distributor, retailer, and fashion coordinator. The key to this teaching skill is the word *appropriate*. You identify many possible frames of reference that can be used in instruction and then make judicious selections from among them, depending on the needs and interest of the students.

To illustrate how having a frame of reference helps you remember material, try the following exercise. Study the following combinations of three letters in order to list them again in about 30 seconds in any order:

HEC
XAT
IPS
XRG
ZZZ
BOR
TAS
LCP
NED

Which combinations of letters did you remember? Undoubtedly it was those for which you have a frame of reference.

- For HEC, you may have thought of Home Economics.
- For XAT, you may have realized the word tax was spelled backwards.
- For IPS, you may have remembered that it was almost IRS or Internal Revenue Service.
- You probably did not recall XRG unless you have some personal frame of reference for remembering it.
- ZZZ may have been remembered because it is different and unusual.
- BOR may have reminded you of Board of Regents or bore.
- TAS may have made you think of the SAT or Scholastic Aptitude Test.
- LCP may not have been remembered unless you had some personal frame of reference for recalling it.
- For NED, you may have realized that the letters spell END — for the end of the list. Or perhaps your name or that of a friend is Ned.

If subject matter is presented using a frame of reference which is meaningful to your students, it will have added relevance and be more likely to be recalled later when needed to help make a decision or to solve a problem.

Illustrating with Examples

Examples are used to clarify, verify, and substantiate concepts. Here are some ways to use examples effectively:

- Start with simple examples and progress to more complex ones.
- Begin with examples relevant to students' experiences and knowledge.
- Build on students' verbal contributions by giving examples to clarify points students have made and to add depth of subject matter.
- Relate examples to the principles being taught or the guidelines being covered.
- Check to see if the objectives of the lesson have been achieved, by asking students to give examples that illustrate the main points.

Rating Scale for Teaching Skills

Person being rated _____   Rater _____

Directions: Use the key to evaluate the teacher on each of the skills. Record in the score column the number that corresponds to the level of competence. Then compute the total score.

KEY: 1 = Inadequate
2 = Improvement needed
3 = Average
4 = Good
5 = Outstanding

1	2	3	4	5	SCORE
Establishing Set					
1. Bored students with a dull, unimaginative approach.	Gained interest of some students with a rather ordinary approach.		Gained immediate interest of students with a stimulating approach.		1. _____
2. Did not achieve rapport and created no interaction among students.	Achieved rapport with some students and gained some interaction among students.		Achieved rapport with students and fostered interaction among the students.		2. _____
Framing Reference					
3. Failed to frame a reference — left students in question as to relevancy of material.	Had some success in framing a reference that helped students understand material.		Incorporated different points of view to achieve an interesting frame of reference with which each student could identify.		3. _____
4. Did not relate frame of reference to objectives to make material relevant to students.	Attempted to relate content to objectives, but this was sometimes unclear.		Related frame of reference to objectives and made students realize the relevancy of material to them.		4. _____
Questioning					
5. Did not use functional questions, did not redirect; discussion monopolized by a few students.	Utilized functional questions to some extent, but some questions required more teacher development before other students joined discussion.		Used functional questions to clarify, justify, and to bring other students into discussion.		5. _____
6. Kept questions on knowledge level and did not encourage higher levels of thinking.	Asked some questions on higher levels but tended to stay with lower level questions.		Used content questions that began on low levels and progressed to higher levels of thinking.		6. _____
Reinforcing					
7. Used only limited verbal reinforcement and did not change voice or expression.	Used some variety in verbal reinforcement but used no other means of reinforcement.		Used a variety of methods of reinforcement including gestures as well as words.		7. _____
8. Overdid reinforcement to point of sounding fake and insincere.	Seemed to be sincere most of the time when reinforcing.		Was sincere in each reinforcement to each student response.		8. _____
Achieving Closure					
9. Did not draw points together or summarize periodically or at the end.	Had some success in drawing points together periodically but had difficulty in choosing when to have final closure.		Achieved closure at appropriate times.		9. _____
10. Did not interrelate parts of material or give students a feeling of progress and achievement.	Interrelated some of the material and gave some students a feeling of progress and achievement.		Successfully pulled parts of lesson together and gave students a feeling of progress and achievement.		10. _____

TOTAL SCORE _____

56

Reinforcing Subject Matter

The purpose of this skill is to further clarify major concepts, generalizations, principles, and key words. You can use repetition effectively to focus, highlight, and direct attention to points that need emphasis. However, students feel belittled and bored when teachers cover subject matter verbatim a second time and with the same media and teaching methods. Varying instructional strategies usually enhances the reinforcement of content. For example, principles of design may be covered in home furnishings and reinforced in clothing selection, table setting, and flower arranging. With each conceptual area, different visual media and verbal examples would be used, and students would participate in different learning experiences and build on previous ones.

Reinforcing Behavior

Your positive reaction to desired student behavior is an integral part of your role as a teacher and facilitator of classroom learning. You can give reinforcement nonverbally through smiling and nodding or verbally with words of support. Praise is often a single word such as "Good," "Fine," or "Exactly." Sometimes you can simply say, "Go on. This is interesting." or, "Tell us more about your idea." Reinforcement is also given by repeating those students' answers that contribute positively to the lesson. When a learner makes a worthwhile comment, you may paraphrase the statement, restate the idea more simply and concisely, or summarize what has been said. When teachers build on students' responses to develop the subject matter further, it is a compliment to students. They feel that their contributions are valued and important.

Both verbal and nonverbal reinforcement reflect concern for students' feelings. It is important to give reinforcement in a variety of ways because students react differently to various types of support. See Chapter 9 for more specific response techniques.

Questioning

The learning value derived from using an educational game, showing a filmstrip, participating in a sociodrama, reading an assignment, or taking part in *any* educational activity depends to a very high degree on your questioning skills. Five general questioning skills are discussed here. See Chapter 9 for more detailed coverage of questioning.

Using Higher-Level Questions

Higher-level questions cannot be answered from memory alone. They call for explaining, using, analyzing, synthesizing, or evaluating rules, guidelines, or principles rather than stating them. Higher-level questions can seldom be answered with only one word. Beginning questions with *how, what,* and *why* generally fosters thinking at levels above recall, or cognitive knowledge.

Using Probing Questions

When teachers probe, they ask questions that require students to go beyond superficial *first answer* responses. You do this when you:
- Ask students for more information or what their replies mean.
- Require students to justify or defend their responses.
- Refocus the students' or class's attention on a related issue.
- Prompt students or give them hints.
- Bring other students into the discussion by getting them to respond to the first student's reply.

Using Student-Initiated Questions

If the classroom environment is nonthreatening and students are interested and motivated, they will usually ask questions that can be used to enhance a lesson. Replying to students' questions can add depth to the subject matter of a lesson. However, replying to students' questions at length should meet the needs and interests of a sufficient number to justify the time spent doing this. Teachers need to be careful not to let students' questions and their own responses extend beyond the point of educationally diminishing returns. In answering a question, be careful not to look at and speak only to the student who asked the question, but rather maintain eye contact and talk with the entire class to keep the students' attention. So that your answer has maximum value, repeat the question or ask the student to do this.

Students often ask questions that lead their teachers into talking about topics different from those related to the purpose of the lesson. Sometimes students delight in seeing how long they can keep their teachers off the subject. Students realize that they cannot be held responsible for material that was never covered in class. Limited discussion about topics not included in the curriculum can add interest and serve as a motivating force, but avoid topics that are too personal, that are *highly* controversial, or that stimulate extremely emotional reactions. Issues that might be acceptable topics for classroom discussion in one school may be totally unacceptable in another school. You need to sense the appropriate time to conclude the talk about irrelevant topics. You might say, "This is all very interesting, but let's get back to what we were saying about …" Sometimes you may avoid being sidetracked by making a comment such as, "That's an interesting question, but we need to continue our discussion about …"

Balancing Student Participation

You need to be aware of which students have contributed to a discussion and which have not, so you can include the nonparticipating students. You want to provide the opportunity for most of the class to participate. Use a random order to call on students rather than going around the room in a set pattern up and down rows.

Timing

As a beginning teacher you may be tempted to answer your own questions rather than give students sufficient time to think of their own responses. In the absence of a response, you may provide a hint to the answer. Perhaps you would feel comfortable saying something like "Let me put it another way," or "I guess I didn't make the question clear," before rephrasing it or changing it to incorporate a lower level of learning.

Using Silence

Many teachers are frightened by silences or pauses in classroom discussions. Because they feel uncomfortable, they tend to fill silences by talking unnecessarily or by making sounds such as "umm." Silence can be a powerful tool in the teaching-learning process because it can provide students with the opportunity to think about what has transpired. You can use pauses effectively after the following:
- Introductory comments that encourage students to think about their answers.
- Questions asked of students to give them time to think about their answers.
- Questions from a student directed to another student verbally or by a look or gesture.
- Student responses that foster additional remarks from other students.

Pacing

Pacing refers to making a smooth transition from one part of a lesson to another and to balancing the amount of intellectually difficult material presented at one time. You should plan the transition to link one concept to another and to move students from one activity to another. When pacing is effective, students have time to absorb the information, but the lesson does not drag. You should be careful not to cover too many *weighty* cognitive concepts at one time, because students need to be provided with the opportunity to analyze and synthesize. For example, if you planned to cover hue, value, intensity, temperature, force, and color schemes in a ninth grade class in one day, there would be too little time for the students to grasp the material. There also should be several opportunities during a lesson for evaluation and student-initiated questions and comments.

Recognizing and Obtaining Attending Behavior

Successful and experienced teachers use visual cues that indicate student reactions such as interest, boredom, comprehension, and confusion. A facial expression, the direction of the eyes, the tilt of the head, and body posture offer messages that make it possible for skilled teachers to evaluate their performance according to students' reactions. Doodling, yawning, twisting hair, and swinging feet are signs that might indicate it is time to modify the lesson by varying the pace, changing the activity, or introducing a different method of teaching.

Eliciting Feedback

The feedback process may be simply stated as providing "knowledge of results." Teachers sometimes ignore the availability of information accessible to them during the class. Questioning, visual cues, and informal appraisal of performance can be immediate sources of feedback. Teachers can be taught appropriate techniques to elicit feedback from students so they can modify their lessons when necessary. Teachers unconsciously tap a variety of feedback sources, but, unless they are sensitive, they tend to rely unevenly on a limited number of students as "indicators" and to rely unevenly on a restricted range of feedback cues.

Behaviors Contributing to Teaching Effectiveness

Behaviors	Evidences
Helps build students' self-esteem.	• Treats students' questions and imaginative ideas with respect by praising and building on their comments. • Shows students their ideas have value by using them on bulletin boards, displays, and verbally in class. • Helps learners find answers to their own questions. • Teaches learners to praise themselves and others sincerely. • Has students do things occasionally without concern about evaluation or grading. • Guides students in setting goals and evaluating realistically. • Ties evaluation in with causes and consequences (What might happen if … ?).
Provides time and an environment for learning.	• Gives students time to think. • Teaches at a pace appropriate to the content and learners. • Provides sufficient time for practice and laboratory activities. • Begins and ends class with routines that provide security. • Starts with activities that create interest and motivate without threatening. • Ascertains level of understanding by asking appropriate questions. • Gives students hints and suggestions for how to remember material. • Repeats subject matter as needed using different approaches.
Provides examples and explanations.	• Gives examples that show how to solve problems and do classwork and homework. • Illustrates with examples that are relevant and meaningful to the students and their lifestyles. • Uses the chalkboard and transparencies to emphasize major points. • Describes work to be done and how to do it.
Organizes and reviews.	• Makes sure learners know what to do and how to do it. • Relates subject matter to material covered previously. • Tells learners how content will be useful to them now and/or in the future. • Prepares students well for what they'll be doing next.

To find out if students are grasping the subject matter of the lesson, it is more effective to ask questions related to the content than it is to ask "Do you understand?" Some students are reticent to admit to the entire class that they do not understand when it appears to them that everyone else does.

Achieving Closure

Closure helps students formulate generalizations. It is appropriate when the major concepts, purposes, principles, or particular portions of a lesson have been covered so that students can relate new knowledge to past knowledge. Closure is more than a quick summary of the material covered in a lesson. In addition to pulling together major points and helping students see the relationships among concepts, closure provides students with a feeling of achievement. Closure is not limited to the end of a lesson. You can provide closure at specific points within a lesson to help students see where they have been, where they are, and/or where they are going. Questions such as these are helpful in closing lessons:

"How does what we've been talking about relate to …"

"What does this mean to you in your life today?"

"How can you use this information in the future?"

Varying the Learning Environment

In addition to using specific techniques skillfully, you can vary the environment to enhance learning. You increase student interest when you change the seating arrangement and the appearance of the classroom. You can use different accessories or rearrange them, make a new bulletin board or display, and use a fresh teaching method. Sometimes you can hold class in another room or have the students sit on the floor during a class discussion.

Although creating interest through variety is usually not identified as a specific teaching skill, it does enhance the teaching-learning process. When you vary your habitual patterns, student attention often increases. For example, you can vary your interaction style or the way in which you move around the room, or even your appearance. A new hair style or fashion worn by the teacher may serve to heighten student interest in content areas completely unrelated to personal appearance. A variety of media, materials, and methods of teaching is also important in creating and maintaining student interest.

Self-Evaluation

Viewing a videotape of yourself can be enlightening! You may discover habit patterns that include distracting gestures, annoying facial expressions, and repetitious verbal interactions. Becoming sensitized to habits such as jiggling change in your pocket, pushing eye glasses up, twisting hair, rocking on your feet, or saying the same words over and over for reinforcement can help you change these behaviors. Try for greater variety in your demeanor and elimination of annoying, repetitious mannerisms.

Microteaching

Microteaching in its purest sense means developing expertise in using teaching skills, practicing one at a time. You may be videotaped with a small group of learners while establishing set. This teaching skill is critiqued and played back as often as necessary. Then you are videotaped again while establishing set again. This procedure is repeated as often as necessary.

A second teaching skill, perhaps using examples, is isolated and worked on next until a desirable level of expertise is achieved using this skill. The process continues until a predetermined level of competence has been achieved in using each of the teaching skills.

In many situations, this pattern may have to be modified. Time, equipment, class size, and other variables affect the procedures used. Perhaps two or three teaching skills are worked on during each videotaping session. Seeing yourself teaching via videotape will highlight your strengths and weaknesses as nothing else will. Self-evaluations as well as peer and supervisor evaluations that point out areas in which you excel and areas in which you need to improve are essential for successful microteaching experiences.

Teaching skills are tools of the trade — and they are also tricks of the trade, in the legitimate sense that they make one teacher succeed where another, equally informed and well-intentioned, fails. The skills can be summarized at length, as in the preceding; but their secret comes down largely to the art of communication, or *interchange*. Learning is not a one-way street. Teaching skills are the things that facilitate the transfer of knowledge from teacher to student, but the feedback generated in the process is also a constant and invaluable guide to the teacher in reaching the desired target.

Evaluation

Chapter 8

Teachers who want to evaluate their students' achievement fairly and honestly provide a broad base on which to determine final grades. A variety of evaluative methods is fairer because different students do well on different types of measures. A variety of evaluative methods gives all students an opportunity to do well occasionally. Thus, student achievement may be based on homework assignments, work done in class, projects, reports, laboratory experiences, self-evaluative instruments, and tests. The proportional weight given to each evaluation in determining the composite grade should be made clear to students so that they can establish priorities.

Using Tests

In addition to determining grades, test results can also be used to analyze students' strong and weak points, to provide a basis for initiating a conference or counseling session, and to help students see the relationships among the concepts covered in the text. Teachers can also use test scores to determine which topics they have covered most adequately and which methods of teaching they have used most effectively.

The frequency of testing depends on the concepts being covered. When only one or two tests are given in a course, undue emphasis may be placed upon them. It is a good idea to give tests at the beginning of the class period. When students are told they will be given a test at the end of the period, they are likely to spend class time in worrying or cramming rather than paying attention to the business at hand. Surprise or pop tests foster student resentment against both the teacher and the subject matter, and increase the probability that students will cheat. Although not all students will study for announced tests, students should have the option of deciding this for themselves. Furthermore, one of the purposes of giving a test is to encourage students to review and clarify concepts. Obviously, the purpose will not be served if the students do not know that they are going to have a test.

Since cheating is a difficult problem to handle, take precautions to minimize its occurrence. See pages 175-176 for specific suggestions for coping with this problem. As a test score increases in importance in determining a final term grade, the likelihood that students will cheat also increases. Therefore, you want to provide opportunities for self-evaluation and to figure term grades on a broad base of quizzes, assignments, reports, and projects. Pressure to cheat is lessened when students realize that neither one very high test score nor one very low score will have a great impact on their overall averages.

Guidelines for Constructing Achievement Tests

The following guidelines relate to writing variations of teacher-made achievement tests. Specifics that pertain exclusively to constructing a particular type of test item precede the examples given for different possibilities.

1. As you write test questions, keep a tally to be sure the behavioral objectives are covered in proportion to the instructional emphasis given to each. Also check to see that achievement of each objective is measured so that some test questions come up to the level of learning of the corresponding objective. However, none of the test questions for a given objective should exceed the level of learning of that objective.

2. Similar types of test items should be grouped together. For example, all simple two-response true-and-false questions should be grouped in one section of the test, and all multiple choice questions of the one-correct-answer type should be grouped in another section. Write separate directions for each section. This organizes the test so that students do not have to keep changing their orientation and thinking process from question to question. Within each section, arrange items so they are grouped by subject matter.

3. Write test items so that an obvious pattern of answers does not emerge, such as *true, true, false, true, true, false,* and so forth. At the same time, questions ought to progress in difficulty, beginning with easier questions. This enables students to experience an initial success that may motivate them to proceed through the test with a positive attitude. Difficult items usually take longer to answer. Students may have a tendency to devote so much time to answering harder questions that little or no time remains to complete the test.

4. Word test items and directions clearly and concisely. If the vocabulary is too difficult, the item may be assessing whether the students understand the meaning of specific words rather than the concepts involved. On the other hand, when the vocabulary is too simple and monotonous, students may be insulted or bored and, consequently, make careless errors. Test-wise students or ones who are particularly adept in syntax will have a decided advantage if there are grammatical clues that give away the right answer. This possibility can be eliminated by using ''a (an)'' and ''(s)'' with nouns and verbs where plurals or verb tenses could indicate the correct responses.

5. It is important that both visual and verbal examples used in class and statements from the text do not reappear on a test precisely as they were originally presented. Using the exact wording of the textbook or the same pictures or samples used in class does nothing to determine whether students can interpret, apply, or analyze subject matter.

6. Use quantitative statements in place of qualitative ones whenever possible because they are clearer. Words like *more, less, sometimes, often, seldom, generally*, and *usually* may be interpreted in various ways by different students.

7. If you have to use negative statements, call attention to the negative word by underlining or capitalizing it. Avoid negative statements if at all possible.

8. Avoid parenthetical clauses and phrases. Although your intent in placing additional material in parentheses may be to clarify by giving an example, in actuality this might cause confusion.

9. Complete each question on one page. If you continue an item onto the succeeding page, this may confuse students and cause paper shuffling.

10. Plan the test so the majority of students have enough time to finish. Objective items tend to provide more extensive sampling per unit of time than do essay questions. However, objective tests have a tendency to become highly factual and to place a premium on memory alone, whereas essay questions provide an opportunity for students to organize and express their thoughts. The subject matter and objectives will affect the types of questions used.

11. Indicate clearly the point value of each test item. This can help students determine the amount of time and effort they should allow for completing their responses.

12. Be sure each test question is independent of all other questions on the test. Answering a question correctly should not depend on having answered a previous question correctly.

13. Check to be sure that the answers to questions are not inadvertently provided in other items on the test.

14. Give a point of reference for attitudes, theories, and philosophies. For example, instead of stating, ''Experience is the best teacher,'' you might write, ''John Dewey believed that ideas must be judged by experience.''

15. The scoring of tests is simplified when questions are arranged and written so that answers can be checked easily and quickly. Responses to objective questions can be written to the left of each item so that you can place an answer key next to the answer column for rapid scoring. You might want to use a separate answer sheet when tests are longer than one or two pages.

True-and-False Items

Because true-and-false questions are fairly easy to write, they are frequently used in tests. However, caution should be observed in constructing true-and-false items so that they will be clearly understood and guessing will be minimized. There should be approximately the same number of true items as false items. When almost all the answers are either true or false, students may become more concerned with an answer pattern than with the content of the items.

The letters *t* and *f* can be easily confused; therefore, use + for true and 0 for false to save time in grading and to avoid potential arguments when tests are returned. It takes more time to read *true* and *false* when the students write out these words. Or you might want to provide an answer column and direct students to circle either T or F.

Correction-type responses and responses that require giving reasons for false answers minimize guessing better than simple two-response items. They also give you a better assessment of student learning.

The following examples show different types of true-false items. The level of learning progresses from knowledge to comprehension to analysis. Many educators erroneously believe that objective test items can be written only at the knowledge level.

■ *True-False — Simple Two-Response Choice (with knowledge-level examples)*

Directions: If the statement is true, place a + in the blank to the left of the item. If the statement is false, place a 0 in the blank.

   +   1. Advance meal planning contributes to wise consumer planning.

   +   2. The selection of the grade of a food product depends upon its intended use.

   0   3. Federal regulations require that recipes be given on the labels of canned food products.

■ *True-False — Correction-Type Response (with knowledge-level examples)*

Directions: If the item is true, write + in the answer column. If it is false, correct it by writing, in the space provided at the left, the word you would substitute for the underlined word to make it a true statement.

   +   1. Most of the design principles we use were developed by the ancient <u>Greeks.</u>

<u>proportion</u> 2. A large design in a fabric to be used for draperies in a small room is an example of poor <u>balance.</u>

<u>transition</u> 3. Curved lines that create rhythm are referred to as <u>opposition.</u>

■ *True-False — Series of Statements Based on a Given Situation (with comprehension-level examples)*

Directions: Mary and Bob have bought an old house that needs redecorating. The rooms in the house are small. Mary and Bob want to make these rooms appear larger through effective decorating.

The following is a list of changes they are considering. If the change would make a room appear larger, put a + in the blank to the left of the statement. If the change would make the room appear smaller, put a 0 in the blank.

   0   1. Use dark colors on the walls.

   0   2. Use intense colors on the walls.

   +   3. Paint the baseboard, molding, and woodwork the same color as the walls.

   0   4. Paint each room a different color.

   +   5. Use mirrors for wall decorations.

   +   6. Choose furniture that is small in scale.

■ *True-False — With Reasons for False Answers (with comprehension-level examples)*

Directions: If the statement is true, place a + in the blank to the left. If the item is false, place a 0 in the blank and then, below the item, give the reason why it is false. Credit will be given only if the reason you supply is correct — true and to the point. You do not have to give reasons for items marked true.

   +   1. On a limited budget, it is more practical to buy furniture that is open-stock than that which is custom-made.

   +   2. Other things being equal, wood veneer of seven ply will be more durable than solid wood.

   0   3. Scotchguard is a finish applied to upholstery fabric that helps to minimize color fading. *It helps fabric to resist soil and stains.*

■ *True-False — Analogy (with analysis-level examples)*

Directions: If the analogy is true, circle the letter **t** in the answer column. If the analogy is false, circle the letter **f**.

(t) f 1. Vitamin A is to night blindness as vitamin D is to rickets.

t (f) 2. Iron is to milk as vitamin A is to carrots.

(t) f 3. Vitamin C is to healthy gums as calcium is to strong bones.

Multiple Choice Items

Multiple choice items usually consist of an introductory statement or question, called the *stem*, followed by a series of words, phrases, or sentences that are called *alternatives*. The stem should consist of a completed idea, not just a single word. All the multiple choice stems in one group should be in the form of either a question or an incomplete statement. Some educators prefer the question form because it is a natural method of inquiry.

Use four to seven plausible alternatives below each stem. Each multiple choice question in one section of the test should have the same number of alternatives for a unified effect. The correct alternatives, as well as the distractors, or incorrect responses, need to be homogeneous in content and form. Distractors should seem plausible or they become *giveaways* and affect the validity of a test. Remember, too, that when students are in doubt, they frequently select the longest choice. Use alternatives such as "all of the above," "none of the above," "two of the above," and so forth infrequently. This type of response is often confusing and can increase the probability of guessing correctly.

The first three types of multiple choice items are illustrated with knowledge-level questions. The last three use analysis-level questions.

■ *Multiple Choice — Single Best Answer*

Directions: In the blank to the left of each item, write the letter corresponding to the *one* answer that best completes each statement.

  b 1. Dry a 100 percent wool sweater:
    a. In the sun.
    b. On a flat surface.
    c. In a dryer.
    d. Near a heat outlet.
    e. On a hanger.

■ *Multiple Choice — One Incorrect Answer*

Directions: Circle the letter of the *one* item that *incorrectly* completes each statement.

1. Fortified whole milk is a good source of:
    (a.) Vitamin C.
    b. Phosphorus.
    c. Calcium.
    d. Vitamin A.
    e. Vitamin D.

■ *Multiple Choice — Variable Number of Answers*

Directions: For every item that correctly answers the question, black out the corresponding letter(s). All, some, or none of the answers may be correct.

1. Which of the following foods contain vitamin C?
    a. Citrus fruit
    b. Eggs
    c. Milk
    d. Bell peppers
    e. White potatoes

■ *Multiple Choice — One-Answer Analogy*

Directions: Black out the letter corresponding to the word that *best* completes the sentence.

1. Strength is to nylon as heat resistance is to:
    a. Acetate.
    b. Cotton.
    c. Linen.
    d. Polyester.
    e. Rayon.

■ *Multiple Choice — Most Inclusive Item without Stem*

Directions: Circle the letter that corresponds to the most *inclusive* item in each group. In other words, choose the item that includes all the others listed in that particular group.

1. a. Educational background
    b. Job experiences
    c. Organizational affiliations
    d. References
    (e.) Resume

2. a. Chef
   b. Caterer
   c. Food laboratory tester
   d. Food-service semiprofessional employee
   e. Dietitian's assistant

■ *Multiple Choice — Most Dissimilar Items without Stem*

Directions: In the blank to the left, write the letter corresponding to the one item in the group that is *not* associated with the others listed. In other words, choose the item that is dissimilar to the others in the group.

___d___ 1. a. Flying a kite
  b. Riding a bicycle
  c. Jumping rope
  d. Modeling with clay
  e. Playing on a jungle gym

___a___ 2. a. Assembling and gluing model airplanes
  b. Playing with toy trucks in a sandbox
  c. Putting together wooden puzzles
  d. Building with blocks
  e. Playing with push-pull toys

Matching Items

Matching tests are used to show the association of or relationship between two elements such as words and definitions, events and persons, examples and principles, or causes and effects.

The matching test typically consists of two columns. Each column should be homogeneous in form and content. For example, items referring to the function of nutrients should not be mixed in the same column with those indicating the best sources of nutrients. Columns should be labeled according to content.

It is recommended that from five to ten items be used in a matching question. When possible, place the longer items in the left-hand column and the shorter responses in the right-hand column. This helps students identify the correct answer quickly. Responses in the right-hand column should be arranged in some logical order such as alphabetically, numerically, or chronologically. This also reduces time spent in locating a correct answer.

The chances of guessing may be reduced by providing a greater number of responses than items or by allowing for response alternatives to be used more than once. However, avoid using one response more than three times or the validity of the test might be affected. This should be specified in the directions in order to minimize confusion for students. Grading is quicker when responses are recorded as numbers rather than letters because numbers are easier to read.

■ *Matching-Identifying Illustrations*

Directions: Match the illustrations in Column A with the terms in Column B. Use terms in Column B only once. (5 points)

COLUMN A	COLUMN B
Illustrations	*Terms*

Column A illustrations:

___2___ a.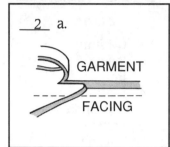
GARMENT / FACING

___4___ b.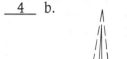

___1___ c.
INSIDE CURVE

___5___ d.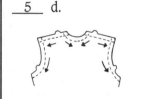

___7___ e.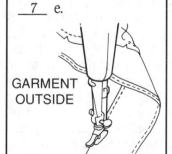
GARMENT OUTSIDE

Column B terms:

1. Clipping and grading
2. Grading
3. Hemming
4. Slashing
5. Staystitching
6. Trimming
7. Understitching

■ Matching — Definitions

Directions: For each function in Column A, locate the nutrient in Column B associated with it. Place the number corresponding to the best choice in the blank to the left of each item in Column A. Use a number only once. (8 points)

COLUMN A	COLUMN B

Primary Functions

  9   a. Keeps gums healthy; aids healing of skin injuries

  8   b. Helps prevent night blindness

  6   c. Builds and maintains body tissues

  7   d. Steadies nerves; aids digestion

  1   e. Builds strong bones and teeth

  10   f. Regulates the deposit of minerals in bones and teeth; prevents rickets

  2   g. Prevents goiter

  3   h. Helps form hemoglobin in red blood cells

Nutrients

1. Calcium
2. Iodine
3. Iron
4. Niacin
5. Phosphorus
6. Protein
7. Thiamine
8. Vitamin A
9. Vitamin C
10. Vitamin D

Completion Items

Fill-in-the-blank, or completion, items are statements in which one or more words are omitted. One-word or single-expression answers such as *credit rating, installment loan,* and *bait and switch* are preferred. They tend to be more objective than answers written in phrases or sentences. Only a significant word should be omitted from the sentence; the resulting blank should occur at or near the end of the statement. In that way, the major thought is presented before the blank appears. It is necessary to achieve a balance between providing too little information and too much, so that completion items are truly discriminating. All blanks should be of uniform length throughout the test so that students will not be encouraged to respond to an item because of the presumed length of the omitted word.

Scoring can be facilitated by using numbers or question marks in the blanks within the sentences and by placing response blanks to the left of the completion items to form an answer column.

■ Completion — Incomplete Sentences

Directions: Fill in the blank to the left of each sentence with the *best* word or words to complete the statement.

  credit union   1. An institution that offers limited cash installment loans only to its members is a(n) (1) .

  banks   2. The majority of noninstallment cash loans is provided by (2) .

  percentage rate   3. The amount of interest you pay in a finance charge is determined by the annual (3) .

■ Completion — Analogy

Directions: Fill in the blank to the left of each sentence with the *best* word or words to complete the statement.

  blue   1. Violet is to yellow as orange is to (?) .

  red   2. Green and orange are to purple as yellow and blue are to (?) .

  analogous   3. Pink and red are to a monochromatic color scheme as yellow, yellow-green, and green are to a(n) (?) color scheme.

Identification Items

The identification test item typically requires the students to label or locate parts of a diagram or to give specific information about a picture or an object. Pictures, diagrams, and actual objects are more vivid than verbal descriptions and provide interest and variation in testing procedures.

Sketches and diagrams should be drawn clearly and large enough to be seen easily. It is important that lines and numbers indicating various parts of a diagram are easy to understand. Illustrations used for testing should be different from those that were used in class. Directions about how students are to proceed should be clear and explicit.

■ *Identification — Passing Around Articles*

Identification tests can also be designed so that actual food products, kitchen utensils, small equipment, sewing machine attachments, samples of clothing-construction techniques, or pictures are passed from one student to another in a planned-sequential order. Gauge when it is time to say "pass" by ascertaining when most of the students have completed the identification on which they are working. An essential in using this technique is to be certain that all students understand that they must *pass* at the designated time. Otherwise, some students will accumulate articles while others will not have any to work on. A variety of rotation systems for passing articles can be used. There should be the same number of items (or only a very few more) as there are students taking the test. To begin, each student should be given either one or two articles. Students should be reminded that items may not necessarily be received in numerical order and that they must write their responses in the correct places on their test papers. After the rotation, the items may be placed on a table so that one student at a time can reexamine them.

This technique lends itself to many variations. Numbered swatches of fabric might be passed for identification by their common names. Pictures representing various periods of furniture design could be mounted, numbered, and used in a similar manner. A question that applies to a large number of items might be asked, such as "What is wrong with each of the following?" Students would respond to samples such as these when the items were passed around: staystitching on a seam line; staystitching continuous around a neckline; a dart marked on the right side of fabric; notches cut inward; pins placed on the cutting line of a pattern; a pattern pinned off-grain; a pattern placed on selvage instead of a fold.

Essay Questions

Essay questions can be used to evaluate a student's ability to use higher mental processes. These processes include: interpreting information, applying rules and principles, analyzing causes and effects, evaluating and developing an original plan. In addition to controlling student guessing to a greater extent than some types of test items, essay questions may more closely approximate the use of information and skills in life situations.

Essay questions are relatively easy to construct, but they do require considerable time for the students to respond and for the teacher to grade. Essay questions are often criticized for having a limited sampling of subject matter, an inconsistency or subjectivity in scoring, and a premium placed on quantity rather than quality of response. These weaknesses can be minimized through the use of several techniques.

■ *Guidelines for Writing Essay Questions*

1. State short-answer and essay questions so that they can be graded objectively. This necessitates stating them so that students who are prepared know what is expected in the answer. For example, if students are asked to "discuss the Basic Four food groups," they might respond in a variety of ways. But if they are asked to "analyze the dietary intake record below, according to the Basic Four food groups and the basic nutrients provided by each food group," students should know how to respond, and you can establish objective criteria to evaluate their answers. An answer key that you develop as you make out the test should include the major points that a student is expected to cover and the relative weight or point value of each.
2. Balance the difficulty level of questions so that sufficiently prepared students can complete their answers in the allotted time.
3. Require students to answer all items. When students have the option of answering three out of four questions, one student may not know anything about the problem he or she has omitted while another student may have been prepared to answer all the questions. Obviously, this test would not determine both students' comprehension of the subject matter fairly or to the same degree.
4. Keep in mind that a lengthy response does not necessarily represent comprehension of the subject matter or a high level of thinking. A brief answer may result from recalling material or thinking analytically and critically.
5. Grade the content of an essay question without regard to handwriting, spelling, or grammar. You might assign these a separate grade.
6. Read the first answer on all the papers and check it according to the established criteria for grading. Group the papers according to the adequacy of the response. Then reread and assign point values to the first question on all the students' papers. Repeat with the second question on all papers, and so forth.

■ Sample Essay Questions

It is easy to develop essay questions incorporating levels of thinking above the knowledge level. For example:

- Describe the differences between guidance and discipline. (Cognitive-Comprehension)
- Make a complete nutrition label for one of these food products, using a U.S. RDA chart to help you. (Cognitive-Application)

    box of enriched cereal

    can of dietetic peaches

    food bar as meal substitute

Note: "You should not offer students a choice of essay questions, but you can provide choices within an essay item when the alternatives are unrelated to the major purpose of the question. In this example, the crucial element is to apply what is known about nutrition labels in general rather than what is known about the nutritional content of a specific food item."

- Analyze the blueprint on display for factors relating to high and low building costs. (Cognitive-Analysis)
- Develop an instrument for rating television programs for children. (Cognitive-Synthesis)
- Evaluate this spending plan for the family situation described below. (Cognitive-Evaluation)

Home economics education students might be offered a choice of concepts for writing a lesson plan. The objective in this example would be to determine the students' ability to plan for teaching rather than to determine the students' knowledge of a given topic. Students could choose the subject matter they know best in demonstrating their ability to plan lessons.

Tests for Students with Limited Reading Ability

Students who read at a level below their grade placement are penalized when emphasis is placed upon traditional pencil-and-paper methods of evaluation. However, when test questions are read to these students and their responses are based on visual stimuli, many of them are not at a disadvantage. Oral questions should be asked as concisely as possible and repeated more than once. Test materials can include photos, drawings, models, or actual items. Students may be asked for simple oral or written responses, or they may be required to give reasons for their answers. Written responses can best be handled with an answer sheet constructed so that students have only to check off

a correct item or write in a number, letter, word, or short phrase.

Practical tests and lab work are appropriate for measuring skills in areas such as food preparation, clothing construction, and child care. The most important point to remember in using these types of tests is that definite criteria must be established so that the results can be scored in objective terms. Well-developed checklists and rating scales are appropriate for measuring student performances on a skill test or on work done in a laboratory experience.

Sample Tests for Poor Readers

Examples follow of test items that could be answered easily by poor readers. The questions are arranged in order of difficulty from the easiest to the more difficult, as they should be. Most questions have four possible responses, as is recommended for multiple choice items. Students of very limited academic ability may only be able to choose from two alternatives. Choosing from among three alternatives is a little more difficult.

■ Food Service

Directions: Circle the one in each pair that is better.

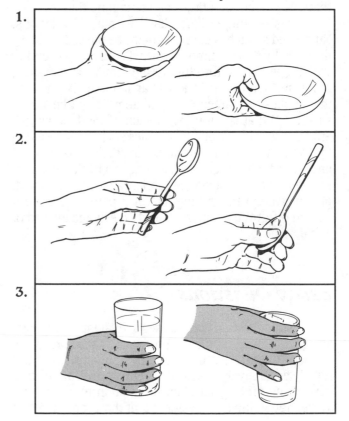

4.

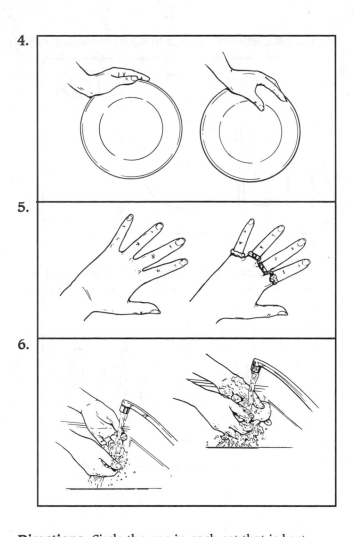

5.

6.

Directions: Circle the one in each set that is best.

7.

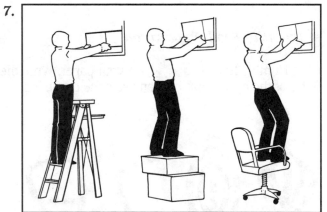

8.

9.

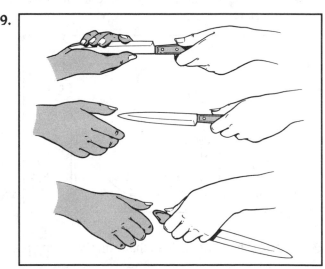

Directions: Circle the last step in cutting a layer cake in half.

10.

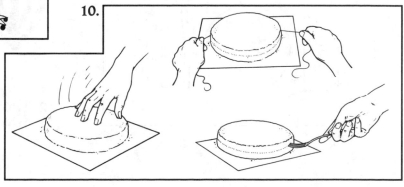

■ Table Setting

Simulated table settings can be sketched, drawn, or pictured on large pieces of construction paper, poster board, or transparencies, so that they can be viewed simultaneously by the entire class. The questions can be asked orally. Student responses are recorded on answer sheets.

1. Write the letter showing the place for a water glass.

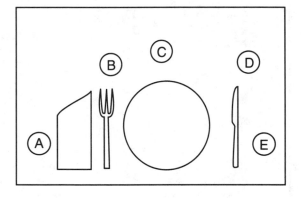

2. Write the letter showing the place for a bread and butter plate.

3. Write the letter of the item that is in the wrong place.

4. Write the letter of the item that is in the wrong place.

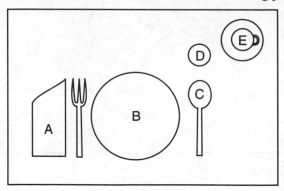

5. Write the letter of the item that is in the wrong place.

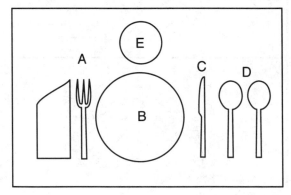

■ Quantity Food Preparation

Number from 1 to _____ on your paper. Write the letter of the beater that best answers the questions.

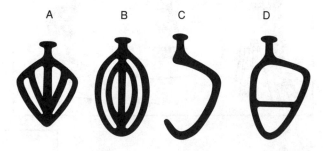

1. Which beater would be used for beating egg whites?
2. Which beater would be used for mixing bread dough?
3. Which beater would be used for mashing potatoes?

Number from 1 to _____ on your paper. Write the letter corresponding to the muffin that best answers the question.

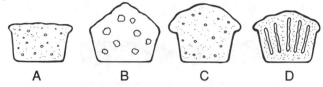

A   B   C   D

1. Which muffin was mixed correctly?
2. Which muffin was mixed too much?
3. Which muffin was baked in an oven that was too hot?

■ *Wallpaper Selection*

Use four or five real rolls of wallpaper that are clearly lettered A, B, C, etc. Ask questions appropriate for the pattern of each sample. Or display a larger number of wallpapers that are divided into groups. Ask questions that students can answer by writing the letter corresponding to the most appropriate wallpaper for the situation described. (Wallpapers are lettered because the questions will be numbered.)

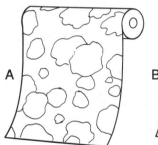

Shiny, pink surface with water stained pattern

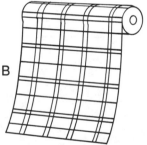

Bold, bright plaid in red, orange, and yellow

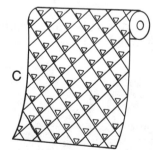

Small all-over print in blue and green

Large, bold print in red and green

1. Which wallpaper would be best where it might get splashed? Why?
2. Which wallpaper is best for a small bathroom? Why?
3. Which wallpaper would be least suitable for a room with dormer windows? Why?

Checklists, Scorecards, and Rating Scales

Checklists, scorecards, and rating scales can be used by students to evaluate themselves or their peers and by teachers to evaluate students' work. Often there is value in having both the teacher and students use the same device to judge the same product or performance and then to compare their evaluations. All three types of evaluation instruments can be used in the cognitive, affective, and psychomotor domains and in all content areas of home economics.

A wide variety of checklists, scorecards, and rating scales can be found in textbooks, periodicals, and commercial publications. It is also a relatively easy matter for teachers to develop their own checklists and scorecards. However, constructing a rating scale is much more difficult and time-consuming. A valuable learning experience consists in having teacher and students work together to develop instruments for evaluation other than rating scales.

Checklists

Checklists are simple evaluation instruments that consist of a list of qualities to be considered and checked off or questions to be answered with a yes or no response. Because checklists are easy to construct and easy to respond to, they tend to include a fairly large number of subconcepts for consideration. The checklist on page 72 can be used to evaluate a laboratory meal.

Scorecards

Scorecards consist of a list of characteristics or factors and possible point values that might be assigned to each, proportional to their importance. The evaluator assesses the attributes in question and determines the score to assign. The scorecard on page 72 could be used to evaluate meals.

You can see that it lacks the depth of content of some other types of evaluation instruments. Scorecards are often narrow in scope; therefore, they are appropriate for judging individual food products, one dimension of human interaction, a single work habit, one step in clothing construction, or a single toy.

The chief limitation of checklists and scorecards is that they have no descriptions of quality, and checklists have no provisions for making interim ratings. The primary advantage of scorecards and checklists is that their use requires students to think about the factors listed for consideration.

■ Checklist for Evaluating a Laboratory Meal

Directions: Evaluate your group's laboratory experience by answering each of the following questions and checking the appropriate column.

Did we:	YES	NO
1. Plan a well-balanced meal?		
2. Stay within our budget?		
3. Use any foods that are out of season?		
4. Forget to order any food when planning?		
5. Have enough to eat?		
6. Have food left over?		
7. Plan for all the tasks we needed to do?		
8. Need equipment we had not planned for?		
9. Use more dishes and utensils than we needed?		
10. Wash utensils as we cooked?		
11. Keep the counter top neat and clean as we worked?		
12. Waste any food in preparation or cooking?		
13. Have all the food ready at the same time?		
14. Serve the meal at the appointed time?		
15. Waste time in preparing the meal?		
16. Serve an appealing and appetizing meal?		
17. Prepare food that tasted good?		
18. Set the table attractively?		
19. Forget anything that should have been on the table?		
20. Use acceptable table manners?		
21. Include everyone in the table conversation?		
22. Leave the cupboards and our lab section in order?		
23. Hand in our bills and written plans on time?		
24. Work well together as a group?		
25. Share fairly the amount of work to be done?		

■ Scorecard for Evaluating a Laboratory Meal

Directions: Score each aspect of your meal by placing a number in the appropriate column. This number cannot exceed the highest possible score given. Add comments in the last column. Total your scores.

Selection of Food	Highest Possible Score	Your Score	Comments
Nutritional balance	40		
Variety of textures	15		
Pleasing combination of flavors	15		
Pleasing combination of colors	15		
Foods in season	15		
Total Score	100		

Rating Scales

Rating scales are a more highly refined measuring instrument than checklists or scorecards because rating scales include descriptions of various levels of quality. This provides for rating on a continuum. The verbal descriptions, against which work is judged, are usually given at three quality levels providing a five-point continuum because verbal descriptions are assigned 1, 3, and 5 points. In-between ratings are assigned 2 and 4 points. Occasionally two verbal descriptions are given providing a three-point continuum. Care must be taken that each level includes all the aspects described in every other level.

If you were going to use rating scales to judge clothing-construction projects, you could develop an instrument for each of the techniques used: marking, staystitching, sewing darts, and so forth. When each technique is evaluated as it is finished, points can be recorded and later cumulated to determine a final grade at the completion of the project. Both you and the students know how well their work is progressing, and steps can be taken to improve the quality, if needed.

One of the techniques to be evaluated in most clothing-construction projects would be hemming. Three levels of quality might be described.

In this example, the description of quality for each aspect ranges from unfavorable (left) to favorable (right). If the hem being evaluated had some of the characteristics described as highly desirable in the right-hand column and some of the characteristics described in the middle column, the point value assigned would probably be 4. Blanks should be provided to indicate the number of points assigned to each feature that is evaluated and for the total score.

■ Rating Scale for Evaluating a Clothing-Construction Project

Directions: Rate your clothing construction project on each of the factors listed by placing 1, 2, 3, 4, or 5 in the blank to the right. If the quality corresponds to the description in the first column, assign 1 point; if described in the second column, give 3 points; if it falls between the two, record 2. Add these points to determine the total score.

HEM

1	2	3	4	5	Points
Stitching Conspicuous and/or uneven stitching.		A few stitches show on right side and some uneven.		Inconspicuous, even stitching	____
Choice of stitch Unsuitable choice of stitch for fabric.		Not the best stitch for fabric.		Suitable choice of stitch for fabric.	____
Depth of hem Should be considerably deeper or narrower. Uneven in depth.		Should be somewhat deeper or narrower. Some variance in depth.		Appropriate depth for garment. Same depth all around.	____
Ease of fullness Fullness eased off-grain and/or tucked.		Fullness eased slightly off-grain and/or some tucks.		Fullness eased with grain and no tucks.	____
Appearance when hanging Hangs unevenly.		Hangs fairly evenly.		Hangs evenly.	____
				TOTAL	____

■ *Rating Scale for Evaluating a Laboratory Meal*

Directions: Rate your laboratory experience on each of the factors listed by placing 1, 2, 3, 4, or 5 in the blank to the right. If the quality corresponds to the description in the first column, assign 1 point; if described in the second column, give 3 points; if it falls between the two, record 2. Add these points to determine the total score.

	1	2	3	4	5	Points
A. MENU						
1. *Use of Time*	Meal elaborate. Not prepared easily in time available.		Meal somewhat complicated. Prepared in time but workers rushed.		Meal simple. Easily prepared in time available.	_____
2. *Cost*	Excessive. Foods out of season and expensive.		Moderate. Some unnecessary expense involved.		Reasonable. No extra or unreasonable expense involved.	_____
3. *Contrasts*	Little or no contrast in color, texture, flavor, temperature.		Some contrast in color, texture, flavor, temperature.		Good contrast in color, texture, flavor, and temperature.	_____
4. *Suitability*	Food preparation too difficult and involved unavailable equipment.		Food preparation suitable for student abilities or available equipment but not for both.		Food preparation suitable for both student abilities and available equipment.	_____
5. *Nutritive Value*	Menu not very nutritious. Did not include enough foods from the basic food groups.		Menu included some of the basic food groups. A few items could have been substituted for less nutritious foods.		All basic food groups included. Meal was very nutritious and well balanced.	_____
B. WORK PLAN						
6. *Time Schedule*	Time needed to complete tasks not indicated, inaccurate, or unrealistic.		Time needed to complete tasks indicated fairly realistically.		Time needed to complete all tasks given accurately.	_____
7. *Sequence of Tasks*	Sequence not given or illogical.		Logical sequence given for part of work such as preparation, service, or cleanup.		Logical sequence given for all tasks.	_____
8. *Division of Tasks*	Division of tasks among group members unfair or not clearly indicated.		Division of tasks indicated but somewhat unequal or lacking in detail.		Fair and equitable division of tasks indicated for each member of the group.	_____
C. MARKET ORDER						
9. *Lists*	Did not include all foods needed, quantities not stated or unsuitable.		Most of foods needed included, quantities questionable for number served.		All foods needed included in realistic quantities.	_____
10. *Cost*	Not given, given for only part of the foods, or inaccurate.		Cost of foods fairly accurate, cost of meal not summarized.		Costs given, summarized, reasonable, within budget.	_____
					TOTAL	_____

In this chapter, there are examples of checklists, scorecards, and rating scales that could be used to rate laboratory meals. They consider essentially the same qualities, although the emphasis is somewhat different in each. However, it should be noted that a rating scale encompasses greater depth of subject matter and necessitates the use of a higher level of thinking to make selections on the continuum. The evaluators are forced to think about their reasons for making certain ratings.

Combination Checklist/Scorecard/Rating Scale

Many times the characteristics of several types of evaluation tools are combined into one instrument. A rating device with the characteristics of a checklist, scorecard, and rating scale might be best for you in some situations. Subconcepts, questions, or statements are listed that the evaluator rates by assigning numerical scores based on a range of point values, or on a continuum.

The following instrument pertaining to oral reports can be used in peer evaluation. The one concerned with "How do you rate as a family member?" emphasizes the affective domain.

■ Instrument for Evaluating an Oral Report.

Directions: Rate each statement below, as it relates to your group's oral report, by placing the number of the word or words that best describes it in the space provided. Briefly explain or support your rating in the space below each statement.

SCALE:

Excellent	Very Good	Adequate	Fair	Poor
5	4	3	2	1

CRITERIA:

_____ 1. Variety of resources were used to prepare report.

_____ 2. Material presented was accurate and up-to-date.

_____ 3. Statements could be verified through facts or statistics given or by sources of information cited.

_____ 4. Information was presented in a logical sequence.

_____ 5. Subject matter was covered adequately for the time allowed.

_____ 6. Provision was made for class members to become involved.

_____ 7. Everyone could hear presentation.

_____ 8. Visuals, if any, were made neatly and could be seen easily by the entire class.

_____ 9. A demonstration, if used, could be seen by everyone.

_____ 10. Group members contributed equally in preparing report.

_____ 11. Group members participated equally in oral presentation.

_____ 12. Class seemed interested in presentation.

_____ TOTAL

■ Instrument for Students to Rate Themselves as Family Members

Directions: Use the key below to rate yourself as a family member.

Key:
Never   0
Sometimes 1
Usually   2
Always   3

_____ 1. I am cheerful at home.

_____ 2. I enjoy doing things with my family.

_____ 3. I have an interest in what others in my family are doing.

_____ 4. I try to understand my parents' viewpoint.

_____ 5. I discuss important matters with my parents.

_____ 6. My parents can depend on me.

_____ 7. I carry out unpleasant decisions and tasks without sulking or pouting.

_____ 8. I make an effort to have my friends know my parents.

_____ 9. I like to tell my parents about my activities outside the home.

_____ 10. My parents can count on me to do my best in sharing home responsibilities.

_____ 11. My parents can depend on me to be responsible for practicing good health habits.

_____ 12. My parents can count on me to use wisely privileges given me.

_____ TOTAL

PART

2

Methods of Teaching

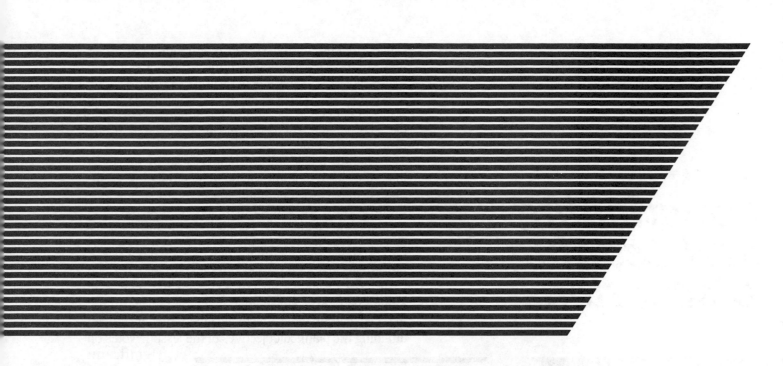

Questioning and Leading Discussions

Chapter  9

care of students' current concerns although these topics may not have been included in the original lesson plan for the day. A sensitive teacher will also recognize when topics may be too personal to discuss in class, when some students may be hurt or embarrassed by certain discussions, and when students are deliberately trying to waste class time.

Skillful questioning, then, is one of the most important keys to a purposeful and stimulating teaching-learning situation. Some educators are able to formulate good questions without a great deal of preplanning. This usually results from having practiced effective questioning techniques over a long period of time. However, you probably will find it helpful to formulate questions before class either by writing them in your lesson plan or by jotting down key words to remind you of the questions you intend to ask. By doing this, you can more effectively guide students toward attaining the planned objectives of the lesson. Notes on significant, preplanned questions serve to limit the number of questions that relate to minutiae rather than to important concepts and generalizations.

You can plan questions that help students to explore ideas and to work toward satisfactory solutions to relevant problems, or you can ask questions that require only knowledge of specific facts. Information is easily forgotten, but developing thinking processes through significant questions that probe for solutions can make an important contribution to the students' education.

The lecture-discussion approach to teaching is the most widely used method at the secondary and college levels. Of course, it needs to be varied with other strategies to stimulate students' interest and hold their attention. Lecture-discussion is often used at the beginning of a class period and is followed by group work, an educational game, a simulated experience, or a hands-on activity. The lecture-discussion and all other methods of teaching are dependent on the questioning skills of the leader.

A discussion without adequate planning of the questions to be asked can be a waste of time. Students enjoy getting teachers off the subject, and it is easier to do this when the questions for a discussion have not been given forethought. Some discussion that strays from the topic for the day can be valuable, but much of it can also be time consuming and hinder you from achieving the lesson objectives. A caring teacher will know when to capitalize on the teachable moment and take

Asking Questions at Appropriate Levels of Thinking

Effective questions place the burden of thinking on the students. Questions can represent the limited levels of thinking such as recalling or recognizing specifics, or the higher and more challenging levels such as applying, analyzing, synthesizing, and evaluating ideas. Generally, it is wise to ask questions at different levels of thinking. The proportion asked at each level depends on the objectives of the lesson. If one of the objectives is to recall cognitive information, then you will ask questions that focus on remembering and recognizing facts. However, because one of the major purposes of education is to help students apply knowledge and develop critical thinking skills, it is hoped that you will plan both objectives and questions that incorporate the higher levels of learning. Questions that require only one-word answers or a simple "yes" or "no" response seldom involve higher levels of thinking, unless they are followed by comments such as "Please *defend* your point of view" or "Please *explain* that to us." Following up on students' replies by asking "Why?" usually fosters analysis-level thinking. If it is possible to answer a question with a "yes" or "no," many students will not give any further explanation.

Some examples of questions above knowledge level are:
- What is an example that illustrates the meaning of the word *compassion*? (Comprehension)
- How can the principles of meat cookery be applied to the demonstration we just saw? (Application)
- What may be the real problems in this situation? (Analysis)
- If you were given this responsibility, what are all of the actions you would consider taking? (Synthesis)
- What decision would be the most satisfactory one for you? Why? (Evaluation)

The sequence of questions asked should be logical and provide continuity in the lesson. The sequence also depends on the subject matter and the background of the students. One approach is to begin with easy questions and move toward more complicated ones. This is effective when the content is complex or when students have difficulty working with abstract ideas. Being able to answer easy questions at first gives students a feeling of confidence, security, and achievement. This may contribute to a positive attitude toward the learning situation and may also affect their desire and determination to be successful in answering more difficult questions.

An example of questions ranging from a basic to an advanced level would be:
- What are the fibers we have studied? (Knowledge)
- What important characteristics does each of them have? (Knowledge)
- If you were to purchase a carpet for a heavy-traffic area in your home, what fiber would be the best to use? (Application)
- Why is this fiber better for this situation than others you might choose? (Analysis)

Another type of questioning sequence is directed toward a problem-solving or a discovery approach to learning. In this case, questioning serves to encourage students to examine the parts of a whole, to clarify a problem, and to ask their own relevant questions.

In order to work toward problem-solving or discovery learning, a teacher might ask:
- How would you describe the experimental approach we used? (Comprehension)
- What might have caused this? (Analysis)
- How can you prove your theory? (Synthesis)

Asking questions such as these encourages students to engage in thinking above the recall level by testing their powers of observation and calling on them to give proof of their theories.

Encouraging Student Participation

Some of the guidelines for effective questioning suggested in this chapter can be implemented immediately. You may need to practice other techniques before they become natural and spontaneous for you.

1. *Students should have sufficient background to answer questions successfully.* It can be very discouraging to say, "I don't know." A sense of timing is important so that the lesson is developed to the point of enabling students to answer questions intelligently. Matching the difficulty of the question level to individual student ability is helpful. Success in classroom discussions is more likely to be attained and students are more likely to feel a sense of achievement when simpler questions are given to marginal students and challenging questions are asked of more intellectually capable students.

2. *Questions need to be clearly worded.* A question like "What do you think about this?" often receives no response or a poor response because students cannot understand the indefinite wording. More structure is offered when the teacher asks, "Why do you agree or disagree with Kim's decision?" It is best to avoid asking "what about" or "how about" questions because they are too vague and too broad.

3. *Variation in wording questions helps create interest.* A few of the phrases you can use to begin questions are: "What might," "Why is there," "Which of," and "If you had." However, avoid introductory words such as "Can anyone give *me*" or "Who can tell *me*," because these phrases tend to discourage participation. Use *us* instead of *me*. "Please share with *us*" elicits a more favorable reaction than "Please tell *me*." The latter sounds as if the student should do something just to please the teacher. Or, simply ask the question without the preface. For example, when you begin a question with "Would you like to," you are encouraging nonparticipation by setting the student up to think "No, I wouldn't like to …" "Can you think of …" likewise makes it easy for a student to respond, "No, I can't."

4. *Directing questions to the entire class, pausing, and then calling on a student by name will help keep class members alert to the discussion and will encourage them to formulate answers.* When a student's name is designated before the question is asked, others realize they probably will not be called on to respond. However, it may be desirable to reverse this order when a particular student's attention has been diverted and the teacher wants to bring the student back into the discussion quickly without calling public attention to his or her lack of concentration.

5. *Do not call on students by going up and down rows or around a circle in a set pattern.* When students know that they will not be asked questions until several others have been called upon, they are less likely to pay attention. However, there is no point in calling on students when their nonverbal cues indicate an inability to answer satisfactorily.

Teacher Responses

If you are animated and interested, you are more likely to obtain student participation than if you do not show these characteristics. In addition to being enthusiastic, there are specific response techniques you can use and behaviors you can develop that encourage meaningful student involvement.

1. *Vary reinforcement given for good answers to encourage student participation.* If you overuse expressions such as "OK," they become monotonous and distracting. Besides, replying with "OK" is like saying, "I heard you." It is a neutral response rather than positive reinforcement and does little to encourage students to participate further or contribute again. Although words like "Right" and "Good" convey positive reactions, if overused these words lose their reinforcement value and sound like "canned," or mechanical, responses. See page 57 for a discussion of reinforcing behavior. Students often become so conscious of teachers' repeated use of certain words or phrases that they listen for them and actually begin to count the number of times they are said. When this happens, students do not hear *what* is being said but rather only *how* it is being communicated. Other annoying habits, such as pacing back and forth or fingering glasses, hair, or accessories, are also distracting to students.

Reinforcement can be given to students by saying: "That's a good answer." "Nice contribution, Pat." "I hadn't thought about it that way." Occasionally paraphrasing students' answers adds variety.

Extending students' answers by adding an additional thought or providing nonverbal acceptance such as a nod of the head also provides positive reinforcement. Skillful teachers can often alter students' answers slightly, so they are more meaningful and acceptable but still give students the feeling that they have made a valuable contribution. See page 81 for *99 Ways to Say "Very Good."*

2. *Try to avoid telling students, "No, that's wrong," because this kind of remark stifles participation.* Students are reluctant to answer questions if they think they might be rebuked. You can indicate that an answer is incorrect, without damaging a student's self-concept, by saying something such as "The question may not have been clear," or "Part of your answer is right, but ..." or "That's an interesting thought; however, you may remember ..." It is also discouraging to be told by a teacher: "I have something else in mind," "I'm thinking of another point," or "There's another answer that is right, too." Replies like these make students feel as if they are playing a guessing game and have to read the teacher's mind. The impression is given that there is only one preconceived and precisely correct answer. In actuality, there may be many responses that are righ or partially right. Students often think of excellent points that their teachers had never considered.

3. *When you follow students' answers with additional probing questions, participation is usually increased.* You might ask students to clarify answers with questions such as "What is an example to illustrate that?" or "What might have caused that to happen?" When you follow up on students' responses this way, students are encouraged to expand their remarks and to justify their answers. This provides additional clarification for the class, and you have increased your opportunity to evaluate students' contributions.

4. *When a student is unable to respond to a question, you might direct another question to the same student.* You can reword the original question or provide a clue to assist the student in answering. For example, your initial question might have been "Why did Tony behave that way?" If no student response is received, you can reword the question: ''Suppose you were Tony. What might have prompted you to act that way?'' Or, "In what ways is this situation similar to a situation we discussed yesterday?" By assisting or guiding students toward correct responses, you can help them feel successful. In this way, students also learn that they are expected to participate in class discussions.

5. *Breadth of subject matter is developed when you bring additional students into the discussion by asking them to respond to the same question just answered by another.* In this way, a variety of view-

points can be presented so that all sides of a topic are explored. You might ask, "What can be added to John's answer, Sandra?" or "What is another side of the issue, Chris?"

Teachers who answer their own questions or interrupt students' answers do not allow students to engage in independent thinking. Often this is done to advance the discussion, but it can lead to a monopolization of class time by the teacher. Students become conditioned not to listen, and future communication may be jeopardized.

The type of questions you ask and the way you ask them reflects your competence as an instructor. Skillful questioning techniques provide the basis for using all methods of teaching effectively. Showing a film, reading a skit, or seeing a demonstration may be nothing more than entertainment unless it is followed by thought-provoking questions that foster higher levels of thinking.

---

99 Ways to Say "Very Good"

1. That's right.
2. That's the way.
3. You're doing fine.
4. Now you have it.
5. Exceedingly well done.
6. That's great.
7. GREAT!
8. FANTASTIC!
9. TERRIFIC!
10. Good work.
11. Good for you.
12. That's better.
13. EXCELLENT!
14. Good going.
15. Keep it up.
16. WOW!
17. Much better.
18. Good.
19. Good thinking.
20. Clever.
21. Exactly right.
22. Nice going.
23. Way to go.
24. SUPER!
25. SUPERB!
26. Keep on trying.
27. WONDERFUL!
28. That's it.
29. That's good.
30. Congratulations.
31. FINE!
32. Right on.
33. TREMENDOUS!
34. Perfect.
35. Outstanding.
36. How clever.
37. That's it.
38. I like that.
39. MARVELOUS!
40. You remembered.
41. SENSATIONAL!
42. You did it that time.
43. That's a good idea.
44. Good job, (Bill/Jane).
45. That's really nice.
46. Keep up the good work.
47. That's much better.
48. You make it look easy.
49. I knew you could do it.
50. You're doing beautifully.
51. That's a clever way to do it.
52. You've got it made.
53. You're learning fast.
54. You're on the right track now.
55. You're doing a good job.
56. You did a lot of work today.
57. Now you've figured it out.
58. Now you have the hang of it.
59. You're really going to town.
60. That's coming along nicely.
61. You outdid yourself today.
62. That's the best you have ever done.
63. I've never seen anyone do it better.
64. You are doing that much better today.
65. You're getting better every day.
66. Keep working on it, you're doing well.
67. You're really working hard today.
68. Nothing can stop you now.
69. You are very good at this.
70. You've just about got it.
71. That's quite an improvement.
72. That's not half bad.
73. You haven't missed a thing.
74. That's the best ever.
75. You did that very well.
76. You've got that down pat.
77. You're really improving.
78. Well, look at you go!
79. I'm very proud of you.
80. You figured that out quickly.
81. I think you've got it now.
82. You really are learning a lot.
83. You certainly did well today.
84. That's better than ever.
85. That was first-class work.
86. You really make my job fun.
87. Now you've figured it out.
88. That's one good way to do that.
89. I'm proud of the way you worked today.
90. I'm happy to see you working like that.
91. Couldn't have done it better myself.
92. One more time and you'll have it.
93. You've just about mastered that.
94. You've got your brain in gear today.
95. Now that's what I call a fine job.
96. You must have been practicing.
97. Congratulations, you got (#) right.
98. It's a pleasure to teach when you work like that.
99. That kind of work makes me proud of you.

REMEMBER:

IF YOU CAN'T SAY ANYTHING NICE TO SOMEONE, DON'T SAY ANYTHING AT ALL!

Leading Stimulating Discussions

A stimulating discussion does not take place because you announce there will be one. Above all, a meaningful discussion is dependent on skillful questioning. Lead questions need to be formulated in advance. It often helps to write these questions down because it is easier to bring a discussion back to the intended focus when a clear direction has been planned.

A discussion is enhanced if the members have a common goal that they select by mutual agreement or through compromise. It is important that every discussion participant respects the rights of all the others. In addition, the overall atmosphere and physical arrangements must be conducive to a comfortable exchange of opinions, ideas, and experiences.

Numerous benefits result from well-conducted classroom discussions. Students learn to listen to other viewpoints and thus broaden their perspectives. They gain skill in tackling an issue rather than in attacking the person discussing the issue. Exposure to a stimulating and "safe" climate for discussion helps participants develop greater sensitivity in communicating with others. There are few substitutes for the satisfaction of a frank, thoughtful, and relevant exchange of ideas.

Selecting a Discussion Topic

Selecting the topic for a classroom discussion requires great care to ensure that it is relevant to the students' lifestyles and is understood by everyone in the group. You may want to encourage students to present problems they hope to solve and subjects they want to discuss. Worthwhile topics offer several facets to explore and also provide opportunities for a variety of viewpoints and perspectives. Discussion topics should be related to a group's real interests, concerns, needs, and experiences.

Initiating a Discussion

You can initiate the main theme of a discussion in a variety of ways. You can provide the needed stimulus through clearly worded and provocative questions that relate to previous experiences of group members, an interesting movie, a stimulating story or article, or an exciting presentation of pertinent data. The problem should be clearly stated, and most members should have sufficient information and background to be able to make positive contributions. If students lack sufficient knowledge or experience relating to the topic, the discussion may be meaningless or even damaging and prejudicial. A stimulating discussion is also based on a firm foundation of student interest and a classroom climate that invites participation. A comfortable, informal atmosphere in which spontaneous humor might surface at any moment is the type of environment that nurtures honest expressions of feeling and opinion.

■ Brainstorming

Brainstorming is one way to initiate discussion. The first step in brainstorming is to gather a quantity of ideas without considering their quality. Participants need to be reassured that their ideas will not be criticized.

An example may be to list suggestions for the theme of an annual employer appreciation banquet or an open house for parents of young children in the cooperative program. As ideas are suggested, the teacher or a student writes them so that they can be seen by everyone. After all ideas are expressed, the participants vote to determine the two or three they like best. Then these are discussed in detail; the advantages and disadvantages of each idea are explored. After this, another vote establishes the *one* idea students think is best. Such a procedure increases the likelihood that the group will be reasonably satisfied with the decision.

If brainstorming is done in small groups, each group may present the two or three ideas it considers its best. After the best of each small group's ideas are listed, an elimination process may be carried out by a vote of all students.

Brainstorming is not designed for use in situations that point obviously to one best solution. Nor is the outcome predetermined by the teacher or student leader. In other words, the group works together democratically to arrive at *a* solution, not at *the* solution.

The Discussion Leader

As a discussion leader, you need to serve as a model of behavior for the students as you listen, encourage student involvement, display interest in the opinions of each individual, maintain good eye contact with everyone in the group, and keep the discussion going through a variety of means. You should avoid monopolizing the conversation, but sometimes you will have to provide direction and guidance. You must be prepared, when necessary, to summarize the main points, make supportive and encouraging comments, or ask pertinent questions. Such sensitivity can prevent the discussion from bogging down or being monopolized by one or two students.

In your role as a discussion leader, more than in any other role you assume as a teacher, you have to be able to think on your feet. At times you may want to rephrase the ideas of the group in clearer and simpler language. However, you need to be careful not to impose your own ideas and values on the class and may have to restrain a desire to express your own feelings and opinions. It is sometimes difficult to let others do the talking, especially when you disagree with what they are saying. Above all, as a discussion leader you need to keep emotions under control.

■ Responsibilities in Leading a Discussion

The leader's main responsibilities are keeping the discussion going and involving everyone, if possible. You must watch facial expressions, for signs of interest, desire to contribute, and waning attention. You need to be sensitive to nonverbal cues such as swinging feet, stares directed at the window or clock, and doodling — evidence of lack of interest. Keep distractions to a minimum to encourage students to pay attention and to participate.

You may want to make periodic summaries, and usually you will be responsible for concluding the discussion. Doing this can take the form of asking the participants to identify the main points, to explain how their ideas or opinions may have changed, or to predict how the discussion could affect students' future behavior.

Seating Arrangements

Experience demonstrates that the people sitting nearest the teacher or discussion leader are the most active participants. People outside this limited area may be hesitant to contribute unless they are skillfully brought into the discussion.

Various seating arrangements can either promote or inhibit communication among group members. It is desirable to have students facing each other. In this way both verbal and nonverbal cues can be detected and acted upon to assist in the discussion process. If possible, ask students to move chairs into a semicircle prior to the discussion.

In most situations, it is better to sit with the students. It is usually better not to stand over the group or behind a podium or desk. Psychologically, this tends to place you in an unapproachable and authoritarian position and diminishes the participation and leadership that can emerge from the group members.

Participants in Class Discussions

It often takes time for groups to develop the kind of rapport necessary for truly democratic and effective discussions. It is important that leaders do not push members too much, but rather give them time to become adjusted to one another and to the classroom environment. Discussion leaders should expect and encourage variety in the group response.

Some quiet people prefer to let others do the talking and still may be participating silently. They may find it difficult to express themselves and consequently become self-conscious in a group of their peers. These individuals may be encouraged to contribute if they are involved in a friendly conversation on a one-to-one basis before or outside class. Questions should be asked of them that require the expression of an idea or opinion rather than a simple "yes," "no," or other one-word answer.

People who monopolize a discussion talk too much and too long and often depart from the subject. They may talk excessively because they are nervous and insecure. Their comments often pertain to personal concerns and interests. In time, others in the group become inattentive or bored and may direct some of their resentment toward the leader.

Allow overparticipators a reasonable amount of time to talk and then ask for others' ideas. A comment such as "Thank you — now let's hear from someone else" has to be made with great tact. In extreme cases it may be necessary to direct questions deliberately to those who are not participating, by calling on them by name, or to allow another student to interrupt.

You can often satisfy the need for attention of students who tend to dominate discussions if you use methods that contribute to the progress of the class. You can ask students to operate equipment that adds a dimension to the discussion, show visual media and other teaching materials, or write points on the board as they are made.

The secure teacher enjoys a good laugh as much as the students. However, when joking has reached the point of interfering with the purpose of a discussion, the teacher who has the respect of students should have no trouble in redirecting their attention. It may be effective to say something like, "That was good for a laugh. Now let's get serious again because this topic is important to all of us."

Any form of humor that is clearly intended to embarrass a group member should be stopped immediately. This usually can best be done by not making an issue of the incident, for that will probably aggravate the situation. Often a frown or some other nonverbal communication indicating disapproval is sufficient to get your message to the offender.

Small-Group Discussions

Small-group discussions in the classroom are important in promoting communication. Students who are reluctant to speak out when in larger groups often participate when in smaller groups. The total group's viewpoints and experiences are expanded and enriched thereby. At the same time, a larger percentage of the students actually contribute and discover that they, as individuals, can be part of a democratic process of decision making based on compromise and mutual agreement.

■ Forming Small Groups

Teachers are responsible for knowing the class as a whole and as a body comprising distinct individual personalities. This background knowledge is important in helping teachers decide when to use discussion methods appropriate to small groups and how to form such groups. Teachers may designate group memberships or allow students to form their own groups. The second course has many disadvantages. Students may be inclined to form their small groups on a basis of friendship. As a result, the intellectual stars, the "I don't cares," the class clowns, and those with various common interests tend to cluster together. The viewpoints expressed and the work produced by such groups may be limited considerably.

Here are several effective methods of group selection:

• Quick Ways

One of the simplest ways to form small groups is to ask students to number off consecutively. The highest number called should be the same as the total number of members desired in a group. Doing this will achieve a random assignment of group members. Organizing students according to their birth months or zodiac signs is another possibility. Listing students alphabetically by first names and using appropriate cutoff points for group formation will also avoid using the traditional last-name method of grouping. If a variety of methods is used over a period of time, students will benefit from having worked with most of their classmates.

• Group Building

To use the group-building approach, tell students to number off by two's ("one, two, one, two," and so forth) until everyone has a number. The students who are "ones" go to one side of the room and those who are "twos" go to the other side. Each "one" is instructed to invite a "two" to join him or her, thus forming pairs. The invited partner should be someone the student does not know or does not know well. When all students have been paired, each pair invites another to join them. If possible, the invitation should go to students not closely known by those extending it. If groups larger than four are desired, this process can be repeated.

This exercise serves as a means of forming groups with members who have never, or perhaps infrequently, worked together. Members gain a feeling of togetherness as a result of mutual decision making in extending and accepting or declining invitations.

Groups formed in this fashion can work effectively on problems that profit from having participants with differing backgrounds and viewpoints. Some examples of these group activities are solving management problems, choosing and preparing for careers, and adjusting to changing male and female roles. This method of group building is especially useful for getting members of newly formed classes better acquainted.

• Related Objects

From a broad subject such as food and nutrition or child development, select a group of objects that can be classified in subgroups related to common function. The items chosen depend on the purpose for which a particular small group was formed. A variety of kitchen utensils can serve as the basis for grouping students to discuss problems related to food preparation, kitchen equipment, or work simplification and time management. The objects chosen to serve as a basis for designating group membership are limited only by one's imagination and resources.

The number of objects used should equal the number of people in the class, and the objects should be chosen so that some serve the same function. The number of student subgroups for the class activity should be the same as the number of subgroups that can be formed by using the objects. After you have displayed all the objects on a table or counter top, tell the students to select one. Then instruct the participants to compare their items and to divide themselves into groups of three or four persons having objects with a common purpose. When the basis for classification is obvious to the students, groups tend to form quickly.

This exercise produces interaction among class members and stimulates thought on an analytical level. At this point, the students should be prepared to work at a task or problem or on assigned questions.

• Puzzle Cutups

Different media, such as related pictures cut from magazines, may also be used to form groups. Choose pictures related to the specific area under investigation. The pictures may be used without a backing material, or they can be attached to something lightweight — a file folder, cardboard, or construction paper. Cut each picture into jigsaw-shaped puzzle pieces. The number of pieces will depend on the desired size of the small groups. One picture is needed for each group.

To organize the class into groups, scramble the puzzle pieces and place them on any flat surface. Then, instruct students to select one piece and locate the classmates who have other pieces that will complete that picture. Through such matching, groups soon form. The teacher can assign specific activities or discussion questions to each group or instruct the groups to turn their pictures over and read the questions on the reverse side.

Activities in housing and home furnishings might use illustrations of different types of housing (individually owned homes, duplexes, mobile homes, apartments), furniture styles, and interior color schemes. Pictures representing various kinds of stores, types of store displays, or various forms of advertisements could provide a stimulating beginning for small-group discussions of consumer economics.

■ Facilitating Small-Group Discussions

After groups have been formed, teachers can use a variety of methods to promote discussion and interaction. Inner and outer circles and buzz sessions help to involve students in small groups.

• Inner and Outer Circles

In this exercise, several small groups of ten to twelve students can be formed (and operate simultaneously) or one group of ten to twelve can participate while the rest act as observers. In either case, directions for one or more groups are given by the teacher from the floor. The purposes of this exercise are to have students listen to others, to give them an opportunity to express their thoughts in a concise manner, and to have them summarize or react to what is said by others.

This is a timed exercise using incomplete sentences or questions relating to specific subjects. To begin the exercise, half of the group is asked to take chairs and form a close circle. The remaining students form a circle around the outside in order to watch and listen carefully to the discussion taking place in the inner circle.

Before the exercise begins, the students in the outside circle are told not to participate in the discussion while they are in that position. The students in the inner circle are instructed to monitor the discussion and to provide as much opportunity as possible for each member to participate.

The inner circle is given the first statement or question and instructed to discuss it for 4 minutes. At the end of that period, the students in the inner and outer circles exchange positions. The students in the new inner circle are asked to react to what they heard the first group say. Two minutes is allowed for this. Then this same inner circle responds to the original statement or a new one for 4 minutes. Positions are again reversed and students now in the inner circle are told to react, in a 2-minute period, to any previous statements with which they agreed or disagreed. This process continues until the students respond to all the statements.

After the exercise is over, you may want to have students express their feelings as you ask specific questions. For example, did the students feel under great pressure to contribute to the discussion? What kind of interaction was there among group members? What were their feelings about silent periods? How did they feel when they heard themselves quoted?

• Buzz Sessions

The term *buzz session* is commonly applied by teachers to the activity of students working in small discussion groups. Three, four, or five students is the most desirable number. If there are fewer, there may not be enough interaction; if there are more, some students may be reluctant to express their ideas and opinions. And the purpose of this form of activity is to maximize student participation.

It is the teacher's responsibility to go from group to group to offer help and to give encouragement. If the teacher is aware of students' progress, she or he will sense the right time to give a warning such as "Take only another minute or two to wind up your discussion." Generally, it is advisable to call time while the students are still enthusiastic about their topics, before their attention wanders.

Buzz groups may be used to formulate replies to letters found in advice columns of newspapers; to offer solutions to situations presented in case studies; to plan menus, time schedules, and market orders; and to develop role-plays and skits. Almost anything that can be done in a class-size group can be done equally well or perhaps better in a buzz group. However, there must be enough depth of subject matter in the chosen topics to warrant the time involved. If the solutions to be suggested or decisions to be reached are not sufficiently thought-provoking, the time spent in buzz sessions may be wasted.

■ Student Discussion Leaders

When students serve as small-group discussion leaders or facilitators on a rotating basis, they have an opportunity to share the teacher's responsibility and develop leadership potential.

At the beginning of the school year, or before small discussion groups are organized, it is desirable to have the class talk about the role of the facilitator and the qualities of a good discussion leader and an effective discussion. Guidelines for both can be established. A poster can be displayed or a duplicated sheet summarizing important points to remember can be given to students. Either serves as a reference for all students. It also gives discussion leaders a basis for evaluating how well they are fulfilling their roles.

The student discussion leader can assist the group by:

- Talking when it is necessary to initiate and guide the discussion, but without monopolizing it.
- Maintaining an atmosphere that is positive, stimulating, and enjoyable.
- Being responsive to the contributions of all members.
- Listening to what is said and maintaining good eye contact with participants.
- Watching the faces and body positions of group members for additional communication cues and using the cues to help each member participate as fully as possible.
- Keeping the goal of the activity continually in mind so that the discussion stays on target; doing this skillfully may require that the leader ask questions and summarize when appropriate.

Structured Discussion Techniques

The purpose of a panel discussion, debate, symposium, or forum is to bring together different ideas and opinions on various aspects of one subject. The audience hears thoughts and opinions that should help each member analyze a timely problem. Although summarizing the material presented is an important part of each of these techniques, the listener is expected to draw personal conclusions from the information presented by forming conclusions, to some degree, independently of the group.

In all these activities, the only people formally involved are the teacher or designated leader and part of the class, but all may participate in follow-up discussions and activities. The success of each depends upon careful planning, preparation, and organization.

■ Panel Discussion

The panel serves to air views relating to a selected topic rather than to arrive at any one decision. The moderator introduces the subject and calls on one of the members to begin. Each panel member, or a small group of students or guests, gives a brief (3 to 5 min-

utes), prepared but informal talk that is usually presented in the form of a question. After each speaker has presented a viewpoint, he or she is free to react to and ask questions of the others.

Following this informal exchange, the moderator usually opens the program to audience participation. The moderator must guide the direction of the discussion, keep it on the topic or on closely related ones, and then summarize the main ideas and the principal sides of the issues.

If a panel discussion is unsuccessful, it is usually because the members have not studied the issue thoroughly or because the topic is too narrow in scope to allow for discussion in depth. Some questions that are appropriate for panel discussions follow:

- What are desirable qualities in an employee?
- Are teenagers today more mature than those of previous generations?
- What should a father's role be in today's world?
- What are some community services that are available to help families?

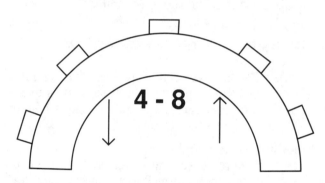

PANAL DISCUSSION

■ Debate

In a debate, the participants are trying to persuade others. Therefore, the topic must be one about which there are fixed positions or definite "for" and "against" viewpoints to be argued. These issues are debated by teams of students who take opposing sides.

A debate begins when one member of the pro team gives reasons for favoring the issue; then a member of the con team gives a case for being against it. This procedure continues until each team member has had an opportunity to present evidence and supporting facts. Each should select the strongest possible arguments, make reference to statistics, and quote experts where relevant. This will give authority to the debaters' remarks.

After the prepared speeches, team members have a chance to respond to the statements of their opponents. During this exchange, a new issue cannot be brought up but new supportive material may be used. Debaters need to investigate the topic thoroughly beforehand so that they can answer questions and defend remarks they and their teammates make. The chair or moderator summarizes briefly, mentioning only the highlights. A class discussion may follow the debate.

A debate topic is given in the form of a positive or negative statement. Controversial issues such as the following lend themselves to debate techniques:
- Women have been (or have not been) liberated.
- Parenthood should be (or should not be) licensed.
- Abortion should be (or should not be) available on demand.
- One year of full-time employment should be (or should not be) required of all freshmen before admission to college.

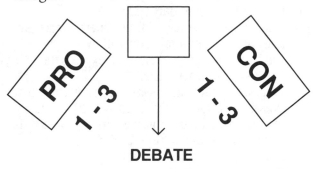

DEBATE

■ *Symposium*

In a symposium there is one problem under investigation, and each participant is qualified to present one aspect of it. Usually the participant's expertise has been gained through personal experience. Speakers are given specified lengths of time for their presentations, and after all of these the participants exchange ideas or ask questions of one another. Following this exploration of viewpoints by the speakers, the class may also enter into the discussion. The symposium, when used correctly, ensures that several aspects of the topic will be presented and, consequently, that the audience gains an overall view of the subject.

The teacher, student leader, or chairperson has the responsibility of introducing the participants and their subjects within the general topic, of summarizing after all the prepared talks have been given, and of leading the ensuing discussion among the speakers. Some topics suitable for symposiums follow:
- *Careers in Home Economics:* Speakers who are employed in semiprofessional and professional areas of home economics could be asked to tell about needed skills and abilities, desirable personality traits, educational requirements, duties and responsibilities, salaries, and chances for advancement in their respective fields.

- *Mothers Manage Resources Differently:* A mother who is not employed outside the home, one who works part-time, and one who has full-time employment could share ideas about how they use their money, time, and energy differently to meet their individual and family needs.
- *Meeting the Needs of Special Children:* It may be possible to ask parents and siblings of mentally retarded, physically handicapped, or intellectually gifted children to discuss how they meet the special needs of these family members.
- *Single-Parent Families:* Both male and female representatives from Parents Without Partners may be asked to tell about the problems they have encountered and the solutions they have found most satisfactory in rearing children alone. Students who live with only one parent may also be willing to give their viewpoints on this topic.

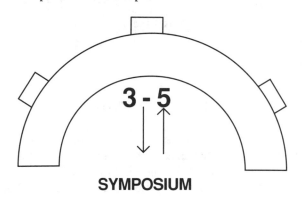

SYMPOSIUM

■ *Forum*

In a forum, two, or occasionally three, speakers offer different points of view about a somewhat controversial issue. A forum is more formal than a panel discussion because the participants do not interact with each other after the prepared speeches, but rather answer questions posed by the class or audience. Listeners have an opportunity to express their own ideas and to ask the forum participants to react to them. The moderator must be adept in changing the direction of the dialogue if it becomes dull, if one or two individuals monopolize it, or if the discourse becomes irrelevant. The moderator summarizes briefly and clearly by reiterating the major contributions.

A forum may be used effectively to introduce a new topic because the speakers are well informed about the topic. The audience is encouraged and expected to ask questions. This does not necessitate their having a very extensive knowledge of the subject matter. Some possible topics for a forum are:
- Men's roles have changed more in the last decade than women's roles.

- People should avoid eating foods to which preservatives have been added.
- Financial problems are the leading causes of marital failure today.
- Cohabitation has more disadvantages than advantages.

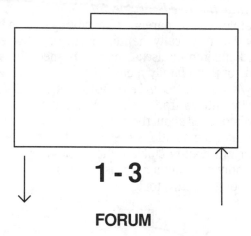

1 - 3

FORUM

Evaluating Class Discussions

Teachers can make improvements in leading meaningful class discussions by periodically thinking about and answering the following questions:

1. Was the discussion carefully planned so progress could be made toward meeting stated objectives?
   a. Was the discussion focused on worthwhile objectives that were clear to the participants and accepted by them as important?
   b. Did the students help determine the objectives and/or discussion topic?
   c. Was the approach to the topic stimulating and challenging?
   d. Did the discussion move fast enough to be interesting but slow enough to provide for sound, analytical thinking?
   e. Were the physical arrangements of the room managed to promote student participation?
2. Was the discussion appropriate for the students involved?
   a. Did the discussion present a true-life problem or a situation that was relevant and meaningful to the group?
   b. Was the discussion related to concepts or topics that had been covered previously?
   c. Did the class members have the background information and experience necessary to make valuable and purposeful contributions?
   d. Was the vocabulary and language used appropriate for the group?
   e. Was there adequate discussion on essential ideas to arrive at some broad generalizations?
3. Were students helped to arrive at their own conclusions and to make their own decisions?
   a. Were students led to explore all sides of the issue?
   b. Were they encouraged to support their conclusions with evidence?
   c. Were they guided to explore the bases for their beliefs and values?
   d. Were they led to consider the possible consequences of their decisions?
4. Were interpersonal relationships supportive and conducive to student participation?
   a. Was there evidence of friendliness, acceptance, sincerity, and mutual cooperation?
   b. Did students seem to feel free to express their ideas and to defend their beliefs?
   c. Were ideas that students initiated treated seriously?
   d. Was it possible, when students digressed from the purposes of the discussion, to refocus their attention without hurting their feelings?
   e. Did at least three-fourths of the group participate?
5. Were the students given an opportunity to evaluate their growth and gain a sense of progress?
   a. Were students led to formulate generalizations that related to previously established objectives?
   b. Was the discussion summarized clearly and concisely?

It is advantageous to you as a teacher to gain feedback from your students to help you evaluate and improve your teaching competence. You can occasionally ask students to answer the preceding questions for the purpose of evaluating a class discussion. The questions can be reworded so the word *you* is substituted for the word *student*. Be sure to let students know that you appreciate their comments and input by thanking them for *their* participation in the evaluation process, by using their ideas when feasible, or by explaining why you cannot use a particular suggestion that has been offered.

Simulated Experiences

Chapter 10

As a teaching aid, the term *simulated experiences* applies to a variety of means for taking subject matter off the printed page and bringing it to life, chiefly in the form of small-scale dramas, or slices of real life. The major simulated experiences described in this chapter include:

- *Skits,* in which students take part in problem situations by reading lines from prepared scripts.
- *Sociodramas,* which emphasize interpersonal relationships for which only a very sketchy outline is provided.
- *Role-playing,* which involves the acting out of roles that are defined in part by convention and students' existing knowledge of the types of characters they portray, even though there may be no formal dramatic framework, as in a skit.
- *Case studies,* which can be presented in the form of letters, records, or real life stories.

Through simulated experiences, students discover meaning that a textbook can only state; the difference is that between doing and merely being told about doing, a case of action speaking far louder than printed words. In sociodramas, moreover, one is not only involved but involved on one's own terms — free to interpret the assigned role by drawing from one's own experience. So subject matter is made relevant on a personal level.

Skits

Using skits in classroom teaching provides an excellent opportunity to involve students actively, to add variety to classroom teaching, and to plan meaningful follow-up activities ahead of time. If teachers write or distribute the skit themselves, they have an opportunity to include slower learners by asking them to read the parts with fewer and easier lines. It is advisable to give out scripts to students in the skit a day or two in advance of the time they will be used. By doing this, students have an opportunity to read the lines several times and are able to give a smoother and more meaningful reading in class. A stand-in may be chosen to become familiar with the skit in case one of the actors is absent on the appointed day.

Teachers may want to change the names in a skit to fit the local situation — to use the names of students in the class, the name of their school, and the names of commercial concerns in the local community. This heightens student interest and may make the situation seem more realistic and pertinent. Using props also adds interest. When skits are first used in a particular class, teachers may supply or suggest the props. Later, students can be encouraged to bring them.

When teachers are familiar with the contents of a skit, they are in a position to give the class points to look for, to suggest topics that may be discussed after it is read, and to suggest follow-up activities in advance. This kind of guidance helps students see the purpose and relevance of the skit.

Teachers can encourage students to plan their own follow-up activities. Planning stimulates analytical thinking, increases student interest and participation, and serves to motivate students to higher levels of achievement. Of course the points to look for, the discussion questions, and the class activities will depend upon previous learning and the students' interests, needs, abilities, and maturity.

Creating Your Own Skit

A skit reading will be nothing more than a reading unless the teacher provides opportunities for making it a meaningful experience. Students often enjoy writing their own skits and may lead the follow-up discussion as well. This has the advantage of involving all class members, of including topics that are of real concern to students, and of showing them that their contributions are worthwhile and important.

Skits in which the lines are more or less spontaneous may also be presented to the class. The plot, the first line for each character and the essence of the dialogue are planned in a general way by class members working together in small groups. A skit of this type could be used in studying various nutrients. Each group of students could select a specific nutrient and, through a short drama, illustrate the following about it:

1. Historical interest and/or discovery
2. Deficiency symptoms
3. Sources
   a. Foods
   b. Others

The teacher will need to provide reference materials and resources to enable students to look up appropriate information to include in this type of skit. A typical skit emphasizing vitamin C may include a scene from Vasco da Gama's trip from Portugal around Africa to India, on which 62 percent of the crew died of scurvy. Later, on the first English expedition to the East Indies, three of four ship captains saw their crews so disabled by scurvy that they were barely able to navigate. The fourth ship, whose daily ration included doses of lemon juice, was untouched by the disease. Soon all British sailors were required to drink lime or lemon juice, and eventually they became known as limeys.

In the skit about vitamin D, it could be brought out that George Washington, who escaped the more serious and crippling effects of rickets, lost his teeth early in adulthood and had to replace them with wooden pegs. Nor were women, as a group, spared such misfortune. To include information about the history, deficiency symptoms, and food sources of vitamin A, the students could act out a scene in which early Greeks, troubled by night blindness, were told by Hippocrates to eat liver dipped in honey. Later, fishermen blinded by the sun glaring on the water ate the livers of codfish and sea gulls to improve their sight. The Greeks and fishermen were not only preventing night blindness but were contributing to their health by getting enough vitamin A, which had been stored in the livers of animals for future use.

In the skit about riboflavin, which promotes growth, it could be shown that the average American man and woman today are several inches taller than their ancestors. By bringing out interesting facts such as these, you will help students remember the material better, and they will see that what is studied in home economics really does influence one's life.

See pages 91-93 for the scripts and follow-up activities for three skits: *This Communication Will Self-Destruct*, *How to Lose a Job Before Getting One*, and *Camera-Shy*.

Sociodramas

In skits, the participants read the parts and portray the roles of the characters that are delineated for them. In sociodramas, the students are free to interpret roles as they actually feel and perceive them. Since the dialogue is spontaneous and unrehearsed, participants usually react as they really would in similar situations. Sociodramas are used when studying problems related to personal or social relations, family living, or any area of human development involving interpersonal relationships.

The primary advantage that sociodramas have over skits is that they take little or no preparation time before class. Skits must be written or at least, in most cases, duplicated and distributed. Since a sociodrama is an extemporaneous portrayal of a situation in which only the first few lines and the general plot or theme are planned, what the participants say and do cannot be anticipated. Therefore, one distinct disadvantage of sociodramas is that the follow-up cannot be planned in advance. Only very general guidelines such as these can be given ahead of time:

- What seem to be some of the underlying and basic causes of conflict between the characters as they are seen in this scene?
- Which of the reactions and behaviors shown by the characters are typical of mature and immature individuals?
- What are some ways in which this situation could be improved?

How to Use Sociodramas

One principle of using sociodramas in the classroom is that a student should never be forced to be in one. Participation should be completely voluntary. However, when teachers know their students well, they can sense which ones would like to take part despite their hesitancy to say so publicly. These students may be encouraged and cajoled into participating with just the right lighthearted approach.

This Communication Will Self-Destruct

The following skit could be used in a family living course or in any other home economics class in which interpersonal relationships are emphasized.

Characters: Toby and Dana, who may be friends or husband and wife

Setting: Toby and Dana's kitchen

TOBY: What time will you be ready for dinner?

DANA: In just a minute.

TOBY: Dinner is almost ready.

DANA: I'll be there as soon as I can.

TOBY: Dinner is ready. I'm dishing up.

DANA: Hold it. I'm almost through.

TOBY: How can I hold dinner? It will get cold — or burn.

DANA: I'm hurrying.

TOBY: Do you know how much time I spent cooking this meal? I was trying to please you.

DANA: You are *so* impatient!

TOBY: Me? You're selfish! All you think of is yourself. You're just like your mother.

DANA: Well, now, I consider that a compliment. It's certainly better than being like *your* mother.

TOBY: Now, what's wrong with *my* mother?

DANA: She's nosy.

TOBY: Now, just one minute. I think you …

Behavioral objectives:

- Identify barriers to effective communication.
- Give examples of barriers to effective communication.
- Explain how a destructive argument differs from a constructive argument.
- Point out barriers to effective communication in the foregoing dialogue.

Points to look for:

- Being too vague
- Using poor timing
- Arguing destructively
- Giving criticism poorly
- Lacking consideration for another person

Discussion questions:

- What could Dana have done to avoid the argument?
- Was Toby unreasonable? Why, or why not?
- What did Toby say that led this conversation into a destructive argument?
- What issues came into the argument that were not related to the main topic?

- How did both Toby and Dana use poor timing in this situation?
- How could both Toby and Dana have handled the situation more effectively?

How to Lose a Job Before Getting One

The following skit could be used in a class on gainful employment or career education or in a comprehensive class on personal development. Sometimes exaggerating a scene will add humor to a situation and help clarify the basic ideas. Satire may help students identify the main points being illustrated in a skit. This type of humor usually appeals to junior and senior high school students.

Characters: Ms. Wilson, personnel manager for Eatmore Restaurant, and Betsy Smith, an interviewee at the restaurant for a job as a waitress

Setting: Ms. Wilson's office, where Betsy has just arrived — 15 minutes late, chewing gum, and dressed in a very tight and revealing outfit

---

BETSY: Gee, Ms. uh, uh. Is it Martin or Wilson? Oh yes, I remember, it's Ms. Wilson, right? Sorry to be late to tell you all about myself, but I got a huge run in my hose and, of course, I had to go back and get a different pair. You know, the panty hose they put on the market these days isn't worth …

MS. WILSON: Yes, I understand, Ms. Smith. Now, I have your application in front of me and would like to talk to you about some of your answers and about why you want to work for us. Your Social Security number was left off your application. Do you have a Social Security card, Ms. Smith?

BETSY: Oh, yeah. Well, you see, I was in such a hurry when I filled out the application that I didn't have time to find it. I changed purses; you know what that means!

MS. WILSON: I see. Do you have your card with you now?

BETSY: I think so. (She digs at length through the items in her purse, taking some of them out and putting them on Ms. Wilson's desk. She finally finds the card.) Yeah, here it is!

MS. WILSON: Thank you. Now, it says here that you graduated from high school, but it is very difficult to read the name of the school.

BETSY: Oh, gosh, I sure did have trouble with that! I didn't see that it said to print until after I'd already filled in all that other old stuff. So I had to mark it out. I graduated — just barely — from Central High School. My mom was so surprised and pleased.

MS. WILSON: Everything else seems to be here. Tell me, Ms. Smith, why would you like to work here with us?

BETSY: Oh, I don't know. I guess it's the only thing open now, and a person gets in the habit of eating, you know. (She laughs boisterously.) Besides, I heard the pay was pretty good here, huh?

MS. WILSON: What do you think would be a fair salary for your work?

BETSY: Well, I used to work for the Good Food Restaurant down the street; they're awful people to work for. You have to keep your hair tied up all the time. And the people that manage the place are impossible. Sometimes I'd have to stay ten or fifteen minutes after closing time to help them clean up. Sometimes they didn't pay me for the extra time, either. They paid me $400 a month and that wasn't enough for all I had to put up with. I was the best waitress they had, but they just didn't realize it or appreciate me!

MS. WILSON: Thank you for coming in for an interview, Ms. Smith. As soon as we've made a decision, we'll call you. Don't bother calling us. If we need you, we will get in touch with you. Good-bye.

BETSY: Thanks a lot. Oh, if you can't get me at home, I'll probably be at City Hospital. My Aunt Mary is going to have her gall bladder out. She's …

MS. WILSON: I'm very sorry to hear that. Now, Ms. Smith, my secretary will show you out. Good-bye.

Discussion questions:

- What did Betsy do that created a poor impression? How could she have made a more favorable first impression?
- Why would an employer be unlikely to hire Betsy?
- What traits did Betsy show in this scene that indicate that she may be a poor employment risk?
- What traits are desired of employees in any type of work? How may a person reveal some of these characteristics during a brief interview?
- Why should prospective employees refrain from asking about salary early in an interview? How could they bring up the subject without being too obvious or direct about it?
- Why is it inadvisable to criticize previous employers?
- How can people answer questions honestly and fairly without it hurting their chances of getting a job?

Classroom activities:

- Reenact this scene showing how Betsy could improve her chances of getting this job.
- Write minidramas planting good and poor features of job interviews, such as being on time (neither late nor early), having necessary information available, and asking appropriate questions. Identify the features of each interview situation that would create a favorable and an unfavorable impression. Discuss which interviewee would be most likely to land the job and why.
- Draw stick-figure or cartoon posters showing proper and improper interview techniques.
- From a grab bag, select the name of a job in which teenagers are likely to seek and find employment. For each job, list appropriate and meaningful questions that the interviewee might ask the employer to increase the likelihood of getting the job.
- Practice filling out job applications. Discuss why each item of information is requested. List points to follow in filling out applications to help "sell" oneself.
- Suggest appropriate attire to wear when applying for various types of work. Discuss why the clothing worn for one kind of job interview may be inappropriate for another.
- Give examples of questions interviewers might ask prospective employees applying for a variety of jobs.

Camera-Shy

Many concepts related to consumer education can be introduced, using the following skit. Those that will be covered depend upon the students' previous experiences and the depth in which consumer buying will be studied. Some concepts that are suggested by the skit, entitled *Camera-Shy*, include selling techniques; types of selling — door-to-door, catalog, department stores, specialty stores, and discount stores; comparative shopping; types of credit and credit costs; contracts; and consumer protection.

Characters: Bernard Brown, a high school senior
Mr. John Blabb, a high-pressure camera salesperson

Setting: The front doorway of Bernard's home

MR. BLABB: Hi, sucker — I mean, sir. Congratulations. I have heard that you're graduating from high school this spring. I'm John Blabb, and a representative from Classy Camera Company. Of course, you've heard of our wonderful and outstanding company, haven't you? Well, of course, you have.

BERNARD: Well … er … I might …

MR. BLABB (Interrupting): Great! Our company has a very special offer and it is only available to graduating seniors. You may be wondering why we're offering such a fabulous buy. At Classy Camera, we feel that you deserve a little something extra as a graduate-to-be.

BERNARD: That's nice. What are you ... ?

MR. BLABB (Interrupting again): We're offering a marvelous, fully automatic camera at a cost you simply wouldn't believe. I'm sure that you'll want to start to develop your skills as a photographer and record the important coming events in your life.

BERNARD: But, I wasn't planning to learn photography, I don't even know how to focus a camera.

MR. BLABB: I was just coming to that. For a very limited time only, we are offering a free course in photography with the purchase of our camera and a few necessary accessories. You're probably thinking, "How can those nice people afford to do that?" Well, we feel that high school graduates deserve a reward and gift for their great accomplishment.

BERNARD: Oh, that's nice, but what would I have to ...

MR. BLABB: Here's our Classy Camera catalog. We're offering combinations of cameras and accessories in the sets numbered seven and eleven. They are only $89.98. Think of all that for eighty-nine dollars. Set thirteen is really a super buy. Monthly payments are so easy — just $5.49 a month — less than 20 cents a day. Just think of that bargain!

BERNARD: When would I get my photography course?

MR. BLABB: It will be scheduled when you receive your camera set. Due to a delivery — but your wait will be well worth it. Now, if you'll just sign here and indicate which of the camera sets you prefer, I'll get your order off immediately. In fact, if you hurry, I can make the next mail pickup.

BERNARD: I think that I like this one best, but ...

MR. BLABB: Good, just check it — no, I'll be glad to check it for you. Have you signed the agreement? Good, good! I must hurry so you'll be sure to get in on this great deal and receive your camera on time. Good-bye, Mr. Brown.

BERNARD: Good-bye — and thank you.

Discussion questions:

- What techniques did Mr. Blabb use that helped him make this sale? What other techniques are sometimes used to persuade people to make purchases they had not planned?
- What should Bernard have found out before signing the contract agreement?
- What responsibilities do consumers assume by signing contracts to buy on credit?
- What are some of the advantages and disadvantages of using credit?
- What does this expression mean: "It is just as important to know how to spend money as it is to know how to earn it"?

Follow-up activities:

- Plan and give sales talks in an attempt to persuade class members to buy particular products. Use typical selling techniques and subtle methods of persuasion. Analyze the sales pitch used in each mock situation to determine what was said that might influence a consumer to buy the item. Discuss what might have influenced the consumer not to buy the product.
- Write a short story or make a tape describing the misfortunes of an individual or a family that has overextended its credit obligations. Suggest solutions to the problems described.
- Collect and discuss magazine and newspaper articles that seem to support the concept of a cashless society.
- Compare the cost of buying different products on credit in several local business concerns and with a variety of credit cards.

Through the discussion and activities following the skit, the teacher may guide students into formulating generalizations similar to these:

1. Selling techniques may be effective in persuading consumers to buy, or in dissuading them.
2. Consumers have a choice in deciding where and from whom to buy.
3. People who plan expenditures are more likely to derive satisfaction from them than people who do not plan.
4. Buying on credit costs money but allows consumers to use goods and services while paying for them.
5. Laws and government regulations cannot protect individuals in all aspects of consumer buying.

The teacher may say something like, "Who will be the younger brother? Nobody? Oh, come on, Mark, I imagine you could play the part of a ten-year-old boy very well!" (This would be particularly appropriate if Mark really has a brother about this age.) If Mark declines this personal invitation, the teacher could reply, "Well, we'll just have the sociodrama without a younger brother." This would be preferable to making a student feel self-conscious and uncomfortable. The first time a sociodrama is used, the class "hams" may be the only volunteers. However, after two or three successful sociodramas, the more reserved and retiring students are likely to want to take part too.

A sociodrama depicts a situation involving interpersonal conflict. In order to include episodes that will be most meaningful to the class members, the teacher could ask, "What are some problems students your age may have at home in getting along with other family members?" Of course, this would be a better and more ethical question than "What are some problems you have in getting along with your family?" Actually, most of the time the impersonal question will result in the same response but will lessen the likelihood that the class period will become a "show and tell" session of family secrets.

A typical ninth-grade class may list problem areas such as these:
• Using the telephone
• Sharing a bathroom
• Having to take care of younger brothers and sisters
• Doing chores around the home
• Disagreeing with parents about dating
• Setting curfews

A student could write on the chalkboard the ideas suggested by class members. Then the students can vote for the two or three items that they believe are most likely to be sources of conflict. Those that receive the most votes would logically be the concerns to be included in the sociodramas.

The class may decide which and how many family members should be portrayed. After the volunteer cast is selected, the teacher will take the participants into a corner of the room, into an adjoining room, or into the hallway near the open classroom door — to any place where there is some degree of privacy but where the teacher can also be near enough to know what the rest of the class is doing. Actually, this planning session will take only a few moments because the participants decide only how the drama will begin and plan just a few of the opening lines. From then on, the dialogue and action should be spontaneous; the students say and do what comes naturally to them.

Teachers have a key responsibility in stopping sociodramas as soon as they sense that the participants are straining for their lines and before the action becomes tedious. The teacher may say something like, "Thank you. Let's stop here and talk about this situation."

Follow-Up

If no discussion follows the sociodrama, it will become only a means of entertaining the class. The purpose of the follow-up is to lead the students in formulating generalizations that can guide them in solving problems similar to those depicted in the drama. The students can be given guidance in many ways. The participants may be asked to analyze the feelings and emotions they experienced during the enactment of the scene. Then, through skillful questioning, the teacher may lead the students to a better understanding of others' responses and reactions.

After a discussion of how the situation might have been handled better, another scene could be dramatized, incorporating the suggestions for improvement. The same players or another group of students could take part in the replay.

Students may reverse roles to gain greater empathy for the feelings of others. For example, the person who played the part of a teenager in the first dramatization may play the part of a parent in the next one.

Advantages of Sociodramas

A sociodrama provides students with an enjoyable and common experience on which to base a meaningful discussion and follow-up activities. In addition, teachers gain valuable insight into their students' maturity levels because the participants in a sociodrama are likely to reflect the emotions they really feel in similar situations. Students also see that others have problems very much like their own. If not used too often, sociodramas add variety and interest to classroom teaching.

Cautions in Using Sociodramas

On rare occasions, the teacher may want to stop a sociodrama because the participants become very emotional about their roles or they become overly self-conscious. Self-consciousness often manifests itself in giggling. This is most likely to happen if the problem situation being acted out is one about which the students feel embarrassment. If this problem persists, the teacher may not want to use this method of teaching at all. However, it is recommended that the teacher use the technique several times before discarding it because it has many advantages. If teachers are enthusiastic and excited about using sociodramas, this will undoubtedly be reflected in their students' attitudes toward them.

Variations

Several unique ways of creating situations for sociodramas are available to teachers. One possibility is that they, or students, could read or tell a short story. Class members could then act out the ending of the dramatization based on this material, without prior discussion of how it will or should end.

Another variation is to use pictures of people who are obviously involved in interpersonal problem situations. Students can enact the scenes as they sense and feel them. Of course, the follow-up discussions described previously will enable these dramatizations to become the bases for meaningful learning experiences.

Role-Playing

Most educators do not make a distinction between sociodramas and role-playing. However, as the terms are used in this book, there is one difference. In sociodramas, students interpret the parts being played in the way they actually feel them or desire to play them. There is not even a subtle suggestion that a role should be interpreted any certain way. However, in role-playing, students are more likely to feel a commitment to portray a character's role in a way that matches what is expected of a person in that particular situation.

For example, when role-playing an employment situation in which one student is serving food to another, the students undoubtedly sense that there is a correct and an incorrect procedure to follow. The players may purposely plant errors in their ways of serving and being served, but there is still the knowledge that there are right and wrong ways. Another example might center on a consumer thinking about making an expensive purchase using credit. In this situation there would be an expected pattern of behavior including certain questions the student knows should be asked.

Other situations typically used in role-playing may involve babysitters asking parents for specific information and prospective consumers asking salespeople questions about specific features of certain products. Situations such as these are usually acted out with maximum benefit after students have gained some background knowledge about the topic.

Case Studies

Case studies are stories or scenarios. They provide a vehicle for involving students in solving problems that are similar to those they face in their real lives. If problem situations are realistic to students, they will want to discuss them in class. Providing a common basis for discussion is preferable to talking in class about students' personal problems or publicly discussing personal and family situations. Case studies, then, are effective for teaching in the affective domain. Students may obtain additional insight into the various facets of their lives and acquire experience in considering their personal problems in more objective ways.

Students are encouraged to use the higher levels of thinking by analyzing the situations provided and by planning creative solutions to the problems presented.

Case studies can be used in many ways. They can be read aloud by the teacher or students, or presented by means of an audiotape or videotape and analyzed in a class discussion. The stories can be duplicated for each student, who is then asked to write answers to the questions provided. Different students' responses would be kept anonymous and could be presented to the entire class for analysis and comparison. Case studies can be analyzed in small groups. Each group might have the same scenario or the groups might have different situations to analyze. In either case, the small groups' conclusions and recommendations can be shared with the entire class to provide the basis for further discussion.

Case study simulations may be presented in personal letters, letters to editors of newspapers and periodicals, and advice-column letters. Other formats for case studies may include narratives, log or diary entries, dialogue excerpts, and simulated counselor or personnel records. The studies will vary in length depending on the type of problem presented, the amount of information to be provided, and the attention span of the students.

Newspaper and magazine articles often provide appropriate case study material. When the teacher or students write the stories, it is motivating to use the names of local places such as streets, schools, and shopping centers to make the situations seem more relevant and meaningful. Published case studies can also be localized by making substitutions for the proper nouns used in the original story.

Scenarios may be open-ended or they may include the outcome or decision that was made. The follow-up activities or questions asked about the situations are actually as important as the case studies themselves. Regardless of whether the ending is provided, case studies can be examined for alternative solutions, along with predictions of possible outcomes. When the material is used in this way, students are given experience in critical thinking and decisionmaking.

The questions used to help students analyze case study situations are extremely important. An effective technique for maximizing the value of this method of teaching is to give students points to look for in the case studies, or to provide them with follow-up discussion questions before reading about the situations. There are four steps in the decision-making process that students can use in analyzing the case studies provided in this chapter:

1. **Identifying the problem.** What exactly is the problem? What additional information is needed?
2. **Identifying alternative solutions to the problem.** What are all the possible solutions?
3. **Examining and weighing the consequences of the possible solutions.** What might happen if this is done? What might happen if another alternative is chosen?
4. **Deciding on a solution.** Of all the alternatives, which provides the best solution? Why? In view of all the consequences, why is this the best thing to do?

Students can continue the following scenarios by acting out the solutions proposed by class members. The questions following each story foster higher order thinking.

Giving the Teacher a Hard Time

April, Jill, and Yolanda were the only ninth graders in the 4th period Food Science class taught by Mrs. Marsh. The rest of the students were eleventh-grade males. The three girls constantly dissolved into peals of laughter whenever any of the guys even looked at them. One day the girls were standing and talking to each other when Mrs. Marsh came into the room. She politely asked the girls to sit down and stop talking. They became very quarrelsome and antagonistic. April loudly defied Mrs. Marsh and suddenly Jill and Yolanda also started criticizing her. The remainder of the class, the upperclass students, looked embarrassed.

Discussion questions:
- Who were the upperclass students embarrassed for?
- Why did the girls become so agitated?
- Would the reaction have been the same if the class had been made up of only ninth-grade girls? Why, or why not?
- Would the situation have been the same if the three students were male? Defend your answer.
- What would be more socially responsible behavior?

Does Popularity Have a Price?

Ted had only been enrolled at City High for two weeks. He recently transferred from a small school in a rural area and was eager to make friends. Regardless of how Ted tried to meet people, his efforts were in vain. The best thing going for Ted was his advanced status in Mr. Duncan's Physical Science class. Ted was particularly good in physical science because he had covered the material last year in his old school. One day, during a quiz, Mr. Duncan stepped out of the room. Ken, a popular student, asked Ted to give him the answer to the test. Ted really wanted Ken's approval.

Discussion questions:
- What should Ted do? Why should he do that?
- Why might Ted be finding it so difficult to make friends in his new school?
- Does cheating make Ted or Ken a better person? A worse person? Defend your answers.
- Who could get hurt in this situation? Why?
- How could Ted make a socially responsible decision and still not "lose face?"

Some So-Called Friends May Not Really Be Friends

Carol and Jackie started running around together at the beginning of their freshman year. They had attended different middle schools so they did not know each other very well until Project 600, freshman orientation. The girls quickly formed a friendship. Soon after Carol's mother met Jackie, she informed her daughter that she did not like Jackie's attitude. Carol's mom said she thought Jackie seemed "wild." Carol was furious with her mom and argued in her friend's defense. Some weeks later, Jackie came over to spend the night at Carol's house. Late that night, Jackie pulled out a bottle of gin. Although Carol was stunned, she nevertheless shared the contents. The girls were feeling the effects of the alcohol when Jackie proposed that they sneak out the back door and go to a party she'd heard about. Carol was unsure, but she followed Jackie to the back door anyway. They were half-way down the steps when Carol's mom called out to her.

Discussion questions:
- What should Carol do? Why?
- Who is responsible? Why?
- Should Carol be allowed to spend the night at Jackie's house? Why, or why not?
- If you were Carol, and you were allowed to make a decision regarding your own punishment, what would you do? Why?
- How could Carol have prevented this situation from occurring?

Photo Situations

In photo situations, pictures provide the common basis for discussion. In other words, a discussion is built upon what students feel about and read into a picture. Usually, but not necessarily, the pictures depict interpersonal relationships. If the picture is available in multiple copies of a textbook or periodical, all the students can view it at the same time. Some educational materials provide color transparencies, along with teaching suggestions, that can be easily used with an overhead projector. If a photo is too small for the entire group to see easily, the teacher can move around the room with the picture or make a transparency of it. After students analyze the scene, the teacher can start a discussion by asking pertinent questions. The example below illustrates how a photo situation can be used:

Photo situations require that the teacher ask questions based on student responses. For instance, in the example below, a student may have replied to the first question by saying, "The child pleaded with her mother not to leave." The teacher could develop this idea by asking an additional, more probing question to carry the thought further, such as "What are some ways of helping children to feel secure so that they are able to cope better when a parent leaves the house?"

The success of skits, sociodramas, role playing, case studies, and photo situations as methods of teaching depend primarily upon the teacher's ability to ask significant, relevant, and thought-provoking questions that promote meaningful discussions.

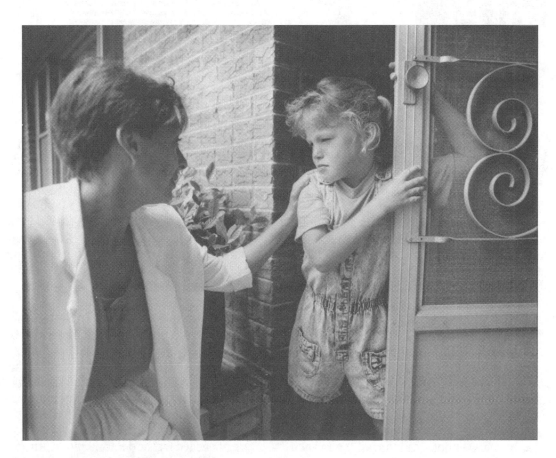

- What may have occurred prior to this scene?
- How could this situation be handled? If it were to occur often, how could it then be handled?
- Describe the feelings and conflicts that the parent may be experiencing?

Demonstrations

Chapter 11

Demonstrations can be very helpful in providing maximum opportunities to learn. They can be used to show procedures, to explain new techniques, to establish standards for individual and group work, and to illustrate methods when time is limited. Demonstrations also save money by controlling laboratory expenses. However, it is frequently better not to give a demonstration than to give one that is poorly executed. If there isn't time to give a really well-planned demonstration, there is probably another way of presenting the material, such as through a film, filmstrip, or video tape.

The purposes or objectives of the demonstration should be absolutely clear to the person preparing and giving it as well as to the students viewing it. Many behavioral objectives for demonstrations will be in the psychomotor domain since the students are usually expected to repeat the procedure viewed or to adapt it to a similar situation. Students may apply the knowledge gained through the demonstration in a laboratory experience, at home, or in on-the-job training.

Planning Demonstrations

There are five essential steps to follow when planning a demonstration:

1. **Outline the material to be covered and determine the way in which it is to be presented.** A concise outline should include an introduction, the major concepts to be covered, and a summary of the main points. It is wise to review the outline and to be thoroughly familiar with its contents. Practicing the introduction will help you begin smoothly and with confidence.

2. **Develop a sequential plan.** A time schedule is helpful; in many cases, such as with food preparation, it is essential. Allow sufficient time for questions and discussion. List all the items needed for the demonstration and check to see that they are all available before starting. Students can often help with the pre-preparation or presentation of the demonstration. However, student participation also needs to be planned.

3. **Determine the steps that can be done ahead of time or eliminated from the actual demonstration.** Pre-preparation of materials and premeasurement of ingredients can help make a demonstration run smoothly and efficiently. Student interest will be lost if too much time is spent on repetitious and time-consuming tasks. However, care must be taken that none of the essential steps is omitted. A happy balance is reached when enough of the actual procedure is shown so that the viewers understand what is happening, but it is not so time-consuming that they become bored.

When there is insufficient time in food demonstrations to prepare and completely cook a product, a finished or partially finished product may be made in advance. Through such a procedure, all the preparatory steps can be viewed and the finished product can be sampled in a limited amount of time.

4. **Select the best equipment for the demonstration and practice using it.** Be sure that the equipment needed for the demonstration is in good working order and is positioned conveniently for working and viewing. Equipment should be placed close enough to the central work area so that you do not distract students by walking back and forth; yet the arrangement of equipment should not obstruct their

view. A stationary or portable overhead mirror may help students see the entire procedure, particularly if the group is large.

5. **Plan to display the finished product.** If food is to be sampled, have utensils out and make provisions for a clean counter or tabletop for serving. If the demonstration is such that the product demonstrated can be hung on a bulletin board or displayed on a table or tray, make these arrangements ahead of time. The display may be very simple, but it should be effective. The impact of the demonstration is lost if the end product does not sell itself.

Demonstration Techniques

Here are some guidelines for giving effective demonstrations:

- Be prepared, so that the action will begin quickly. Opening remarks should be brief and to the point.
- Maintain good body posture and avoid leaning on work areas. Using proper work heights contributes to good posture and lessens fatigue, an especially important consideration if the demonstration is repeated during several class periods.
- Work at a pace that allows the students to follow the details of each step of the demonstration.
- Practice techniques ahead of time so that manipulation becomes almost automatic.
- Use both hands whenever possible but try to avoid crossing your hands and arms.
- Work in full view of the students. They may become inattentive if they are too far away to see clearly or if equipment or materials obstruct their line of vision.
- Keep the work surface neat and well organized throughout the demonstration. When the work surface is cluttered with equipment or other items, attention is diverted from the demonstration.
- If the process or technique being shown is repetitive and time-consuming, plan to do enough so that the technique is understood but do not spend time completing the entire operation. Either have the demonstrated work partially done beforehand, with enough left unfinished so that it can be adequately shown and completed, or do only part of the work from the beginning and have a sample completed to show as the finished product. To save time and to be more comfortable, thread needles for hand sewing ahead of time.
- If the nature of the demonstration is such that it should be viewed closely (for example, clothing construction techniques), provide sufficient space and a seating arrangement so that everyone will be able to see easily. If the group is too large to permit everyone to see simultaneously, demonstrate to part of the class at a time. To avoid discipline problems, make provision for the other students to be occupied constructively.
- Items should be passed around after the demonstration. If items are passed during the demonstration, the students' attention will be diverted so that continuity and interest are lost.
- References or resources may be provided for student use if demonstrations are complex or detailed, if students need more help, or if students are absent at the time of the original demonstration. Some possibilities include: printed illustrations and directions, step-by-step bulletin boards and posters that can be used over again, duplicated sheets with detailed directions or diagrams, and folders with samples and directions that students can use individually or in small groups. Students can also be referred to filmstrips, loops, and programmed instructional materials after the demonstration has been completed. However, if additional materials are available after every demonstration, students may come to expect and rely on them. Therefore, it may be neither necessary nor advisable to have illustrative samples after those demonstrations in which the concepts presented are relatively easy to understand.
- Use every possible opportunity to set a good example and to illustrate proper procedures and safe practices, even though you will not actually call attention to all of them in the course of any one demonstration.

Specific Techniques To Use In Food Demonstrations

Food and nutrition courses provide opportunities to demonstrate various food preparation skills, as well as the proper use of tools and equipment, safety precautions, and sanitation procedures.

■ Getting Ready To Demonstrate

- Cover supply trays, assembled food products, and previously prepared displays. This will create interest and an element of surprise.
- Dress as students are expected to dress during laboratory lessons. This may include wearing an apron or brushing and fastening the hair so that it is away from the face. A teacher may want to wear a uniform or lab coat while demonstrating, to create a professional and authoritative image. Clothing should be simple without long ties or sleeves that could dip in the food or be dangerous near equipment. Jewelry should be kept to a minimum or removed.

Planning Sheet for Demonstrations:

1. Meeting: 2. Date:

3. Location: 4. Projected Size of Audience:

5. Major Concepts:

6. Objective(s):

7. Introduction — Establishing Set:

8.

List of all consumable supplies needed:	List of all equipment needed:

9.

Preplanning and preparation steps to be done:	When	Completed (check when done)

10.

Outline of steps in the demonstration:	Points to be discussed during the demonstration (narrative):

11.   Closure or Summary:

12.   Evaluation: (How did it go; what to do differently next time)

- Wash hands well before beginning and call attention to the fact that this is being done.
- When possible, use low-cost foods that are high in nutritive value. This will not only stretch the department's budget but also show students how to cut costs. You will also have an opportunity to incorporate some subject matter relating to nutrition.

■ *Preparing and Mixing Foods*

- When preparing food in a mixing bowl, leave the bowl on the table for the mixing process. A damp cloth placed under the bowl eliminates slipping and minimizes noise. Using a clear mixing bowl allows students to see the contents. When necessary, the bowl may be lifted and tilted to provide a better view.
- Give food on a spoon a firm shake in the palm of the hand so that the material falls into the bowl. This is preferable to hitting a spoon or beater on the side of a bowl.
- When pouring a mixture from a bowl, be careful that fingers do not come in contact with the food. Use a flexible scraper to remove the mixture quickly and easily.
- Place a damp cloth or pastry cloth under a cutting board to prevent slipping. When working with flour, put in a container the extra flour that will be used on the board or cloth.
- When fresh eggs are to be used, have extras on hand in case they are needed. Because eggs are not always separated without getting some yolk in the white, break or separate only one at a time into a cup or small dish. Then transfer each egg to the bowl or mixture to which it is to be added.
- When spreading a mixture on bread, leave the bread on a board and use an assembly-line technique.
- Clean greens in advance and store them in plastic bags or clean, wet dish towels to save time during the actual demonstration.
- Turn meats with tongs or two forks to minimize splattering.
- Clean up spilled food immediately. Do not put food that has been spilled on the working surface back in the bowl you are using.

■ *Being Efficient and Organized*

- Put ingredients and equipment needed for the recipe in the order of use.
- Put trays in numbered order so they can be located easily. As an aid, use cards that list the supplies to be placed on each tray. Protect cards and recipes by placing a sheet of clear plastic over them.

- Remove a used tray from the table before a clean one is put in its place.
- After each piece of equipment is used, place it back on the tray, not on the counter or tabletop. This makes cleaning up more efficient.
- Place the wastebasket next to the table, not under it, so you will not have to duck to find it.
- Line the wastebasket with a bag or newspaper to make cleaning up easier.
- Complete the demonstration with a clean, cleared work surface. This may serve as the display area.

■ *Using Equipment and Appliances*

- Put canisters, measuring equipment, rolling pins, and other items to the side when not in use. If these are placed in front, the students' view will be obstructed.
- After a small appliance has been used, remove it from the demonstration area.
- When an electric mixer is used, remove the used beaters to a tray before the bowl is moved.
- Have a spoon holder or saucer on the range for used utensils.
- When lifting a lid from a hot pan, turn it away from the body and place it upside down on the working surface.
- Turn pot handles away from the front of the range.
- Stand to the side of the range when opening the oven door.
- Use potholders to pull out oven racks or to remove hot food from the oven. Leave potholders at the range but not near the burners or heating elements. Do not use paper towels or dish towels as potholders.
- Use pans whose sizes are appropriate to burners and units.
- Turn off the burner or unit when the cooking process has been completed. Students may be shown how to use the heat retained in electric units for cooking and warming foods.

Commentary and Remarks During Demonstrations

- It is not necessary to talk every minute during a demonstration, but extremely long pauses may make it difficult to hold the attention of the group. When it is unnecessary to describe the process being demonstrated, use the time to add depth to the subject matter at hand. Present supplementary material or ask thought-provoking questions.

- Use impersonal pronouns and articles such as "this," "a," or "the." This eliminates the need to use the possessive. It can be awkward to refer to "your greasy bottom" or "our liver."
- Avoid saying "The next thing I'm going to do is …" Use impersonal terminology such as "The second step is …" It is unnecessary and distracting to announce every movement you will make.
- Complete a sentence or thought before turning to something else.
- Stop talking when moving from one place to another, when turning away from the group, or when handling noisy equipment or materials.
- A good time to summarize what has been shown is when the product is being prepared for display.

Involving Students in Demonstrations

- Encourage students to ask questions and tell about personal experiences related to the topic being demonstrated. Ask them to give reasons for using different procedures, for variations and substitutions, and for alternative methods.
- If it is a food demonstration, make sure that students have the opportunity to sample the product. It can be frustrating to watch food being prepared for an entire class period only to have the bell ring and the food whisked away. Capitalize on the motivation built into the fact that teenagers like to eat!
- Let students take turns being assistants. One or two students might help throughout the entire demonstration, or students can be called on to perform one or two steps. Teenagers seem to enjoy cleaning up and washing dishes when they are away from home! Serving and passing food can be a meaningful learning activity for students with limited social experience. For example, they can be prompted to serve a guest, if one is present, first.
- Organize advanced classes so that students give demonstrations individually, in pairs, or in small groups. Establish criteria for evaluating these demonstrations, which can be an integral part of almost any subject-matter area being studied. Students can demonstrate such varied procedures as preparing formula and feeding an infant; using, cleaning, and caring for large and small appliances; making accessories and decorative items for the home; and repairing furnishings and equipment. See the evaluation chart below.
- Encourage students to show the class the procedures and techniques used for extended learning experience projects. These demonstrations could be brief and presented during class-sharing sessions.

Evaluation of a Demonstration

Use the key below to rate the demonstration (possible points = 50):

KEY: 5 = Excellent   4 = Very good   3 = Good   2 = Fair   1 = Poor

POINTS BEING CONSIDERED	5	4	3	2	1
1. Was well prepared					
2. Organized materials and equipment efficiently					
3. Worked so all students could see					
4. Kept work surface neat and clean					
5. Displayed skill in using the technqiue demonstrated					
6. Maintained appropriate pace					
7. Maintained an informative commentary during demonstration					
8. Involved students in the demonstration					
9. Reflects favorable image through appropriate attire and demeanor					
10. Completed demonstration within time limit					
TOTAL POINTS					

Games for Learning

Chapter 12

The types of games that can be used in teaching range from those that are simple and can be played within a relatively short period of time to those that are complex and time-consuming. All games require some degree of knowledge and many games involve a certain amount of chance. Chance enters into games when cards are drawn; when rewards are granted and penalties imposed, as in board games; or when dice, spinning wheels, or similar devices are used.

Simulation games are currently popular. They serve to isolate a portion of a life situation from its complex environment. The simulation is designed so that the players can experience some of the daily responsibilities, decisions, consequences, and pressures inherent in life or in a given situation. Through these means, people are helped to make decisions, to approach problems in a new way, and to explore areas that are new to them without suffering the consequences one is likely to encounter in life.

Since students either play according to predetermined rules or establish the guidelines themselves, the teacher is no longer the authority or judicial figure. Games, then, are one form of student-directed learning.

When implementing games in the classroom, caution must be taken so that winning does not become more important than learning. Games should not dominate the curriculum. As with other methods of instruction, if games are overused, they become ineffective.

Games that are used for reinforcement of information previously covered can be fairly uncomplicated. Commonly known card games, TV quiz shows, popular board games, and word games that involve decision-making experiences are somewhat more difficult to devise because they are more comprehensive and complicated. However, a number of well-known board games can be or have been adapted for educational use. A variety of games is available today. Many of these games are designed to simulate life situations in areas relating to consumer issues, interpersonal relationships, and the clarification of values and goals.

It is very important that the purpose and the rules of the game be clearly stated and understood by all players. If the rules are in writing, the students can begin the game themselves, and they have a reference immediately available if a question should arise. When a player's response to a question is challenged, textbooks, periodicals, or appropriate charts and tables should be available for students to check the accuracy of the answer.

The teaching power of a game is limited only by the instructor's imagination and ability to plan meaningful follow-up questions or activities. The games and the follow-up activities can help students find pleasure in learning and, therefore, serve as a means of motivation.

Games are an excellent vehicle for fostering higher levels of thinking, particularly analysis, as students figure out commonalities among careers, foods, and other variables. Following is a discussion of some noncommercial games that are especially suited to the home economics classroom.

Match 'Em

Match 'em is an easy game to assemble and to explain to students. The purpose of the game is to identify common equivalent measures used in food preparation when dividing or increasing a recipe.

A set of thirty playing cards is needed. Old playing cards can be backed with colored paper, or construction paper can be cut up in card-size pieces or 3-by-5-inch index cards can be used. A measurement is written on each card. For example, one card may have one-half cup and another card eight tablespoons. The finished deck must include fifteen sets of equivalents.

Directions: Lay all playing cards face down on the table. Turn two cards face up on each play. If the cards are equivalent measurements (not identical), the two cards are placed in a stack in front of the player. If the cards are equivalents, the student gets another turn. If a player does not turn up two equivalents, the next player takes a turn. When all of the cards are matched, the matches should be checked against an answer sheet. The student with the greatest number of matches wins.

A variation of this game can be played to enhance vocabulary by matching terms that mean the same thing, such as self-esteem and self-confidence, encouragement and support, creativity and imagination, uncertain and apprehensive. It is also possible to play Match 'Em with foods rich in the same nutrients, such as oranges and grapefruits, fish and poultry, bread and cereal, yogurt and cheese, lentils and dried peas.

Card Games

Familiar card games can be used as a form of student-directed review. The rules can be simple or complex depending on the specific learning objectives for the lesson. After a card game has been played, students may want to change the rules to provide variety. The game becomes more interesting as student involvement is increased.

To play the card games described in this chapter, make a deck of 52 cards with pictures of various foods or garments that illustrate different lines, colors, and textures. Pictures of architectural and furniture styles can also be used, but it may be necessary to have some duplicates of the styles. You can use the same general style more than once, but use different pictures. You could also make 52 cards by writing on them characteristics or brief descriptions of children at various age levels; different fibers; and a variety of clothing styles, careers, and employment skills. To show how card games can be used as an educational learning experience, the area of food and nutrition has been selected for illustrative purposes here. Pictures of foods that are good sources of one or more of the following nutrients can be used: protein, fat, carbohydrate, vitamin A, B-complex vitamins, vitamin C, iron, and calcium. Some empty-calorie foods may be included. Two wild cards might be added for variety, making a total of fifty-four cards.

Cards can be made by cutting pictures of food from magazines and attaching them to small index cards. If multiple sets of cards are desired, labeled sketches of foods should be drawn in rectangles of playing-card size on a master sheet. After these sheets have been duplicated, the individual pictures are cut out and attached to a firm backing.

Each of the game variations described here could be adapted to other content areas such as these:

Child Development — developmental characteristics of a certain age group such as a four-year-old:
- playing in small groups with three or four friends
- beginning to share possessions and toys with "special" friends
- asking for things instead of snatching them
- seeking approval with comments such as "I'm good, aren't I?"

Family and Peer Relationships — verbal behaviors that contribute to negative communication:
- arguing
- criticizing
- putting down someone's idea
- blaming

Nutrition — foods rich in a certain nutrient such as vitamin A:
- apricots
- cantaloupe
- broccoli
- carrots

Textiles — characteristics of a certain fiber such as cotton:
- absorbent
- wrinkles
- durable
- can be laundered frequently

Clothing Selection — lines, colors, and textures appropriate for certain body types such as the tall and slender shape:
- contrasting belt
- western yolk
- warm and bright colors
- bulky fabrics

Housing — architectural characteristics typical of a certain style such as Dutch Colonial:
- gambrel roof
- dormer windows
- story-and-a-half construction
- clapboard or shingle siding

Interior Design — characteristics of a certain period of furniture such as Chippendale:
- mahogany
- cabriole leg
- pierced and carved splat back
- Chinese influence

Four of a Kind — three to four players

The object: to make as many books as possible. Each book is to consist of four cards having pictures of foods that represent good sources of the same nutrient or foods from the same food group. Wild cards can represent any food in a group or any nutrient designated by the player holding that card.

Directions:
1. Deal each person seven cards. Form a discard pile by turning one card face up. Place the remaining cards face down in the center of the table.
2. When individual players take turns, they may draw two cards from the pile that is face down or pick up the entire discard pile. The discard pile may be picked up only if the top card can be used to form a book. After completing a move, the player must put one card face up on the discard pile.
3. Place each book on the table as it is made. A book can be made and placed on the table only during a player's turn, not during anyone else's turn.
4. The game is ended when a player has no playing cards left, after having discarded. Play is also ended when there are no cards on the pile from which to draw and when the discard pile cannot be picked up by anybody. The player who has the greatest number of books wins the game.

Fishing for Food — two or more players

The object: to get cards that make a nutritious meal including foods from each of the basic food groups. The first person to do this wins.

Directions:
1. Scatter cards face down on the table.
2. Each player draws any five cards from those on the table. The remaining cards are left face down.
3. During each player's turn, one card is drawn and one card is discarded face down with the others.
4. Play continues until there is a winner.

Nutrition Points — two or more players

The object: to identify correctly the food group, the number of servings required daily, and the function of the major nutrient in the foods appearing on the cards.

Directions:
1. Stack cards face down. Each person turns up a card from the pile.
2. Score in the following manner:
   a. One point for identifying the food group of the item pictured on the card.
   b. Two points for stating the number of servings of the food required daily.
   c. Three points for telling the function of the major nutrients in the food.
   d. Minus the specified number of points for incorrect answers.
3. When the players have gone through the entire deck, the person having the greatest number of points is the winner.

Trading Game — three or more players

The object: to collect cards that are all in the same food group or nutrient-dense with the same vitamin or mineral.

Directions:
1. Deal the entire deck of cards to the players.
2. Players trade cards in any direction across the table by holding the card or cards face down and calling out the number of cards they want to trade. A player trades with a person who wants to exchange a like number of cards.
3. The first person who collects nine cards in any one of the basic food groups receives ten points. At the end of the game, two points are deducted for any card displaying foods with empty calories. The first person to reach 100 points is the winner.

Truth or Bluff — three or more players

The object: to get rid of all the cards in one's hand.

Directions:
1. The entire deck of cards is dealt.
2. In turn, each player places one to four cards face down on the table and states what the cards are. For example, the student can say, "These two cards are in the meat group." This may or may not be true.

3. The player on the left can either accept the statement or challenge it. If the statement is accepted, play proceeds to the next person. The discarded cards remain on the table. When the play is challenged, the cards must be shown. If the truth was told, the challenging player must take the cards laid down by the preceding player plus all the cards in the discard pile. If the cards were misrepresented, the player who tried to bluff must take these cards and the discard pile.
4. The first player without any cards wins the game.

Nutrition Solitaire — one person

The object: to place 16 cards representing foods that are good sources of protein and vitamins A and C in a square. The square should have vitamin A-rich foods across the top, vitamin C foods at the bottom, and protein foods on the sides. The four cards in the center can represent any nutrients. Designated nutrients can be changed for different games.

Directions:
1. Place all of the cards face down on the table. Turn up one card at a time and place it where it should be, according to the designated rules.
2. The player automatically loses if a card is turned up and its line is filled. For example, if a card picturing an orange is turned up, but the line for vitamin C is filled, the player loses.
3. In order to find places for more cards and to complete the square, the player can remove from the square and discard any pair of cards in the same food group. For example, the player may take away two in the meat group, or two in the fruit and vegetable group, and so forth.
4. The game is won if the player gets the proper layout of cards. The game is lost when the player turns up a card and its designated line is full and when the deck of cards has been played through once.

Zingo

This is an action-oriented game that can be used to review terms used in most home economics content areas. Zingo can be adapted for use in naming pieces of clothing construction and kitchen equipment; identifying clothing construction terms, nutrients, and furniture styles; and defining cooking terms. A card is needed for every student. Each card should consist of 16 different words or terms. Not all cards will have the same terms. For those cards that do have the same variation of terms, the placement of words must be different. Small squares of construction paper can be used as covers for responses.

A series of questions corresponding to the words or terms on the cards is needed. Some samples are: (1) What is the spool called that holds the bottom thread while you are machine sewing? (2) What is the diagram called that shows you how to place your pattern pieces on the fabric? (3) What do you use to find out how many inches (cm) there are around your hips, waist, and chest?

Directions: This game is a variation of bingo. When a question is read, the word or term that correctly answers it should be covered with a paper square. Players have "Zingoed" when they have covered a vertical, diagonal, or horizontal line on the game sheet. Four corners do not count.

There is one best answer for each question. The accuracy of the winner's answers should be checked. If there is an incorrect choice, the questioning continues until another Zingo winner is found. It is the teacher's responsibility to make this game a valuable learning experience by explaining why a choice may have been incorrect and by giving additional examples to illustrate correct responses.

ZINGO			
Body language	Gestures	Poise	Attention
Conversation	Listening	Respect	Timing
Eye contact	Grooming	Posture	Introductions
Facial expression	Grammar	Smile	Rambling

Some variations of Zingo include:

Cooking Terms

Fillet	Parboil
Cream	Poach
Dredge	Simmer
Fold	Sauté
Julienne	Core
Knead	Broil
Marinate	Baste
Pare	Braise

Wellness Concepts

Stress management	Cholesterol
Aerobics	Eating disorders
Obesity	Heart rate
Nutrition	Self-esteem
Walking	Drug-free
Saturated fat	Relationships
Blood pressure	Prevention
Lifestyle	Mental health

Clothing Construction Equipment and Terms

Tracing wheel	Guide sheet
Thimble	Gauge
Pattern	Shears
Needles	Layout
Pins	Measuring tape
Iron	Shears
Bobbin	Carbon paper
Sleeve board	Pressing cloth

Home Economics Tic-Tac-Toe

Tic-tac-toe is a simple game to set up and play in class. The grid for the game can be drawn on the chalkboard or on a poster board. If poster board is used, cardboard "X's" and "O's" can serve as markers for the squares. The teacher or a class member can serve as the questioner and scorekeeper.

The class can decide upon an equitable means of selecting the team that goes first. The questioner then asks the first member of this team a question. Team members are not allowed to consult each other about answers. When students answer questions correctly, they place their team's mark on the grid. Team members may consult about where to place the marker. Whether or not the student answers the question correctly, the next turn goes to the other team. When a question is missed by one team, a student on the next team gets an opportunity to answer the same question. Turns for answering questions are rotated among team members.

A score of 5 points is given to each team for every marker it has on the grid. A bonus of 10 points is awarded to the team that goes tic-tac-toe. The team with the greatest number of points wins the game.

Hidden-Clues Puzzle

Hidden clues is a word game that can be used in a variety of ways. Teachers, as well as the students, can develop hidden-clues puzzles very easily. First, an important concept consisting of approximately five to twelve letters is chosen. Then words are selected that are related to the major concept. Each of these supporting words or subconcepts must contain at least one of the letters in the mystery word. Letters in the related words need to be scrambled. Finally, in the letter blanks supplied for each of the related words, circle the letter used to make the surprise answer. The following is an example of one puzzle.

Directions: Unscramble each of the following groups of letters to form two words related to consumer economics.

EHKCC	Ⓞ _ _ _ _
TENITRES	_ _ _ _ Ⓞ _ _ _
TPYNAME	_ _ _ _ Ⓞ _ _
TBDE	Ⓞ _ _ _
PPNRLICEI	_ _ Ⓞ _ _ _ _ _ _
OTEN	_ _ Ⓞ _
RYLAAS	_ _ _ _ Ⓞ _
ONAL	_ _ Ⓞ _
TSOC	_ _ _ Ⓞ
IFCNANE	_ Ⓞ _ _ _ _ _
NOYEM	_ _ Ⓞ _ _
RCGEHA	_ _ _ _ _ Ⓞ _

Now arrange the circled letters to discover the mystery answer. These two words are important to every consumer: _____ _____ .

Answers

check	principle	cost
interest	note	finance
payment	salary	money
debt	loan	charge

The mystery answer is: *credit rating.*

After the puzzle is solved, the relationship of each of the words to the mystery answer should be discussed. It would be an added challenge to have students formulate a generalization using some of the hidden-clue words.

Go Forth

Go Forth is a board game involving skill and chance. The object of the game is to answer correctly as many questions as possible. It can be played by two or more players and one questioner-scorekeeper.

The materials needed for the game are:

1. **Board** — The playing board should be approximately 9 inches by 14 inches or larger. Poster board or cardboard provides a firm backing. A board rendition similar to the diagram at the end of this chapter can be made. Sketches and phrases should be keyed to the specific subject.
2. **Number cards** — Colored construction paper is suitable for all of the cards used in the game. Numbers are to be written on cards that measure approximately 1-1/2 inches square. Four cards numbered 1, 2, and 3, and one card numbered 4 are needed.
3. **Stars** — Stars are drawn on 1-inch-square cards. Approximately 50 cards are needed.

4. **Dots** — Dots are drawn on 1-inch-square cards. Approximately 50 cards are needed.
5. **Question cards** — Questions to be asked during the game should be typed or written on one side of cards about 2 inches by 3 inches or on small-size index cards. Write on the cards content questions and the number of spaces that a player can advance for giving a correct answer. Label one-third of the cards in the deck with 1, one-third with 2, and one-third with 3. The numbers may or may not relate to the difficulty level of the questions.
6. **Markers** — Disks or other objects are needed to serve as markers for players' board positions.

It is recommended that the board, card, stars, and dots be machine laminated or covered with clear adhesive shelf-type paper to increase their durability and to preserve them.

Directions: Before beginning play, shuffle the number and the question cards separately and place them on the board in the appropriate spaces. Appoint a questioner-scorekeeper to read the questions that are drawn by the players. The cards are not to be seen by the players.

1. Draw a number card and advance the number of spaces indicated.
2. Select a question card and hand it to the questioner-scorekeeper to be read aloud. If the question is answered correctly, draw a star. If the question is answered incorrectly, draw a dot.
3. Continue to draw question cards, taking turns.
4. If players land on a crossover, they have a choice of continuing on the same path or taking a shortcut.
5. When players land on a "count your dots" square, they should count the number of dots received for incorrect answers. If the count is five or more, they need to go back to the starting position and begin again. If players have ten or more dots when they arrive at the finish, they must begin again.
6. The game ends when the first player crosses the finish line. The player with the largest number of stars wins the game.

Crossword Puzzles

Crossword puzzles can be excellent devices for student self-evaluation and for reviewing key concepts of previously covered subject matter. There are computer programs that fit selected one-word clues into a grid, number the cells appropriately, and fill in the unused blank spaces in the puzzle.

You want to choose a concept for the puzzle topic that is broad enough in scope to have many words associated with it. Then list as many words as possible related to this topic. Ideas can be obtained by using a book index or thumbing through the pages of a text or reference book.

Write either definitions, questions, or fill-in-the-blank statements appropriate for each of the words used in the crossword puzzle. These should be clearly worded and consistent in format. A feeling of confusion often results when statements, questions, and completion items are interspersed. If the completion format is used, place the blanks at or near the ends of the sentences. See page 66 for more information about writing fill-in-the-blank items.

Students who are especially adept in language arts or particularly enjoy working crossword puzzles may like to make some to share with the class. This can also be done in small groups. The discussion that relates to making the puzzles could serve to reinforce subject matter concepts.

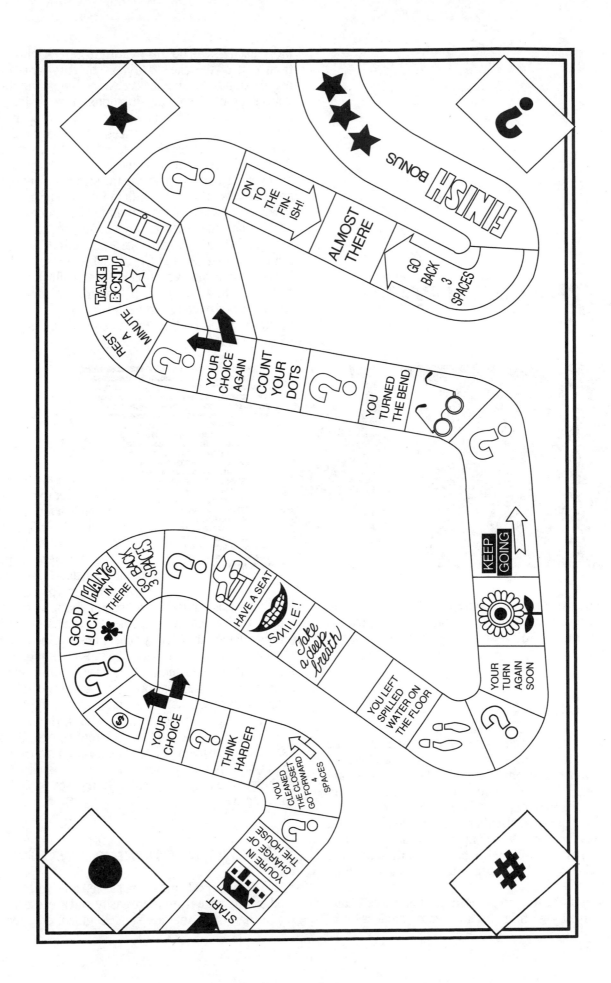

109

Display Media

Chapter 13

Various media can be used in the classroom to introduce, reinforce, summarize, or highlight material and to stimulate interest in the home economics curriculum.

Chalkboards

Chalkboards in the form of slates date back to the time of the oldest schoolhouse in America, and stories about Abraham Lincoln "cipherin' " on his slate are well known. Today, some form of the chalkboard can still be found in almost every classroom. If at all possible, needed material should be put on the chalkboard before class. Teachers lose contact with the class when they turn their backs to write on the board, and if the process takes very long, students may become bored and inattentive.

The chalkboard can be used most effectively during class time by writing only key words or ideas on it.

Most teachers can do this by turning only slightly away from part of the class. Having students write on the board can also be an effective way of engaging them in various problem-solving situations. If extensive material has been put on the board before class time, it can be covered by pulling down a screen hung above the chalkboard. By doing this, students will not be distracted by the material before it is to be used, and information can be revealed a little by moving the screen up at appropriate intervals. Thus, students are not likely to be overwhelmed by seeing a lot of writing all at once, and they will not become distracted by reading ahead.

The chalkboard is an excellent place to put reminders that need to be available for several days. These may include vocabulary lists to which words are added as they are used, behavioral objectives to be accomplished over a short period of time, dates of school events such as FHA/HERO meetings, or assignments with due dates.

Flip Charts

It takes considerably longer to put written material in a flip chart than on a chalkboard, but flip charts are fairly durable and can be used indefinitely. Because of their durability and the time and money involved in making them, it is advisable to use flip charts with subject matter that is relatively stable. Principles of furniture arrangement or the Dietary Guidelines for Americans are practical for a flip chart; clothing fads or changing fashions would make such a chart obsolete in a relatively short time. Pictures, cartoons, or sketches can be used in flip charts to add interest but they must be large enough to be seen throughout the classroom. If the lettering is too small, its use is limited. Different colors should be used to emphasize important words, but more than three colors on a page can create a "busy" visual effect so nothing is really emphasized. Avoid yellow — it doesn't show up well.

Selecting and Making Flip Charts

- Use a large pad and, if possible, one with a spiral edge. The pages turn more easily and are less likely to tear than those that are stapled, glued, or taped.

- If the flip chart is to contain writing, select the kind with ruled lines or a grid printed lightly on the pages. This eliminates the need for ruling guidelines in pencil and then having to erase them.
- Be sure the writing is large enough to be read easily at the greatest distance from which it will be viewed. Measure carefully and rough out lightly in pencil what is to be written. By doing this, the ends of lines will not be crowded and few words will have to be divided.
- Do not put too much writing on any one page. A large amount of written material that is cluttered and lacks variety does not encourage anyone to read it. Avoid having a sentence carry over from one page to another.
- Put a protective sheet of paper betwen the page on which writing is being done and the next page, so that ink will not leak through.
- Use the flip chart on an easel or other brace where it is high enough to be seen by everyone in the room. Place it so the pages can be turned without having to move the flip chart.
- Number pages near the lower edge of each sheet and make an index on the cover of the flip chart including the pages devoted to each topic. This may eliminate wasting class time and boring students by unnecessarily flipping through pages to locate certain sections.
- Affix your name to the outside cover so the flip chart will not be misplaced and can be identified readily when stored with those belonging to others.

Three T's for Flip Charts

You have seen presenters who spent more time talking to their flip charts than to their audiences. These tips will help you next time you are in front of a group using a flip chart:

- **T**alk to the audience, not to the flip chart.
- **T**urn toward the audience.
- **T**ouch the item on which you want the group to focus.

Practice before you are in front of the audience.

Flannel Boards

A wider range of illustrative materials can be used with a flannel board than with a flip chart or chalkboard. Visuals for a flannel board can be prepared in advance so that they are ready when needed. Once made, items can be filed and used many times over. It is efficient to keep flannel-board materials and accompanying notes or lesson plans together in large, heavy envelopes that have been marked clearly on the outside to identify their contents.

The flannel board and the articles on it can be moved from place to place, providing a high degree of flexibility that some other media lack. Items can be rearranged for comparisons, they can be added sequentially, and they can be taken away. Therefore, a whole process or any part of it can be reconstructed. Charts, diagrams, and graphs can be built as learning proceeds. Thus, materials can be used to suit the immediate needs of the situation.

Making Flannel Boards

Cotton flannel, because it is very inexpensive, is usually used to cover lightweight plywood, very heavy cardboard, or composition board. Actually, any napped or fuzzy fabric such as velvet, corduroy, or felt can be stretched tautly to cover the board and taped or tacked securely on the wrong side of the board. It is also possible to sew two pieces of flannel together, perhaps of different colors, in pillowcase fashion, and to slip the board inside so it fits snugly. This provides a reversible flannel board of different colors with a case that can easily be removed for cleaning. A flannel board measuring approximately 30 by 40 inches is of sufficient size to be seen by an audience of 150 to 175 people. A board of this size is not difficult to move about, although a somewhat smaller one might be equally suitable for classroom use. But if the board is too small, the variety of ways in which it can be used is limited.

Preparing the Illustrations

Magazine pictures should be glued or rubber cemented, with a product that will not leave buckles or ripples when dry, to a background such as construction paper or very lightweight poster board. Magazine paper is too lightweight and flimsy to be used without backing, and unmounted illustrations of this kind create an unfinished appearance. Care should be taken not to use backing materials that will be too heavy to stay on the flannel board securely. Other illustrations that do not need framing, such as figures from pattern catalogs, can be backed with old file folders.

At least one-half of the back of the mounted illustrations should be covered with a napped fabric. The fabric should be glued with the napped side up. When the prepared article is placed against the flannel board, it will stay in place because the two napped surfaces have an affinity for each other. For added assurance that the materials will stay in place when positioned, they can be stroked gently with an *upward* motion of the hand, and the board should be tilted backward slightly.

Using Flannel Boards

Flannel boards can be used to clarify, illustrate, reinforce, introduce, or summarize information.

■ To Clarify Concepts Through Visual Stimuli

As with all media, the educational value of flannel boards depends upon the teaching skills employed in using them. Flannel boards can help students who do not verbalize well to clarify concepts through visual stimuli. For example, pictures of foods of different colors, textures, and temperatures can be used to teach principles of meal planning. Silhouettes of objects like vases, bowls, candlesticks, plaques, and plants can be effective in demonstrating formal and informal balance, lack of balance, emphasis, pleasing proportions, and various types of rhythm. Students can use the flannel-board illustrations to practice and criticize their own arrangements.

Students may study the theoretical relationship between line and design in dress and the apparent size of the body without being able to visualize specific lines in actual garments. For that reason, a flannel board of pattern-catalog silhouettes can be very helpful in clarifying these concepts. Students can be asked to group pictures of garments from one side of the board with the lines displayed on the other side. Students can also be asked to point out garments appropriate for different body types, to analyze the effects of color and texture on apparent body size, to determine which garments could be recycled to be fashionable, and to suggest ways to accessorize the clothes for a variety of effects.

Computer-generated drawings of houses can be backed with flannel to be used when discussing the kinds of families living on a typical residential street. As each of the following family configurations is discussed, the appropriate number of dwelling units can be placed at varying intervals along the block (see page 114):
• 6 units with married couples; 3 with children
• 2 units with people living alone
• 1 unit with a single-parent family
• 1 unit with a combination of people living together

■ To Illustrate Sequences or Progressions

Flannel boards are especially effective for showing a sequential series or progression of events. Principles of furniture arrangement can be illustrated by placing the various pieces until an entire room or home exemplifies pleasing balance, appropriate groupings, and workable traffic patterns. Felt can be cut to scale and used without any backing to represent various items of furniture. Rooms can be marked off with tape or strips of fabric pinned in place to indicate walls, windows, and doors. A soft lead pencil can be used to mark off 1-inch squares on the background flannel.

A flannel board makes an excellent medium for explaining the color wheel. Poster board can be cut in the shape of numerals and colored to show the primary, secondary, and tertiary hues. As the colors are defined, the numbers can be put in place — 1 for the primary colors, 2 for the secondary colors, and 3 for the tertiary colors. Color harmonies can be illustrated with markers. Later, the numerals can be replaced with colored circles so students can arrange them without the numbers.

■ To Reinforce, Introduce, or Summarize Subject Matter

Flannel boards are effective for introducing, reinforcing, and summarizing subject matter. One could be titled "What Is a Parent?" As terms like teacher, counselor, nurse, personal shopper, recreation leader, cook, gardener, and chauffeur are mentioned, appropriate pictures can be put on the flannel board. When students think of roles for which there are as yet no illustrations, they can be asked to bring representative pictures to class to add to the flannel-board collection.

Another flannel board, to which illustrations can be added as students suggest ideas, might be titled, "Mr. Blueprint, Consider Our Needs." Pictures or sketches representing things to consider when planning a home can be placed around a blueprint or house plan. A piggy bank or play money can be used to represent finances; families with many, one or two, or no children can represent size of family; and a young couple and an older couple can represent age of family members.

A jigsaw puzzle can be employed to review cuts of meat by using two colors of construction paper, flannel, or felt for the tender and less tender portions. The pieces can be fitted together in the shape of a cow. As each cut of meat is placed, it can be discussed in relation to the anatomy, development, and movement of the animal.

Principles of commercial buffet-food service, such as a salad bar, can be illustrated by using cutouts to represent dinnerware, specific food items, dressings, and other accompaniments. Later, small groups of students could be given different menus and asked to illustrate appropriate table settings for these menus on the flannel board. Cutouts of plates, utensils, and other necessary pieces can be traced from the actual items.

By adding, shifting, and removing parts of a flannel board, the teacher will be able to clarify concepts. Students can work individually or in small groups with flannel-board illustrations to experiment until the best solution to a problem is demonstrated.

"A FAMILY PORTRAIT"

MARRIED COUPLE

MARRIED COUPLE WITH CHILD(REN)

MARRIED COUPLE WITH CHILD(REN)

SINGLE PARENT WITH CHILD(REN)

MARRIED COUPLE WITH CHILD(REN)

PERSON ALONE

MARRIED COUPLE WITH CHILD(REN)

"OTHER"

PERSON ALONE

114

Bulletin Boards

Bulletin boards can be effective in supplementing classroom teaching, emphasizing certain areas of subject matter, teaching by themselves, creating interest in a topic, and making a classroom more attractive. However, these objectives will be realized only if the bulletin-board display attracts attention. A bulletin board that is left up more than two weeks will have little, if any, educational value. Ideally, bulletin boards or parts of them are changed about once a week. Current events, community celebrations, important school events, or contemporary verbal expressions may provide timely themes.

Some educational materials, such as teacher's resource books or binders, include descriptions and illustrations of bulletin board ideas. Newspaper and magazine advertisements often stimulate ideas for creative and catchy bulletin boards. Games such as football and chess may provide a frame of reference for conveying an idea. For example, the slogans *Cheer for ...* or *Team up for ...* with an illustration of a megaphone, or *Make the Best Move* with the silhouette of a chess figure or a checkerboard background, could be used in many ways.

Tips for Saving Time

Making bulletin boards can be a valuable learning experience for students working individually or cooperatively in small groups. Looking for pictures of foods representing each of the food groups can be a meaningful activity for younger students, while showing steps in the decision-making process, with written explanations, may be appropriate for more advanced students. Finding pictures that illustrate warm and cool color combinations, formal and informal balance, and different principles of design can be a worthwhile learning experience, and students' examples can be used to create attractive bulletin boards.

Magazine pictures should be mounted for a professional and finished appearance. Unmounted pictures tend to look messy and *tacky*. Pin marks that make pictures look worn can be avoided by placing pins or small tacks so they brace the illustration rather than make a hole in it. The pins near the lower corners are slanted upward and the pins near the upper corners are slanted downward. Tacks can be inserted so that the cap portion, rather than the nail-like part, hold the paper firmly in place. Tape can be rolled in loops, with the adhesive side out, and used on the back of lightweight illustrations to fasten them to the bulletin board. This gives a neat appearance and can create a three-dimensional effect if the pictures are not flattened against the background surface.

A photocopy machine may be used to enlarge drawings, and cutouts, silhouettes, cartoon characters, and large line drawings can be made easily by utilizing an opaque projector. The poster board on which a picture is to be drawn is fastened to the wall or bulletin board. The opaque projector is moved forward or backward until the desired size of the image is obtained. The picture is traced directly on the poster board and can be cut out later, if desired. It is also possible to use transparencies with an overhead projector for the purpose of providing images to trace. Children's coloring books are excellent sources of simple line drawings, especially of animals.

There are software programs that produce large-letter captions. It is also possible for students to make lettering or captions for an assignment in an art class that could be used later in a home economics class. Ready-made letters are relatively inexpensive and come in a variety of sizes, colors, and styles. To make lettering straight, a very light guideline can be penciled on the bulletin board background, a yardstick can be pinned in place and the letters lined up with it, or a string can be fastened across the board to form a straight edge.

Color

Color is important in creating mood, providing associations, and strengthening the theme or message of a bulletin board. Pastels would be more appropriate than harsh colors for a bulletin board titled *Parenting Partners*. Yellow, white, and clear bright colors are more appropriate than tan or gray for conveying the idea of cleanliness. Green and red or orange and black suggest specific seasons of the year. Certainly, "stop" written in red and "go" written in green are more effective than they would be in the reverse colors!

Usually it is desirable to use only three main colors: one for the background, one for the lettering, and one for the illustration mountings. Of course, pictures will contain a variety of colors, but the effect of these will be small in proportion to the basic colors of the display. When large areas have too many colors, the bulletin board is likely to lack unity.

Principles of Design

The most effective display is simple and uncluttered, with a clear message. It is better to rotate illustrations than to use too many at one time. A bulletin board should provide interesting treatment of space and a variety of shapes to attract attention. This usually calls for unequal proportions. Informal balance is generally more eye-catching than symmetry.

A variety of textures can add interest. Background materials may be burlap, felt, tissue paper, corrugated cardboard, or any other substance that will add textural variety without detracting from the primary purpose of the bulletin board. Real objects like empty milk and egg cartons, cereal boxes, and other containers can be tacked in place from the inside. Small toys, first aid items, clothing accessories, kitchen utensils, and doll furniture are just a few of the items that can be used to add a three-dimensional effect.

Lettering

The lettering should be easy to read and in keeping with the theme. A word in the caption may be written in a different lettering to emphasize a point. Block letters would be appropriate for a bulletin board on children's toys, while delicate script would be better for a display of different types of invitations and replies. The examples shown below illustrate lettering that strengthen and weaken the message.

Lettering should be easy to render. Obviously, cutting out individual letters is very time-consuming.

However, if this is done, letters can be saved, and eventually a substantial file can be accumulated. Storing each of the twenty-six letters and various punctuation symbols in a separate envelope, folder, or box makes them easier to locate when they are needed.

Captions

Bulletin board captions can do much to attract attention, create interest, motivate students, and reinforce subject matter that has been covered by other methods. Popular song titles, advertising slogans, proverbs, or contemporary expressions can be used. Captions might capitalize on a play on words, current events, or special lettering. A bulletin board can also be made without a caption, encouraging students to suggest a suitable title. Teachers can ask students to suggest labels for parts of the bulletin board, thus using it for a learning experience. Many of the bulletin board ideas that follow could be used this way.

■ Letters for Emphasis

- YOU **AUTO** CONSERVE FUEL: Use students' driving and car-maintenance tips for conserving gas. Cartoons might be used to illustrate these points.
- GOOD GROOMING FROM A TO Z: Use colorful construction paper to make the letter Z large enough to cover most of the bulletin board. Center the Z under the title and mount pictures showing well-groomed boys and girls or grooming aids across the top and bottom and down the center of the letter.
- BOWL THEM OVER: Use the cutout of a bowling ball. Mount pictures that depict characteristics of a succesful job interviewee such as effective communication, being well prepared and organized, good grooming, and appropriate attire. Mount pictures on construction-paper bowling pins that seem to be flying in various directions.
- STAIRWAY TO: Adapt this caption to career education, better use of resources, or any other topic. Position each letter on a different "step" so that it leads into the main title.

■ Plays on Words

- NO "LION," GOOD GROOMING COUNTS: Write *hair, nails,* and *clothes* in appropriate spaces around a picture of a lion or a toy lion. Put the word *clothes* near the animal's tail, to which a pert ribbon or bow tie has been fastened.

- GET READY, GET SET, SEW!: Display patterns, showing the number of pieces, that would be appropriate for a first clothing-construction project. This caption could also be used with a display of items needed for an approaching unit in clothing construction.
- WHAT TYPE OF LEARNER ARE YOU? Tack up kitchen tools and equipment to illustrate the following:
  Are you a (*strainer*)? Keeps important material?
  Are you a (*sponge*)? Soaks up a lot?
  Are you a (*sifter*)? Blends knowledge together?
  Are you a (*corer*)? Gets at the core of the matter?
  Are you a (*chopper*)? Cuts up a lot?
  Are you an (*egg beater*)? Gets things mixed up?
  Are you a (*funnel*)? Goes in one ear and out the other?
- GIVE A HOOT. DON'T POLLUTE: Mount a cutout of an owl. Use pictures that show lack of concern for the environment and ecology, such as cans thrown along a highway, a crowded room full of people and cigarette and cigar smoke, and a campfire left unattended.
- PROTEIN MOO-O-VES YOU: Picture a cow in the center of the board. Place illustrations of meat, poultry, fish, egg, and milk products around it.

■ Seasons and Holidays as Themes

- DON'T GET SPOOKED: Drape a sheet in the form of a ghost and pin it to the background of the bulletin board. Use terms appropriate for the situation, such as "Study for test Oct. 13," "Hand in progress report Monday," or "Complete notebook by Friday."
- MARCH IN WITH SPRING GARDENING: Use the silhouette of a drum or drummer on one side of the board. On the other side mount pictures of vegetables appropriate for spring planting in a home garden. This theme could be used with a community or neighborhood spring clean-up activity.

■ Titles with Multiple Uses

- SEEDS WORTH SOWING: Outline the bulletin board with packages of plant seeds. In the center of the board, develop ideas for various concepts. For example, in consumer education, include: staying informed, reading tags and labels, determining quality and quantity, paying promptly, keeping records, and handling merchandise carefully. For career education, use words such as: honesty, loyalty, dependability.
- HAPPINESS IS ... USING YOUR MONEY WISELY ... HAVING A JOB: Use a happy-looking cartoon character. Arrange items around it that are things for which teenagers like to spend their money — snack foods, clothes, makeup — or use items pertaining to the world of work, such as a job-application form, Social Security card, paycheck stub.

- DEVELOP GOOD HABITS: Outline the bulletin board with an old film or filmstrip. In the center, mount pictures illustrating the topic. For grooming include: brushing teeth, washing face, shampooing hair, caring for clothes, and choosing food wisely. For management, use pictures illustrating desirable study habits such as: good light, TV and radio off, working at a table or desk, sufficient sleep, and scheduling work.
- TOOLS OF THE TRADE: Mount actual items or illustrations of the tools necessary for completing a certain task or job. For clothing construction, mount sewing equipment such as a measuring tape, tracing wheel, carbon paper, seam guide and zipper foot. In food preparation, you might include measuring spoons and cups, spatulas, peelers, and other small equipment.
- GUIDEPOSTS IN BUYING: Mount a large posted sign in the center of the board. Change the label on the sign to indicate the area of study and arrange appropriate pictures or models around it. For instance, when the guidepost says "insurance," use replicas of a home, car, and hospital to illustrate kinds of insurance; play money or dollar signs to illustrate the cost; a calendar to illustrate length of coverage, and so forth.
- STEPPING-STONES TO ... KEYS TO ... FOOTSTEPS TO ... PUZZLED ABOUT ...: Use cutouts of stones, keys, footprints or puzzle pieces to mount words and pictures appropriate for the specific theme. For example: for *Good Health* use nutrition, cleanliness, rest, exercise. For *Happy Family Living* use words such as security, understanding, affection, common goals.
- OPEN THE DOOR TO ...: Place a simple silhouette of a door in the center of the display. Around it mount large keys cut from construction paper. Give the keys labels relating to topics such as friendship, communication, health, and careers. In a cooperative program, words such as courtesy, dependability, cooperation, respect, and cheerfulness might be used.
- DON'T FIDDLE AROUND: Use a picture or sketch of a fiddle or violin as the center of the board. For a display on decision making or management, write the steps in problem solving on pieces of paper mounted around the fiddle. This idea could be used for an FHA/HERO chapter membership drive. Add *Join FHA/HERO* and pictures of chapter activities from previous years. The theme could also be used as a reminder to *Bring Your Materials Monday* for a clothing construction project and to display the items needed.

Some other titles and illustrations that can be used to remind students of school events, important dates, and assignments, or to join school groups are: *Don't Forget* — with a silhouette of an elephant; *Don't Poke Around* — with a picture of a turtle; *Count Down For* — with a cutout of a rocket; *Hop to It* — with a sketch of a rabbit; and *Be Wise* — with a drawing of an owl.

■ *Introducing Home Economics*

At the beginning of the term, a bulletin board can be used to convey the idea that home economics encompasses a wide variety of subject matter, to encourage participation in FHA/HERO and other activities, or to foster interest in home economics-related careers. The following bulletin boards could be used to serve such purposes:

- WE'LL BE BUSY AS BEES: On the horizontal layers of a simulated beehive, list the conceptual areas of home economics that will be covered. Place cutouts of bees around the hive. This idea would be suitable for use with elementary or middle-school students.
- FOCUS ON ...: Use the silhouette of a camera, and mount and label pictures depicting child development, home management, family living, consumer education, and other areas of home economics.

- SOMETHING TO CROW ABOUT — HOME ECONOMICS: Use a sketch of a rooster that seems to be telling the good news about areas of home economics to be studied.
- DIAL A CAREER IN HOME ECONOMICS: Use a cutout of a telephone dial or a game spinner. Around it place pictures of people in home economics-related occupations.
- BE ONE OF THE BUNCH ... JOIN FHA/HERO: Make a bunch of grapes from purple felt or construction paper. A green stem and a few leaves can be added for interest.
- SEW UP A CAREER IN HOME ECONOMICS: Make the option with heavy yarn or broken lines to suggest stitches, or "sew" the words into a backing using heavy yarn. Use pictures to depict various career opportunities in home economics or to show areas in which students are working if the class is part of a cooperative program.

Bulletin Board Ideas

Personal Development

- A FRIEND IS A PRESENT YOU GIVE YOURSELF: Line the bulletin board or display space with gift wrapping paper. Add ribbon to make the board look like a gift box. In class discuss what the caption means.

- FRIENDS ARE LIKE FLOWERS — YOU CAN'T HAVE TOO MANY: Mount construction paper cutouts of flowers, flowers of tissue paper, flower seeds, and/or the silhouette of a watering can. Label the items with characteristics suggested by class members such as sense of humor, honesty, tact, dependability.

- CASH IN ON A GOOD PERSONALITY: Simulate a store computer register. On green rectangles that suggest dollar bills coming out of the drawer of the register, write appropriate words suggested by the students such as friendliness, cooperation, sincerity, loyalty.

Family Relationships

- LOOKING AT FAMILIES: Feature eyeglasses, along with pictures of families varying in type, gender, age, race, and number. Label each picture as to the type of family represented, such as nuclear, single-parent, extended, blended, unrelated, single-person, and so on.

- FAMILY TIES — THE TIES THAT BIND: Cover the bulletin board with brown wrapping paper and attach string or ribbon to create a wrapped package. Add several bows. Mount pictures of different types of families engaged in a variety of activities that help to strengthen families, such as spending time together, communicating with one another, sharing household tasks, or celebrating a special tradition.

- COMMUNICATION CLUES — CRITICIZE CAREFULLY: Draw stick figure cartoon characters or find pictures that seem to convey effective communication skills, such as choosing an appropriate time and place, keeping calm, avoiding accusations and threats, and listening well.

Child Development

- WANTED! BABY-SITTER: Mount a mirror under the title. List qualities necessary for successful baby-sitting. Complete the bulletin board with "Do You Qualify?"

- PLAY IS THE BUSINESS OF CHILDREN: Mount pictures of children playing quiet and active games, cutting and pasting, painting, listening to stories, playing with clay.

- PUZZLED ABOUT TOY SELECTION? Mount pictures of toys on construction paper cut in the abstract shapes of puzzle pieces. Complete with suggestions or guidelines for choosing toys.

Food and Nutrition

- Always
  Be
    Clean:
Display various articles or pictures of items that are associated with cleanliness and sanitary food preparations.

- GET UP CROWING: Mount a picture of a rooster crowing about the attractive breakfast illustrated.

(Continued on next page)

Food and Nutrition (Cont'd).

- AIM FOR GOOD NUTRITION: Mount an arrow and the facsimile of a bullseye. On the circles of the target, write the food groups or the nutrients — vitamins, minerals, proteins, fats, and carbohydrates.

- IT'S NOT WHAT YOU'RE EATING — IT'S WHAT'S EATING YOU: Mount pictures of overweight people and slender people along with high-fat, high-calorie foods and high-fiber, low-calorie foods.

- BE WISE ABOUT THE EGGS-SENTIALS: Use a picture of an owl hooting about the nutritive value of appealing egg dishes.

Housing and Interior Design

- MAKING A HOUSE A HOME: Use a floor plan or outline of a house in the center. Around it mount pictures depicting scenes such as family members enjoying a meal together; parents giving their children tender, loving care; children playing; a child caring for a pet; a family entertaining friends.

- YOUR COLORFUL ENVIRONMENT: Tack up an artist's palette. Around it, place large simulated dabs of paint labeled with words such as home, neighborhood, family, friends, church, recreation. Utilize labels suggested by class members.

Home Safety

- BETTER SAFE THAN SORRY: Use a picture of a teddy bear wearing a bandage or sling. Around it mount suitable line drawings showing children playing in the street, electrical cords and fans within children's reach, a child playing with a potentially dangerous item, or other appropriate scenes.

- **S**ensible
  Safety
  Safeguards: Display articles and pictures of items such as locks, railings, labels for poisons, and repaired electrical cords.

- MENACES IN THE HOME: Mark off the bulletin board to look like a house. Arrange scissors, poison labels, matches, medicine containers, a frayed electrical cord, and other appropriate items or pictures of them in each room of the house.

Clothing and Textiles

- ONE BUYS THE COMMONPLACE BUT YOU CREATE THE ORIGINAL: Have the students take turns displaying the patterns, fabrics, and notions they have chosen for a sewing project.

- **S**uper
  Swift
  Sewing: Use pictures or pattern envelopes of easy-to-make garments with few pattern pieces. Also tack up swatches of fabric that require a minimum amount of work.

- TENDER CARE MEANS LONGER WEAR: Use pictures or real items illustrating the subcaptions: save and read hangtags, repair immediately, store properly, follow washing instructions, remove spots and stains quickly.

- THE GUIDE SHEET — YOUR MAP TO CLOTHING CONSTRUCTION: Separate and label parts of the guide sheet such as views, layouts, and steps in construction.

Consumer Education

IT'S IN THE BAG: Tack up a large paper bag with "Spending Plan" written across it. On each of three packages, wrapped like gifts and protruding from the top of the bag, write *resources, fixed expenses, flexible expenses,* and *savings.*

TIMELY TIPS: Mount a facsimile of a clock. Around it place pictures or captions relating to concepts such as maintaining a good credit rating: shopping for interest rates; comparing goods, prices, and guarantees; or steps in decision making.

THERE'S MORE TO CREDIT ... THAN SIGNING YOUR NAME: Write the word credit in green or red letters, using the opposite color for the rest of the words. Use a cutout of a wallet and a picture of a person who looks as if an agreement is being signed. If such a picture cannot be found, a contract could be used instead. Mount mock dollar bills so that they look as if they are flying out of the wallet.

LOOK AT THE LABEL: Display enlarged food, energy guide, or clothing labels. Point out information that is of value to the consumer. Discuss how this information can be used to help make satisfying consumer decisions.

Exhibits

Making an exhibit can be a class endeavor, a small-group project, or an FHA/HERO activity. Exhibits can serve to provide educational information, to create interest in home economics activities, to interpret the program to others, and to bring favorable publicity to the department or organization. Making a display can help students develop creativity, a sense of responsibility, the ability to work well with others, and leadership skills.

Places Exhibits Can Be Used

In the classroom, an exhibit may be used to show students' work. Although the types of projects exhibited by students may differ over a period of time, everyone should have an opportunity to display an assignment at some time.

There are often showcases that can be used for exhibits in the hallways, the main office, or a lobby of the school. Displays can be planned for Parent-Teacher Association (PTA) meetings, back-to-school nights, and the school or public library. A city hall or county courthouse may have facilities for showing exhibits. Museums and shopping malls often welcome displays made by students.

Sometimes store windows can be used. A local furniture store may provide excellent opportunities for students studying home furnishings to create room arrangements and to decorate display areas and windows. A local jewelry store or china shop might provide space and materials for a table-setting display. Students' projects can be exhibited at a local fair where the home economics department may have a special booth.

Making Effective Exhibits

An exhibit should have only one theme, simply communicated. Writing is kept to a minimum with only enough key words to convey the message clearly. A few large items attract attention better than many small ones. It is desirable to use real objects, but if that is impossible, models are preferable to pictures. The colors and background used should strengthen the theme of the display and attract attention without being overwhelming. Sometimes the effectiveness of an exhibit can be increased if the viewer is permitted to touch the item on display.

Some ideas for exhibits in which real objects can be used are:
- Children's clothing with growth features and alterations, or home-sewn children's clothing.
- Toys and books for children of various ages.
- Low-cost, high-nutrition foods.
- Home projects such as refinished furniture and home-made furnishings.
- Home accessories made from inexpensive or recycled materials.

Well-planned, attractive, and effective exhibits can help bring status to the individuals and groups that prepared them as well as to the department. There is much potential value in exhibits for changing the traditional image of home economics and for establishing good public relations. If teachers avail themselves of every opportunity to inform others about home economics, the discipline will grow in numbers and prestige.

Audio and Visual Media

Chapter 14

Educators today have a wide variety of methods, media, and materials available to enhance their teaching and complement the variety of learning styles prevalent among their students. Of course, different teachers prefer different media, just as individual students like some approaches better than others. By using a variety of strategies, teachers are better able to interest and motivate more students. Any method or media that is used too frequently loses its appeal.

The first time a teacher shows a film, the students usually react enthusiastically. If a film were shown the next day, the reaction could be expected to be considerably less enthusiastic. The third day, the response might even be negative no matter how good the film is. Reactions similar to the following might be expected:

The first day: "Oh, boy! We're going to see a movie!"

The second day: "Oh, we're having a film *again* today."

The third day: "What? *Another* film? Not again! Is that all we're ever going to do in here — see films?"

Video/Television

A videotape player connected to a television monitor can bring realistic, up-to-date information and situations to the classroom. Videos can be purchased, TV shows taped and shown during classtime, or videos can be made by students or teachers. Videotapes can be viewed by an entire classroom of students, by a small group of students, or by individual students. As with other instructional materials, the teacher needs to be familiar with technological equipment and materials before using them.

Students today have grown up on electronic media, television, and videotapes. There are statistics that  show many students have spent more total time watching TV than they have going to school. Videotapes and TV are inherently interesting and motivating because they are part of non-school life, are up-to-date, and touch on contemporary topics of concern. As with any teaching method or media, variety is essential. Even television and videotapes lose their appeal if used too often.

Videotapes

Quality videotapes can be purchased on almost any topic you would want to cover in the home economics classroom. These range from human sexuality topics to hands-on psychomotor skills areas. Videos showing real-life situations pertaining to concerns of students, which may be analyzed and discussed by a group, are especially useful. Videos showing details of skills taught in the home economics classroom may be viewed by students as frequently as necessary until the skills are learned. This frees the teacher from having to repeat demonstrations frequently.

Videotapes are inexpensive compared to films, but the money spent on them can add up quickly because they are so readily available. Teachers at the local school or district level often pool their resources to buy tapes and then share them.

Videotapes, as well as all other teaching media and learning materials, must be selected to enable learners to achieve planned objectives. Previewing is necessary to assure that these objectives are met, as well as to give students guidance for viewing the tape. This guidance for viewing may be in the form of questions that will be discussed later, points to look for, or telling students how the content relates to follow-up activities in which they will be involved. Previewing videotapes is easy because it can be done at school or at home.

Commercial Television Programs

Television shows can be recorded and shown later during classtime. The entire show can be viewed or only relevant portions can be selected for viewing and discussion. Please see page 123 for guidelines for using commercial television in the classroom. Copyright laws do not permit the teacher to keep a tape recorded from television for repeated use. Tapes recorded from television must be erased after the initial use.

Commercial television shows are excellent for use in affective areas of learning such as family relations, parenting, interpersonal relationships, work-family interface issues, self-esteem, and communication. There is a danger, however, in using situations that are totally different from the lifestyles of your students. Students may have no frame of reference for relating to some television families and individuals who seem too good to be true and unrealistic. Commercial television programs are also appropriate for use in demonstrating food preparation techniques, remodeling housing, and being successful in work situations. As with any media, guidance for use, clear directions, expected outcomes, and follow-up activities have to be planned, communicated, and implemented.

Camcorders

Camcorders can be used to record video instructional materials. Some ideas for their use are:
- The teacher can videotape a lesson for viewing by students when a substitute teacher is in the classroom.
- Classroom sessions can be videotaped for later viewing by students who are absent or need review.
- Presentations of guest speakers and student reports may be recorded for later replay, or to show to other classes.
- Laboratory lessons can be videotaped and used later to evaluate management principles and efficiency.

- Children in the child development laboratory can be videotaped and segments of the tapes used to analyze the developmental level of the children and to plan developmentally appropriate activities.
- Tapes can be made to illustrate interactions such as positive verbal guidance techniques, giving criticism, guidance vs. discipline, and constructive and destructive arguments. These tapes can be used to teach communication concepts and to assess students' sensitivity to communication skills.
- Student skits, role-plays, and demonstrations can be videotaped and used for self-evaluation or later for discussion. They can be shown to other classes now or in the future.
- Highlights of field trips or FHA/HERO meetings and activities that are videotaped by one or more students can be viewed later by other students.
- Student activities can be videotaped and used to market the home economics program with potential students, parents, administrators, and school board members. Involve a large number of students including males, school leaders, and a variety of age groups. Remember that it is appealing to youthful students to see slightly older students because it makes the younger ones feel important and more grown-up. Young teens want to be older teens.

All equipment for using videos must be compatible. Although other sizes are available, the most common video equipment used in the classroom is 1/2 inch VHS.

Films

As with a videotape, a film should always be previewed before it is shown to a group, unless it is familiar from prior use. Without any orientation to the film, students may respond to it as entertainment and overlook its educational value. This orientation is particularly important if the clothing styles, car models, and background furnishings to be seen are out-of-date. If educators admit these things ahead of time, but also point out that the subject matter is still valid and reliable, learners will be more likely to view the film in a positive manner. Of course, a certain amount of preoccupation with outdated fashions is to be expected. Everyone should be able to enjoy a good laugh from seeing them if this does not overshadow the more desirable aspects of the film. The countdown numbers can be another distraction. If at all possible, begin showing the film at the title frame to avoid them.

Guidelines for Off-Air Recording of TV Programs for Educational Purposes

In March of 1979, Congressman Robert Kastenmeier, Chairman of the House Subcommittee on Courts, Civil Liberties and Administration of Justice, appointed a Negotiating Committee consisting of representatives of education organizations, copyright proprietors, and creative guilds and unions. The following guidelines reflect the Negotiating Committee's consensus as to the application of "fair use" to the recording, retention, and use of television broadcast programs for educational purposes.

1. The guidelines were developed to apply only to off-air recording by non-profit educational institutions.

2. "Broadcast programs" are television programs transmitted by television stations for reception by the general public without charge. A broadcast program may be recorded off-air simultaneously with broadcast transmission (including simultaneous cable re-transmission) and retained by a non-profit educational institution for a period not to exceed the first forty-five (45) consecutive calendar days after date of recording. Upon conclusion of such retention period, all off-air recordings must be erased or destroyed immediately.

3. Off-air recordings may be used once by individual teachers in the course of relevant teaching activities, and repeated once only when instructional reinforcement is necessary, in classrooms and similar places devoted to instruction within a single building, cluster or campus, as well as in the homes of students receiving formalized home instruction, during the first ten (10) consecutive school days in the forty-five (45) day calendar day retention period. "School days" are school session days — not counting weekends, holidays, vacations, examination periods, or other scheduled interruptions — within the forty-five (45) calendar day retention period.

4. Off-air recordings may be made only at the request of and used by individual teachers, and may not be regularly recorded in anticipation of requests. No broadcast program may be recorded off-air more than once at the request of the same teacher, regardless of the number of times the program may be broadcast.

5. A limited number of copies may be reproduced from each off-air recording to meet the legitimate needs of teachers under these guidelines. Each such additional copy shall be subject to all provisions governing the original recording.

6. After the first ten (10) consecutive school days, off-air recordings may be used up to the end of the forty-five (45) calendar day retention period only for teacher evaluation purposes, i.e., to determine whether or not to include the broadcast program in the teaching curriculum, and may not be used in the recording institution for student exhibition or any other non-evaluation purpose without authorization.

7. Off-air recordings need not be used in their entirety, but the recorded programs may not be altered from their original content. Off-air recordings may not be physically or electronically combined or merged to constitute teaching anthologies or compilations.

8. All copies of off-air recordings must include the copyright notice on the broadcast program as recorded.

9. Educational institutions are expected to establish appropriate control procedures to maintain the integrity of these guidelines.

Advantages of Films

Films are particularly useful for showing sequential events or stages that in actuality have considerable time lapses between them, such as developmental levels of children or steps in clothing construction, food preparation, or housekeeping. Movies also provide a common experience on which to base a discussion about interpersonal relationships. Films can be especially valuable in providing students with experiences that they would not ordinarily have, otherwise. For example, a film might show how a certain food is used around the world or how clothing styles reflect various worldwide cultures. Often, films can be stopped so that students can predict the outcome and then compare their ideas with those of the film producers. Films, unlike filmstrips, do not lend themselves well to skipping sections, although they can be shown in parts, perhaps on two consecutive days, to permit some intervening discussion.

Sources of Films

Educational films are readily available from a wide variety of sources. A school district may have a media library from which films can be borrowed. Professional organizations, universities, and nonprofit associations often lend, rent, or sell educational films. They are also available, usually for the payment of postage, from companies whose major purpose is to distribute media produced by commercial business concerns. Naturally, media financed by large companies will contain some reference to their products. However, this seldom creates a problem, and students can be asked to suggest other brand-name products with similar characteristics. When borrowing or renting films, it is the educator's professional responsibility to see that they are returned promptly since schedules for their use are usually made many months ahead. If media are kept longer than planned, others may be inconvenienced and disappointed. When scheduling films, it is important to keep in mind that they have to be shown in a darkened room. This may present a problem in a room that is not air-conditioned if the weather is hot in the early fall or late spring. Blackout shades prevent the circulation of air through open windows.

Efficient educators keep annotated bibliographies of films that have been used so they can be shown in the future without previewing. Index cards cataloged into general subject-matter areas can be used to file valuable information such as the name of the film, source, rental fee, length, grade levels and courses for which it is appropriate, evaluation of the film, guide questions, and follow-up learning experiences. It is a wise practice to keep a record of films previewed and judged not good enough for use, so that these will not be reordered in the future.

Slides

A teacher can use slides in the order that best suits the needs of a particular group, make comments about the slides as they are shown, and ask and answer questions while they are being viewed. A teacher with little skill in photography can take slide pictures or make them. The beautiful and true colors in slide projections make slides especially effective in portraying natural scenes and color harmonies. Slides are an excellent medium for showing detail in close-ups of period furniture, storage arrangements, and window decorations.

One of the most outstanding advantages of slides is that they can be used to show items of interest in the local community, such as architectural styles and features, people at work in home economics-related careers, and extended learning experiences. Using slides of local scenes has great motivational value because students can identify with what they are seeing. Viewing pictures of others' projects may stimulate students to think of meaningful projects of their own and increase their desire to do well on the projects they choose.

Slides can be synchronized with audiotapes for a rather formal presentation. Although the tape recorder can be stopped at any time, this method may stifle a spontaneous exchange between the presenter and the audience.

Processed slides can become quite costly but instant slides made from transparencies are inexpensive. These can be used for titles and headings, simple line drawings, and brief written directions. Students working cooperatively can make their own instant slides to accompany their group project reports. This gives students a non-traditional way of contributing to a group effort. It encourages innovation and involves students in ways that help develop a sense of achievement.

To make instant slides, mark a sheet of paper into rectangles measuring 1-3/8 inches in width and 7/8 inch in height. Write, type, or sketch the material needed for a slide within these boundaries. Be sure to use a medium that will etch well and then process through a transparency-producing machine. Cut the rectangles apart, leaving a margin of sufficient size to place the slides in frames. The frames can be from commercially processed slides that are unusable, although frames designed specifically for making instant slides can be purchased. Keep in mind that the heat from the projector lamp can cause this type of slide to become distorted or to burn if projected for too long.

Most camera stores sell blank slides that you can write a few words on or use to make a simple line drawing. Slide photos can also be taken of posters for title frames.

Slides are placed in a carrousel or slide holder so that the pictures are upside down and the wrong sides are facing the direction in which they will be projected. Care should be taken to ensure that slides will be projected correctly because confusion and wasted time may result when slides have to be arranged as they are shown. It is easy to preview slides with a small hand projector designed for this purpose. The preview session provides an excellent opportunity for planning the commentary and the answers to questions that will be asked during the presentation.

Filmstrips

Filmstrips can be previewed easily, shown in part or whole, depending on class needs, and reexamined with a minimum of effort. Filmstrips are suitable for use with large and small audiences. They can provide close-up views of work that might be difficult to see clearly in a live demonstration. The medium can also cut down on the cost and time involved in an actual demonstration. Students can catch up easily, after an absence, by viewing a filmstrip individually or in a small group. A room does not have to be darkened to see a filmstrip, but it is desirable to show it in dim light. Manuals or teacher's guides and student materials that provide additional information are frequently available. Filmstrips are easy to store. They are made in a wide variety of subject areas and are often made available to schools without charge by commercial concerns. They can also be purchased at reasonable cost from various textbook and media publishers.

Filmstrips are available with and without sound. Sound filmstrips require the use of a sound filmstrip projector or a tape recorder. Tapes can be synchronized with filmstrips to provide continuous sound. Silent filmstrips may have captions on each frame and/or a written script to be read. A filmstrip is inserted in the projector upside down as it comes off the roll.

Although filmstrips have many advantages, they are not without limitations. Frames are in a fixed order and cannot be rearranged unless they are cut apart and made into slides. Filmstrips are not easily repaired. Those that are free usually contain elements of commercialism.

As with films, the educator should in some way point out to the learners the purposes for which a filmstrip is being viewed and its relevance to other learning. As with slides, the teacher can ask and answer questions and lead a limited discussion as frames are shown.

Students can be asked to read the captions aloud. They are more likely to remain attentive when called on in a random order. Some students may enjoy participating by operating the projector.

Outdated commercial filmstrips can be used to make personalized ones. Students working in groups enjoy using their own filmstrips in giving oral reports. This activity encourages creativity and resourcefulness. Soak the old filmstrip in a solution of half liquid bleach and half water for about 10 minutes. Then use a soft rag to rub off the original images. Allow the clear film to dry. Write or draw on it with a pen suitable for making transparencies, or use a grease pencil if the material is not to be used again. Sprinkle the filmstrip with talc, powder, toothpaste, or corn starch if you have difficulty with the ink adhering. Four holes arranged vertically on the filmstrip constitute one frame. Because this space is so limited, use only very simple line drawings and messages with few words and letters. Students enjoy these filmstrips when they relate to a school event or local activity.

Transparencies

Transparencies are easy to make and store in regular file folders, can be shown in a well-lit room, allow the teacher to face the class while showing them, and can be projected as large or small as desired by simply moving the projector backward or forward and focusing it. Overlays, up to about five or six sheets, can be used to build a concept sequentially. For example, a series of centrifugal circles can be placed, one at a time, to show how love grows and broadens as an individual matures. To facilitate their use, overlays can be taped together in sequence on one edge or fastened into a cardboard frame.

Many textbook and educational companies sell full-color transparencies and reproducible black-and-white transparency masters. Color transparency packets come with a variety of teaching suggestions and activities to use with each transparency. Some commercial transparencies may be framed, which helps keep them flat and easy to handle and provides a place to write notes. However, frames can make the transparencies rather large for storage in regular file folders.

Making Transparencies

Transparencies can be made by passing a sheet of acetate and the original through a heat-sensitive machine that is designed for making copies. This particular process transfers the image on the original to the acetate by etching it. Special sheets of acetate, marketed specifically for use with this machine, must be used for making transparencies. Most modern photocopy machines have this capacity; some commercial machines can make color transparencies.

When typing copy to be reproduced for a transparency, elite and pica size type are usually too small to project well unless shown on a very large screen. Instead, use software that has large-size lettering capacity or use a photocopy machine to enlarge your typed or word processed copy.

Because transparencies are rather expensive, you may want to reproduce as much material on one sheet as possible, even if all of it will not be shown at the same time. Material relating to different concepts or for use with different classes may be fastened to a background sheet of paper with transparent tape, which will be invisible after processing. These small transparency items can be cut apart and the pieces can be slipped (temporarily) into clear plastic folders for projection. This process can help to cut down on cost without creating an overcrowded and cluttered visual.

Another type of transparency, which is considerably less expensive, can be made easily with clear, stiff plastic such as that bought by the yard. Plastic project-folders measuring 8-1/2 by 11 inches are inexpensive and can be split in half to provide two sheets. Felt-tipped pens, grease pencils, or special pens marketed for making transparencies can be used to write and draw on the plastic. Most colors, except occasionally yellow, reproduce and project satisfactorily. Because grease pencil rubs off easily, it is used when the material on a transparency will be removed. Grease pencil may be advantageous when figuring problems such as interest rates because the writing can be erased quickly and easily by rubbing it with a tissue or soft cloth, and then other problems can be worked on the same sheet of acetate. The transparent sheets of plastic are also ideal for tracing pictures and sketches.

Color

Color can be added to a black-and-white etched transparency with markers, special pens, tapes, and adhesives produced specifically for this purpose. It is advisable to check the colors of tapes and adhesives by projecting small samples because colors do not always project the same as they look in the package. Acetate sheets for transparencies can be purchased in several colors so that the entire background will be viewed in one solid hue. This can add variety to presentations and may be helpful in categorizing concepts or organizing materials into subtopics.

Ideas for Transparencies

In studying textiles, cartoons or stick-figure sketches make effective transparencies for portraying the characteristics of various fibers. For food and nutrition, a nutrition label taken from a package can be reproduced to show a group how to use the pertinent information found on the label. Newspaper ads can be made into transparencies for use in studying consumer education.

Some topics that can be handled easily and effectively with transparencies are:

- *Family Relations.* Centrifical circles can be used to show how love grows and changes as an individual matures. The center circle can be self-love; the next, love of parent or caregiver; and on to love of humankind.
- *Child Development.* Transparencies and overlays could be used to evaluate how clothing features, eating utensils, closet arrangements, bathroom accessories, and furniture can foster or hinder independence and self-reliance in young children.
- *Grooming.* Overlays can be used to show the effects of different hairstyles on various face shapes. A series of overlays can also be used to illustrate application techniques and effects of makeup.
- *Design.* Overlays of various colors could be used to illustrate different color schemes when planning an outfit or decorating a room.
- *Housing.* Floor plans of small homes with identical dimensions can be used with different overlays to illustrate room and furniture arrangements, provisions for privacy and storage, and traffic patterns.
- *Management.* Sketches containing potentially hazardous conditions and ways of eliminating them can be identified and discussed by the viewers.

Audiotapes

Audiotapes and recorders can be used by teachers and students for class presentations and special projects. Tapes can be synchronized to be used with slides, filmstrips, transparencies, exhibits, and displays. They can also be coordinated with examples of step-by-step procedures such as many of those used in clothing construction, food preparation, or craft making. Tapes are particularly well suited to conducting interviews and can make an immediate experience of an interview with a special person who cannot come to school.

Tapes are often an integral part of individualized study units, such as modules, learning packages, and programmed instruction. They also provide an easy method of reviewing previously covered material.

Technology in the Classroom

Ruth Browning, Ph.D.
Chairperson, Home Economics Education Department
Indiana University of Pennsylvania

Technology in the classroom is a tool for teaching and learning. Just as pencils and pens are common tools today, we can visualize that in the future there will be a computer and a VCR at each student workstation.

In the home economics classroom, technology is used to teach home economics curricular objectives and sometimes is part of the curricular objectives. Technological equipment is used to provide information, to guide learning in small steps in a sequential manner, and for evaluation. However, one of the most important things a school can do is to help students become users of technology, not just recipients of lessons using technology.

Technological equipment has varied uses in the classroom. Videos are excellent for viewing and analyz-

ing real-life situations. Computers are useful in providing instruction and analyzing facts and data. The potential for combining computers and videos for learning activities utilizing a process known as interactive video is exciting. Simulations using computer-controlled interactive video can provide continuous feedback to the learner and the instructor. Teachers also find computers useful for maintaining classroom and department records and for preparing instructional materials.

As with other instructional materials, the teacher needs to be familiar with technological equipment and materials before use. Guidance for use, clear directions, expected outcomes, and follow-up activities must be planned, communicated, or implemented.

Computers

Using computers in home economics provides preparation for living in a technological society and enables students to see that computer skills are useful not only on the job but in managing home and family responsibilities. More importantly, computers are one of many tools available for instructional use. They can add variety to the learning and make learning more enjoyable. Computers encourage teachers to spend more time on objectives involving calculations of numbers such as dietary analysis and budgeting. Using a computer to analyze diets and budgets makes learning these concepts fun as laborious calculations are performed instantly by the computer. Computer use tends to motivate many special needs students.

To use computers effectively, the teacher will need to devote time to learning how to use computers. Most will benefit by enrolling in a class or workshop to get started. Once concepts of computer operation and the terminology associated with computers are understood, a variety of options exist for further learning. Classes and workshops are available. However, before enrolling you should investigate carefully the objectives of the course. Classes or workshops frequently focus on one aspect of using computers such as programming in a specific computer language, or the use of a specific software package such as word processing, database, or spreadsheet. You need to be certain the course or workshop will be useful to you.

Another effective way to learn computer applications is to sit down at the computer and learn to use one software program at a time by following readily available tutorials or guidebooks and reference books which accompany the program. This is very time-consuming but one only learns to use computers by using them and solving problems as they are encountered. Joining a local users group, composed of persons who use the same type computer that you use, puts you in contact with persons who can help if you cannot solve a problem without help. School computing coordinators are also good sources of help.

Computer Selection

Selection of a computer, whether for home or school, involves careful analysis of how the computer will be used. Several components are essential. These include the computer itself, keyboard, monitor, storage device (hard or floppy drive), and back-up storage. These components are normally sold as a package, but you may need to seek assistance as there will be choices in computer makes, models, sizes, and options. School computing coordinators, home economics teachers who use computers, or other computer users are sources for advice.

Before purchasing a computer, it is essential to determine how you will use the computer. Identify the software available for the desired use. Although all computer makes have word processing, database, and spreadsheet software, there may not be other software available that is appropriate for home economics.

Some schools have policies about computer purchase and usage. Your school computing coordinator will be able to inform you regarding school computing policies. Some schools equip specific classrooms with computers; other schools establish computer laboratories that may be reserved by a teacher for use of an entire class; other schools encourage placement of one or more computers in classrooms where they will be used routinely in an individualized manner. Some schools have adopted policies that a single make of personal computer will be purchased.

In consulting with the school computing coordinator, you should question and analyze how specific software may be utilized in a computer laboratory situation. Many school computer laboratories are equipped to teach programming, business, or word processing applications and may be very limited for home economics use. You will need to know the school policy for securing software for specific home economics content, and you will need to know if home economics software is available for the makes and models of computers in the laboratories. Another home economics teacher, a county home economics extension agent who uses computers, and analysis of software catalogs can provide guidance on software availability for specific makes and models of computers. You will also need to analyze software in relation to course objectives to make certain software is available for the specific goals or objectives of your class.

Even though a school has a policy of purchasing a single computer make, most administrators can be convinced to purchase other makes if specific types are needed for specific classroom instruction and use. Likewise, teachers who can show that they can make more effective use of one or several computers in a home economics classroom than in a large computer laboratory can convince administrators to place computers in the home economics classroom.

You also will need to determine the type of printer to purchase to produce hard copy or printed copy. This decision will depend on the projected use and the amount of money available. Three types of printers currently available are:

- **Dot matrix printer** produces print and graphics using small dots to create characters. This is the least expensive type of printer. Quality of print varies from what is obviously computer printing to near letter quality.
- **Daisy wheel printer** produces print that is identical to that of a typewriter. It will not print graphics.
- **Laser printer** produces high quality print in a variety of type styles and sizes and also prints graphics. It prints the whole page at one time and is excellent for publishing pamphlets, newsletters, and materials for publication. It is expensive.

If you plan to use a computer for communication or networking with others, you will also need a modem and a telephone line. A modem is a device which is used to send data over telephone lines and is necessary in order to communicate with computers in other locations. Other equipment may be needed for special purposes such as a FAX machine for sending and receiving mail from others, or a plotter to make line drawings for housing designs and blueprints.

Software Selection

Quality of instruction depends on the quality of the software. Software must be selected which will enable students to attain specific course objectives. Excellent software is a waste of money if it does not focus on the instructional objectives of the class.

Some sources of information about software include:
- Catalogs and advertisements.
- Journals and publications.

- Exhibits at professional meetings, conferences, and computer fairs.
- Software stores.
- Educational resource centers.

A growing trend is for textbook publishers to publish software and other instructional resources to accompany textbooks. Such courseware is usually well coordinated.

■ Ways to Purchase Software

Most software is purchased as a single copy for a singler user. The software comes with documentation, the instructions for use and reference information. Sometimes a second or back-up copy is included. This permits one person at a time to use a program.

Software which is frequently used in group instructional situations may sometimes be purchased in packages, for example, a package of ten copies, at a reduced price. A package usually contains a single copy of documentation and may include an instructional booklet for each copy of the program.

Site licenses may be purchased for some software. Site licenses are usually expensive but permit unlimited use of a program at a single site or school.

Some software may also be obtained at little cost. Public domain software or programs that are not copyrighted are available. These are most frequently available through computer users groups, electronic bulletin boards, or from educational resource groups. The only cost is postage and the cost of a disk.

Shareware is also available. It is similar to public domain software except that the user is asked to pay a small fee to the developer. Information services have shareware.

■ Back-up Copies, Copyright Laws, and Warranties

Computer software must be protected from damage. A back-up copy should be kept in a secure location. The back-up copy can then be located in case the disk in use becomes defective.

Commercial software is copyrighted, making it illegal to copy it for distribution to others in the school unless a site license is obtained or to copy it for friends. However, it is legal to make a back-up copy, which is not used but stored for use in case the original disk becomes damaged. In the event a software program is locked so a copy cannot be made, it is usually possible to obtain a second copy at a minimal cost if the damaged original is returned. Some companies provide a back-up copy with the original purchase. Publishers of software have enormous investments in the development of quality software. Schools have both a legal and a moral obligation to enforce copyright laws.

Replacement copies can only be obtained by the software owner. Therefore, it is important to return the warranty card when new software is acquired. This registers the owner so you are eligible for assistance regarding program updates or new versions which may usually be purchased at reduced cost. Some companies publish periodic newsletters which are mailed to registered owners.

Care of Hardware and Software

Well-cared-for hardware and software lasts a long time and is relatively maintenance free. However, moisture, grease, and dirt are detrimental to computers. Computers should be located away from food preparation or other areas where grease, liquids, and food are found. NO FOODS OR LIQUIDS SHOULD BE PERMITTED NEAR A COMPUTER. Liquids will ruin computer chips instantly. Food or pieces of dirt can also cause problems. Occasional dusting is all that is normally needed. A cover placed over the computer when not in use will help to keep it dust free.

A high-quality surge protector should be used to connect the computer and peripherals to the power source. A surge protector protects the computer from electrical power surges. The surge protector is placed between the computer and the wall socket.

Service agreements for computer service and maintenance may be purchased. However, service agreements are expensive. Many schools prefer to "self insure" and pay for needed repair and replacement costs. This is usually much less expensive than having a maintenance agreement for numerous pieces of equipment.

Software must be handled with care. Clean hands are necessary. Teach students to avoid touching the shiny parts or bending disks. Disks should be kept away from magnetic fields which can erase them. Disks should be stored in a relatively cool, dry place in an upright position. Plastic or wooden storage boxes may be purchased for storing disks in an organized manner.

General-Purpose Software

Three general-purpose types of software dominate the software field: word processing, database, and spreadsheet. All makes and models of computers have these three software packages available — some have many different programs of each type. These three types of software have a variety of uses, including many applications for home economics.

Nearly all schools have some computers and general-purpose software programs available. Following are ways in which a teacher can incorporate computer assignments into classroom instruction using these programs. Both databases and spreadsheets necessitate an understanding of how the program works and a time commitment to initial preparation of assignments.

Word Processing

Word processing is a tool for writing. Any project or assignment which requires writing can be completed using word processing. Written work is easy to revise, correct, or edit, and completed copy looks neat and professional when printed.

■ Suggestions for Student Assignments

- Write a letter of complaint to a manufacturer of a product.
- Write a letter of thanks following a field trip.
- Prepare written reports or outline oral reports.
- Publish a newspaper for expectant mothers giving suggestions on care of children, or any other topic relevant to home economics.
- Describe self and family in relation to stages of the life cycle.
- Develop a plan for minimizing family conflicts regarding use of limited space at home.
- Write a paragraph which identifies long- and short-term personal goals.
- Describe the steps of decision making and apply these to a specific situation.

■ Suggestions for Teacher Use

- Prepare information sheets for students.
- Prepare study guides, worksheets, assignments, or tests.
- Write letters to parents concerning student progress.

Database

A database is an organized collection of information. Databases are designed to store information in an organized, accessible manner. A library card catalog and a telephone book are databases. Cookbooks and data about food nutrients are examples of databases used in home economics.

Databases — either commercial, teacher prepared, or student developed — can be used as tools to develop critical thinking skills as students sort large amounts of information to find patterns or identify trends. In today's society knowing how to find and interpret information is as important as knowing facts. Using a database, students can develop inquiry skills to categorize, organize, access, manipulate, and evaluate information. Students should begin using a database by seeking facts and answering lower level cognitive questions. Then the teacher should present opportunities for responses to higher level questions involving analysis, synthesis, and evaluation.

■ Suggestions for Student Assignments

Either the students or the teacher can prepare the following databases:

- Compare the average daily usage of water in various parts of the world. Answer questions such as: Who uses the most water? Who uses the least? Compare this information to living standards, levels of development of society, and how water is obtained. Analyze what influences personal use or waste of water.
- Compare the amount of Vitamin A or any other nutrient in a selected list of foods. Determine types of foods that contain the most Vitamin A. Make recommendations for inclusion of Vitamin A foods in the diet.
- Categorize and enter information from nutrient data on cans or boxes of products prepared by different companies, such as canned green beans or chocolate cake mixes. Then sort and arrange data by categories. Evaluate results and answer questions such as: Do all products of the same food have the same nutrients? Are there differences in relation to nutrients (i.e., food value) and total weight? Which product would you purchase? Why?
- Maintain records of student membership, vital information, and achievement in FHA/HERO.

■ Suggestions for Teacher Use

- Keep and update inventory of department equipment and supplies.
- Maintain student records such as names, addresses, phone numbers, book numbers, and locker assignments.

Spreadsheet

A spreadsheet, originally an accounting ledger, is a large grid with columns and rows. It is used to calculate numbers and make predictions based on numerical data. Calculations of all types can be made once figures are entered. This includes addition, subtraction, multiplication, division, or any combination of these. Additionally, most spreadsheets have functions which automatically determine averages, sums, and square roots.

Spreadsheet use requires critical thinking both to set up and to use. If one does not understand the mathematical concepts underlying the calculations, then one cannot develop a spreadsheet assignment or effectively use a spreadsheet.

■ *Suggestions for Student Assignments*

- Compare the prices of selected foods in various stores.
- Calculate the cost of a recipe or meal.
- Develop a budget for a FHA/HERO project.
- Calculate the impact on savings if money is invested at varying interest rates.
- Calculate how much water and money are wasted by a dripping faucet.
- Calculate the cost to operate an appliance such as a hair dryer for a certain period of time.
- Calculate the cost of burning a 60 watt bulb for a period of time. Compare with the cost of a 100 watt bulb for the same time period.
- Develop a family budget for a year. Consider both fixed and flexible expenses. Once the budget is completed, analyze the effects of an increase in income, how regular savings can multiply, an increase in rent, a decrease in earnings (for example, a wage earner is laid off or an expected bonus is not received), and an increase in car insurance or gasoline costs.
- Compare the cost of energy used by various refrigerators or other appliances over the expected life of the appliance. Analyze this cost in relationship to the original purchase price of each appliance.

■ *Suggestions for Teacher Use*

- Maintain a gradebook.
- Prepare charts, tables, and schedules.
- Prepare and maintain a department budget.
- Estimate expenses and income for projected fund-raising projects.
- Prepare a budget for a field trip.

Software for Specific Instruction

Software can be obtained for a variety of specific purposes. Although some classes in the secondary schools have as their goal to teach students about computers, the purpose of using computers in home economics is to teach home economics content with the aid of the computer. All subject areas of home economics have available software. Both the quantity and quality is increasing rapidly.

Good software programs combine information, realistic decision making, and games with graphics and animation. Such variety tends to stimulate and hold the interest of students.

Types of Software Programs

Computer-assisted instruction software is available in a variety of formats with a variety of purposes:

- **Drill-and-practice programs** review and reinforce facts. In many ways they are "expensive flash cards;" however, they enable the student to work independently, freeing the teacher for other tasks. Repetition of drill-and-practice programs often provides reinforcement of factual information for slow learners in a method that is both fun and challenging. Drill-and-practice programs are easy to write. Teachers with limited programming skills can develop drill-and-practice programs rather easily. Likewise, students with programming skills can learn desired home economics content by writing programs for use by other students. Modifying a test program to count number of right and wrong answers can be a challenging assignment for students with programming skills.
- **Tutorial software** is designed to present information and teach facts or concepts. Tutorials are much like reading a textbook on the video screen. Any home economics content can be developed into a tutorial. However, most tutorial programs give information and then ask questions about the information, providing instant feedback and reinforcement of learning. Depending on student response, the program can branch as in programmed learning to provide more information, elaborate on concepts, or move quickly to new information. Tutorials are time-consuming to develop but use rather simple programming concepts so that a teacher or student could develop them. Many tutorial programs related to specific home economics objectives are available.
- **Simulations** are imitations of real-life situations or fantasies designed to teach real-life concepts. Programs must be accurate representations of reality and need a complex system of data, based on how an actual real-life situation operates. Examples of simulations are a trip to the grocery store, a family finance situation, and problems of securing nutritious food on a trip through space. Simulations help students learn content and provide practice in making decisions and analyzing alternatives. The best simulations require

advanced thinking skills as the user manipulates variables to see how decisions impact on other circumstances.

- **Learning games** have a clear set of rules, clear goals, a winner, and are designed to be fun. Some games resemble simulations. Games should help students learn worthwhile concepts and be based on facts.

Other types of programs available for home economics include:

- **Computerized cookbooks** are a form of a database. In a computerized cookbook, recipes usually are categorized by type as in printed cookbooks. However, recipes usually can also be located by a search for specific ingredients such as cheese or pumpkin. Quantities frequently can be changed, such as halving or doubling, before printing the recipe for use.
- **Printing and publishing programs** are used to create stationery, greeting cards, or graphics for writing letters of thanks or appreciation or for awards. They also are used to create banners announcing activities or headings for newsletters and newspapers. Graphics created by these programs may be used to add interest to any printed materials. Although software exists for laying out a newsletter or newspaper for reproduction, it is common to cut and paste up articles and graphics for reproduction via a photocopy machine.
- **Authoring programs** enable teachers to develop computerized lessons without programming knowledge. An authoring program permits teachers to enter information, questions, quizzes, and graphics into a structured format which students can then use on the computer.

Computer software must enhance the curriculum. However, teachers must supplement computer learning with thought-provoking questions, stimulating activities, and discussion designed to encourage student thought at the higher cognitive levels.

Applications for Consumer and Homemaking Education

Software is available for all subject areas of home economics. However, specific types of programs dominate or seem most appropriate for use in various subject areas. Software for specific purposes is usually easy to learn to use or guides the user through the program.

■ Family and Child Development

- Tutorials are numerous for various aspects of family living and child growth and development. These are appropriate for learning facts or reinforcement of learning related to specific objectives.
- Software programs are appropriate choice activities in child care and development laboratories. Preschoolers can use the computer independently. With minimal instructions, they can select, insert disks, and turn on the computer. Some programs for preschoolers focus on academic skill development through drill and practice with numbers and letters. There are, however, programs which children control by drawing, placing letters on the screen, or adding notes to a musical composition. These types of programs support the need of children to actively explore and manipulate. Drawing programs encourage construction of lines, squares, rectangles, curves, and other shapes about which preschoolers learn. Interactive graphics programs such as Terrapin Logo (produced by Terrapin, Inc., Cambridge, MA) and Delta Drawing (produced by Spinnaker Software Corporation, Cambridge, MA) are appropriate for older preschool children and teach basic concepts of computer languages.

■ Food and Nutrition

- Diet and recipe analysis is the most frequent use of computers in the home economics classroom. Such programs make the laborious calculations of nutrients for diet analysis quick, interesting, and fun. When selecting a diet analysis program, it is essential to ensure that the database is large enough and complete enough to serve the needs of specific classes. Many diet analysis programs are very limited.
- Cookbooks and recipe storage permit quick retrieval of recipes which can be printed and taken to the food preparation laboratory. This eliminates the problem of recipes and cookbooks becoming splattered with food.
- Numerous games, tutorials, and simulations are available for teaching food and nutrition. Many are effective for teaching and reinforcing specific objectives.

■ Management of Resources and Consumer Education

- Tutorials on purchasing and managing money are numerous. Some simulations are available in this area. Specific programs need to be explored carefully to make certain they are consistent with objectives and encourage student learning.
- Programs for financial record keeping encourage budgeting and analysis of family spending. Some of these programs incorporate tax preparation, automatically categorizing expenditures and deductions.

■ Housing and Interior Design

- Some tutorials and furniture layout simulations, with predrawn floor plans and furniture templates, are available. However, software in this subject area is less plentiful than in the other areas of home economics.
- Drawing software programs, such as computer-aided design (CAD), are the most effective programs for design. However, these programs are expensive and require considerable time for the user to learn.

■ Clothing and Textiles

- Software for clothing and textiles is varied in content, including tutorials and simulations. Pattern layout and sewing techniques are common.
- CAD software is available for fabric print design.

Applications for Occupational Home Economics

Software and computers used in home economics occupations are larger (more kilobytes or megabytes), more powerful, and more sophisticated than the personal or microcomputers used in most classrooms and homes. Although students can learn basic concepts on personal computers, occupational home economics programs are more effective if computers and software of the type actually used on the job are available for instruction.

Many businesses and industries have computers designed specifically for their industry or specialized software written for their specific needs. Some uses of computers in home economics occupations are as follows:

- **Child care and family agencies** maintain personal records of clients, including participation and attendance, names of parents or guardians, health records, and payments made by clients and government programs. Such agencies also use computers to maintain staff and payroll records and to compile data for reports.
- **Hotel and restaurant management businesses** make reservations via the computer. Virtually all records of staff, payroll, and inventory are computerized, along with bills and payments. Food orders in restaurants are entered into the computer and every transaction converted into needed information for processing orders and maintaining inventory. Menu and recipe standardization, cost control, and nutrient analysis are other uses of computers in restaurants.

Likewise, hospital food services use computers for these same purposes — especially for developing and maintaining special diets.

- **Clothing and textile producers** utilize CAD systems for clothing and fabric design. Patterns are made on specialized computers which convert and draw patterns in all sizes. Computers are used to determine the layout of pattern pieces on fabric so as to use the least amount of cloth. A small reduction of two or three percent in the amount of fabric used per garment can result in savings of hundreds or thousands of dollars. Computerized cutting of fabric is more accurate and faster than older methods.
- **Housing design** also uses CAD computers and software. Architects draw house and building plans, as well as all blueprints for reconstruction, via the computer. Likewise, interior layouts are produced using computers, and plotters are used to make hard copy of these drawings.

Software Evaluation Criteria

All software must be selected carefully so that it is useful for the specific purpose intended. The most important criterion is that software and hardware are compatible — the hardware is of size and type to run the software. See the chart, "Criteria to Software Evaluation," on page 134.

Utilization of Computers

Computers can be used for group or individualized instruction, for interactive videos, for classroom management and preparation of instructional materials, and for communications.

Group and Individualized Instruction

How teachers plan for computer use depends upon how and where computers are available and the teaching style of the teacher. If large group instruction with computers is to be the teaching method, then there will need to be a computer available for each student to use — or a minimum of two students per computer. Two students can usually work together satisfactorily. Likewise, software will need to be available for each computer.

The use of individualized instruction or learning centers requires less investment in computers and software. This usually means that computers can be avail-

Criteria for Software Evaluation

	Yes	No	NA
Computer and software compatability:			
1. Software will run on computer available (i.e., size, model).			
2. Needed peripherals are available.			
3. Documentation is clear and comprehensive.			
Relationship to objectives and instruction:			
4. Objectives of software are consistent with course objectives.			
5. Program can be used for instruction or reinforcement of instruction.			
6. Worksheets, activity sheets, and tests based on objectives are included.			
7. Additions or modifications can be made by the teacher if appropriate.			
Subject matter:			
8. Subject matter is accurate.			
9. Subject matter is appropriate for intended users.			
10. Subject matter is logically organized and sequenced.			
11. Subject matter is free of race, ethnic, sex, or other stereotypes.			
Technical concerns and ease of use:			
12. Program is free of technical errors.			
13. Instructions are easy to follow.			
14. Frame display is clear and easy to read.			
15. Graphics are clear and contribute to program.			
16. Program response time is adequate.			
17. Program menu can be easily accessed for help or to change activities.			
18. Program has ability to branch or loop depending upon performance of student.			
Student interaction:			
19. Program provides for maximum meaningful interaction.			
20. Cues and prompts are adequate.			
21. Students can use program with minimal assistance.			
22. User can control the pace and sequence of program.			
23. Program stimulates creativity.			
24. Feedback is appropriate and non-threatening.			
25. Positive reinforcement is provided.			
26. Program helps students understand wrong answers.			

able in the home economics classroom. A computer learning center in the classroom can be established with one or more computers. Clear, detailed instructions of how to operate the computer and how the computer is to be used are needed. Although detailed materials for individualized instruction are time-consuming to develop, once developed they can be used repeatedly.

Individualized instruction is an excellent classroom management plan when needs and abilities of the students are diverse. Assignments can be developed at the level of the students. Slow learners and special needs students can take as much time as needed to complete the assignment. More capable students can be provided more challenging assignments.

Interactive Video

Interactive video combines the use of videodisc or videotape and a computer. Interactive video utilizes the visual impact of a photographic image and the interactive capability of the computer. This technology provides the potential to provide high quality visuals and detail for study of content such as historic costume or furniture. Actual situations placed on videodisc or videotape are a powerful teaching tool, allowing students to analyze and make decisions related to the situations. When a student makes a decision concerning the situation, the computer program responds to the student's response with questions or possible results regarding the situation. Situations on employability attributes, decisions to be made when caring for children, or family interactions and communications are examples of the type of program well suited to interactive video.

An interactive authoring system enables the teacher to create a computer lesson that will interact with videotape. The teacher enters information to be learned, directions, and questions for the learner. At appropriate points in the lesson, examples or simulations on tape may be accessed for analysis. Teachers may use either segments of commercial videotapes or self-made videos to create the lesson.

Closely related to interactive video is digital image processing. An image is entered into the computer, such as through a video camera. Then by using a library of images or through computerized mathematical calculations, the original image can be changed. For example, a newly built house can be landscaped by adding trees and shrubs and moving them until a satisfying landscape is created. The new house owner can then follow this plan in doing the actual landscaping. Another use is to take a picture of an individual considering a weight-loss diet. Mathematical calculations made by the computer can show how the person would look at a different weight — for example, forty pounds lighter.

Classroom Management and Instructional Materials

In addition to providing instruction and learning experiences for students, various computer programs and equipment can be used for classroom management and preparation of instructional materials. Many suggestions for teacher use of general purpose software programs — word processing, databases, and spreadsheets — were presented earlier. However, specific programs dedicated to a single purpose, such as maintaining a gradebook, keeping student records, maintaining inventories, and printing address labels, are available for purchase.

Several specific purpose programs and aids to instruction for teacher use follow:

- Reading analysis programs are designed to determine the grade level of reading materials.
- Crossword puzzles and word searches can be developed using specific programs for this purpose.
- Testing programs are available which allow teachers to create quizzes and tests from a test bank of hundreds of true/false, multiple choice, completion, and essay questions. Teachers can also add their own questions to the test bank. The programs will create multiple versions of the same test, along with answer keys. The tests are printed out and copied for use as a paper and pencil test. Some testing programs enable students to actually take the test on the computer. These programs keep track of the correct answers and provide immediate feedback to the students on achievement.
- Graphics can be added to materials created on the computer through the use of many clip art programs. Another method of using graphics is through the use of a scanner. A scanner is a piece of equipment which is connected to the computer. It copies a picture or photograph, then stores it via the computer for use when needed in producing materials.
- A large screen (25") television can be connected to a computer (with an RF modulator) and used in the front of a classroom to project computer images. Although the image is somewhat fuzzy, it can be used satisfactorily. For example, used with a word processing program, brainstorming ideas can be entered into the computer and then printed for distribution.
- A large screen projector may be purchased for the specific purpose of projecting computer images on a large screen. The most effective is a pad which is connected by cables to the computer and placed on the surface of an overhead projector.

Communications

By adding a modem to a computer and connecting it to a phone line, information, data, and resources beyond the classroom are easily accessible. Such telecommunications hold many opportunities for learning activities. Some examples are:

- Electronic bulletin boards provide announcements and current information.
- Home Economics Extension services have an elaborate database which can be accessed to secure up-to-date information on home economics topics.
- Large database communications computer services such as Compu-Serve, GEnie, AppleLink, and The Source provide forums to communicate with others on topics of interest. Shareware software is distributed free through these networks with the request that if you use a program you will send a small fee to the developer. Electronic mail is available through these services. Electronic connecting with other classrooms and schools in foreign lands offers the potential for increased understanding and communication with students of other cultures.

Impact of Computers on the Family

Computers affect family life in many ways as the use of computers in our society expands. Following are some ways that computers impact on our lives and homes:

- Airlines make reservations and seat assignments via computers.
- Hospitals maintain patient records with computers that are frequently connected to large data banks. This makes detailed information about previous illnesses and treatments readily available to caregivers in different hospitals or in the future.
- Pharmacies maintain records of drug purchases of individuals with computers. The programs can also provide warnings if a client has incompatible prescriptions.
- Supermarkets and other stores use computers to read product information codes when checking out purchases. Inventory is maintained and orders processed using this data.
- Banks maintain accounts using computers. Bank machines enable persons to conduct business and obtain information about their accounts during hours when the bank is closed.

- Microwaves, washing machines, and other appliances in the home contain silicon chips which are actually computer processors.
- Electronic devices which use batteries or solar power are available for use as address and phone number books, spelling checkers, and games. Many are small enough to carry in a shirt pocket.
- Grocery guides, attached to shopping carts, can provide store directories to help shoppers locate items. These electronic devices also provide information about special prices and available foods.
- Interactive computers in stores can increase speed of service. For example, upon entering a store customers can place their orders in the computer and then pick up and pay for their orders at the check-out counter. A similar service permits customers to order groceries from home and then pick them up at the drive-through supermarket. Payment can be processed through an electronic computer directly to the bank. Other interactive computer systems in stores can provide consumer product information and recommend specific products based on user responses to questions regarding planned use of the product. When combined with video, the customer can view the product and how it may be used.

Computer Uses in the Home

Students asked to brainstorm where computers are used or projected for use in everyday life could generate a long list. In addition to the ideas previously listed, other possible uses for computers are as follows.

■ Safety and Security

- Locks may be computerized with plastic cards or code numbers entered at each use.
- A voice synthesizer may warn of danger such as a break-in, a malfunctioning furnace, or poor air quality.
- Automatic draperies open and close depending on temperature and outside light.

■ Home Management

- Financial records and electronic checkbooks may be kept by a computer program which also compiles income tax records.
- Analysis of utility costs may be done on the computer.
- Inventories of collections and valuable possessions may be computerized.
- Stock market and investment information is readily available to the home computer user via phone line.

- A home computer connected to a telephone line to the bank could authorize payment of bills.
- Bank statements could be received on the home computer.
- Connected to a phone line, computers can be used to seek information, make purchases, or communicate messages.

■ Family Health

- A computerized sensor can monitor breathing rates of a sleeping child, sending the message to a parent in another room.
- First aid information can be accessed via phone lines in case of an emergency.
- Family health records can be maintained using a computer.

■ Food and Nutrition

- Daily menus can be analyzed for nutrient content. This would be of special interest to athletes and persons on special diets.
- Fast foods can be ordered by computerized phone for delivery to the home.
- A few grocers publish computerized lists of foods which may be ordered by phone, picked up at a drive-through location, and paid for by electronic funds transfer.

■ Home Education and Information Access

- Large data banks provide access to encyclopedias and other needed references.
- Computerized card catalogs provide information as to the location of specific books and how to access the books on the computer.
- Computers are important education and communication devices for severely physically disabled individuals who may be able to operate a joystick or other electronic sensor through body movement.

■ Entertainment

- Chess enthusiasts can play games via computer with persons in other locations, or a game can be played with the computer itself.
- Hobby enthusiasts can communicate with others and trade information and ideas.

Home Office

- Jobs which utilize computers and electronic mail could be done at home. This would eliminate commuting costs and enable workers to live in locations far from their job. See "Issues Related to Working at Home" shown below.

The Future

Technological multimedia will expand in the 1990's. Audio, text, numerical data, and graphics will be increasingly combined to produce quality classroom learning resources. Communication networks will expand and become more common, enabling access to virtually unlimited sources of information. Communication networks will provide access to classrooms in far-away locations, allowing students to communicate easily with students of other countries and cultures.

Robots will do many repetitive jobs in the home and provide increased independence and employability for the physically disabled. Already industrial robots are performing common tasks such as assembling and painting cars. Industrial robots have been developed which assist in food preparation such as making pizzas and french frying potatoes. Robots in the home will perform tasks such as sweeping the floor, cleaning the bathroom, and mowing the lawn.

A computer the size of a book and costing less than $100 will make it realistic for each student to have their own computer. Thus, computers will be as common among students as calculators are today.

Issues Related to Working at Home

Although many jobs could be done at home using a computer and a phone line for communication, there are many issues related to family life and family management which merit consideration in the home economics classroom. The following questions can serve as the basis for classroom discussion on work-at-home issues:

- Will working at home reduce pollution because of less commuting to work? Or will more energy be used in heating and cooling homes?
- Will children who see parents working at home develop a respect for work and its responsibilities?
- Can family members work together on the same job? What would be the advantages or disadvantages of several family members working together on a single job?
- What kind of self-discipline is needed to work at home without direct supervision? Would working hours be more flexible?

- Can an individual concentrate on work responsibilities and be productive while caring for children or other family members?
- What effect would increased contact among family members have on the family unit?
- What impact would working at home have on other businesses? For example: restaurants where workers congregate for lunch, public transportation which transports commuters, clothing stores which sell business-style apparel.
- How will the amount of pay be established? Will workers receive benefits? Will employers pay less to persons working at home? What impact could this have on income earned by women and single-parent families?
- Will workers feel isolated? Will new patterns of social interaction develop as persons have less contact with persons in the workplace?

PART 3

Organization for Learning

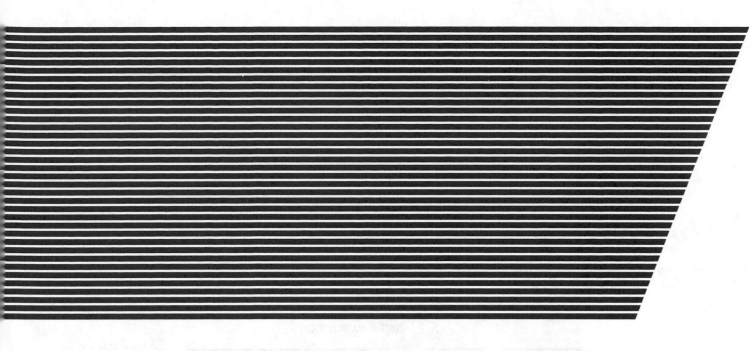

Laboratory Experiences

Chapter 16

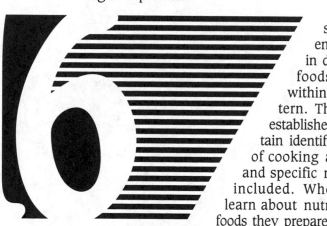

Laboratory experiences can provide excellent opportunities for student participation in planning and carrying out learning activities, applying principles, and practicing desired behavior. To be truly educational, laboratory experiences need to be based on concepts that have been covered in class. Basically, there are three general types of laboratories: productive, experimental, and observational.

Productive Laboratories

In productive laboratories, the emphasis is on developing psychomotor skills and gaining experience in managing resources. Although the final product may be important, the processes used to produce it are equally important.

Planning

Laboratory experiences require careful preplanning and scheduling. Tasks need to be coordinated so that precious class time is not wasted, so that all students have jobs that are challenging and meaningful, and so that situations are as realistic as possible. For these reasons, it is usually more effective to prepare and serve complete meals in food laboratory lessons than it is to make only one food product. After all, how many times in everyday life are there four or five people to make one salad, one pie, or one vegetable dish? If a student's sole contribution during an entire class period is to separate an egg, this person is likely to feel very frustrated and look upon home economics as a waste of time. If the meal-project approach is used, there may be fewer laboratory sessions because of the time and expense involved, but each student will have a more realistic and meaningful experience.

Students should be given some choice in deciding what foods to prepare within a meal pattern. The pattern is established so that certain identified principles of cooking are involved and specific nutrients are included. When students learn about nutrients in the foods they prepare and eat, the study will be more meaningful than when nutrition is studied as a separate unit. Instead of studying about calcium, thiamine, and vitamin A in a nutrition unit preceding food preparation, these nutrients can be covered in a meal pattern that includes a milk-rich food, a quick bread, and a green salad. The importance of calcium can be reemphasized, and protein and vitamin C can be studied when preparing foods within a meal pattern of a fruit salad, a meat-extender dish, and a milk-rich dessert.

Appropriate principles, such as those used in milk cookery, are studied and then applied through laboratory experiences. When using the meal-pattern approach in food and nutrition laboratories, it may take a week to complete the appropriate learning activities. If a one-unit kitchen group in a home economics class is divided into subgroups consisting of two or three students, the schedule might be like this:

140

MONDAY

Group A Plan own menu in quantity to serve the large-unit kitchen group, select recipes, make out market order, develop work schedules.

Group B Follow same procedure as Group A with own menu.

TUESDAY

Group A Pre-prepare as much food as possible for serving the next day (Wednesday).

Group B Pre-prepare as much food as possible for serving on Thursday.

WEDNESDAY

Group A Complete final preparation. Serve meal to entire unit kitchen group. Clean up with help of Group B.

Group B Work on assignment relating to meal pattern for the week or evaluate management skills and preparation techniques used by Group A. Enjoy meal. Help Group A clean up.

THURSDAY

Group A Work on assignment relating to meal pattern or evaluate management skills and preparation techniques used by Group B. Enjoy meal. Help Group B clean up.

Group B Complete final preparation. Serve meal to entire unit kitchen group. Clean up with help of Group A.

FRIDAY

Group A Evaluate laboratory experience and complete related assignments.

Group B Follow same procedure as Group A.

Of course, if funds will not permit serving all students on both days, the meal can be planned for only the two or three students in one group. However, bear in mind that planning and serving meals for four or five is, for most students, more like their present home situations. It is also possible to serve only one subgroup in a given week and to serve both subgroups another week to vary the quantities in which students prepare foods.

A work schedule should be developed that designates the tasks to be performed by each student and the time at which each should begin. Asking students to make time schedules that are unrealistic can greatly diminish student enthusiasm for home economics. The following example provides enough detail to show the teacher that each student has specific tasks to perform, that the sequence is logical, and the approximate time allowed for each step is appropriate.

MENU

Citrus Mold

Individual Hamburger Pizzas

Milk

TUESDAY — PRE-PREPARATION DAY

Student A	Student B
1:00 — Comb hair, put on apron, wash hands.	1:00 — Comb hair, put on apron, wash hands.
1:03 — Cook hamburger meat.	1:03 — Prepare gelatin using ice cubes.
1:18 — Prepare other ingredients for pizza sauce.	1:15 — Prepare orange and grapefruit slices.
1:25 — Cook sauce, stirring occasionally.	1:25 — Add fruit to gelatin mixture.
1:35 — Begin to clean up.	1:30 — Clean lettuce and store.
1:42 — Check out.	1:38 — Help with cleanup.
	1:42 — Check out.

WEDNESDAY — SERVING DAY

Student A	Student B
1:00 — Comb hair, put on apron, wash hands.	1:00 — Comb hair, put on apron, wash hands.
1:03 — Roll hamburger buns flat.	1:03 — Warm pizza sauce.
1:08 — Pour pizza sauce on buns, bake at 350° for 10 minutes.	1:06 — Unmold gelatin salad.
1:12 — Help set table.	1:12 — Help set table. Place salad on lettuce leaves.
1:16 — Pour milk.	1:18 — Serve meal.
1:18 — Serve meal.	1:33 — Begin to clear table.
1:33 — Begin to clear table.	1:35 — Rinse dishes and help put them in dishwasher.
1:35 — Rinse dishes and help put them in dishwasher.	1:42 — Check out.
1:42 — Check out	

It is often helpful to have a poster, indicating a general time schedule, to which students can refer. After observing this chart based on a 45-minute class period, it should be obvious to students that they have to use every minute to their best advantage.

If the teacher will allot 2 or 3 minutes for a check-out at the end of a foods laboratory session, many problems that are associated with leaving a disorderly laboratory can be avoided. At the designated check-out time, students should be in their kitchen units with drawers and cupboard doors open. Then the teacher can observe three or four items, varying the items checked for each laboratory session, to see that they are clean and in the proper place. Only after this quick check are the students in that kitchen group dismissed to go to their next class. This procedure ensures that the facilities are left in order for the next group using them.

While students in one group are preparing their menu, the others can be engaged in worthwhile activities. These might include reading about, and answering questions pertinent to, foods and nutrients emphasized in the meal pattern for that week; planning menus for a day to accompany the one being served; and observing and evaluating the students who are working in the laboratory at that time. Students in one subgroup may evaluate those in another subgroup by completing checklists or rating scales relating to laboratory work habits or by conducting time and motion studies. For example, the students who are not serving on a particular day could draw or be given a scaled sketch of their group's kitchen. On this, they could trace the movements of the other group members who were serving that day. Lines drawn in different colors might show the pattern made by each of the working students. Later the movements can be analyzed by pointing out unnecessarily repeated movements or by explaining what could have been done differently to conserve time and energy.

Evaluation

Whether students are evaluating themselves or other students, the methods used should be changed frequently. After students have used the same rating device several times, they tend to lose interest in it, which affects the quality of their evaluations.

■ Evaluating a Foods Laboratory Experience

See pages 72 and 74 for a checklist and a rating scale that could be used to evaluate food and nutrition laboratory lessons. Scorecards are particularly appropriate for judging individual food products because scorecards are used for evaluations that are narrow in scope. See the scorecards shown above.

Scorecard for Muffins

Directions: Score your muffins <u>excellent</u> if they have all the qualities listed for that characteristic. If less than excellent, score them good, fair or poor. Total the points and put that number at the bottom.

Appearance
Golden brown color. Gently rounded top that is pebbly, not smooth.

☐ Excellent 4   ☐ Good 3   ☐ Fair 2   ☐ Poor 1

Flavor
Pleasing. Slightly sweet. Delicate.

☐ Excellent 4   ☐ Good 3   ☐ Fair 2   ☐ Poor 1

Texture
Uniform. No tunnels. Slightly moist.

☐ Excellent 4   ☐ Good 3   ☐ Fair 2   ☐ Poor 1

Tenderness
Breaks easily without crumbling. Tender and light.

☐ Excellent 4   ☐ Good 3   ☐ Fair 2   ☐ Poor 1

TOTAL SCORE _____

The following, with open-ended questions, suggests another format. These instruments can be used by individual students, students working in groups, or the teacher. On evaluation forms used during consecutive laboratory lessons, you can emphasize different concepts such as nutrition, cost of the menu, and meal service. Appropriate questions can be developed for other concepts, as well.

- MENU
  1. What factors contributed to a pleasing menu?
  2. How could the menu have been improved?

- WORK SCHEDULE
  1. In what ways was the work schedule helpful?
  2. What time-saving principles were used by members of the group?
  3. How could the work schedule have been improved?

- MARKET ORDER
  1. In what ways was the market order well planned?
  2. How could the market order have been improved?

- PRINCIPLES OF COOKING
  1. What principles of cooking were practiced because of the choice of menu?

2. What new principles were learned by the group during this laboratory session?

- TABLE SETTING
  1. What were the good points about the table setting?
  2. What points could have been improved?

- CLEANUP
  1. In what ways was the cleanup managed efficiently?
  2. In what ways could the cleanup have been managed better?

- PERSONAL WORKING RELATIONSHIPS
  1. In what ways did members of the group work well together?
  2. How could the work load have been distributed more fairly?
  3. How could personal relationships be improved among group members?

■ Evaluating a Clothing Laboratory Experience

In all types of productive laboratories, students will be most highly motivated if they have some opportunity for selecting their projects. Some teachers may not feel that they can handle the situation in a clothing construction laboratory if all the students are using different patterns, but students can be offered choices among alternatives. A number of patterns appropriate for different ability levels can be designated as those from which students may make their selections. It is unjustifiable to cover concepts relating to line, design, and color and then to expect everyone in a class to make identical garments.

It may be easier for a teacher to evaluate specific features while a garment is being constructed than to judge many completed projects all at one time. By using periodic evaluations, students are helped to see the strengths and weaknesses of their work as it progresses and to make improvements as they continue. There is also value in having students judge their work as it progresses and compare and discuss their evaluations with the teacher.

It is recognized that simple evaluation devices imply that all the qualities listed are of equal importance. This may not necessarily be true. However, if comments are given, this shortcoming can be minimized. By using a series of checklists, points can be accumulated to help determine a final grade. Provision must be made for adjusting the total point value when all the identified clothing construction techniques are not included in all students' projects.

The following checklist on staystitching would be appropriate for use with beginning students; the one on facings shown, on page 144, for more advanced students.

STAYSTITCHING: Rate the quality of your staystitching by placing a check mark in the appropriate column. Total the points assigned and put this number in the space provided. The highest possible number of points is 30.

Desirable Qualities	Comments	Excellent 5	Very Good 4	Good 3	Fair 2	Poor 1
1/2 inch from seam allowance						
Even distance from cut edge						
Stitched in proper direction						
10-12 stitches per inch						
Proper machine tension						
Same color thread as garment						

TOTAL POINTS _____

FACINGS: Rate the quality of your facings by placing a check mark in the appropriate column. Total the points assigned and put this number in the space assigned. The highest possible number of points is 30.

Desirable Qualities	Comments	Excellent 5	Very Good 4	Good 3	Fair 2	Poor 1
Intersecting seams pressed open and flat						
Seams graded with wider seam allowance toward right side of garment						
Seams clipped or notched as needed						
Understitching straight and 1/8 inch from seam allowance						
Understitching through facing and both seam allowances						
Clean finishing done without tucks						
Facings pressed flat						
Hand-tacking inconspicuous						
Facing cannot be seen from right side of garment						

TOTAL POINTS _____

■ Evaluating Other Laboratory Experiences

In addition to food and nutrition and clothing and textiles, productive laboratories are appropriate in all home economics areas. Some examples follow:

Content Areas	Products to Make
Child Development	• Toys and baby sitting kits • Baby sitter's information booklet to record for each family the names of doctors, emergency numbers, and names and phone numbers of friends and relatives who could be called for help
Family Studies	• Message board • Family tree • Organizer for bills and receipts • Family album
Resource Management	• Reusable fabric grocery bags • Window quilts • Carryall for household supplies
Housing and Interiors	• Decorative accessories • Furniture (refinished or recovered)

Entrepreneurial classes that are interdisciplinary in nature are becoming increasingly popular. Home economics, business, and technical education classes may work together to plan and produce products to sell, to advertise, and to market. Students assume roles such as designers, business managers and assistant managers, salespeople, and cashiers. Students work together to evaluate the entire procedure and make recommendations for other entrepreneurial experiences.

Experimental Laboratories

Problems researched through experimental laboratory sessions often dictate that scientific methods be used. Using experimental methodology helps give home economics status in the eyes of those who think of it only as "stichin' 'n eatin'." Preferably, students will experiment to seek answers to questions rather than to prove facts already clear to them. The learning experiences suggested here can be developed using scientific and experimental methods.

Students should realize that experimental methodology requires a control for each experiment. If a comparison is to be meaningful, it must be a comparison of the effects different procedures have on samples of the same test object. For example, to check the effect chlorine bleach has on nylon fabric as compared with nonchlorine bleach, three samples of the fabric must be tested: one with each bleach and, for the control, one with no bleach.

Food and Nutrition

- Conduct experiments to determine the effects of various food-preparation techniques on different food products. For example, compare the color, texture, and flavor of vegetables prepared by steaming, boiling, and microwave methods. Prepare piecrusts using a variety of techniques and different fats. Compare the results for taste, appearance, and cost. Hard-boil and hard-cook eggs to determine if there are differences in flavor, texture, and color. Vary the baking temperature and the amount of beating for the same cake or muffin batter and note differences in shape, texture, and color. Vary the temperature and method of cooking small samples of tender and less tender cuts of meat. Draw generalizations from these experiments.

- Weigh three differently priced varieties of ground beef so as to make three exactly equal portions of each, or nine meat patties in all. Cook one sample of each variety to the same degree of doneness by frying; then cook one of each by broiling, and then by charcoal broiling. Weigh each portion after cooking to determine the amount of fat lost. Compare and contrast for flavor and appearance. Draw conclusions from this experiment. Using the same method of preparation, quality, and quantity of ground beef, salt the patties before, during, and after cooking. Report on what you learned by doing these experiments.

- Follow each of these procedures: Gently spoon sifted flour into a cup and pack flour into a cup without sifting, tapping frequently. Sift each of these and remeasure. Determine procedures to be followed when measuring flour. Predict what might happen when preparing baked products if these procedures are not followed.

- Use standardized tables of substitutions to interchange several food items in a recipe. Evaluate products made for possible variations in quality and nutritive value. Explain why each of the foods listed in a table of substitutions can be exchanged for the other. Determine if all substitutions are reciprocal.

- Experiment with different spices and flavorings on a variety of food products to find out which have a high degree of acceptance. After preparing foods using different condiments in varying amounts, ask a panel of judges to rate the products on a continuum. Use these ratings to develop special dishes designated as "Some of ＿＿＿ High School's Favorite Recipes."

Clothing and Textiles

- Use a variety of cleaning agents, common household products, and methods to remove different types of spots and stains, such as those caused by fruit juices, coffee, chocolate, grease, lipstick, blood, and ink on a variety of fabrics. Utilize the findings of the experiments by removing common spots and stains on different types of fabrics.

- Experiment with a variety of fabrics made from different fibers and with various finishes to ascertain the effects of several laundering techniques. Before beginning, outline the size of each fabric sample on a piece of paper, indicating the lengthwise and crosswise grain. Wash in hot, warm, and cold water for different time periods to note if there is shrinkage and, if so, how much. Press fabric swatches at several temperature settings to note effects on different fibers and finishes. Keeping the fabric, type of soil, and water temperature the same, experiment using cold-water detergents, soaps, bleaches, presoaks, enzyme-spray products, and stain removers in stick form to compare results and cost. Establish guidelines for washing family laundry.

- Dry fabrics of varying fiber content and with different finishes, using a clothes dryer set for several time and temperature readings. Remove some fabrics immediately after the cycle is finished and leave others to cool in the dryer. Hang items such as knit shirts, underwear, and washable slacks on a clothesline, using a variety of techniques. Determine which methods minimized puckering, stretching, and the amount of pressing needed. Make a list of suggestions for machine-drying and line-drying clothes.

- Conduct weathering experiments with fabrics of different fiber content. Hang some swatches indoors where they get a lot of sun and leave others outdoors. Note changes in color, strength, and the degree of disintegration after established periods of time. Make generalizations about fibers that are most and least suitable for curtains, draperies, and outdoor areas.

Consumer Education

- Compare a variety of commercial products designated for cleaning ovens, washing windows, polishing furniture, cleaning and waxing floors, and shampooing carpets. Consider the results, time and energy required to do the job, and cost involved. Compare and contrast commercial products designed for one purpose with common all-purpose household products, such as ammonia, for cleaning ovens and windows. Block off the floor in the home economics laboratory into several equal sections that receive about the same amount of traffic. Try various types of cleaners and floor waxes on each portion. Compare and contrast the sections of the floor one, two, and three weeks later. Make a generalization about the cost of household products in relation to their effectiveness.

- Use several varieties of household cleaning-equipment items such as different types of vacuum cleaners, mops, and rug shampooers. Determine the variety of tasks for which each can be used. Compare and contrast the items for efficiency, cost, care required, and features such as warranties and local service facilities.
- Compare and contrast baked products such as cakes, muffins, and pies made from scratch with those made by using convenience foods. Consider flavor, texture, appearance, cost, ease of preparation, time involved, and freshness after varying lengths of use. Suggest situations in which it would seem advisable to buy a specific food product already completely prepared, to use a mix, or to make the product from scratch. List the advantages and disadvantages of using convenience foods.

Management

- Store different types of foods in the refrigerator and freezer using various products for wrapping, such as plastic bags closed with metal twisters, foil, waxed paper, and heat seals, as well as different types of containers. Leave some products (such as carrots) uncovered in the refrigerator and (ice cream) uncovered in the freezer. After specified periods of time, compare the products for flavor, texture, and freshness. Experiment with freezing eggs, tomatoes, and potatoes in different forms. Establish guidelines for storing and freezing different food items.
- Practice making a bed until the most efficient system is determined. Demonstrate to others how to make the bed this way. Then have time trials or relay races to see how fast a bed can be made while meeting standards of performance established previously.
- Use these two procedures to clean rooms that get about the same amount and type of use:
  a. Clean the ceiling, walls, and draperies first; dust the furniture next; vacuum the floor last.
  b. Vacuum the floor first; dust the furniture next; clean the ceiling, walls, and draperies last.
  Check the rooms three days later. Establish an efficient procedure for cleaning rooms.

Evaluation

The most educationally valuable part of any laboratory experience should be the evaluation. It is during this time that generalizations are formulated and conclusions are drawn about the work done. Questions are posed, such as "Why did this happen (or not happen)?" Without evaluation, the laboratory activity tends to become an end in itself, if not just busywork. If students follow instructions and carry out an experiment without making generalizations about what they have done, they are unlikely to acquire the understanding originally intended.

Observational Laboratories

In observational laboratories, the teacher must furnish guidance so that students have a clear understanding of what they should be noting. The student views situations and phenomena so that certain concepts will become clearer. Usually students are expected to draw conclusions and to make judgments about what they have observed. Although learning experiences of an observational nature are most often associated with child development, they are actually relevant in studying all areas of home economics.

Food and Nutrition

- Have a "treasure hunt" to point out unsafe practices that have been planted in a roped-off laboratory kitchen or drawn in a sketch. Use items such as these:
  a. Potholder near a burner
  b. Pot handle turned toward the front of the range
  c. Coffee pot cord extending over the edge of the range
  d. Unlabeled bottles containing poisonous chemicals stored under the sink
  e. Knives left on the counter top
  Develop a set of guidelines for kitchen safety.
- Observe mold as it develops and grows. Leave vegetables, fruit, or meat in the refrigerator for extended periods of time. Moisten bread, place it in a closed container, and leave it in a warm and humid place for several days. Using the findings from the experiment, make a list of suggestions for storing these foods.
- View a display showing the different forms in which milk is available commercially and the various types of cheeses. Have a tasting party. Compare costs and nutritive values. Suggest ways in which each of the forms of milk and cheese can be served and used in cooking.

Consumer Education

- Observe eggs, both in the shell and as raw eggs displayed on a small plate, in the grades and sizes that are available locally. Note differences. Break a fresh egg and an older egg into separate saucers. Compare shape, height, and thickness of yolks and whites. Also view various grades of meat, poultry, and canned fruit or vegetable products. Determine factors that would affect the selection and use of each of the grades by comparing appearance, texture, flavor, and cost.

- Visit a grocery store to observe the location and placement of specialty and novelty items that are unlikely to be on a shopping list. Note the position of staple foods, dairy products, and nonfood items. Discuss the techniques used that may influence a consumer to buy more than was planned. Discuss factors that influence the choices a person will make when grocery shopping.

Management

- Observe demonstrations by classmates or guest speakers in which they exhibit efficiency and skill in performing specialized tasks such as decorating cakes, setting in sleeves, or dovetailing kitchen chores. Notice techniques used to save time and energy.
- Watch classmates make the same single dishes or simple meals in a U-shaped, L-shaped, and one-wall kitchen (or whatever layouts are represented in the home economics department). Trace the steps of the cooks on scaled floor plans of the kitchens. Measure the total length of the lines drawn. Determine in which types of kitchen the cook walked most and least. Discuss whether that necessarily makes this the best type of kitchen. Why, or why not? Other than the shape of the kitchen, what influenced how much the cook walked? What conclusions can you draw from this time-and-motion study?
- Use the layout of a local grocery, with the fixed location of various types of products, to trace in colored pencil or with string the probable route followed by a consumer using a disorganized and jumbled shopping list. Make a grocery list, including the same items, that fits the arrangement of this store. In other words, list the products to be bought so the consumer can begin at one end of the store and go up and down each aisle once, without backtracking. Measure the distances covered by shoppers using the different procedures. Decide which part of the store should be visited last, just before checking out, and why.

Child Development

- View children's TV programs. Develop a checklist for judging programs for children of various ages. Rate some programs using the checklist. Make a list of suggestions for improving the programs and send it to the appropriate networks.
- View a display of children's clothes that illustrates features such as these:
  a. Expansibility — clothes that grow with children
  b. Self-help items — clothing that enables children to help dress and undress themselves
  c. Special features — mittens or feet that are part of sleepwear or outerwear
  These clothing items may be borrowed from a store or brought to class by students. Discuss the desirable and undesirable features of each garment from different standpoints:
  a. Ease of putting on and taking off the garment
  b. Self-help features
  c. Comfort
  d. Washability and ease of care
  e. Durability
  f. Safety
- Relate scenes observed in a laboratory at school, or in a child-care facility, in which children seemed to illustrate social and emotional maturity or immaturity for their presumed ages. Tell whether adults, involved in the situations where immature behavior was displayed, seemed to handle them well or poorly.
- Observe preschool-age children, other than one's own brothers or sisters, in any three of the following situations:
  a. At play
  b. At mealtime
  c. Being dressed or undressed
  d. On a shopping trip or other outing
  e. Going to bed for a nap or for the night

Observe the children on a playground or in nursery school, Sunday school, the neighborhood, a store, or their homes. Use the same child for all three observations or use different children. In the observation report answer questions such as these:
  a. How old were the children? If you do not know for sure, how old do you think they were? What were they doing that helped you judge their ages?
  b. How did the children react in these situations? Why did they react these ways?
  c. What provisions were made to let the children do things for themselves? Did they? Why, or why not?

- View videotapes of children in a child-care facility and rate the performance of student teachers, aides, and other appropriate adults using an instrument that contributes to objectivity. A few of the characteristics you might consider are included in the rating scale shown on page 148.
- Visit child-care facilities and observe the children, teachers, toys, equipment, furnishings and kitchen facilities. Note the precautions taken to maintain the children's health and to promote their safety. Evalu-

ate the child-care facilities visited, by answering questions such as those in the box on page 149. However, fill out the checklist after leaving, not while visiting, the child-care center.

By going over questions like these before visiting child-care centers, students have been given some guidance toward making their observations meaningful experiences. It is recognized that many other points could be included in such a checklist. These questions are suitable for students with very limited experience in child development and serve to help them become aware of only a few of the features to consider in selecting a child-care facility. Furthermore, these are questions that one should be able to answer by observation only, without having to distract the facility employees by asking them to furnish additional information. Students can be encouraged to add their own questions to a checklist like this one.

Performance Rating Scale

DIRECTIONS: Please circle the number that best indicates the performance described as weak (1), below average (2), average (3), strong (4), or outstanding (5). Omit items that do not apply.

I. Demonstrates human relation skills in dealing with self and working with others such as pleasantness, courteousness, confidence, positive attitude, effective communication with children and others.

1	2	3	4	5
Does not demonstrate any human relation skills.		Demonstrates some human relation skills.		Demonstrates a variety of human relation skills.

1	2	3	4	5
Does not communicate effectively with children or others.		Occasionally communicates effectively with children or others.		Communicates effectively with children and others through techniques such as using first name, noting clothing, and praising efforts.

II. Utilizes various techniques in working with children with respect to the principle of human development such as working individually with each child, allowing each child to work at own pace.

1	2	3	4	5
Does not use any techniques in working with children with respect to principles of human development.		Occasionally uses some techniques in working with respect to the principles of development.		Uses many techniques in working with children with respect to the principles of human development.

III. Demonstrates methods of guidance such as direct and indirect guidance, positive verbal guidance.

1	2	3	4	5
Does not give direct guidance when needed.		Occasionally uses methods of direct guidance.		Utilizes a variety of methods of direct guidance such as leading or showing physical contact which restrains or reassures the child.

1	2	3	4	5
Does not give indirect guidance.		Occasionally uses methods of indirect guidance.		Utilizes a variety of methods of indirect guidance such as setting stage for activities, choosing appropriate toys and activities, scheduling of activity and rest.

1	2	3	4	5
Does not use positive verbal guidance.		Occasionally uses positive verbal guidance.		Uses positive verbal guidance such as: Please sit down; It's time to go outside now.

In observational laboratory lessons, students are not physically involved, as they are in productive and experimental laboratories. However, with appropriate guidance and direction in observation, students should be just as involved intellectually, and should be learning just as much, as in other types of activities.

Features to Look for in a Child-care Facility

Answer the following questions with a yes or no and be prepared to justify your answers.

1. Is the child-care facility licensed?
2. Is there adequate space indoors to move about freely while skipping, running, and dancing?
3. Is there adequate space indoors to build with blocks, to play house apart from the group, and to paint without being jostled?
4. Is there adequate space outdoors for running, climbing, and tricycle riding?
5. Is the outdoor equipment suitable for the developmental levels of the children attending the facility?
6. Is there some place outdoors for playing quietly if children choose to do this?
7. Are the toys and equipment sturdy, clean, and safe?
8. Are there blocks, balls, dolls, housekeeping toys, dress-up clothes, large- and small-wheel toys and puzzles easy enough for young children to do?
9. Are there easels, paint, clay or dough, crayons, scissors, and plenty of paper for many uses?
10. Are there games and toys that help children learn about shapes and sizes?
11. Are there tables and chairs that are the right size for working comfortably with both feet on the floor?
12. Does the program seem to meet the needs of growing children?
13. Are there quiet times for rest, stories, conversation, and refreshments?
14. Are there free play periods when children can choose what they want to do?
15. Is there time for the children to make things for themselves and to grow in creativity and independence?
16. Are the work periods of short duration so the children do not lose interest?
17. Do the teachers seem to show interest in the children as individuals?
18. Do the teachers seem to be constantly alert to the safety of the children?
19. Are the children supervised constantly?
20. Do the children seem happy?

Teacher Guidance

Laboratory lessons require careful planning by both the teacher and students if the activity period is to run smoothly and available time is to be used to the best advantage. If the lessons preceding laboratory work have provided students with essential background material, most students should be able to work with a reasonable degree of independence and cooperation. However, students do not need to know everything about a subject before participating in a laboratory experience. In fact, if too much time is spent on meal planning, table setting, and kitchen management before the first foods laboratory lesson, the teacher may have failed to capitalize on the inherent motivation students have for this type of activity. The best procedure seems to be to guide students into selecting comparatively simple activities at first, so they can have a sense of achievement, and to provide just enough background in the subject beforehand to enable them to carry out the planned activities successfully. Related concepts can be covered in greater depth as the unit progresses and can be interspersed between subsequent laboratory lessons.

Students who ask for help loudly and repeatedly tend to monopolize the teacher's attention. If, however, the instructor makes the effort, there are procedures that can be used so that all those who need individual guidance are likely to get it. In some classrooms, students write their names on the chalkboard as they need assistance. The teacher helps them in the order in which their names appear on the list. Another system that can be used is to have a set of numbered cards the students may pick up in order. The teacher gives guidance to pupils who have requested it by calling out their respective card numbers in sequence order.

The problem of students becoming overdependent upon the teacher can be a very real one. Sometimes, rather than answer students' questions directly during a laboratory lesson, the skillful teacher can ask questions of the students instead, until the correct responses become apparent to them. Students can be guided to ask, "Is this what I do next?" rather than "What do I do next?" The first question suggests that the student has given the problem some thought and has tried to arrive at a suitable solution. The latter question suggests that the student has come to expect the teacher to do most of the thinking and problem solving.

During the laboratory period the teacher should supervise all the groups, making sure that guidance is not limited to only a few. This gives the teacher an opportunity to observe the managerial processes used and the interpersonal relationships among students.

Managing Laboratories

The teacher who is secure and has the students' respect will not hesitate to pitch in and help clean up the lab. If students realize that the lab is really theirs and not the teacher's, they are likely to take pride in it and cooperate in keeping it orderly.

Cleanup charts can be used so that duties are rotated every few days or once a week. The following might be suitable for an all-purpose laboratory. Students can suggest the jobs that need to be done because these will vary from one situation to another.

MANAGEMENT MATRIX					
Duties	**Weeks**				
	9-1	9-8	9-15	9-22	9-29
Check roll	1	8	15	6	13
Straighten supply cabinets	2	9	16	7	14
Dust	3	10	1	8	15
Put chairs and tables in order	4	11	2	9	16
Sweep floor	5	12	3	10	1
Water plants	6	13	4	11	2
	7	14	5	12	3
STUDENTS					
1. Booker	5. John	9. Angelina	13. Rachel		
2. Jim	6. Marty	10. Beth	14. Jeff		
3. José	7. Lisa	11. Camille	15. Eva		
4. Jana	8. Anita	12. Eileen	16. Sandy		

At the end of a unit or the term, devise a system that will ensure that all students have some responsibility in the final cleanup. For example, when classes have concluded their work in the food and nutrition laboratory, make a list of all the jobs that must be done in order to "close up shop." Include as many tasks as there are students in all the classes that have been using the lab. Then duplicate the list and cut one copy into strips. Each student draws a slip from a bag or box. On the master sheet, a copy of the list that has not been cut into strips, write students' names next to the jobs for which they are responsible. By doing this, you can check later to see how well each student has performed the assigned task. Those who have done poorly can be asked to do their jobs again, and those who have done well can be complimented and thanked.

Disadvantages of Laboratory Lessons

Laboratory work may present problems for the novice teacher who does not yet realize how much longer it takes teenagers to complete a project than it does adults, or how much longer it takes a group to perform some tasks than it does a person working alone. If a class is large, there may not be room or sufficient equipment for everyone to work at once, and the teacher may not be able to provide continuous guidance. If the teacher does not supervise adequately, the students may not practice the skills they are supposed to be mastering. Furthermore, the freedom and informality in a laboratory situation may lead to excessive talking and wasting time if students are not highly motivated and if planning and organizing have been haphazard.

Unfortunately, laboratory experiences often result in low-level projects that are neither challenging nor motivating. Making an apron usually has much less appeal to a teenager than making an item of clothing that is popular at the time and will be worn where peers of both sexes congregate.

Laboratory lessons are expensive, not only in a financial sense but also in terms of time, material, equipment, and facilities. When laboratory sessions become everyday routine, little learning takes place in spite of the practical experience gained. When teachers rely on too many laboratory lessons, they fail to provide the variety and stimulating environment that challenge students and foster creative activity.

Advantages of Laboratory Lessons

Laboratory lessons provide an excellent opportunity for students to have input into the teaching-learning process by direct participation in planning, organizing, and carrying out individual and group projects. Students are encouraged to be creative and resourceful and to manage their resources advantageously. They are also provided with opportunities to generalize and to apply generalizations in new situations.

Laboratory lessons can furnish favorable circumstances in which students may practice desired behaviors under supervision and with guidance. Students work with concrete problems rather than with abstractions. In addition, laboratory experiences may help clarify concepts for those who have difficulty with verbalizations. For many, the greatest advantage of laboratory work may be the experience of working and learning to get along well with others in a democratic situation.

Community Resources

Chapter 17

A variety of community resources is available to all teachers. The quality and quantity of these vary from community to community. Numerous benefits can be derived from identifying and tapping local resources. Channels of communication can be established between people in the community and students and teachers in the home economics program. Local residents and agencies often become sources of support for your program. Community members can serve on your advisory council.

Involvement in the community can provide subject matter with realistic learning situations and practical applications that would not otherwise be available. Students often become more motivated and involved in course work when they have contact with people and places outside the classroom.

Planning for Resource People and Field Trips

There are several guidelines to keep in mind when inviting resource people into the classroom or when planning field trips with students.

1. As long-range plans for classes are being made, begin to identify resource people and field trips that can become integral parts of the learning activities. Valuable suggestions may be obtained from students, co-workers and other school personnel, newspaper items, and the advertising pages of the telephone directory.

2. Contact resource people well in advance of the time you would like to have them work with the students. The initial contact may be made through a personal visit, telephone call, or letter. After agreement has been reached about an appropriate date, time, and place, a letter of confirmation including this information should be sent. It is equally important to specify exactly what material is to be covered. Many resource people find it helpful to know the general background of the class and the extent of preparation in the subject matter that students will have before the guest's contact with the group. Resource people may suggest or ask that students view a specific film or filmstrip; read a selected story, case study, or article; or be introduced to specific information before they come to speak. This ensures that the students and the speaker have a mutual frame of reference. There may be opportunities for individual students or student committees to assume some of the responsibility for identifying community resources and contacting appropriate personnel. This not only helps the teacher, but also provides the students with valuable experience.

3. Field trips outside the school usually involve detailed planning to obtain permission from school administrators and parents and to arrange transportation. For field trips that are longer than one class period, there may be additional planning involved to determine the cost of the trip, set departure and arrival times, obtain additional chaperons, and make provisions for meals, if necessary.

4. Students should be adequately prepared for guest speakers and field trips. Students can discuss what they hope to learn and formulate some questions they would like to have answered by speakers or during field trips. Having each student write one or two questions to be asked usually increases participation during question-and-answer periods, but it might also result in questions that sound rehearsed. At any rate, it is advisable to encourage students to ask questions about points they do not understand rather than to allow them to rely on you to keep a discussion going.

5. Students may need to be reminded that their behavior, when a guest comes to class or they go on a field trip, reflects on the entire school. Encourage students to be courteous and helpful to visitors. On trips away from school, it may be wise to remind students not to make negative comments about what is observed while on the site and not to sit down in a furniture store or in a private home unless invited to do so.

6. When a resource person has finished talking to the group or it is time to conclude a field trip, some words of thanks from both the teacher and the students are appropriate. It may be advisable to remind students beforehand to stop and informally thank a speaker for having come or a host for having let you visit. In fact, you can use all such occasions to help students learn socially acceptable behavior.

7. After a speaker or field trip, a thank-you note is appropriate. It is helpful and can be effective if a student or a student committee assumes this task. You may want to read over student-written thank-you notes before they are put in final form and mailed.

8. When resource people come to the classroom, there are several things that can be done to help make the visits pleasant and profitable:
   a. The school office should know when guests are expected. If at all possible, assign someone to meet guests at the office.
   b. When speakers are introduced, sharing a little of the persons' background with the class can help guests establish rapport with the students.
   c. People invited to the classroom are not always accustomed to public speaking and may direct their voices to the teacher rather than the students. Consequently, if you sit near the back of the room, speakers are more likely to project so everyone can hear. You also have more control over student behavior from this position in the room.

9. Occasionally a guest speaker does not come as scheduled, or plans for a field trip have to be canceled at the last minute. Therefore, it is advisable to have alternate plans ready for the class period. Sometimes a lesson planned for two or three days in the future can be used.

Resource People

A variety of people in diverse professions and occupations can make contributions to home economics programs. Some to consider are: disabled persons, the parents of disabled people, first-generation immigrants or people of different ethnic background, interior designers, builders, architects, real estate and insurance representatives, credit bureau employees, merchandising personnel, religious leaders, social workers, counselors, and lawyers. In addition to providing expertise in specific areas, many of the people mentioned can serve as effective resources in career education. The responsibilities, opportunities for advancement or specialization, and satisfactions and limitations of their positions can be explored.

Beauticians and cosmetologists might be invited to class if they avoid a commercial approach. Doctors are excellent resource people; however, their schedules frequently rule out speaking engagements. A nurse, whose schedule may be less demanding than that of a doctor, could also provide an authoritative and professional viewpoint. Retired people often have more flexible schedules than those who are employed full-time; consequently, it may be easier to arrange meeting times with them. Inviting older citizens to serve as resource people can help to minimize the so-called generation gap and at the same time provide older citizens with the satisfaction of making a valuable contribution to the community.

A change in format from the customary lecture and question-answer period can add to a presentation considerably and provide a stimulating frame of reference for discussion. Students might act out a hypothetical counseling situation with the resource person. Other topics that could be used are problems related to dating, engagement, and marriage; personal financial crises; unexpected or unwanted pregnancies; or child abuse.

A panel discussion can be an excellent way of involving a number of resource people in one classroom presentation. A panel of people of different ages and responsibilities might discuss how they manage their time, money, energy, and other resources. A panel of parents might discuss the responsibilities of child rearing or special problems in caring for children.

Field Trips

Field trip opportunities are available in most communities. Trips to places of business, museums, institutions, private residences, recreational facilities, and state and federal offices offer interesting educational possibilities. Many manufacturing plants, research organizations, clothing retailers, department stores, and furniture and appliance stores welcome visits by students. Such field trips can promote a better understanding of merchants' and manufacturers' roles in the business world and in the local community.

Various local facilities for the care of young children and the elderly could be toured. Retirement and nursing homes, as well as public and private child-care centers, are interesting and informative places to visit. Some of the following might be observed or noted: special provisions for caring for a specific age group, the type and diversity of activities offered, the approximate cost, and the concern shown by personnel.

Concern about community problems can provide a basis for a variety of field trips. Inadequate playground facilities, community centers that have deteriorated, or poor methods of refuse disposal could serve as focal points for involving young people. One possible result of such field trips is that students may be motivated to analyze existing problems, collect additional information, and propose — and possibly become involved in — satisfactory solutions.

Comparative shopping trips can be enjoyable and informative. Depending on the specific products, features, and services being investigated, students can be divided into investigating teams. Each team could be responsible for going to a different type of retail establishment and checking the same or comparable items for particular features. For example, in comparison shopping for a particular appliance, the following points could be identified: brand name, special features, directions given for use, warranty, certification or endorsement by various organizations, cost, and finance charges if purchased on credit. When students return to class, each team can report its findings. Thus, a considerable amount of information can be shared. Students could decide which would be the best buy for a variety of given situations. They could also be asked to defend their choices.

Making full use of community resources offers you a variety of ways to reinforce and expand the content of your course and to motivate students and help them grow.

Scheduling Alternatives

Although it may be very desirable to have a resource person come to class or to take a field trip, circumstances and scheduling may prohibit it. There are alternatives that can be considered. If a resource person can speak to only one class, an audiotape or videotape could be made and played for other classes. The tape could become part of a library to be used as an additional resource or for individualizing instruction. A person who is unable to visit the school might be able to speak to a small group of students or the teacher at his or her residence or place of business. In this case, the interview could be taped on a camcorder cassette recorder. If a field trip cannot be scheduled for an entire class, it may be possible for a group of students or the teacher to go outside of school hours and take pictures for slides. The slides and information about the trip can be organized into an interesting classroom presentation.

Establishing an Advisory Council

The advisory council becomes an important vehicle of communication by bringing ideas from the community to the home economics department and by interpreting the home economics program to the community. The advisory council serves only in an advisory capacity. It is not a policy-making board. The major tasks of the council are to assist in collecting and interpreting information for use in program planning and evaluation, to make recommendations and offer suggestions to school authorities and personnel, to help plan and evaluate the home economics program, and to help interpret the home economics program to the community. All vocational home economics teachers are required to work with an advisory council. Some advisory councils serve only one school, while others are organized to provide input to all the home economics programs in a town, city, or school district.

The composition of the council is directly related to its effectiveness. If it is to communicate advice and the opinions of the community accurately, it must be representative of the entire community, drawing members from families of different ethnic and socioeconomic groups and from families of differing composition. These might include intact families with children, single-parent families, families with females employed in the home, families with females employed outside the home, and single-homemaker families. However, if the advisory council is to provide effective interpretation of a program to a community, to obtain community support, and to promote home economics projects in the community, it also must include well-known, influential people. You might consider some of the following:
- A school administrator (who may prefer to serve as an ex-officio member)
- Business and professional people
- A Chamber of Commerce representative
- Local employment office personnel
- Civic and church representatives
- Health and welfare representatives
- An extension home economist or 4-H agent

- Newspaper personnel, such as the editor of the Family Living Section
- A professional home economist in business or at a university

Once the overall desired composition of the council is determined, suggestions for individual members can be made. You want the council to be large enough to represent appropriate constituencies and organizations in the community, but not be so large that it is unwieldly. Eight to twelve individual members usually constitute a workable size group.

The American Association of School Administrators, a section of the National Education Association, has recommended these cautions in trying to achieve a successful advisory council:

- The council should be organized during developmental stages, not when a program is in trouble.
- There needs to be a crystal clear understanding of the functions of the council.
- The cooperation of the parent-teacher association should be secured in organizing an advisory council so duplication of effort and competition is avoided.
- The advisory council needs to understand thoroughly its relation to the school board.
- The lay advisory council should not be a rubber-stamp organization to approve policies and issues agreed upon by the superintendent and the board that are only submitted to the council for approval.
- Professionals, including school administrators, should be included on the council, but not be allowed to assume central or dominating roles.
- Time limits need to be set for both short- and long-term committees.
- Lay groups have to be treated with sincerity, frankness, and honesty, and council opinions and suggestions need to be received with dignity and respect.

Duties and Responsibilities

It is advisable to make some preliminary preparations so that the council can function effectively. It is a helpful first step to make arrangements for members to become acquainted with each other. The members of the advisory council need to know the purposes of the council — why it has been organized and what its role and limitations are. In addition, members need to have background information about the home economics program and the guidelines that have been used to plan the current program. With this preparation, the council members will be able to participate fully and meaningfully.

Some specific duties and responsibilities of your advisory council might be to:
- Set up short-term and long-term goals for the program.

- Help keep the curriculum up to date.
- Make plans for growth and expansion of the program.
- Help secure, through donations and discards, materials and equipment that are needed.
- Give advice, encouragement, and support.
- Act as public relations liaison with the community.
- Assist in the evaluation of the program.

In addition, advisory councils for occupational programs may also assume some of these responsibilities:
- Help determine home economics-related occupations in the local area for which training is needed.
- Recruit students that are in need of the training (with the help of the vocational guidance counselor, if there is one).
- Help find suitable training positions and/or provide jobs for students.
- Create good rapport between industry, business, and the home economics education program.
- Assist in securing permanent job placements for graduates.
- Make suggestions for other types of programs needed in the community.

Planning Advisory Council Meetings

Meetings of the advisory council need to be well planned. Members are busy people who want to feel their input is worthwhile. The meetings should deal with relevant topics about which the council is knowledgeable. Responsibility for planning the meeting, making the arrangements, and taking care of the follow-up may rest with you, with the chairperson of the advisory committee, or with another responsible individual. Regardless of who assumes responsibility for making the arrangements, keep the following tips in mind:
- Send an invitation and an agenda to the members.
- Meet in the Home Economics Department so council members will see student projects, displays, bulletin boards, and evidence of class and FHA/HERO activities.
- Plan to serve refreshments, perhaps prepared by students, that are low fat, high fiber, low sodium, or in some way reflect concern for and indicate the study of nutrition.
- Duplicate or make transparencies showing information that would assist the council in discussing concerns.
- Send a summary of the meeting proceedings to council members, along with a thank-you note that is personalized.
- Follow up on suggestions made by the council. This may involve working with individual council mem-

bers, talking to administrators, contacting other teachers, working on learning experiences and future plans for the department, and discussing ideas with students. It may not always be possible to take action on all suggestions made, but it is important that suggestions be explored. Either by way of a memo or a report during a future council meeting, you should report to members of the council the outcomes of their suggestions.

Home economics teachers have many additional means of communicating an accurate image of the profession. Some of these within the school include bulletin boards, display cases, library displays, and assemblies, open houses, and parent-teacher association meetings. Programs emphasizing a variety of aspects of home economics can be prepared for local business personnel, community organizations, and civic groups. Exhibits are appropriate for community centers, public buildings, and county and area fairs. The task of expanding and improving the image of home economics is the responsibility of each individual in the profession. For more information about marketing your program, see Chapter 29.

Basic Skills and Cross Credits

Chapter 18

A great deal of publicity has been given to the disappointing results of student performance on national, regional, state, and city academic achievement tests. Widespread reports have circulated about the inability of high school graduates to write an intelligible letter, fill out an application form acceptably, and make correct change. These limitations and other concerns such as the increasing cost of education have been partly responsible for the movement back to basics. Basic skills are those in language, reading, science, and math. Although home economics teachers are not specifically charged with the responsibility of teaching English, writing, or math, all professionals in an educational setting need to work together to reinforce basic skills.

If teachers do not take time to reinforce basic language, reading, science, and math skills, the result may be that students will not learn all the home economics subject matter. Also, by not emphasizing both subject matter and basic skills, the implications for students could be that English, math, and science have no application in other courses or in the real world.

Basic Skills

As an interdisciplinary area of study, home economics provides practical application of basic skills in real-life situations. Home economics links basic academic skills to skills needed for personal and family day-to-day living. When students use basic skills in home economics classes, they recognize that everyday life requires the ability to read, write, and apply math and science concepts.

Home economics teachers can work with other teachers to reinforce subject matter from course to course, planning to teach certain concepts simultaneously. Many researchers have pointed out that students learn more and are more highly motivated when the subject matter is relevant to their lives and to their personal goals. There are a number of concepts that can be taught simultaneously in home economics and English and math. Using credit in making consumer purchases can be correlated with computing interest in math classes. Math problems can be worked in occupational and cooperative education classes dealing with subject matter such as commercial food preparation, interior design, and clothing-care services, to reinforce computation skills emphasized in a math class. Students can write letters of application, complete job-application forms, and write summary reports at work when business correspondence is taught in an English class.

Students can reinforce language arts skills and expand their vocabularies in any home economics content area by developing word games such as scrambled letters, word searches, and crossword puzzles using appropriate computer software programs. The games need to be structured so that students have to provide definitions and/or examples to verify their knowledge and understanding of the vocabulary used.

Math Skills

In many content areas of home economics, it is important that students do some basic math computation and use calculators to solve problems and to assimilate subject matter. Converting standard measurements to metrics, managing money, understanding paycheck statements, figuring income tax, computing the cost of credit, making price comparisons, and purchasing fabric and making alterations in clothing construction are but a few of the areas where some basic knowledge of math is needed.

Many stories are told of students who have an aversion to math. Nevertheless, math is frequently used in everyday life. You can help students see how knowing basic math procedures and using a calculator can facilitate reaching some goals that may be important to them, such as using credit to make a consumer purchase. Work a sample problem on the chalkboard and then have students individually compute a similar problem. Put math problems related to specific subject matter on flash cards. Have students use a pocket calculator to determine unit prices, to figure the cost of credit, or to tally grocery expenditures. Students could compute the cost of having a baby and rearing a child to their present age or to 18 years of age. Students can be helped to be realistic about what it costs to live — rent, utilities, transportation, and so forth — and their potential salaries with and without education beyond high school. The potential for home-based and employer-based income can be computed and compared.

Computer Skills

Very good computer programs are available for diet analysis. Software is also available for career exploration, developing life coping skills, personal and family financial planning, income tax return preparation, comparison shopping, home safety checks, and other home economics-related areas. Computer programs can be used to help students develop study, communication, math, and consumer skills. For more about computers and technology in the home economics classroom see Chapter 15.

Science Skills

There are many opportunities to show how science principles relate to many aspects of everyday life. For example, it is possible to demonstrate the relationship between physical well-being and an adequate diet, as shown in animal feeding experiments. Demonstrate the principles behind different methods of food preservation; after different time intervals, compare the quality of the preserved food with food products that have not been preserved. Frozen foods that have been wrapped correctly and incorrectly can be stored for a period of time and later evaluated for flavor and texture. (Compare these findings with preservation of prehistoric animals frozen for thousands of years.)

Divide students into three groups. Have each group eat the same amount of measured popcorn, crackers, or cookies. Have one group jog around the room or jump rope until the students have burned up the number of calories eaten. Have one group walk slowly until the corresponding number of calories has been used. Have the third group sit quietly until the same number of calories has been burned. Guide the students in drawing conclusions and making generalizations from this "experiment." Students can also be guided in computing their 10-second target heart rates after 20 minutes of aerobic exercise.

Demonstrations can be conducted to illustrate the nutritive composition of some food such as the oil in peanut butter, the starch in potatoes, and the sugar and fat in selected fast foods. Illustrate different chemical reactions in food preparation when various food substances are combined, such as the production of carbon dioxide when baking powder and water and baking soda and an acid are mixed, and the reaction of easily oxidized cut fruit when treated and not treated with an acid. Students can make yogurt to determine the effects of acids and enzymes on milk products.

Conduct experiments to identify various textile fibers by using burning and acetone tests. Test flame-retardant properties of different fabrics; compare the effect of correct and incorrect laundry procedures used on fabrics to which flame-retardant chemicals have been added by the manufacturer. Demonstrate how water conditioners work in hard water. Do weathering experiments on fabrics of different fibers.

Social Studies and Family Life Education Skills

Students can trace customs in their own families to their cultural heritage and share these customs with the class. Students can read about ethnic foods and tell about food customs unique to various regions of the United States.

TV programs and commercial films can be identified that promote gender-role and culture-biased stereotyping. Students can write letters to producers pointing out these facts. Students can read published articles on teenage pregnancy, right-to-life and pro-choice advocates' activities, homosexual couples' rights to adopt children, and similar topics to separate value judgments from facts.

An assignment that is correlated with work in English class can require reading literature that reveals family life in authoritarian, matriarchal, single-parent, and disadvantaged families. Family lifestyles of historical figures and people well known today can be compared and contrasted.

Writing Skills

Evaluating written assignments can be time-consuming and tedious work. However, writing does provide students with the opportunity to develop communication skills needed throughout life, to organize their thoughts in a logical manner, and to receive constructive criticism.

In addition to the traditional subject-matter reports and term papers, there are many other opportunities for students to do written assignments. Some of these include: keeping a journal or diary; summarizing a reading assignment; evaluating a lab or project; writing job-application letters; developing written directions; composing book reviews for childrens' books or books of interest to one's peers; and writing letters to congressional representatives, to the editors of newspapers and magazines, and to retailers, manufacturers, and service organizations.

Some points to keep in mind when formulating written assignments follow:
- Select topics of interest to students, ones that are highly motivating and have evident relevance to their lives.
- Have students submit an initial assignment to be critiqued but not graded at the beginning of the term.
- Review with students grammar and spelling errors frequently made in written assignments.
- Have a speaker whom students respect stress the importance of written communication skills in everyday life.
- Have resources available, such as a dictionary and a thesaurus, and teach students to use them.
- Give clear directions that provide structure for the assignment.

Reading Skills

Numerous research studies have indicated that student comprehension of reading material is not solely the interaction of the student and the text but the interaction among the student, the text, and the teacher. Teacher intervention makes a difference in students' reading comprehension. Reading assignments can present problems for students with inadequate reading skills and a lack of familiarity with the subject matter.

Teachers can take several different approaches to provide some solutions for reading problems:
- Spend time helping students become acquainted with the reading resource materials that will be used in the classroom. For example, when using a textbook it is important for students to understand the layout, index, table of contents, headings, questions, chapter summaries, footnotes, and purposes of italicized words.
- Use materials as they were written but make adjustments in the instructional strategies used. For example, familiarize students with vocabulary and content by giving pre-instruction. Provide advance organizers that are summary statements of chapter content to help facilitate comprehension and recall. Define key words and use them in a context sentence. Suggest that students focus on the title and the first sentence of each paragraph since these give direction to the content that follows.
- Develop a list of questions to be answered or discussed later. These can be given before students begin reading, at the end of each paragraph or section, or at the end of the entire reading selection. Questions can be formulated to require higher levels of thinking.
- Formulate follow-up questions so students have to read all of the material to answer them. Questions that are planned to require the higher levels of thinking are more effective than those that ask the student only to pick out isolated bits of information. For example, for assigned reading on the types of maturity, students might list the types simply by copying the subtitles or headings. On the other hand, if students were asked to give examples other than those provided in order to illustrate the various types of maturity, comprehension of the subject would be required. The latter example is likely to require a total reading of the material.
- Use reading assignments to stimulate higher levels of thinking. In assigned reports often students retell the plot without analyzing the story for deeper meanings or applying it to their own lives. Questions such as the following foster critical thinking: How does the message in this novel or biography apply to your own life? What is the author pointing out about character development? How is the main character's personality similar to and different from your own?
- Write directions of your own at appropriate reading levels. Short sentences and short words help reduce the reading level. Unfamiliar words can be used if they are defined, thus, enriching the students' vocabularies.

Well-chosen reading materials can spark student interest, and they can even serve as a form of encouragement to students to pursue some subjects in greater depth. Therefore, judging the appropriateness of written resource materials is an area of concern to many teachers. Resource materials may include textbooks, paperbacks, magazines, and newspapers. For more about reading materials, see Chapter 23.

Career Skills

Concepts in career education include evaluating one's own personal characteristics, abilities, strengths, and weaknesses in relation to different career options. Students can explore various career choices and paths related to each of the subject matter areas of home economics. Teaching strategies can be structured that help students gain employability skills such as dependability, punctuality, courtesy, tact, and cooperation. Employability skills also include setting goals, making satisfying decisions, communicating positively, planning effectively, managing resources efficiently, maintaining harmonious human relationships, and evaluating objectively the results of efforts.

Learning experiences can be planned that foster reading, writing, and verbal communication skills by having students participate in the following:
- Reading and summarizing career information.
- Reading and replying to real or fictitious help wanted ads.
- Filling out job applications.
- Writing letters of inquiry about positions and letters of job acceptance.
- Developing appropriate resumes for jobs requiring different skills.
- Practicing telephone etiquette for business situations.
- Role-playing a variety of interviewing situations, giving and accepting criticism, asking for time off, and resigning from a job.

Cross Credits

Math and science have always had a high standing in educational priorities. This has continued as the public has become more concerned about the preparation of American youth in the basic skills areas. Special commissions, government agencies, and mass media have been influential in increasing graduation requirements in traditional disciplines. This movement has also brought attention to the fact that many vocational classes require a high level of proficiency in math and science. This focus has supported the growing trend toward granting through applied courses some of the required math, science, social studies, and art credits needed for graduation.

The National Commission on Secondary Vocational Education reporting in *The Unfinished Agenda, The Role of Vocational Education* recommended the following:

> Students should be allowed to satisfy some requirements for high school graduation — for example in the areas of mathematics, science, English, or social study — with selected courses in areas of vocational education that are comparable in the content coverage and vigor.

The areas of cross credit in which home economics teachers have been most successful are science credit for nutrition or for food science, mathematics credit for consumer education, social science credit for family studies, and art credit for interior design. It is recommended that you work to implement cross credit courses by first gaining the support of the teachers in the other discipline — the content area in which you want your course to "count." Teachers who have overloads are most likely to be receptive to this idea. It is also very important that your proposed course have academic credibility and reinforce basic skills vigorously. Present your ideas to your administrators and/or school board members only after you have conducted an extensive review of curricula, developed a curriculum for your particular situation, and completed a needs assessment indicating probable future enrollments.

References

"Building Basic Skills." *Momentum.* Cincinnati, OH: Southwestern Publishing Company, 1989.

Holsey, Lilla G. and Vila M. Rosenfeld. *Science Competencies Vocational Education.* School of Home Economics, East Carolina University, Greenville, NC, 1985.

Home Economics Basic Skills Guide, Grades 7-12. Los Angeles Unified School District, Mission Hills, CA: Glencoe Publishing Company, 1986.

Miller, Sandra W. and Charlotte R. Tulloch, editors. *Teaching Basic Skills Through Home Economics.* Development by the Basic Skills Subcommittee of the Home Economics Research Committee, American Vocational Association, and published by the Home Economics Association, Washington, DC, 1989.

Rosenfeld, Vila M. and Lilla G. Holsey. *Mathematics Competencies in Vocational Education.* School of Home Economics, East Carolina University, Greenville, NC, 1985.

The Unfinished Agenda: The Role of Vocational Education in the High School. The National Commission on Secondary Vocational Education. The Ohio State University, National Center for Research in Vocational Education, Columbus, OH, 1984.

Using Basic Skills

1.0 PERSONAL DEVELOPMENT/FAMILY RELATIONS

1.10 Reading
1.11 Reading Stories of Family Situations
1.12 Reading Terminology

1.20 Writing
1.21 Writing Letters & Stories
1.22 Writing Social Notes
1.23 Writing Invitations

1.30 Communicating
1.31 Communicating Verbally and Nonverbally
1.32 Communicating Effectively with Family Members
1.33 Communicating by Telephone
1.34 Communicating with Manners
1.35 Communicating: Listening

1.40 Using Numbers
1.41 Using Numbers in Individual and Family Situations

1.50 Perceiving
1.51 Perceiving Others' Feelings

2.0 MANAGEMENT

2.10 Reading
2.11 Reading Schedules
2.12 Reading Telephone Directory
2.13 Reading Directions
2.14 Reading Abbreviations/Symbols
2.15 Reading Terminology
2.16 Reading Charts and Graphs
2.17 Reading Stories about Management

2.20 Writing
2.21 Writing Directions
2.22 Writing Messages

2.30 Communicating
2.31 Communicating Goals
2.32 Communicating Plans

2.40 Using Numbers
2.41 Scheduling Time
2.42 Ranking Goals & Values
2.43 Computing Costs

2.50 Perceiving
2.51 Perceiving Time
2.52 Perceiving Unsafe Conditions
2.53 Perceiving Problems
2.54 Perceiving Alternatives

3.0 FOODS/NUTRITION

3.10 Reading
3.11 Reading Menus
3.12 Reading Food Labels
3.13 Reading Recipes
3.14 Reading Directions
3.15 Reading Terminology
3.16 Reading Charts and Graphs
3.17 Reading Stories About Foods

3.20 Writing
3.21 Writing Menus
3.22 Writing Recipes

3.30 Communicating
3.31 Ordering Food
3.32 Communicating Food Preferences and Needs

3.40 Using Numbers
3.41 Computing Calories
3.42 Metrics
3.43 Measuring Weights and Volumes
3.44 Computing Food Costs

3.50 Perceiving
3.51 Perceiving Flavors/Aromas/Textures/Appearance
3.52 Perceiving Portions
3.53 Perceiving Quality

(Continued)

Using Basic Skills (continued)

4.0 CONSUMER EDUCATION

4.10 Reading
- 4.11 Reading Labels
- 4.12 Reading Advertisements
- 4.13 Reading Terminology
- 4.14 Reading Stories of Consumer Experiences

4.20 Writing
- 4.21 Writing Orders
- 4.22 Writing Letters about Consumer Concerns
- 4.23 Writing Checks
- 4.24 Writing About Consumer Experiences

4.30 Communicating
- 4.31 Communicating: Selling a Product
- 4.32 Communicating with Salespeople

4.40 Using Numbers
- 4.41 Computing Unit Cost
- 4.42 Making Change
- 4.43 Computing Total Cost
- 4.44 Bank Balances

4.50 Perceiving
- 4.51 Perceiving Quality
- 4.52 Perceiving Quantity

5.0 WORLD OF WORK

5.10 Reading
- 5.11 Reading Newspaper Advertisements
- 5.12 Reading Stories about Work
- 5.13 Reading Terminology

5.20 Writing
- 5.21 Writing: Applications and Forms
- 5.22 Writing: Resumes
- 5.23 Writing: Researching A Job

5.30 Communicating
- 5.31 Communicating through Interviews

5.40 Using Numbers
- 5.41 Computing Salary

5.50 Perceiving
- 5.51 Perceiving Workers
- 5.52 Perceiving Work to be Done

6.0 CLOTHING/TEXTILES

6.10 Reading
- 6.11 Reading Labels
- 6.12 Reading Directions
- 6.13 Reading Stories About Textiles & Clothing
- 6.14 Reading Terminology and Symbols
- 6.15 Reading Charts

6.20 Writing
- 6.21 Writing Directions

6.30 Communicating
- 6.31 Communicating through Clothing

6.40 Using Numbers
- 6.41 Body Measurements
- 6.42 Computing Yardage
- 6.43 Metrics
- 6.44 Computing Cost of Project

6.50 Perceiving
- 6.51 Perceiving Textures
- 6.52 Perceiving Quality
- 6.53 Perceiving Color Differences

Developed by:
Home Economics Educators of West Virginia

Through a Project with
The Division of Specialized Allied Studies
The Department of Home Economics
Marshall University
Huntington, WV

Cooperative Learning

Chapter 19

Patsy J. Hallman, Ph.D.
Professor, Department of Home Economics
Stephen F. Austin State University

Cooperative learning is a term used often by both classroom teachers and educational theorists. But what does it really mean and why is it important? Basically, cooperative learning refers to an approach in which students work on learning activities in small groups and receive rewards or recognition based on the group's performance. The students work together to maximize the learning of each member of the group. They discuss the material to be learned with each other, help each other to understand it, and encourage each other to work hard. Within cooperative learning groups, students are responsible for learning the assigned material and for making sure that all the other members of the group learn the material, too.

Cooperative learning has three successful components:

- **Interdependence.** Group tasks are structured so that students must be concerned not only about their own learning, but also about the learning of each member of the group — "we sink or swim together." This interdependence may be encouraged by a variety of techniques such as the assignment of roles to individual students, the sharing of materials within the group, and the preparation of a joint answer or report by group members. If the group meets a collective goal, such as all members scoring 80% on a test, then all members of the group receive the same recognition or reward from the teacher or peers.

- **Individual accountability.** Each member of the group is personally responsible for learning the skills and facts related to the group task and each member must be prepared to demonstrate mastery of the assigned work. The teacher may randomly ask one member of the group to explain how to solve the problems, select one answer sheet from the group to evaluate, or give a quiz to all group members. Students receive individual scores for use in assigning grades.

- **Social skills.** Certain behaviors are needed for working successfully with others. Skills such as listening, sharing, encouraging, resolving conflict, and checking for understanding are necessary for group work to succeed. In cooperative learning, these skills are called *social skills*. The teacher should include instruction in social skills and have groups focus on one skill at a time.

The Value of Cooperative Learning

Cooperative learning is a teaching strategy that is applicable to all subject areas and to all age groups. Educators throughout the United States, as well as in countries around the world, are promoting cooperative learning because they believe it increases learning, builds self-esteem, and improves interpersonal skills. Research suggests that students enjoy school more when they learn in groups. In addition, job success largely depends on a person's ability to work cooperatively with others.

The foremost authorities on cooperative learning are David Johnson, Roger Johnson, and Edythe Johnson

Holubec. They have reported in numerous publications that cooperative learning experiences tend to promote higher achievement than competitive and individual learning experiences. Their research results hold for all ages and for all subject areas. The Johnsons point to increased retention, greater use of higher level reasoning, more accurate perspectives, and increased motivation to learn. In addition, students demonstrate higher self-esteem, greater cooperation, more positive attitudes toward teachers and school, greater peer support, and more positive heterogeneous relationships. As a result, the Johnsons have built theoretical models, conducted research to validate theory, and created procedures for teachers and administrators to use in implementing cooperative learning.

Vasquez and others have developed a cooperative learning training program for the Association for Supervision and Curriculum Development. They emphasize that cooperative learning is a superior teaching strategy for creative problem solving, for conceptual learning, and for developing more effective communication skills. They also emphasize that students who participate in cooperative learning experiences develop improved social skills. Within a specific classroom, student participation is greatly increased with the use of the strategy.

Writing in *Phi Delta Kappa*, Cohen points out that cooperative learning is an important means of accommodating the increasingly diverse school populations. It is recommended for inner-city classrooms, bilingual and multilingual classrooms, and other heterogeneous settings. Cooperative learning provides a structure for learning in which all students, regardless of ability, may achieve success.

Overall, the proponents of cooperative learning emphasize that more learning takes place when students work together in groups than when they work separately as individuals. While cooperative learning may not be appropriate for all lessons, it can be used effectively in most lessons if simple modifications are made in traditional lesson plans. See the chart below for examples of home economics lessons that lend themselves to cooperative learning. Home economics teachers can use cooperative learning to help students reach content objectives while practicing the social skills that are essential for positive relationships with families, friends, co-workers, and community members.

Examples of Home Economics Lessons Which Lend Themselves to Cooperative Learning

Family Living
- Setting family goals
- Improving family communication
- Managing multiple roles
- Handling family crises

Child Care and Development
- Caring for infants
- Meeting toddlers' needs
- Analyzing parenting skills
- Choosing day-care facilities

Food and Nutrition
- Analyzing diets
- Planning healthy menus
- Preparing a family meal
- Selecting appropriate foods for children and/or elders

Clothing and Textiles
- Planning a wardrobe
- Using the elements of design
- Recycling clothing
- Selecting outfits appropriate for work

Consumer Education
- Analyzing consumer rights and responsibilities
- Making effective consumer complaints
- Buying a used car
- Setting up a "first" apartment

Management
- Making decisions
- Reaching personal goals
- Using resources
- Conserving energy

Housing
- Comparing whether to rent or buy a home
- Arranging furniture
- Organizing storage space
- Making simple household repairs

Family Health
- Managing stress
- Avoiding health risks
- Planning an exercise program
- Preventing accidents

Career Education
- Identifying interests and skills
- Applying for jobs
- Getting along with co-workers
- Balancing work and family life

Cooperative Learning as a Teaching Strategy

When teaching strategies are classified as either presentation strategies or interaction strategies, cooperative learning appears as an interaction strategy. It provides opportunities for students to work together — discussing materials with each other, and helping and assisting each other to learn.

Within a lesson, cooperative learning is most often used as an activity that follows the presentation of new material by the teacher. Working within groups, students apply knowledge that was taught during the lesson. For example, a home economics teacher might introduce the concept of self-esteem. After telling students the objectives and purposes of the lesson, the teacher presents basic information about self-esteem. This might include how self-esteem differs from self-concept, how self-esteem develops, and some characteristics of people with high self-esteem and low self-esteem. Students might be asked to read selected pages from a textbook to learn additional information about self-esteem. Then, using the cooperative learning strategy, the teacher divides the students into small groups to develop a plan for improving a teenager's self-esteem. When the work of the group is completed, some form of individual accountability is provided. For example, the teacher might randomly select one member of each group to report on the rationale of the group's plan.

Although cooperative learning is similar to group activities that teachers have always used, it differs in several important factors. In cooperative learning activities, group members take responsibility for the learning of other members as well as for themselves. They must have the opportunity for face-to-face promotive interaction, explaining what they are learning to each other and helping each other understand and complete assignments. In addition, group members have to utilize social skills that are needed for working well together. The teaching methods for cooperative learning are specifically defined and structured.

Cooperative learning is different from competitive and individual learning in both student activities and evaluation criteria. In both competitive and individual learning, students do not work with their peers as partners in learning. In fact, in competitive learning students work against each other to achieve success. They may be graded on a curve, which requires them to compete with their peers in speed and accuracy. Their goal is personal achievement rather than achievement by the entire group. In individual learning, students have no reason to interact with others in the class and no concern whether others are successful. In contrast, the evaluation criteria for cooperative learning provide rewards for group success, as well as for individual success. These differences cause many educators to support the theory that more learning takes place in structures designed for cooperation than in structures designed for competition or for individualized learning.

The Teacher's Role

As teachers begin to use cooperative learning strategies, they discover that their role in the classroom changes. Students no longer view teachers as the main source of information and the solvers of all problems. Instead, teachers become facilitators or classroom managers as they organize lesson content and learning environments to maximize learning for all involved.

The Johnsons have identified the roles and responsibilities of the teacher using cooperative learning as follows:

1. Grouping students.
2. Planning lessons.
3. Emphasizing social skills.
4. Monitoring groups.
5. Facilitating student processing.
6. Evaluating progress.

Grouping Students

When using cooperative learning groups in a classroom or laboratory, you will have to make decisions about the size and composition of each group, the arrangement of the room, the distribution of materials, and the assignment of roles.

■ Size of Group

To determine the size of each group, consider the class size, the characteristics of the students, the group assignment, and the lesson topic. For example, in a large class seated in an auditorium, groups of two would probably work best. On the other hand, in a regular classroom with 24 students, groups of four — with desks turned so that the students face each other — may easily be formed.

Experienced teachers recommend groups no larger than five for optimum participation; groups of three or four are usually preferable. Students often stay with the same group for several assignments to foster group commitment.

■ Group Composition

Generally, classroom groups consist of randomly assigned students or homogeneous groups of students with similar ability levels. However, an important goal of cooperative learning is to facilitate learning in heterogeneous groups. To help you form heterogeneous groups, you may use these criteria:

- **Ability**. Representation from high, average, and low performers creates a group which has the potential for successful work and simulates a real-life work situation. Thus, a group of four students should include one high performer, one low performer, and two average performers. To determine levels of ability, you may use previous semester grades or recent evaluations of projects, reports, or quizzes.
- **Characteristics**. Groups also need a fairly equal distribution of students according to gender, grade level, racial or ethnic background, social status, and personality traits.

Sometimes it is helpful for students to have one friend in their group. If you are unaware of friendships, develop a sociogram or simple questionnaire which asks students to list the four classmates, in priority order, with whom they would most like to work in a group formed for a specified purpose. See page 84 for other ways to form small groups.

■ Room Arrangement

The room arrangement affects the success of the group. When groups of two are formed, the desks need not be moved. For larger groups, the desks are usually clustered so that the students may work facing each other. For example, four desks may be arranged so that they create a mini-table. The large tables found in many home economics laboratories also promote successful group work.

Plan a room arrangement that encourages face-to-face interaction and there will be greater student participation. Experts say face-to-face interaction also increases learning.

■ Materials

One way to ensure successful cooperation is through limited distribution of supplies needed to accomplish the group task. For example, you might distribute only one instruction sheet or worksheet to a group so that the members have to pull in close to each other. Or divide a set of materials among the group members so that each person has to share in order for the group to produce the whole set of materials.

■ Role Assignments

Some lessons lend themselves to role assignments of individual group members. A group of three students might include a leader, a recorder, and a checker. The leader would be responsible for total participation, the recorder responsible for the paper work, and the checker responsible for seeing that all group members understand the concepts and skills studied. Some teachers use these assignments: facilitator, reporter, and summarizer.

If the group task is to evaluate the quality of purchased apparel, the group might need one person in charge of the garments, another to record the comments, and a third to monitor participation and time allowances. In this instance, the role assignments could be: materials manager, recorder, and checker.

In a foods laboratory, one person may be the cook, one the cook's helper, and one the assistant. Although each student is assigned specific tasks, all the students are responsible for understanding the skills needed for the preparation of each product.

Role assignments may not always be appropriate for group work. In a class on toy safety, each student may be responsible for checking each toy, contributing to the evaluation list, and discussing the toy's features. After each toy is examined and a list of positive and negative features prepared, each student may sign the report to indicate agreement. The cooperative learning strategy of asking each member of the group to sign the instruction sheet to indicate agreement with the report and/or knowledge of the facts promotes personal integrity and responsibility among group members.

Planning Lessons

Before cooperative learning groups are asked to begin working together, detailed lesson plans are needed. You may choose to modify existing lesson plans to accommodate the essential components, or you may choose to use a totally new form. See the lesson plan adapted for cooperative learning groups on page 166. This plan allows the teacher to present new information, then place students in groups to apply the information. By contrast, the lesson plan shown on page 167 illustrates a class structured for an entire period of cooperative learning work.

Regardless of which type of lesson plan you use — the modified traditional one or the one designed just for cooperative learning, the following elements will be needed in the plan:

- **Grouping Decisions**: The size and composition of each group as well as the arrangement of the room must be determined for each cooperative learning experience.

- **Academic Task**. Structuring the task so that students reach the academic objectives may be the most important aspect of the lesson plan. A well-prepared task is stated so that all students clearly understand it. The task must be broad enough to demand enough work to make the grouping worthwhile. It also needs to be a multiple-ability task in order to accommodate the various abilities represented in a heterogeneous group.

Many teachers have found that handing out a printed instruction guidesheet, with the task clearly outlined for each group, helps to reduce frustration and increase productivity.
- **Criteria for Success**. You must decide how the students will know if they have been successful with the assigned task. For example, the group work on self-esteem may be considered successful if each group

---

Traditional Lesson Plan Modified to Use Cooperative Learning

CLASS   Apparel   **UNIT**   Management

LESSON TITLE   Wardrobe Planning

BEHAVIORAL OBJECTIVES:
   Apply principles of effective wardrobe planning.

INTRODUCTION:
   Direct students' attention to a large poster of an empty closet. Ask students to brainstorm items which a teen would put into the closet. Explain lesson objective and purpose.

LEARNING EXPERIENCE:
1. Present an illustrated lecture on wardrobe planning using the following outline:
   a. determine need
   b. inventory what you have
   c. sort and treat garments
   d. try new combinations
   e. plan for additions
   Use transparencies and demonstrate sorting.

2. Involve students with these questions:
   - What is an adequate wardrobe?
   - Is the best dressed person the one with the most clothes? Explain your answer.
   - How does a plan contribute to a satisfying wardrobe?

3. Ask students to move into Cooperative Learning Groups to complete the following task:
   TASK: Plan a wardrobe for the next season for Jim who is a 15-year-old football player, loves to camp out, is active in church, and is able to spend an average amount on clothing. Record your plan on the attached worksheet.
   CRITERIA FOR SUCCESS: Completed plan must illustrate each of the steps taught.
   INTERDEPENDENCE: Each individual will be given one unique reference: text, handout, article. Each signs the final report.
   INDIVIDUAL ACCOUNTABILITY: Randomly selected group member will explain the group's plan and the steps involved.
   SOCIAL SKILLS: Total participation.
                  Encouraging supportive behavior.

CLOSURE:
            Process the groups with a discussion of how well the groups functioned. Process the class on the usefulness of the outlined steps in planning for an individual's wardrobe.

RESOURCES AND REFERENCES NEEDED FOR LESSON PRESENTATION:
   - Transparencies on wardrobe planning.
   - Assorted clothing for demonstration.
   - Textbooks and reference materials for groups.
   - Worksheet for each group.

lists specific ways for a teenager to build self-esteem. For the group evaluating the quality of purchased garments, success may be defined as completing an evaluation form for each garment. Worksheets should be signed by each group member to indicate agreement.

- **Interdependence**. Every cooperative learning experience needs a structure and a plan that requires students to work together to complete the assigned task. This can be encouraged by having each group member responsible for teaching a procedure to the others, by limiting the materials available so group members have to share, by assigning roles or jobs to each group member, or by requiring a group product or worksheet that shows that all students have participated in completing the task.
- **Individual Accountability**. The plan must include a way of assessing whether each student achieves the objectives of the lesson and develops the required skills. This can be measured in a variety of ways, such as random questioning by the teacher, student explanation of a solution or demonstration of a skill, completion of individual worksheets, signatures on a group worksheet, or filling out a checklist or scorecard.

- **Social Skills**. The development of social skills necessary for productive group work is an ongoing process. Therefore, you should structure expectations for specific behaviors in each lesson. These expected behaviors are usually those which the class has agreed to work to improve, or you may have identified behaviors that need attention during your observations of group work. See page 168 for additional information on social skills.
- **Monitoring**. You will want to identify how the group work will be monitored. Informal observation is most common. Occasionally formal, written monitoring is used to collect data on special skill development and/ or needs. See pages 168-169 for more information on monitoring.
- **Processing**. The term *processing* is used in cooperative learning to indicate cooperative evaluation of group work. It is the final step in the lesson plan. The evaluation of progress toward both academic objectives and social skills objectives is important to successful group work. Usually processing takes the form of discussion within the cooperative learning groups or with the entire class. During processing, the group may assess how well the members are working

together, plan strategies for improving their effectiveness, and set new goals for the next cooperative learning experience. Processing appears in a cooperative lesson plan in the position of closure in a traditional lesson plan. See page 169 for additional information on processing.

Emphasizing Social Skills

Students need to be taught to work effectively in groups. As a teacher using cooperative learning strategies, you may have several questions about teaching social skills. You may ask: "What social skills shall I teach?", "How shall I teach social skills?", and "When shall I teach these skills?"

■ Skills Needed for Group Work

The chart on the right lists some social skills identified by teachers who use cooperative learning. Use your own judgment about the skills that your particular class needs. By adding to and subtracting from these suggestions, you can develop your own master list.

Using your master list, prioritize the skills. Teach those skills you feel are most essential first. Some home economics teachers begin with the first three skills on their list. As work progresses, you will add to the list. Students are excellent resources for determining what social skills are needed for their groups.

■ How to Teach Social Skills

When you teach social skills, help your students understand how people act when they work successfully in groups. Begin by discussing the rationale of a specific skill and defining expected behaviors. Some strategies to use are:
• Modeling
• Role-playing
• Demonstrating
• Making posters
• Analyzing studies
• Practicing

Questions sometimes help students understand an abstract concept such as encouragement or support. For example, a teacher may ask, "What does *encouragement* look like?" Students may respond by smiling, nodding, giving the "thumbs up" sign, or patting each other on the back. Then the teacher may ask, "What does *encouragement* sound like?" Students may say, "Good idea," "That helps," "That's interesting," or "Great!"

Common Social Skills for Cooperative Learning

• Encourage new ideas.
• Give everyone a chance to talk.
• Work quietly.
• Participate in the group.
• Listen.
• Respect the opinions of others.
• Share materials.
• Fulfill your role assignment.
• Use supportive phrases to encourage others.
• Contribute to the product.
• Complete work on time.
• Criticize constructively.
• Summarize information.
• Question ideas and suggestions.
• Stay on task.

As students begin to work cooperatively in groups, the need for certain behaviors will emerge. From these obvious needs, you and your students may write guidelines for expected behavior within the class.

■ When to Teach Social Skills

Some home economics teachers have the class practice essential social skills in cooperative groups before they begin serious work toward an academic objective. Others identify needed skills and either model or role-play them when they assign the task for specific group work. As students work on their group task, they are expected to practice the assigned social skill.

Some teachers prefer to teach social skills as a part of the processing that follows each group experience. Others simply stop class work and teach a skill when the need arises using the teachable moment. No matter when you choose to teach social skills, it is important that students consciously practice the use of these skills as they interact with one another.

Monitoring Groups

While the students are working in their groups, you will be needed as a resource person, as a validator, and as an evaluator. Move quietly around the room observing and helping groups as needed by:
• Answering questions that arise.
• Clarifying the assignment.
• Explaining words, processes, or equipment use.
• Demonstrating a process or skill.
• Encouraging the practice of social skills.
• Questioning students to promote higher level thinking skills.
• Reminding groups to follow the class guidelines.

You also can use this time to evaluate the progress of the groups' work, listening for supportive comments and body language as the students work together. Record examples of the students' use of social skills for later feedback to the group.

Be alert for any problems that groups may have in accomplishing the assigned task or using social skills. If intervention is required, encourage groups to solve their own problems by asking questions and making suggestions. The goal is to help students develop their own problem-solving skills.

Facilitating Student Processing

Processing means student evaluation of group results and behaviors. It is the final stage in each cooperative learning activity. During this phase, the groups can review what they have learned about both the academic task and the social skill. There should be time for processing within groups and then each group can share with the entire class. This acts as a student-generated review of the assignment and creates a sense of unity.

During processing, groups can discuss how the members were helpful to the group and what they could do to make the group even more successful. For example, one group may suggest ways to communicate more effectively with each other. Another group may develop a list of words and phrases to use to be more supportive of each other. Or a group may decide to work on increasing the questioning of each other in order to have more participation from certain members.

This is the time to share your observations with individual groups or the entire class. You might give each group an observation sheet that you have marked and let them analyze their practice of the assigned skill. If the group work has resulted in an unacceptable level of noise, you might lead a class discussion on problems created by the noise level and ideas for ways to reduce it.

Evaluating

Evaluation of progress toward academic objectives is an integral part of cooperative learning. Teachers are responsible for assessing every individual's progress toward reaching the academic objective. Evaluating social behaviors that produce successful group work is equally important in cooperative learning. However, determining fair and accurate methods of assessment may be a challenge for teachers who are just beginning to use cooperative learning strategies.

Some teachers assign two grades to students. They evaluate and grade the group's product — a report, a single set of answers agreed to by all group members, a decision on which the group has reached consensus, or a tangible creation such as a display. In addition, they give an assessment of each student's individual work, such as responses to questioning, a worksheet, a demonstration, a homework assignment, or a quiz. In this way, students receive two grades: one for group work, and one for individual mastery of the concept or skill.

Teachers who use the two-grades method believe that the ability to work productively in groups is as important to life success as is mastery of technical skills and information. Thus, a teacher may use cooperative learning groups when students are evaluating ways to discourage the use of harmful drugs. A group grade could be assigned to each member based on the group's presentation of a workable plan for action in the high school, junior high, or middle school. Then the teacher could ask students to write a short essay on the harmful effects of drugs and assign a second grade to each student.

In teaching with cooperative learning groups, as in any teaching, feedback to students is important. Since feedback should occur as soon as possible, you will want to monitor work as it progresses and not wait until it is completed. Both individuals and groups need to know the quality of their work to assure optimum learning. In addition, group work becomes more appealing to students if their product is evaluated promptly.

Teachers also may choose to provide rewards to groups for successful completion of the group assignment. Rewards may take the form of extra points to individuals, special recognition for the group, opportunities to view a special video or visit in the community, or other motivational activities that prove successful in a particular class. Some teachers use certificates, ribbons, bulletin board displays, and nutritious refreshments as rewards. Others believe that the group work itself provides sufficient reward for students.

Implementation

See the chart on page 170 for some specific tips for implementing cooperative learning strategies in your classroom, laboratories, and FHA/HERO activities. Start slowly. Students need to adjust from working competitively or independently to working cooperatively with one another. Persevere. Remember it takes time to learn new skills and behaviors.

When you introduce a cooperative learning activity, it is important to explain the group task and the expected behavior in words that are clear to students. For example, in a lesson on self-esteem you may say, "In your groups, please analyze the case study presented

Tips for Using Cooperative Learning

1. Begin using cooperative learning with only one class.
2. Select a class and a lesson which you know well.
3. Plan in detail.
4. Validate your plans by explaining them to a colleague.
5. Practice giving clear directions.
6. Prepare detailed instruction sheet or worksheet for groups.
7. Set up a practice lesson for training and to validate plans.
8. Start with small groups of only two or three students.
9. Teach social skills as a key to group success.
10. Model expected behaviors.
11. Post expected behaviors in a prominent place in the room.
12. Allow time for group processing.
13. Leave the room set up all day for group work, if possible.
14. Plan to reward groups that reach their goals.

in the worksheet you have received. The case study involves a person who has low self-esteem. Each of you should take responsibility for reading the case study and contributing at least one suggestion for change in the person's practices. Group leaders will take responsibility for getting a suggestion from every group member. Recorders, please write each suggestion on the case analysis form. Monitors, please observe the group's work for expected behaviors. Remember that today we are working on tactful expressions of disagreement. When your case analysis is complete, sign the form to show that each member of your group agrees with the report."

Many school districts provide teacher training in cooperative learning. Some workshops offer a conceptual model that may be used with any lesson in any subject area. Other programs provide specific lessons and strategies for implementing cooperative learning. Many articles and books are available on the subject. In addition, some administrators are implementing cooperative learning strategies at faculty meetings and district meetings.

Cooperative learning is much more than dividing students into small groups and giving them a task to do. It is specifically designed to promote group interdependence, individual accountability, and social skills. Students learn to work together to maximize the learning of each member of the group. They develop both academic and social skills that they can utilize in family life, the workplace, and the community. Some educators believe that nothing is more basic than to empower students with the ability to work together in solving the problems facing our society.

References

Cohen, E.G. "Continuing to Cooperate: Prerequisites for Persistence." Phi Delta Kappa, Vol. 72(2), October 1990, pages 134-138.

_____. Designing Groupwork. New York: Teachers College Press, 1986.

Edwards, C. and J. Stout. "Cooperative Learning: The First Year." Educational Journal, January 1990, pages 38-41.

Ellis, S. S. "Introducing Cooperative Learning." Educational Leadership, January 1990, pages 34-37.

Hall, H. C. and S. W. Miller. "Home Economics Teacher Education into the 21st Century." Journal of Home Economics, Vol. 81(2), Summer 1989, pages 7-13.

Johnson, D. W., R. T. Johnson, and E. J. Holubec. Cooperation in the Classroom. Edina, MN: Interaction Book Company, 1988.

_____. Circles of Learning: Interaction in the Classroom. Edina, MN: Interaction Book Company, 1986.

Johnson, D. W. and R. T. Johnson. Learning Together and Alone. Englewood Cliffs, NJ: Prentice Hall, Inc., 1987.

Johnson, D. W. Human Relations and Your Career. Englewood Cliffs, NJ: Prentice Hall, Inc. 1987.

Kagan, S. Cooperative Learning: The Structural Approach. San Juan Capistrano: Resources for Teachers, 1989.

Schultz, J. L. "Cooperative Learning: Refining the Process."Educational Leadership, January 1990, pages 43-45.

Slavin, R. E. Using Student Team Learning. Baltimore: John Hopkins University Press, 1986.

Vasquez, B. T., R. E. Slavin, M. D'Arcangelo, and L. J. Kiernan. Cooperative Learning Series Facilitators Manual. Alexandria, VA: Association for Supervision and Curriculum Development, 1990.

Motivation, Discipline, and Student Responsibility

Chapter 20

Motivation and classroom discipline go hand in hand. Students who are motivated and interested in their work are unlikely to present major behavior problems. Providing purposeful and stimulating learning activities that will interest students is a challenge that must be met in order to achieve an environment conducive to learning. Classroom discipline, curriculum, and teaching are interrelated and need to be considered simultaneously. Motivation and discipline can not be separated from teaching and learning.

Motivation

Dealing with students' attitudes toward school and their interpretations of subject matter may necessitate learning about the lifestyles of students in the class, as well as their views of the environment. Sometimes it is appropriate to indicate situations when the subject mat-

ter is likely to be especially valuable. A teacher might begin a lesson with "You will be able to use this information when ..." or "You will need to know this if ..." or "It will help you at work to know ..."

Teachers need to realize that they teach through their verbal behavior and their actions. Anything teachers say or do may significantly change a student's self-concept, feelings, and attitudes, either for better or worse. Undoubtedly, you can recall an instance in which something a teacher said had an enormous impact on your self-concept. Remember that a positive self-concept is one of the prime factors in motivation and achievement.

Enhancing Students' Self-Concepts

Teachers are not likely to motivate students by saying "I like you." You need to show that you care. Learn students' names as quickly as possible and speak to them by name. "Hi Chris" shows more interest than just "Hi." Teachers have to establish an atmosphere of mutual respect and trust that makes each student feel worthy. Teachers do not get the respect of students by demanding it. Esteem and honor must be earned. One way to start is to take time to listen to what students have to say and to use their ideas and suggestions whenever possible. Teachers who are receptive to students' feelings show this with remarks made in a positive manner. If a student seems to disagree with a statement another has just made, you might say, "John does not seem to see it that way. How do you feel about it, John?" Wise teachers also bear in mind attitudes previously expressed and show this recollection by making a comment such as: "Yesterday Marie expressed the opinion that ..." When you remember a student's contribution and refer to it later you are, in essence, saying "Your ideas and thoughts are important. You are important and worthy." When you take a student's present or past comment and build or "piggy back" on it, you are helping to build self-esteem. Motivating students and building their self-confidence is partially dependent upon consistently listening to what they have to say.

Self-concept is also related to the students' realistic selection of objectives. When students are given a choice of problems to work on and are told that these are ranked in order of difficulty, low achievers typically select either the easiest or the most difficult. They choose from among the simpler items because of their lack of self-esteem or, conversely, from the more difficult because they reason that nobody else in the class can handle the problem, either. The incentive and rewards for achieving at such a high level may be so great for these students that they become unrealistic about the situation. Average or above-average achievers are likely to select problems of medium difficulty.

When students of average or above-average ability are unsuccessful with their problems, they generally select easier and less challenging ones the next time they are offered a choice. In other words, failure in one situation affects one's self-concept and the goals one sets for oneself. The old saying "Nothing breeds success like success" has wide implications for teachers. It is their responsibility to help students choose projects and assignments from which they can gain a sense of challenge, achievement, satisfaction, and success. Of course, it is also necessary to give students enough guidance and help to enable them to accomplish their tasks reasonably well in relation to their backgrounds, previous experience, skills, and overall abilities.

Teachers' Behaviors That Affect Student Motivation

It is important to realize that students, like teachers, behave in terms of what seems to be true. Teaching and learning are accomplished not necessarily according to what the facts are, but according to how they are perceived. A sense of acceptance or rejection can be communicated to students by their teacher's posture, gestures, and demeanor. The teacher who frequently stands with arms folded may inadvertently be conveying the message, "Don't approach me. I'm unapproachable." Similarly, the teacher who is always sitting behind the desk rather than occasionally getting physically close to the students may be communicating, "I really don't care about you," or "I am the authority in this room." Slouching and slumping may reflect indifference and boredom, whether real or imagined. On the other hand, maintaining good eye contact, smiling, and giving students your full attention may communicate to students, "I think you are important."

Some factors that tend to lessen motivation in the classroom are overemphasis on the acquisition of knowledge and on memorization of facts, disapproval of curiosity, a great deal of negative criticism, rejection of suggestions for additional or alternative activities, overreliance on the lecture method of teaching or on textbooks, and highly authoritative approaches to maintaining discipline. The teacher who asks, "Why did you do it *that* way?" is more likely to suppress a desire to learn than one who asks, following an unsuccessful student effort, "What do you suppose happened?" Other kinds of remarks teachers sometimes make that adversely affect motivation are:

"This is how *you* do it *in* my class."
"I tried it once. It won't work."
"You know you should not have done it like that."

Unfortunately, many experiences in school stifle students' enthusiasm for learning because of expectations of conformity — disapproval of breaking the traditional mold.

Teacher behavior that is inconsistent, distant, cold, and rejecting is far less likely to enhance self-concept, motivation, and learning than behavior that is warm and accepting and consistent. Self-confidence and self-respect are strong motivating forces. The teacher who realizes this will take every possible opportunity to help students feel wanted, worthwhile, and positive toward themselves. It is important to acknowledge that *all* students have the same need for recognition, attention, and achievement.

Comments on Students' Work

Writing comments on students' papers is well worth the effort. In fact, a personal comment usually has much more motivational value than the grade assigned to the work. A written remark, such as "I am disappointed because this is not up to the standard I have come to expect from you; I'm sure that you'll do your usual quality of work on the next assignment," should certainly encourage the student to do better. A teacher's sincere pride in a student's paper can be reflected by writing something like "I am very pleased with the way your work continues to improve. Keep it up!"

It is recognized that it takes a great deal of time to write remarks appropriate for each student, but personal comments usually have very positive effects on student achievement. A research study was conducted by Page in which a large number of students' papers with grades ranging from A to F were divided equally into the following three groups: those on which only a grade was written; those on which a stereotyped comment such as "Keep up the good work," "Needs improvement," or "You can do better" was written; and those that contained statements showing personal and professional concern for the individual student. On the next assignment, the students who had been given only a grade the first time made the least progress; the students who had received personal comments made the most improvement. In fact, those students in the latter group who had done failing work on the first assignment made the greatest improvement of all the students in the study.

When evaluating students' work, it is advisable to both begin and end with positive comments and to intersperse negative remarks between the favorable ones. Negative criticisms are more likely to be accepted and acted upon if they are preceded by positive ones. Finishing with a positive comment leaves the student with a better feeling than ending the evaluation on an unfavorable note. It is almost always possible to find something good to say about any project.

Extrinsic Versus Intrinsic Motivation

Extrinsic rewards are those that are not directly related to an achievement itself. Though they result from the achievement, they are really something extra. Examples include: giving a student $5 for every grade of A earned, promising new clothes if grades are raised in a certain subject, or making a down payment on a car if the student stays in school until graduation. In the classroom, students may be given food to eat if they work on their assignments quietly all period, or they may be promised a party if they finish their clothing construction projects on time. They are being motivated by external forces.

Intrinsic motivation comes from within the individual. It means wanting to do well for its own sake, and it brings a sense of self-satisfaction and self-fulfillment.

Many parents and educators shudder at the thought of motivating students extrinsically because the rewards have to cease at some time and, in life, people are not necessarily compensated for all their accomplishments. However, there is always the possibility that extrinsic motivation may evolve into intrinsic motivation. This is likely to happen if, in working for an extrinsic reward, the student also gains a sense of personal achievement and if the reward is as closely related to the accomplishment as possible.

Classroom Discipline

Discipline in the classroom is a form of negotiation between the teacher and students. When discipline is thought of as control, uniform behavior and a quiet room may result, but there will also be limited creativity and less flexibility. When discipline is thought of as punishment, negative and aggressive responses are likely to surface. Students often react with behavior that seems to say, "Let's see how much we can get away with —

how much we can bother the teacher. Let's get 'teacher's goat' and make life miserable.''

When discipline is thought of as a student responsibility, attainable goals are more likely to be set and reached. Self-reliance is an important component of effective classroom discipline — for both the students and the teacher.

There are no hard-and-fast rules for having effective classroom discipline. The reason is that there are differences from one area of the country to another, from one school to another, and from one class to another. Effective solutions depend on the types of learners, teachers' personalities and abilities, the curriculum, and the unique interaction of all of these.

Problem students usually represent only a small proportion of the student population. However, for inexperienced teachers, one or two difficult students can seem like a classroom full of problems. Think positively. The majority of students are conscientious and hard-working.

It is not easy to teach in all schools, and not all classes are easy to teach. In some schools, the motivation to learn is high, and the environment in classrooms is relaxed and informal. In schools where the student population is more difficult to handle, teachers have to work harder to get and maintain students' attention.

If you are a new teacher in a school or if there is an administrative change in a school where you have been teaching, it is best to find out the school policies on discipline. Determine what type of support you can expect from administrators. Of course, that is a resource you would use only when you had tried other approaches.

Teachers need to realize that there are some factors that influence classroom discipline over which they have limited control. These include not only school policies but also administrative support, the overall school atmosphere, the backgrounds of the students, parental support, class size, and room configurations.

The Teacher's Self-Concept

Teachers need to formulate a philosophy of discipline with which they are comfortable and which is compatible with their teaching style and personality. Teachers who are uncertain about their own self-worth, their knowledge of the subject matter, and their ability to teach effectively express these conflicts in their own insecure behavior in the classroom. This, in turn, produces additional trouble. Teachers need enough self-confidence to be able to set with the students reasonable limits of student behavior and to follow through with predetermined action if students respond inappropriately.

Insecurity on the teacher's part may be evidenced by a controlling manner with aggressive and harsh disciplinary actions or by passivity. Teachers who are passive for personal reasons usually fear failing. Teachers who reach out and take risks are risking the possibility of failing occasionally.

The saying, "You usually get what you expect," is often a self-fulfilling prophecy when it comes to a teacher's classroom discipline. Students who are expected to be cooperative usually are, and those who are expected to misbehave often do. The teacher's attitude is of utmost importance.

Teachers who cannot manage their classrooms certainly cannot enjoy teaching. They often become the "burned out" teachers who leave the profession. Unfortunately, though, some remain teaching. These teachers have a negative influence on students and give the profession a "bad name."

Getting Off to a Good Start

The importance of "setting the right tone" in your classes at the beginning of school cannot be overestimated. During the first few days, students size you up, the class, and the situation. They test you to determine the limits you place on various forms of behavior and whether they will like or dislike the class. In other words, students decide how cooperative they intend to be.

Be in class before the students arrive if at all possible. It is an especially good practice to stand in the doorway at the beginning and the end of class and talk to students. Students need to know they are important and welcome.

Give students something definite and interesting to do the first day of class so they learn at least one new piece of information before they leave the room. Don't worry about how much material you cover the first week of class as long as there is an atmosphere conducive to learning. As you begin to develop rapport with students, involve them in helping you select the subject matter to be covered to ensure that it is helpful to them and meets their needs.

The first five minutes of class is very important in establishing class control for the remainder of the period. Begin class only after you have students' attention. Although you may have to wait a few minutes before beginning, there is little point in starting and then having to repeat what was said earlier.

There is no substitute for being organized when teaching. Disorganization — unscheduled time, poorly plannned activities, and a lack of congruence in the subject matter — inevitably leads to confusion, lack of student interest, and potential behavior problems.

Being Well-Organized

Inexperienced teachers generally have the most discipline problems because they are overwhelmed with routine "custodial" duties, and they find it necessary to spend much more time on curriculum planning than more experienced teachers. New teachers may feel they have insufficient time to work on building relationships with the students. Actually, teachers who have achieved a healthy professional relationship with their students are more likely to be able to foster positive relationships among students. This, in turn, helps foster a more productive environment for teaching and learning.

Teachers of any age need to act like adults in charge of a democratic environment and not like pals to the students. Many students have little discipline at home. They feel secure when they have parameters, know where they stand, and recognize that they will be treated fairly and with consistency from time-to-time and from student-to-student. Students are most likely to conform when they are clear about what is expected of them.

Teachers who have effective discipline are perceived to be good managers and well organized. Organization includes:

- Being well prepared for class, getting the class settled to begin on time, having materials ready to use, and preparing professional looking handouts and visuals.
- Acting deliberately by knowing what needs to be covered, keeping the class moving forward, using an appropriate tone of voice, and being in charge while maintaining a warm and friendly demeanor.
- Knowing the subject matter well enough to provide up-to-date information, being able to explain and clarify it, making it interesting and stimulating, and being able to answer questions.
- Involving students in planning and implementing activities that involve higher levels of thinking.
- Handling misbehavior fairly and consistently without damaging students' self-concepts.
- Being self-disciplined by following school rules, being truthful, and not threatening unless threats can be carried out.

Interacting with Students

Martin and Quilling have suggested that you can set the stage for effective discipline by developing positive interactions that include:

- Listening to the concerns of others.
- Communicating until understanding is achieved.
- Exhibiting a positive regard for people.
- Establishing a give-and-take relationship.
- Being organized and consistent.
- Using other's time efficiently.

- Stressing the positive.
- Respecting the rights and property of others.
- Setting an example.
- Evaluating objectively.
- Admitting mistakes.

As you go about the daily business of working with students both in and out of the classroom, be friendly, warm, and pleasant without becoming a part of their social group. Students want teachers they respect, not buddies. Wearing professionally appropriate attire helps you establish and maintain a professional relationship with students.

■ Handling Discipline Problems

When there is a disagreement between you and a student, avoid arguing with the student in front of the class. A confrontation serves no useful purpose and only disrupts the class activity. There are usually no winners in a confrontation. When a student does not need extra help in establishing personal control and learning the limits of permissable behavior, try to talk quietly to the student at the end of the period, during a free period, or before or after school. Tell the student what behavior you expect. Be positive; focus on the desirable consequences of cooperating rather than on what will happen if behavior is unacceptable.

When it is necessary to correct students for misbehavior, each situation has to be evaluated on its own merits. However, it is important to be consistent in the way problem behavior is handled. Listen to a student's explanation carefully, patiently, and sympathetically. There is doubtful effectiveness in severe discipline, in punishing a class for the misbehavior of one student, or in making the offending student write "I will not ..." 100 times. Lowering a student's grade for inappropriate behavior is also poor practice. The problem is not the student's achievement but the student's behavior. By lowering a grade, you are associating punishment with learning.

If you are sure a particular student is responsible for an act of inappropriate behavior, avoid forced confessions and apologies which only serve to encourage a student to lie. In many instances, you already know the facts. Tell the student you are aware of what was done, and that you do not want to see it repeated.

The longer you wait to assert control in a classroom, the more difficult it will be to establish it. Students sense which teachers will enforce control and which will not. Nevertheless, it is important to keep a sense of perspective and not challenge the perpetrator of every minor offense. You may be the only one annoyed, and sometimes situations become magnified out of all proportion. For example, you can overlook some whispering.

Who knows, the students may be talking about the subject matter. Be *certain* a student made an offensive comment or misbehaved before you take action that might cause a confrontation in class or put you on the defensive with the students. Decide when to go along with a joke. It is important to maintain your sense of humor; you will need it at times.

People sometimes associate control with rules and policies. However, it is important to establish only the rules and policies you intend to enforce. When a multitude of rules are in effect and you try to enforce all of them, you spend a great deal of your time doing so. On the other hand, rules that are not enforced serve to encourage students to challenge other rules.

Be cautious about giving students passes to leave the room. Generally, it is best not to give students passes to leave the room at the beginning of the period. You might say, "You had a chance between classes. Class is beginning now." If students ask for passes to leave the room in the middle of a period, tell them to wait a few minutes. Probably they won't ask again because you have made it clear you do not approve of their missing part of the class. When students request permission to leave the room near the end of the period, tell them to wait until the class is over.

If a class tends to create disciplinary problems, keep your eyes on the students until you establish pleasant yet firm discipline. It is inadvisable to turn your back on an unruly class, even to write on the chalkboard. Make a list of students who are inattentive in class. Work to get them involved. It may also be helpful in especially difficult situations to change a disruptive student's seat to one near you. By having control over each individual in class, you have control over the entire class.

Remember to sit in the back of the room when you have a guest speaker, show a film, or use a videotape. You will be better able to take care of problems from this vantage point than from the front of the room. In front of the class everyone can see you and will be disturbed as you indicate to one or two students that they need to change their behavior. Teachers are responsible for the conduct of students in their classrooms.

Among the most difficult interactions are those in which students deliberately challenge the teacher's authority. If teachers are to meet their professional responsibility, they must try to help students develop acceptable behavior and become involved in the learning process even if these students are uninterested and uncooperative.

■ Handling Cheating

Students' reasons for cheating are varied, and it is not always easy to decide how to handle such problems.

It is impossible to prevent cheating from occurring altogether, but there are measures that can be taken to minimize the problem.

When students respect a teacher and perceive that they are treated equitably, and when rapport is developed between students and the teacher, students are less likely to cheat than when any of the opposite conditions exist. Teachers are responsible for creating an environment that makes it difficult for students to cheat when taking a test. For example, the period during which a test is being given is not an appropriate time for teachers to concentrate on work at their desks to the extent that they are oblivious to students' actions. On the other hand, the teacher who walks around the room and peers over students' shoulders throughout a test period can be very annoying and distracting.

Especially in crowded classrooms, be sure that there is ample space around individual students. This will make it less easy for them to look at others' test papers. If it is difficult to provide sufficient space around students or if cheating is a problem, you may want to develop two different test formats by arranging the same questions in different order. Giving a test on short notice or springing a test may cause students to resent the teacher's actions and make it easier for them to rationalize their cheating by telling themselves it is justifiable.

When cheating is suspected, the teacher must act carefully. Accusing a student of dishonest behavior, in the absence of concrete evidence, will put you in an untenable position and may have a detrimental effect on the student's future actions. The situation can often be handled subtly. For example, a teacher might take the two identical papers of students who sit next to each other and write across them, as if on one sheet: "My, but it is unusual that your two papers are exactly alike." Nothing further may be required. It can be predicted that these particular students will be grateful that an issue was not made of the situation, and they are not likely to repeat the behavior in that teacher's class.

When public accusations and confrontations occur, both parties may emerge blemished regardless of who is right or wrong. Often relationships are strained for too long afterward. Even if a student has cheated, it is important that the incident not affect the student-teacher relationship the next day. The incident is over. Harboring resentment and suspicion is not conducive to a positive relationship.

If several members of a class are involved in cheating, never penalize the entire class for actions of a few by giving another test the next day or making an extra assignment. The infraction is not the responsibility of the entire class. In addition, evaluation and academic work should not be associated with punishment.

All teachers have classroom-control or cheating problems at some time during their careers. It is important not to dwell on the bad days and situations that you might have handled poorly. Instead, think of all the students who do not create problems and of all the good days and good lessons you have had.

Discipline Action Planning

Discipline problems in the classroom can be minimized when teachers establish a well-managed environment for effective discipline and develop and implement discipline action plans. A discipline action plan consists of written expectations of student behavior, identified rewards for students who behave appropriately, and established consequences for those students who do not behave appropriately.

Dennis indicated that teachers would be less subject to "burnout" and job dissatisfaction if they entered the classroom with realistic and preplanned expectations of acceptable student behavior and preplanned consequences for misbehavior that were made clear to students initially. This does *not* mean that a teacher should begin a new school term by reading and distributing rules for behavior — certainly *not* rules that begin with "You should not ..." What a negative tone this sets! Instead, students can help plan for effective discipline that will enhance the learning environment for them and the teaching environment for you.

At the beginning of a new school term you can work with the students to establish criteria for behavior in their class. Three to five *positive* guidelines for behavior are an appropriate number because these need to be stated in general terms to be applicable in a variety of situations. With your guidance the students might establish a list similar to this:

- Respect the rights and property of others.
- Be courteous to others.
- Be cooperative.
- Use good manners.
- Be prepared.

These should be labeled as to class and displayed prominently on a poster for all to see. Rewards and consequences can be established the same way. The sample Discipline Action Plan, shown on page 177, was adapted from one used by Dennis in her research.

Think about these questions as you plan your own approach for having effective classroom discipline:

1. What expected student behaviors were disregarded by the students making this Discipline Action Plan?
2. Which reward(s) would be the best for students who behaved appropriately? Why?
3. Which technique(s) would be the best for correcting a student's behavior? Why?

With present-day lifestyles, schools have to assume a larger role in teaching children to be responsible for *some* of their own education. Too often teachers cheat their students out of opportunities to think by answering their own questions if nobody answers immediately. Teachers can probe for answers or rephrase questions. Given the learning objectives, students often have excellent ideas for learning activities to help them achieve these objectives. In other words, students can help in the curriculum planning process.

The teacher who cleans the lab alone is also assuming responsibility that belongs to the students *and* the teacher. The teacher who thinks of the department as *ours* rather than *mine* is more likely to foster responsible behavior among students.

When a teacher always has a pencil, paper, or book ready for the students who forgot theirs, students will find out that irresponsibility is acceptable. Because employees who are late several times may lose their jobs, teachers who tolerate frequent tardiness are not helping students accept responsibility for their behavior. Basic skills, in one sense, are not only reading, writing, math, and science but also being punctual, courteous, and cooperative. The best way to teach responsibility is to expect responsible behavior of students.

Student Assumption of Responsibility

In assessing accountability in schools, standardized student achievement test scores are often used to determine the effectiveness of the educational system as well as the competence of individual teachers. This approach presents a fallacy because students should assume some responsibility for their learning, too. Continued transference of responsibility from students to teachers or situations causes students to conclude that they do not have to be responsible. Student acceptance of responsibility in the learning process is essential if students are to reach their maximum potential.

In the past, a major role of the family was to teach youth to be responsible citizens. Recent research findings show that first-born children are often given considerable responsibility for the care of younger siblings and for home management tasks. On the other hand, later-born children often develop the idea that someone else is more responsible for their actions than they are. It has been shown that there is a relationship between assumption of responsibilities at home and in school. In addition to ordinal position in the family and assumption of responsibilities at home, it has been found that assuming responsibility at school, not surprisingly, seems to be associated with number of siblings, self-motivation, and high grades.

Teacher Versus Student Responsibilities

Should the teacher be accountable for the student who does not want to learn and who does not attend school regularly? As was said previously, it is the teacher's responsibility to *try* to reach this type of student, but each student brings background factors to the class over which the teacher has no control. Home conditions, family attitudes toward education, aspiration level, academic ability, and self-concept are associated with motivation toward doing well in school. Teachers cannot and should not be held responsible for everything that happens in school. Everyone in a particular class has some responsibility toward what happens in that class.

The teacher has the responsibility of providing learning experiences to help the student achieve objectives, but the student has the responsibility of meeting the objectives. Students can be helped to assume responsibility in the learning process by establishing goals that lead to improved performance. Students may be allowed to select learning activities that interest them, but these activities should not interfere with other students' learning. No student has the right to bother others. Students may need help in learning to respect the rights of others. Students need to be responsible for self-discipline and self-control both in academic activities and personal conduct. They also need to accept the consequences for their decisions about their behavior.

Student Motivation and Assumption of Responsibility

In her dissertation, Douglas wrote about four groups of factors essential for effective motivation in the educational setting. One group consists of physical factors such as lighting, heating, air-conditioning, comfort, and seating arrangement. A second group contains teacher-related variables such as preparation for class and presentation of material that is neither too elementary nor too difficult. A third group includes social and emotional factors such as teacher enthusiasm, demonstrated respect and acceptance of individual students and varying points of view, and peer acceptance. A fourth group includes listening skills to improve interpersonal relationships. Because there is a relationship between motivation and student assumption of responsibility in the classroom, teachers' efforts toward motivating students are efforts which have positive and far-reaching paybacks.

Measuring Student Assumption of Responsibility in the Classroom

Douglas developed and administered the scale shown below to 198 students and 10 of their teachers. She found a high level of agreement between students' and teachers' scores. Interestingly, she found that students who had jobs rated themselves lower than did other students. Perhaps these students were learning the importance of assuming responsibility in employment situations. There is value in having students evaluate themselves regarding their assumption of responsibility in the classroom. It helps them become aware of behaviors expected of a responsible person.

References

Douglas, Carolyn Sue. "Assessment and Analysis of Student Assumption of Responsibility in the Classroom." A Dissertation in Home Economics, Texas Tech University, Lubbock, TX, May 1980.

Martin, Betty B. and Joan Quilling. *Positive Approaches to Classroom Discipline*. Home Economics Education Association, Washington, DC, 1981.

Name _____

Student Assumption of Responsibility in the Classroom Scale

Directions:

Keep the following definition in mind as you read and answer each of the statements below.

Definition: Responsibility involves doing something you know you are supposed to do without having to be told to do so.

The statements listed below are responsibilities a student might show in the classroom. For each statement, decide how often you believe the student you are rating shows the responsibility stated. Then, place a check in the appropriate column. There are no right or wrong answers. There are only your opinions.

Clerical Responsibilities	Always	Often	Sometimes	Seldom	Never
1. Brings necessary materials to class such as paper, pen, pencils, and assignments.					
2. Keeps books in good condition.					
3. Keeps graded papers in notebook.					
4. Corrects mistakes when papers are returned.					
5. Leaves school property in good condition.					
6. Uses own possessions such as books, paper, pen, and pencils.					
7. Writes neatly and legibly.					
8. Helps keep the classroom neat and clean.					
9. Brings a pass to class when tardy.					
10. Promptly returns papers that must be signed.					
11. Promptly returns borrowed items such as the teacher's reference books.					
12. Promptly takes care of fees.					

(Continued on next page)

Student Assumption of Responsibility in the Classroom Scale (continued)

Personal Responsibilities

	Always	Often	Sometimes	Seldom	Never
1. Uses available class time to work on assignments.					
2. Completes assignments on time.					
3. Promptly makes up work missed during absences.					
4. Brings other work to do after completing class work.					
5. Studies for tests.					
6. Asks questions when explanations are not understood.					
7. Uses sources allowed to complete work.					
8. Contributes to class discussions in a positive way.					
9. Is well groomed.					
10. Voluntarily comes for extra help from the teacher when needed.					
11. Is seated when the tardy bell rings.					
12. Is quiet when the tardy bell rings.					
13. Follows directions.					
14. Does work to the best of ability.					
15. Concentrates on the work of the class during the class period.					
16. Avoids disturbing others.					
17. Attends to personal business before class starts.					
18. Obeys school rules.					
19. Obeys class rules.					
20. Asks questions relating to topic.					
21. Accepts results of own behavior.					
22. Follows class routine willingly.					
23. Attends school regularly.					
24. Behaves when visitors are present.					
25. Speaks in a way that is easily heard.					

Relationship Responsibilities

	Always	Often	Sometimes	Seldom	Never
1. Respects the teacher.					
2. Respects the teacher's belongings.					
3. Waits for a turn for the teacher's help.					
4. Is courteous.					
5. Listens to others when they talk.					
6. Respects other students' belongings.					
7. Encourages other students to be quiet.					
8. Allows the teacher to settle problems.					
9. Helps other students understand information.					
10. Cooperates with the teacher.					
11. Cooperates with the students.					

FHA/HERO

Chapter 21

Future Homemakers of America/Home Economics Related Occupations (FHA/HERO) is a nonprofit national vocational organization for young men and women in home economics in public and private schools through grade 12. FHA chapters emphasize consumer and home-making education; HERO chapters emphasize preparation for jobs and careers in home economics occupations.

Future Homemakers of America/Home Economics Related Occupations is the only in-school organization with the family as its central focus. It is a vocational education student organization that functions as an integral part of the home economics education curriculum and operates within the school system. The organization provides opportunities for active participation at local, state, and national levels.

Future Homemakers of America/Home Economics Related Occupations encourages personal growth, leadership development, family and community involvement, and preparation for the multiple adult roles of wage earner, community leader, and family member. Chapter projects focus on a variety of contemporary youth concerns, including teen pregnancy, parenting, family relationships, substance abuse, peer pressure, nutrition and fitness, intergenerational interaction, and career exploration. Involvement in Future Homemakers of America/Home Economics Related Occupations offers members the opportunity to expand their leadership potential and develop *skills for life* — planning, goal setting, problem solving, decision making, and effective communication — necessary in the world of work and the home.

Mission

The mission of Future Homemakers of America/Home Economics Related Occupations is to promote personal growth and leadership development through home economics education. Focusing on the multiple roles of family member, wage earner, and community leader, members develop skills for life through:
- character development,
- creative and critical thinking,
- interpersonal communication,
- practical knowledge,
- vocational preparation.

Purposes

The purposes of Future Homemakers of America/Home Economics Related Occupations are to:
1. Provide opportunities for self-development and preparation for family and community living and for employment.
2. Strengthen the function of the family as the basic unit of society.
3. Encourage democracy through cooperative action in the home and community.
4. Encourage individual and group involvement in helping achieve worldwide brotherhood.
5. Institute programs promoting greater understanding between youth and adults.
6. Provide opportunities for decision making and for assuming responsibility.
7. Become aware of the multiple roles of men and women in today's society.
8. Develop interest in home economics, home economics careers, and related occupations.

Membership

Since its founding in 1945, Future Homemakers of America has involved over 8 million youth. It has a national membership of more than 281,000 young men and women joined in a network of 53 state associations including the District of Columbia, Puerto Rico, and the Virgin Islands. There are 11,000 local chapters.

Future Homemakers of America/Home Economics Related Occupations also has alumni and associate memberships to promote a strong bond between the FHA/HERO student organizations and the community, to act as a resource bank, and to increase the organization's visibility. Alumni and associate members use their talents and enthusiasm with local chapters to:
- Speak on careers or life experiences.
- Serve as judges.
- Serve on evaluation teams.
- Chaperone functions.
- Help organize special activities.
- Serve as a vocational home economics advisory committee member.

Why Have an FHA/HERO Chapter?

Future Homemakers of America/Home Economics Related Occupations helps support the entire school plan for student involvement in worthwhile activities, promotes community involvement, and even provides volunteer services for those in need. It helps promote student, administrative, and community ownership in the home economics program.

FHA/HERO Helps Teachers Help Students

The activities of an FHA/HERO chapter can enrich and extend the home economics curriculum by going beyond the physical limitations and time constraints of the classroom. Academic skills can be reinforced in a non-academic environment. The curriculum may be perceived to be more relevant by providing opportunities to show the relationships between home economics subject matter and real-life situations. Planning a chapter budget, serving nutritious snacks at meetings, and working with children and elders as volunteers reinforce concepts covered in class and provide opportunities to fine-tune skills developed in class.

In addition, teachers profit by having a chapter in these ways:
- There is a ready-made vehicle for teaching decision-making skills.
- There are additional opportunities to build rapport with students through positive interaction in a non-threatening situation.
- The organization helps motivate students and helps to improve attitudes toward school and learning.
- Student leaders emerge who can be helpful in classes, attract additional students to the program, and help promote home economics to parents, administrators, and community citizens.
- Excellent FHA/HERO materials can be used to enhance chapter and class activities, thus, extending the use of resources.
- There are increased opportunities for teaming with other professionals and demonstrating cooperative working relationships.
- Networking with other advisors provides a support system and cadre of educators who have similar interests and concerns.
- There are additional opportunities to promote home economics as a career.
- Teaching is easier and more fun.

Advantages of FHA/HERO for Students

Students profit from involvement in Future Homemakers of America/Home Economics Related Occupations in many ways. Some of the advantages for students are:
- A sense of belonging and purpose.
- Increased opportunities to develop leadership, citizenship, and social skills by serving as officers and committee members, by learning and practicing parliamentary procedure, and by widening their circle of friends.
- Greater understanding of themselves and their relationships with others.
- Many opportunities for learning to work cooperatively with others, for developing a sense of responsibility and commitment, and for exercising decision-making skills.
- The satisfaction of helping others, of performing community services, and of working with others toward common goals.
- Opportunities to attend out-of-town meetings and conferences that expand their life experiences.
- Opportunities to learn more about careers in home economics; to develop skills needed for the world of work; and to establish habits of punctuality, dependability, and cooperation necessary for employment.

- An awareness of the many rolls they have to play in society as members of families and communities and in employment situations.
- Experiences and participation in activities that help build self-confidence and enhance their self-concepts.

Future Homemakers of America/Home Economics Related Occupations often helps convince administrators of the value of the home economics program. It also helps you gain parental and community support for your programs.

The Co-curricular Approach

A co-curricular chapter usually operates in class, but it can meet outside of class during an activity period or after school. In the past, out-of-class chapters were most common, but today they are difficult to schedule because of busing, students caring for younger siblings after school, and student employment.

The co-curricular approach builds on class learnings and goes beyond curriculum requirements. It offers activities that strengthen academic skills. Originally, the co-curricular approach was referred to as the integrated approach because classwork and chapter activities are so closely intertwined. This integration results in meaningful and in-depth chapter activities.

Co-curricula chapter activities are initiated and planned by students, relate to one of the eight purposes of Future Homemakers of America/Home Economics Related Occupations listed on page 180, and provide incentives and recognition that go beyond class requirements. The co-curricular approach provides opportunities for favorable publicity that receive positive reactions in the community and from administrators.

Analysis of Different Structures

The diagrams of circles on page 183 illustrate how Future Homemakers of America/Home Economics Related Occupations and class activities can be separate without overlap, and how they can be integrated and structured in a co-curricula mode of operation.

Organization

In a home economics department with one teacher, the classes that meet each period of the school day constitute subchapters or mini-chapters that are organized separately. Each class chapter president or another designated officer becomes part of the school Executive Council that coordinates school and community-wide activities. The in-class structure can be modified to include students who are not presently enrolled in home economics, but have taken home economics in the past. Sometimes a mini-chapter to accommodate these students can meet before or after school or during lunch or an activity period. Former students may be able to meet during their study halls with a class chapter that is organized the same period.

The chart on page 184 illustrates how in-class chapters might be organized in a three teacher department. The two classes that meet first period with different teachers come together and form one mini-chapter. Only one home economics class is scheduled fifth period so it constitutes a mini-chapter by itself. Teachers share the responsibilities of being advisers for the mini-chapters. In this example, Ms. Green serves as adviser for only two mini-chapters because she is a first-year teacher and because she advises and coaches the cheerleaders.

In some schools, all students enrolled in home economics classes are considered members of Future Homemakers of America or Home Economics Related Occupations. However, members who pay their dues may be called affiliated or voting members. Because some students find it difficult to pay dues, chapters may have fundraisers to pay the dues of all members. Working on the fundraiser can help develop a cohesive and cooperative group.

Advantages of the Co-curricular Approach

In-class chapters provide an ideal means for enriching subject matter covered in class. An individual representing a particular ethnic group might describe family life in that culture, bring representative clothing to class, show pictures of festive occasions, and prepare or serve a typical food item. In a HERO chapter class meeting a panel of employers might discuss characteristics they look for in a potential employee.

In *Techniques For Starting and Maintaining FHA/HERO Chapters* published by the Home Economics Education Association in 1988, the authors have identified the following advantages of the co-curricula approach:
- Conflicts with work and after-school activities are eliminated.
- The relationship between chapter activities and curriculum is more obvious.
- Communication with members is easier since members are more readily available.
- Because every student who is enrolled is a potential member, there is generally greater membership potential.
- The ratio of male and female members can become more balanced.

Analysis of Different FHA/HERO Structures

CLASS   **FHA/HERO**

- Chapter operates as a separate entity.
- Little or no evidence of any relationship between class work and chapter activities.
- Class members and FHA/HERO members find it difficult to explain what FHA/HERO is and its relationship to the home economics program.
- Class extended learning experiences and FHA/HERO experiences have no relationship to each other.
- School and community action by FHA/HERO is independent from classes.

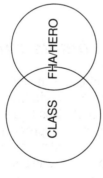

CLASS   **FHA/HERO**

- Class chapter action related somewhat, but there is little or no transfer of learning.
- There are officers for the school chapter only.
- FHA/HERO organization as a structure is separate and not interrelated with classes.
- FHA/HERO experiences may be the same as class extended experiences.
- School and community action may include some joint action of FHA/HERO and classes.

CLASS   **FHA/HERO**

- FHA/HERO is presented as a part of home economics in each class.
- Classes each period organize a mini-chapter and plan chapter-class activities. These chapters are a part of the total FHA/HERO school chapter.
- Each class chapter elects officers and a representative to the Executive Council.
- Class chapters usually hold bi-weekly or monthly meetings.
- The total school chapter may meet once or twice a year.
- Class chapter action extends into the school and community.

FHA/HERO
CLASS

- FHA/HERO is presented as a part of home economics in each class.
- Chapters operate totally within classes.
- All chapter functions tie in with class activities.
- Each class period has independent officers.
- All meetings are planned and held in class.
- Action extends beyond classes in to the school and commuity.

FHA/HERO In-Class Structure for Multi-Teacher Department

Class Periods	Teachers			Mini-chapters	Advisers
	Ms. Jones	Mr. Smith	Ms. Green		
1st	Class	Class	Planning	Ms. Jones & Mr. Smith's classes	Ms. Jones
2nd	Class	Planning	Class	Ms. Jones & Ms. Green's classes	Ms. Green
3rd	Planning	Class	Class	Mr. Smith & Ms. Green's classes	Mr. Smith
4th	Class	Lunch	Class	Ms. Jones & Ms. Green's class	Ms. Jones
5th	Lunch	Class	Lunch	Ms. Green's classes	Mr. Smith
6th	Class	Class	Study Hall	Ms. Jones & Mr. Smith's classes	Ms. Jones
7th	Class	Study Hall	Class	Ms. Jones & Ms. Green's classes	Ms. Green
8th or Activity Period	Department Chair Business	FHA/HERO for former class members	Cheerleader Advising & Coaching	Former class members	Mr. Smith

- More students have opportunities to participate and assume leadership roles.
- Members often continue to enroll in home economics to maintain their membership.

Starting a Chapter

The first step in beginning a new chapter is to obtain an affiliation form from your state adviser. Members affiliate by paying local, state, and national dues, but this may be accomplished through chapter fundraising projects designed to earn money to pay every member's dues. In some schools every student in home economics classes is an affiliated member. Only affiliated members may participate in state and national activities.

As soon as members are affiliated nationally, they begin receiving their own copies of *Teen Times*. You will receive materials, too, to help you in your role as adviser. See pages 185-186 for a list of helpful resources for starting and maintaining an FHA/HERO chapter.

Gaining Administrative Support

The most effective means of getting and maintaining support from your administrators is to obtain their input in the form of ideas and suggestions and to keep them informed of your progress and activities. Invite administrators to attend meetings, to be honorary members, to participate in panel discussions, and to serve on the Home Economics Advisory Council. Administrators are sure to support activities that help build students' self-concepts, enhance and extend classroom learning, and promote good relationships in the community. Remember, too, that your enthusiasm for FHA/HERO can be contagious.

Building Membership

The co-curricular approach offers membership to a large number of students. Tell students how participation in the organization will benefit them personally. Help the members plan interesting and exciting meetings. Help them develop effective recruitment techniques such as one-on-one personal invitations to join, telephone calls to prospective members, and involvement of many members in chapter activities. Ideas for recruitment bulletin boards are found on page 118.

Some people object to the name "Future Homemakers of America." It may be up to you to explain that everyone who is a member of a family is a homemaker — male and female. You can point out that with the very large proportion of working women today, homemaking skills such as parenting, managing resources, and making nutritious food choices are life skills everyone needs to survive.

Some additional suggestions for building membership follow:

- Have a contest to develop effective recruitment materials and award the winner free membership or a free trip to a regional meeting.
- Implement a "Big-Brother/Big Sister" type program for freshmen and transfer students.
- Publicize meetings by having members present "commercials" over the school PA system with the daily announcements.
- Develop a showcase highlighting photos of students at events during the last school year.
- Show a videotape of chapter members participating in appealing activities such as community activities and state meetings.

The Role of an Adviser

An FHA/HERO adviser should be just that — an adviser, not a decision maker. Sometimes as the adviser you need to say "no" to protect students from failure. In your more mature judgment, you may realize a proposed plan is unrealistic. You may also realize that students have to be allowed to implement a particular plan to learn from trial and error. And sometimes students succeed in spite of your negative predictions — that hopefully you have kept to yourself.

An adviser, then, is supportive and helps students develop decision-making skills. An adviser is a facilitator whom students can depend on for guidance. An adviser does not assume the leadership role but helps students develop leadership abilities. Some suggestions for helping students develop leadership skills follow:

- Encourage officers to have written agendas for meetings.
- Assist students in planning and conducting efficient business meetings.
- Utilize committees to facilitate programs or conduct the business of the organization.
- Offer suggestions but have students select their own programs for meetings.

- Help members develop and later evaluate a plan of work and budget for the year.
- Encourage students to make recommendations in writing to the officers elected for the next year.
- Teach students how to write news releases about chapter activities and encourage them to do so.
- Have students take turns leading discussions at chapter meetings.
- Encourage chapter members to volunteer time to worthwhile community activities and organizations.
- Guide students in planning and implementing a special semester event such as a party for elders in a residential care facility.
- Help members plan, carry out, and evaluate fundraising projects.
- Arrange for members to introduce guest speakers and panel members at chapter meetings.
- Have students contact, arrange for, and write thank-you notes to guests.
- Have members participate in and lead panel discussions for meetings.
- Structure group activities so group members work with a variety of different personality types over time.
- Delegate organization responsibilities to involve as broad a base of the membership as possible.

Advisers are the backbone of FHA/HERO, and they make or break the chapter. Student members will need more help and guidance from you at first than they will later. If you are doing most of the work, you are limiting students' potential for developing leadership, organizational, and management skills. It is important to pull back and encourage the students to take the lead.

The best advisers make their students look good by seeing that they get recognition for work well done. Secure educators who serve as youth organization advisers have enough self-confidence themselves to be able to give confidence to students through member participation in positive and successful experiences and favorable publicity.

Sources of Help

A variety of resources are available for FHA/HERO advisers and members. Some of these follow:

- *Handbook for Youth-Centered Leadership* — the most important resource for each FHA/HERO chapter. This handbook has been especially designed to help members and advisers organize and manage a chapter, plan projects, and develop leadership in members. Topics covered include starting and running a chapter; building membership, public relations, and fundraising techniques; down-to-earth management tips for both in-class and out-of-class chapters; simplified tips for planning projects; ideas for team building, officer selection, and committee work; and reference sections on ceremonies, traditions, policies, history, and chapter resources. Directions provide chapter members with experiences in individual, cooperative, and competitive activities. The primary focus is how to run a co-curricular chapter and how to maximize student involvement.

- *Techniques for Starting and Maintaining FHA/HERO Chapters* — a highly recommended publication which also describes many available resources. It is available from the Home Economics Education Association, 1201 Sixteenth Street, N.W., Washington, DC 20036.
- *The Adviser* — a newsletter sent to chapter advisers three times a year. It includes tips for successful chapter management, an ideas exchange, national updates, information about upcoming issues of *Teen Times*, and other useful adviser information.
- *Teen Times* — the national member magazine which is designed to meet the interests and concerns of FHA/HERO members. Project ideas, discussion topics, and leadership ideas are included. Copies are sent to chapter advisers for distribution to all affiliated chapter members four times a year.
- *Guide to Student Fundraising; 129 Ways to Raise Money* — a publication which assists chapters with fundraising projects by showing how to design a project for a specific chapter, plan each phase carefully, promote the projects, and follow through to get the desired results. The fundraising ideas detailed include those to help FHA/HERO members use home economics skills for profit, fund group activities, attract new members, gain recognition, learn new skills, and provide a service to the school and community. It discusses the question: Why raise money? It outlines how to select and plan fundraisers, how to promote the fundraising event, and gives ten tips for assuring a successful fundraising event.
- *Bylaws* — a booklet which provides the governing rules of Future Homemakers of America, Inc. It enables chapter members and advisers to function within the official structure of the organization.
- *Public Relations Manual* — a workbook which gives tips on writing news releases, working with radio and television, giving speeches, and developing a public relations and image building plan for local chapters. It

was developed as a companion piece to the videotape, *Stand Out From the Crowd*, designed specifically to help local chapters plan and carry out local public relations programs.
- *Techniques Workbook* — a booklet which provides over 10 ready-to-use ideas for chapter involvement. It gives ideas for getting members off to a good start, dividing large groups, designing and evaluating workshops, drawing out group ideas, and developing experiences through a variety of activities.
- *Adviser Training Manual* — a publication developed primarily for those who are training home economics teachers to be FHA/HERO advisers. It contains workshop techniques, worksheets, and transparency masters. Activities are grouped according to four skills needed by advisers: understanding organizations, establishing co-curricular chapters, guiding youth-centered activities, and using resources. The manual contains information on establishing adviser training networks, FHA/HERO research priorities, and lists of completed research and articles written about the organization.
- *Skills for Life* — a 10-minute, 16 mm film which shows what membership in Future Homemakers of America means to three young people. The film is narrated by Judy Woodruff, a noted news commentator and former FHA/HERO member. It is appropriate for many audiences, including students, teachers, administrators, parents, and community groups.
- *STAR Events Manual* — a publication which includes eligibility and participation requirements and rating sheets for each of the STAR Events. Guidelines change occasionally. Write to your state adviser for current guidelines or send for the most current manual.
- *Program Handbooks* — handbooks for national programs, such as Student Body, Financial Fitness, Leaders at Work in Food Science, and Power of One. Some are free of charge.

For more information on resources from the national organization, write for the organization's publications catalog at the following address:

Future Homemakers of America, Inc.
1910 Association Drive
Reston, VA 22091
(703) 476-4900

**FUTURE HOMEMAKERS OF AMERICA/HOME ECONOMICS RELATED OCCUPATIONS
(FHA/HERO) CLUB MEETING SCORECARD**

Presiding Officer's Name _____ Date of Meeting _____

DIRECTIONS: The FHA/HERO meeting has been divided into 5 sections that have been subdivided into individual items. Each item has been assigned a maximum of 5 possible points. Score each item with 1 to 5 points as appropriate. The total from all the section items will give a sub-score. Total the 5 sub-scores for the TOTAL SCORE.

	Possible Score	Actual Score

1. OPENING CEREMONY INCLUDED:
  a. Meeting began promptly (5 points)
  b. Attendance taken (5 points)
  c. Creed said in unison (5 points)
  d. Meeting ended on time (5 points)
COMMENTS:
	20	

2. BUSINESS SESSION INCLUDED:
  a. Written agenda distributed (5 points)
  b. Minutes read (5 points)
  c. Parliamentary Procedure used (5 points)
  d. Officers' reports given (5 points)
  e. New business (5 points)
  f. Different members involved (5 points)
 	
COMMENTS:
	30	

3. PROGRAM INCLUDED:
  a. Introduction given (5 points)
  b. Chapter members seemed interested (5 points)
  c. Educational ideas/skills presented (5 points)
  d. Most member's needs met (5 points)
COMMENTS:
	20	

4. RECREATION INCLUDED:
  a. Leader prepared (5 points)
  b. Everyone participated (5 points)
  c. Sportsmanship exhibited (5 points)
  d. Members seemed to enjoy it (5 points)
COMMENTS:
	20	

5. REFRESHMENTS INCLUDED:
  a. 5 points if served
  b. 10 points if served and nutritious
  c. 0 points if not served
COMMENTS:
	10	

Adapted from scorecard developed by Catrennia Williamson, Lubbock, Texas.

	TOTAL SCORE	100	

PART 4

You, the Educator

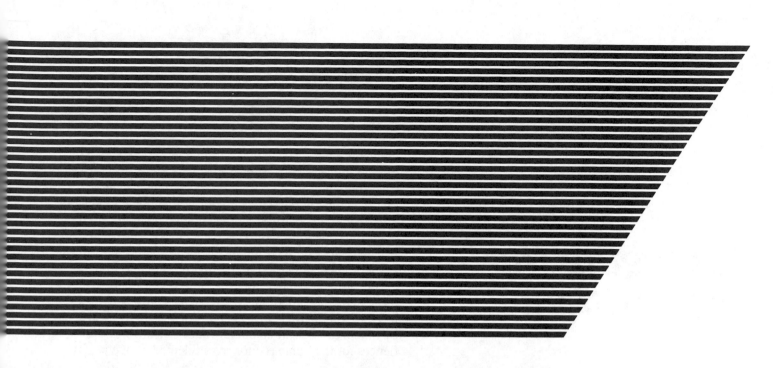

Managing the Department

Chapter 22

In the business world, management is stressed so that businesses can operate smoothly, maintain standards, and balance the budget. Good management practices are important in home economics classrooms for the same reasons. Effective management helps the teacher facilitate classwork and learning and run the department smoothly. This chapter focuses on two areas of management: functional management for effective teaching, and administrative management dealing with records, reports, and finances.

Functional Management

In the home economics classroom, teachers have the opportunity to implement and illustrate many managerial processes. Students who have had an opportunity to work in an attractive department that is efficient and conducive to work will be able to see theory put into practice.

Establishing Good Relations Within the School

Home economics teachers have a responsibility to see that the students and department are not exploited, but many requests can be fulfilled while providing enriching experiences. Common requests are to furnish refreshments for faculty meetings, to prepare a special dinner for the school board, to make draperies for other areas of the school, to repair or launder athletic uniforms, to make robes for the choir or costumes for a play, and to perform a myriad of other tasks. The teacher will have to use good judgment in deciding when to grant or refuse a request. Certainly, the home economics department should not become a service center to the extent that important, planned learning activities have to be curtailed. However, many of the jobs requested by others can be carried out as valuable learning experiences for the home economics students involved.

Students can take turns serving refreshments at meetings, and a small group of students can plan and set the table to facilitate quick service. Appropriate foods can be prepared earlier in the year during a class when procedures for storage and freezing are taught. Students who complete their laboratory assignments faster than others can be meaningfully involved by working on special service projects. For example, students making costumes for a play may also have an opportunity to do some historical research or to apply knowledge of fabric characteristics or of clothing as an expression of identity. Assembly-line techniques used in commercial clothing construction and other needle trades can be used to produce many similar items, such as choir robes.

Organizing and Maintaining Laboratory Space

During the course of a day, many different students use the home economics department facilities. It is important that each group leave the equipment and other resources in good order and condition so that subsequent groups can proceed with their work as planned. It is helpful to post a list of procedures for using department facilities where it can easily be seen. In this way, home economics classes and other groups who use the facilities will know what is expected in the way of leaving the department in order. Make the poster of guidelines for using the department large and attractive with a catchy title that will encourage people to be cooperative.

Labeling cupboards, drawers, and shelves makes it easier to keep equipment in its proper place. Sometimes numbers or dots of different colors can be painted on items to designate the unit kitchens in which they belong. By using plain dinnerware of varying colors for different kitchens, the dishes can be combined for special occasions; afterward, they can easily be returned to their respective units.

Other suggestions that facilitate keeping the department orderly, attractive, and efficient follow:

- Develop a checkout and return system for books, materials, and equipment borrowed by both students and teachers.
- Have a box or drawer that serves as a lost-and-found, and have students check there for misplaced items.
- Provide space near the door for students to leave clothing and books that will not be needed.
- Have duplicate cleaning supplies and equipment so that housekeeping tasks can be performed quickly.
- Conceal supplies and materials needed for future activities by using a decorative screen or one that can double as a bulletin board.
- Put instructional materials in one designated place, once they have been used, so that students, assistants, or aides will know to return them.
- Plan lessons so that more than one class can use the equipment, materials, and supplies while they are out. (This is particularly helpful with food and nutrition classes.)
- As much as possible, repair or replace worn items as quickly as possible.

Most schools require an annual inventory of equipment, utensils, and supplies on hand near the end of the academic year. Usually, forms for this purpose are provided for teachers to complete and turn in. They are kept on file in an administrative office. It is advisable to make duplicates and to keep at least one copy of the inventory in the home economics department. Students can help take inventory, and this activity can be related to on-the-job experiences and clarification of principles of storage and efficient management.

Preparing and Using Professional Files

One of the home economics teacher's most valuable resources should be the files. Materials in the departmental files when a teacher comes to a school, visual aids made with school supplies, and those items ordered in the name of the school are public property.

They should be left in the department if a teacher changes positions. However, obsolete materials should be discarded. Materials that a teacher may buy with personal funds or make with personal supplies and those acquired in college classes belong to the individual teacher.

The files usually contain professional reports and records, lesson and unit plans, teacher-made and commercial teaching aids, newspaper and magazine articles, booklets, pictures, information sheets made available through the Extension Service, and any other materials that are helpful in classroom teaching and individualizing instruction. Whether the teacher is revising an established file or beginning a new one, the filing system should ensure quick location and easy replacement of materials.

Filing Systems

Select a filing system to which folders can be added logically without having to rearrange the established sequence. In an alphabetical arrangement, an extra folder can be slipped in place easily or the materials in one folder can be subdivided into additional categories. No two folders should have the same title. When a numerical system is used, folders are initially placed in alphabetical order and numbered accordingly. As additions or subdivisions are made, numbers are either added at the end of each section or decimal points or letters are added to the original designation, such as 12.1, 12.2, or 12A, 12B. A folder designated "miscellaneous" should either be put in sequence alphabetically or placed at the end of a section. When such a procedure is employed, there is less tendency to fill the folder than when it appears in front.

■ Labels

Labels or highlighter pens of various colors can be used to designate broad areas included in the file, such as child development, clothing and textiles, and career education. The labels may be word processed or typed so that the general subject appears in capital letters or is underscored.

■ Coding

Coding an item facilitates its return to its proper folder. If all materials are coded in the same easy-to-see place, such as the upper right-hand corner of the page, filing can be done quickly. The coding may be placed on a small piece of the colored label used to designate that subject. If an alphabetical filing system has been

191

selected, abbreviations such as CD, C & T, and CE may be used. (See the preceding section.) It is helpful to include on the file folder label any abbreviation used in coding. If two areas could have the same abbreviation, such as consumer education and career education, carry the abbreviation one letter further — CoE and CaE — to minimize confusion. Subheadings may be written out or shortened in code, provided no other folder contains the same abbreviation. If a numerical system is used, coding is very simple, since 1.1, 1.2, and 1.3 would indicate the exact folder to which an item should be returned. Since coding is a time-consuming task, students may be able to help.

■ Cross-referencing

Often an item can be filed logically in one of several folders. A leaflet entitled *Birthday Cakes for Tots* could be placed under child development, food and nutrition for special occasions, baking, or several other headings. Once a decision has been made about where to file a specific item, reference can be made to it in other folders. This cross reference can be recorded by writing on the folder itself, or on some durable material in it, "Also see ... for ...." Name specifically the item to which reference is made so that time will not be wasted by examining an entire folder of materials.

■ Index

An index is to a file what a computer or card catalog is to a library. The index should be double- or triple-spaced so additions can be made to it without retyping. It is advisable to indicate the color designating each area and any abbreviations used. The pages of the index can be preserved by putting them in sheets of plastic. Using an index is more efficient than looking through a drawer full of file folders. Indexes can save time for teachers, students, and aides.

Using Student Assistants and Teacher's Aides

If a school does not have a system for utilizing student assistants, it may be possible to start such a program, perhaps through chapters of Future Home-makers of America/Home Economics Related Occupations or Future Teachers of America. In some schools, students are assigned as assistants to a specific teacher. They earn one-half unit of credit in office management or clerical practice and are assigned grades for their work.

It is advantageous to have a student assistant who has skills in typing, filing, and operating business machines, as well as some background in home economics. There also are many advantages in selecting a student assistant who has previously been in the teacher's classes but who is not currently enrolled in one. This student will be familiar with the procedures used in the department, with the location of equipment and teaching materials, and with the subject matter. If the student is not in a home economics class while serving as a student assistant, the possibility of confidences being revealed to others is minimized. More work can be accomplished if the student assistant is available during the teacher's planning period than when the teacher is in class.

Teacher's aides are widely used in schools today. Usually they are chosen because they like working with people and have competencies that enable them to perform tasks that free teachers from routine work of a paraprofessional nature. Very often those teachers who are able to think of ways to use a teacher's aide are the ones who receive the most help.

The services of both student assistants and teacher's aides can be utilized in typing letters, reports, assignment sheets and handouts to be photocopied, and materials for making transparencies. However, some school administrators request that neither teacher's assistants nor teacher's aides type or grade tests. Their services may be used in making media such as posters, bulletin boards, flannel boards, flip charts, and audio and video tapes. They can set up displays, prepare foods for the supply table, develop composite market orders, partially prepare materials for a demonstration, check students' lockers or tote trays, straighten supply cupboards, file materials, and help take inventories.

In schools where neither student assistants nor teacher's aides are available, there are other alternatives available to the teacher. Students may be able to prepare home economics materials in other classes, such as typing or art, or in school-related clubs. If students are permitted to perform certain tasks traditionally carried out by the teacher, they will help lighten the teacher's workload and at the same time gain valuable experience.

Administrative Management

Organized reports and budgets, although not usually considered to be the most exciting and creative aspects of teaching, are essential to a well-run home economics department. Once a functional system is developed, it is usually easy to maintain.

Keeping Records and Preparing Reports

Accurate and detailed records provide information you can use to document the accomplishments and annual reports that affect the future status of the department. You can use the information to evaluate student progress and to manage the budget in an objective manner. In addition, you are able to evaluate the curriculum and teaching strategies implemented during the year.

It is helpful to keep a file of newspaper clippings and pictures pertaining to activities of the home economics department. Date the articles, indicate the paper they were taken from, and record the names of people appearing in photographs. Students can be responsible for doing this and for writing brief reports summarizing special activities. The reports should identify the event being described and answer these questions — who, what, where, when, and why. A student, perhaps an FHA/HERO member, may be designated as the official department photographer. Natural-looking, unposed snapshots with not more than five persons are most acceptable. At the end of the school year, articles and pictures can be used to provide evidence of departmental accomplishments.

It is advisable to keep a log in which conferences with students and contacts with parents are recorded. Each entry can be brief, including the date, the nature of the meeting, and the main points covered. It is also important to keep a record of the instructional units and the time devoted to each. When reports are due at the end of the school year and plans are made for the next year, this information will be readily available. For future reference, the following should also be on file:

- The number of students enrolled in various home economics courses.
- Class roll and grade books.
- Plan books, including objectives and concepts covered in each course and the length of time devoted to each subject area.
- Records of activities, programs, and achievements relating to FHA/HERO chapters.
- Number of parent/guardian/spouse contacts made.
- Summary of types of extended learning experiences completed and descriptions or examples of one or two.
- Descriptions of one or two new and innovative ideas incorporated into the home economics program that year.
- Copies of annual reports.
- Evaluation devices and test items that can be revised for future use.
- Evaluations of films and the guide questions or follow-up activities used with them as well as with videotapes, filmstrips, skits, and reading assignments.

- Expenditures made in previous years and during the present year.
- Needs for maintenance, repair, and replacement.
- Inventory records of equipment, supplies, videotapes, software, textbooks, and other teaching aids.

The financial reimbursement received by a school and the reputations of both the school and a teacher may be affected by the accuracy and punctuality of reports, particularly an annual report. Reports may be your only contact with the central office administrators; therefore, it is important that information be reported accurately, clearly, concisely, and on time.

Managing Finances

When preparing the budget for the department, it is necessary to allow for repairs and replacements. It is a good idea to keep notes of what is needed as the school year progresses, since you must be prepared to justify all expenditures that are planned.

Involving students in making up the budget helps them realize that the department is theirs as well as their teachers' and can be a valuable learning experience in money-management concepts. In working with the budget, it should become apparent to students that the expenditures per individual are greater in smaller classes than in larger ones. This fact can be related to the cost per person of preparing meals for one or two individuals as compared with preparing foods in larger quantities. When prices are charged for products made and services rendered by students in home economics classes, it is usually required that any profits go back into the program. With guidance, students can help decide how these funds will be reinvested.

During economic downturns, there is a need to keep tight control over departmental expenses. Some teachers are hoping to operate on last year's department budget when cuts are being made in school, district, and state-wide budgets. The problem is compounded when trying to maintain a quality program and increase student enrollment in home economics classes. Thinking of different ways to do things more economically is likely to be a top priority. Some of the following suggestions may be helpful.

- Investigate whether repairs on equipment can be made free of charge by others in school, such as technical education classes or the custodial staff.
- Visit local businesses such as department stores, florists, fabric stores, and other specialty shops to request materials such as fabric remnants and swatches, wallpaper books, rug and upholstery samples, flowers, and ribbons that can be used as teaching aids.

- Save and use manufacturers' coupons when buying supplies, household products, and food for the department.
- Photocopy handouts and student worksheets so both sides of a sheet of paper are used, if the material is readable.
- Use free videotapes, filmstrips, and films rather than give a demonstration to show food-preparation principles and techniques for expensive lessons in an area such as meat cookery.
- Arrange for food demonstrations to be given by home economists from utility companies and by personnel from bakeries, specialty food stores, and catering services.
- Try to secure donations of food or other materials from local businesses.
- Encourage students to think of and use less expensive substitutes for ingredients in recipes, such as store brands instead of nationally advertised brands, crunchy cereals in place of nuts, and canned cheese soup for cheddar cheese sauce.
- Shop for specials in stores if you have the time and if you are not restricted to purchasing supplies from a designated store.

- Identify stores that give school discounts.
- Obtain certain foods needed in quantity, such as dried milk, through the school cafeteria.
- Buy lower-priced seasonal foods in quantity if storage facilities are available.
- Grow herbs that can be used in cooking and as garnishes, and that also make the department attractive. Use garbage such as avocado seeds and the tops of pineapples to grow decorative plants.

Sometimes students ask if they can collect money to buy expensive food items or bring extra foods to use in meal preparation. Teachers should realize that some students may feel uncomfortable because they are unable to contribute, but they would be reluctant to say so. Sometimes students volunteer to bring surplus foods grown at home. Check the school policy to determine whether student contributions of this nature are allowed.

Taking advantage of opportunities to implement good management practices in operating a classroom and department pays dividends in the long run. Once you have invested the time needed to establish good management practices, you have more time to devote to other professional activities.

Selecting Reading Materials

Chapter 23

Among the most important tasks any teacher undertakes is selecting reading materials and guiding students in choosing them to use in classwork, to complete assignments, and to carry out individual and group projects. Because students differ greatly in their reading abilities, their background experiences, and their needs, you will want to provide a variety of reading materials from which students can choose. The concerned teacher will have enough familiarity with the materials and the students to offer guidance to individuals when they are making selections. When a number of students read a variety of sources, they are able to share with each other several ideas and viewpoints, thus enriching the classroom experience.

Evaluating Written Materials

Frequently when teachers are asked to select textbooks and reference materials, they don't know which features to evaluate. One technique that may be used effectively is to select two or three concepts that should be in a text or reference of this type in order to establish criteria for evaluating the coverage of these topics and for comparing the available books. The criteria may be used to formulate a checklist, rating scale, or list of questions to which the evaluator responds by making a judgment based on a continuum. Totaling scores on a continuous scale will provide some measure of objectivity. After the one or two books have been selected that rate highest on the chosen concepts, these texts can be examined in their entirety.

Examining the authorship, copyright date, and publisher's data about a textbook can furnish valuable information. The specific intent of the authors and their point of view should be clear to the teacher after reading the foreword, preface, or introduction. If the book is a revised edition, it is advisable to determine the extent of revision by noting changes in the table of contents, illustrations, format, and several selected pages. A brief discussion of other points to consider when selecting textbooks and reference materials follows.

Subject Matter

The subject matter covered in books and other reference materials must be compatible with the conceptual framework and behavioral objectives established for the course or courses in which the materials will be used. In addition, the proportion of material devoted to various topics needs to be well balanced in relation to the phases to be covered in class. Analyzing the table of contents in a textbook or the major headings in handout material should provide insight into whether the reference work is compatible with the course of study.

The subject needs to be applicable to the geographic area in which it will be used. Material with special appeal to students living in one area of the country will have limited appeal to students living in another region.

Illustrations, too, must be chosen so that students in a variety of geographic situations can relate to them.

Of course, the subject matter, as well as the illustrations should be up-to-date. The presentation must be reliable and authoritative without causing students to feel they are being talked down to or lectured. Written material that seems to say, "This is the only way to do it," will have little appeal and acceptance. More than one point of view should be expressed on controversial issues, and both the advantages and disadvantages of the alternatives explored. Moralizing and value judgments have no place in reference material if it is to be well received by the majority of young people today. Material must be appropriate for the age group that will use it, and must make provision for individual differences among students. As with graphic illustrations, verbal illustrations such as problems, examples, and case studies should be balanced as to race, ethnicity, and gender.

Difficulty in understanding concepts increases as concepts become less concrete and more abstract. The less factual and more abstract concepts are, the more difficult the material is to read and comprehend. *Family* can be an abstract concept. A simple definition of family does not clarify the concept. It is only after much reading, study, and experience that the concept of family becomes clearer.

Reading Level and Writing Style

Studies have shown that when there is a terse writing style, when ideas are presented too compactly, and when the vocabulary is technical, students are discouraged from reading assigned materials. These variables contribute to reading difficulty which affects the comprehension level.

Naturally the reading level and vocabulary have to be appropriate for the students who will use the material. However, material can be written in very simple language and still incorporate the elements of critical thinking. Words that are above the general vocabulary level of the students can be used if the words are clearly defined and used in a context in which their meaning is obvious. In fact, incorporating new words into students' vocabularies is an inherent part of teaching all conceptual areas. A short glossary of terms or a list of words to define may be helpful.

The publisher's materials that are used to promote a textbook usually indicate the general age group for which a textbook is designed. Although specific reading levels designated by grades in school are not generally given, the publisher furnishes valuable information relating to the overall audience for whom the textbook is best suited.

Written materials that are too far above or too far below students' reading levels can be a "turn-off" to students. Generally, short words and sentences are indicative of lower reading levels, whereas long words and long, more complicated sentence structures are found in materials with a higher reading level.

There are a number of tests available that can assist you in estimating the reading level of written material. The Flesch, Fry, Dale-Chall, Danielson-Brian, and Farr-Jenkins-Paterson tests provide fairly accurate assessments of reading level. They have the disadvantage of being somewhat tedious to compute. However, there are computer programs available that compute reading levels quickly.

A rough estimate of grade level can be obtained quickly by using word length and sentence length as indicators:

- Compute the average number of words per sentence in a sample of 100 words.
- Count the number of words having three or more syllables. Do not count the following: proper names; combinations of short, easy words such as *bookkeeper*, and verb forms which are three syllables because of -*ed* or -*es* endings, such as *created* and *trespasses*.
- Add the two figures and multiply by 4/10 (0.4). For example, if there are 3 difficult words (three or more syllables) in the 100-word sample, and the average sentence contains 13 words, the computation is $3 + 13 = 16 \times 0.4 = 6.4$ grade reading level.

Format and Organization

A two-column page of material is easier to read than one wide column. The type should be large and clear enough to be read easily. The paper should not reflect light unduly but should have sufficient gloss to keep it clean. The durability of a book and its thickness and shape have to be considered. A textbook that is overly thick may have a negative psychological effect on students. Books that are unusual in size and shape may be difficult to carry and store on shelves.

Valuable to teachers and students are materials that suggest learning experiences; these activities may relate to general concepts or particular topics in the texts. They provide ideas for the teacher and encourage students to delve further into those areas in which they have special needs or interests. Projects to be carried out at school, in the home, and in the community may be suggested. Case studies, teaching aids, and thought-provoking questions for discussion may be proposed. The learning experiences suggested should appeal to students at various achievement levels and should help the teacher individualize instruction.

TEXTBOOK EVALUATION FORM

Directions: For the textbook you are reviewing, circle the appropriate number by each statement (5 = Strongly Agree, 4 = Agree, 3 = Neutral, 2 = Disagree, 1 = Strongly Disagree). Compute a total score for each textbook reviewed and use the total score for comparison purposes. Pay particular attention to the subtotal for each category, particularly "Appropriateness."

	SA	A	N	D	SD
Appropriateness and Scope					
The author's point of view is acceptable to the school and community.	5	4	3	2	1
The author's point of view is in agreement with the home economics program philosophy.	5	4	3	2	1
The content is at the appropriate reading level.	5	4	3	2	1
The content covers a range of appropriate objectives/competencies/achievement indicators of the home economics course/program.	5	4	3	2	1
SUBTOTAL _____					
Accuracy					
The author is qualified to write the book.	5	4	3	2	1
The content is up-to-date and timely.	5	4	3	2	1
The content will not quickly become outdated.	5	4	3	2	1
The content is accurate.	5	4	3	2	1
The content is sufficient to cover fundamental areas.	5	4	3	2	1
SUBTOTAL _____					
Format					
Attractive format with an appropriate mix of text copy and illustrations.	5	4	3	2	1
Organization of content will facilitate learning.	5	4	3	2	1
Writing style is interesting and upbeat.	5	4	3	2	1
Explanations are clear and accurate.	5	4	3	2	1
Suitable vocabulary is used and defined.	5	4	3	2	1
Learning objectives are identified.	5	4	3	2	1
Illustrations are well-designed and reinforce content.	5	4	3	2	1
Photographs are up-to-date, interesting, and appropriate.	5	4	3	2	1
Printing is clear and easy to read.	5	4	3	2	1
Summaries and/or reviews are included.	5	4	3	2	1
Individual and/or group activities are suggested.	5	4	3	2	1
Provisions are made for individual differences in interests and abilities.	5	4	3	2	1
Table of contents, glossary, and index are sufficiently detailed.	5	4	3	2	1
Cover and binding are attractive and durable.	5	4	3	2	1
SUBTOTAL _____					
Bias					
There is no evidence of:					
Racial bias	5	4	3	2	1
Ethnic bias	5	4	3	2	1
Religious bias	5	4	3	2	1
Gender-role stereotyping	5	4	3	2	1
Age discrimination	5	4	3	2	1
Job denigration	5	4	3	2	1
SUBTOTAL _____					

Illustrations

Illustrations may be used to arouse interest or to teach, but they should be as timeless as possible. This means that styles in hair, clothing, and furnishings must not make the book appear to be old-fashioned in the adolescent's eyes. Pictures showing hemline lengths or fads of any kind should be kept to a minimum. Occasional cartoons, line drawings, and diagrams add variety and interest and tend to minimize the problem of becoming dated.

Illustrations should achieve a balance between females and males and minority-group members so that all readers feel that the book is relevant to and concerned with them. Illustrations also have to appeal to the particular age group by whom the textbook will be used. In addition, a variety of lifestyles, family structures, and economic situations should be portrayed. If pictures depict only middle-class conditions, some students may feel alienated.

Illustrations without captions or descriptive explanations lose much of their educational value. Pictures, sketches, and diagrams should also be placed as close as possible to the related subject matter in the text. Although color illustrations increase the cost considerably, they have much motivational value. It is more effective to have a number of colored pictures distributed throughout material than to have the same number of colored pictures confined to only a few sections. Illustrations should be sufficient in number to break the visual monotony of the printed material but not so numerous that they make it difficult to follow the continuity. It is possible to have so many illustrations that they become a distraction rather than an asset, and they can take up space needed for adequate coverage of the subject.

Cover

The most obvious feature that anyone notices about a book at first, of course, is its cover. The cover can do much to attract a person's interest, to establish a positive attitude toward wanting to read the book, and to stimulate curiosity about what is inside. A colorful cover that is not dated is an asset to any textbook. The cover may convey a contemporary approach that has appeal to the perspective readers or it may dissuade them from wanting to investigate further.

Using a Variety of Reading Materials

There are a variety of types of reading materials available for the general public that are suitable for use in the classroom, such as magazines, paperbacks, and newspapers. One obvious advantage of using different types of written resource materials is that the variety may serve to promote additional interest in the subject matter. When interest is developed, you are more likely to be able to reinforce basic skills. For example, students can read several people's opinions about solving the energy problem or curbing inflation, write a summary of the conflicting viewpoints, and take a stand on which approach would seem to be in the best interests of consumers.

Some suggested activities using paperbacks, periodicals, and newspapers follow. Many of these learning experiences can be adapted for use in studying any home economics subject and simultaneously reinforcing basic skills. In a rapidly changing field, there is no excuse for using outdated reading material. Fortunately, home economics teachers have an abundant supply of up-to-date publications that students can use. However, your ability to use these materials effectively is as important as the quality of the publications themselves. Students need guidance in using periodicals, newspapers, and other written materials to ensure optimum learning. Telling students to read is not enough.

Reading Demands in Home Economics

Readers in home economics content areas have a variety of types of materials with which to cope. These include:

- *Technical terms* unique to the field, such as saturated fat, blended families, bias, and positive verbal guidance techniques.
- *Step-by-step directions* to follow in using a recipe, implementing techniques for constructive rather than destructive arguments, and following a pattern guide sheet.
- *Data* to interpret in family life cycle graphs, fiber characteristics charts, and nutrition labels.
- *Mathematics* to use in measuring, financial planning, and doubling recipes.
- *Chemistry* to use in analyzing food composition tables, detergent labels, and ingredient lists, as well as in removing spots and stains from different fabrics.
- *Reference materials* to use in analyzing family life situations of historical figures or contemporary people in public service.
- *Critical thinking* to use in solving peer relationship problems, evaluating products, and deciding how to handle a touchy situation at work.

Paperbacks and Periodicals

Paperbacks are comparatively inexpensive, often up-to-date, and may have special appeal to the students because they are frequently best sellers or currently popular. Paperback books dealing with consumerism, interpersonal relationships, and laymen's psychological theory are well suited for use in home economics classes. Because of the relative ease with which paperbacks can be obtained, students can read from many sources and share information, thus enriching their experiences. The wide variety of paperbacks available also enables students at various maturity levels and from different cultural and socioeconomic backgrounds to satisfy their diverse needs and interests.

Magazines also focus on a number of issues relevant to home economics and can be used effectively in the classroom. The recency of material in current magazines makes them especially appealing. Articles in them can be shared and discussed; stories can be put on audiotape and left unfinished, allowing students to supply the endings and to compare their conclusions with those of the authors; and pictures can be used by students in making notebooks, mobiles, collages, posters, bulletin boards, and a myriad of visuals of other kinds. Students who regularly receive certain magazines in their homes can assume responsibility for bringing to the attention of the class articles related to topics discussed in class.

Newspapers

Using newspapers in the classroom helps students see the relevance of education. After all, reading newspapers is one of the basic ways to learn about the problems of the world. Although newspapers cannot substitute for textbooks, they are an excellent supplement. Using newspapers in teaching can promote critical thinking. Students can compare articles covering the same issues and situations and look for discrepancies.

The examples that follow illustrate just a few of the ways in which the different components of a newspaper can be used in teaching home economics. Many of these learning experiences could be coordinated with assignments and projects in other subjects.

■ News stories

- Supply headlines for articles, from which the titles have been cut, relating to consumer affairs, family relationships, or child abuse. Compare and discuss the merits of different students' suggested headlines.

- Read newspaper articles to become better informed about local, state, and national efforts to solve problems relating to pollution, ecology, use of resources, storage of nuclear waste, food surpluses and scarcities, unemployment, and other pressing issues. Discuss the responsibilities of citizens to question or support legislation and programs pertaining to these problems.

- Collect articles telling about home accidents. Suggest ways by which these mishaps might have been avoided.

- Hold a press conference in which you pretend to have just discovered another nutrient, developed a new synthetic fiber, or invented a revolutionary household appliance. Write news stories describing how this new product will change consumer practices and affect personal and family living.

- Bring to class examples of news releases from local and national business organizations. Discuss the merits of such publicity to the commercial company and to the consumer. Discuss whether the releases are newsworthy items or advertising disguised as news.

- Submit for publication a news story about the home economics department or FHA/HERO activities for the school or local newspaper. Use appropriate journalism techniques. Write a feature story about a home economics student who has received an award or honor or has been elected to an office or position of status.

■ Advertisements

- Analyze advertisements to differentiate between those that have a primarily emotional appeal and those that provide factual data. Determine what the emotional advertisements are suggesting to the consumer. Underline or circle information that both appeals to the emotions and provides meaningful consumer information.

- Discuss the psychological effects of various phrases such as: for three days only; only two to a customer; must be sold immediately; last chance to buy; stock up while they last; limited number available; hurry, they're going fast. Give examples of other phrases used in advertisements that are designed to persuade the consumer to act quickly. Distinguish between "for sale" and "on sale."

- Compare food ads and plan menus for a week, utilizing as many specials as practical. Determine why grocery stores sometimes sell items below cost; advertise specials; and promote features such as double off on manufacturers' coupons, hours open for business, and bonus gifts such as children's books and dishes that are not directly related to buying food. Discuss the values of advertising to the consumer and to the seller.

- Design advertisements that try to persuade different types of people to buy the same hypothetical product. Create advertisements that appeal to money, beauty, style, and status consciousness. Also create advertisements that attract particular groups such as teenagers, boys or men, middle-aged women, parents, senior citizens, and specific ethnic groups.

■ Classifieds

- Analyze want ads in a newspaper over a period of time to determine the types of employment for which there are the greatest and least demands locally. Analyze the reasons for these findings.
- Select a job being advertised in the want ads of a local newspaper and write a letter applying for that position.
- Spread out the classified sections of several newspapers on tables. Have a scavenger hunt to locate all the jobs advertised relating to specific areas of home economics, such as child development, clothing and textiles, food and nutrition, home management, or any other areas being studied.
- Go to a local newspaper office or to the library and examine want ads of a year ago and of five years ago. Determine if there are any differences in the kinds and numbers of jobs being advertised. Discuss what might have caused these changes.
- Analyze your own employment potential by writing an advertisement to appear in a situations-wanted column. Determine how personal assets relate to different types of employment that might be sought.

■ Columns and Features

- Read letters appearing in personal advice columns and formulate replies. Compare return letters to those written by the columnist. Discuss, in large or small groups, letters appearing in newspapers in which advice is sought and point out the possible effects of different courses of action that could be suggested.

- Analyze comic strips to determine values held by the author as reflected through various characters.
- Read columns that appear regularly in a local newspaper and deal with topics such as nutrition, food buying, consumer affairs, family economics, and household management hints. Take turns summarizing and reporting to the class in your own words the information gained from studying these columns.
- Pretend to buy a few stocks and follow the market every day. Compute gains and losses at the end of a specified period of time. Analyze reasons why some stocks may have increased in value while others may have decreased.

Making Reading Assignments

Students should be given a purpose or direction for their reading. This may be in the form of behavioral objectives outlined for them, points to look for, questions that will be discussed later, or follow-up activities that have been planned. The teacher could say something like: "After reading the material, we will discuss …" or "After reading this you will be expected to …" or "Here are questions for you to answer after reading …"

When offered this type of guidance, students are better able to determine what is important. When students are only directed to read specified pages by a certain date, they have little basis for deciding what material is most pertinent or for knowing what is expected of them.

Teaching Family and Career Skills

Chapter 24

Martha B. Frost, Ed.D.
Associate Professor, The Center for Human Resources
State University of New York at Plattsburgh

Since home and family living cannot be separated from the realities and demands of working, the home economics teacher has a unique contribution to make to the total growth and development of the individual. Certainly, personal and family living patterns affect and are affected by the work people do. Working wives and mothers are a large and permanent part of the work force. More than half of all American women work for pay outside the home, nearly three-fourths of whom are in their child-bearing years. Two-thirds of all mothers are employed today, including 72 percent of mothers with school-age children.

This continuing increase in recent years in the percentage of employed wives and mothers has contributed to problems in work and family role expectations. As a result, employed spouses report frustration with role conflicts, lack of time and energy, and generalized stress. More men are assuming the roles of homemakers. Therefore, both boys and girls and men and women need help in preparing for multiple roles as wage earners, homemakers, and family members.

Home economists, with their concern for the development of the individual and for the well-being of families, are in a unique position to help young people in two vital areas of concern: the ability to balance work and family life, and an understanding of the world of work. Some teachers may include career education as a separate unit in regular home economics classes, while others may integrate family and career skills into the various subject-matter areas, such as family living, child development, and food and nutrition. Whatever approach is taken, career education programs must be adapted to meet the changing needs of students, schools, and communities.

Balancing Work and Family

The home economics teacher can show the interface between home and family responsibilities and school work by demonstrating the balance required to manage the dual roles. A profile of the typical working woman shows that she is in her mid-30's, is married, and has school-age children. She is well educated — over three-fourths are high school graduates, nearly one-third have attended college, and 1 of 6 is a college graduate — and is employed in a traditionally "female" field. Yet, she has primary responsibility for home and family: most available research shows that husbands of working wives assume relatively few household responsibilities.

Child and Elder Care Concerns

Current attitudes make it acceptable for women to work, but research shows that much of the upheaval experienced by families in our society results from the lack of support networks for working women and their families. An important example is the inadequacy of existing child-care services. With fewer than three million licensed day-care slots and more than ten million preschool children whose mothers work, this remains a critical need. Where quality day-care is available, it is prohibitively expensive for many working parents. After-school care for school-age children of working parents is difficult to obtain or scarce, giving way to the latchkey phenomenon which has thousands of children in makeshift arrangements or in self-care. See page 149 for a list of features that can be used to help parents select a child care facility.

Elder care is a growing concern also. More than six million elderly Americans need help with such basics as getting out of bed and going to the bathroom; millions more can't manage meals, money, or transportation. Increasingly, men are shouldering such responsibilities. Still, three-fourths of those caring for the elderly are women, more than half of whom work outside the home and 40 percent of whom still have children at home.

To help wage earners, businesses and schools are increasingly offering on-site child care. Intergenerational care — perhaps a wave of the future — is becoming more widely available. Opportunities for home economists will abound as the number of caregiving programs and agencies also increases.

Household Responsibilities

Dual-earner families also have the stress of household responsibilities, particularly the fact that changes in the work roles of women outside the home have not been accompanied by comparable changes on the home front. Cultural norms influence both spouses' performance in this area, but society expects wives to bear the primary responsibility for taking care of home and family.

Although husbands' efforts at home have increased, wives still do significantly more housework. For example, some studies show that while men do tasks they consider "fun," such as occasional cooking and child care, it is women who regularly assume these responsibilities day in and day out. Men are less likely to do laundry or vacuum. More often, it is the traditionally "male" tasks, such as lawn and car care and taking out the garbage, that remain the responsibility of men. The only wives who report egalitarian sharing of household tasks are typically those who have status, education, and money equivalent to their husbands'.

A real problem for two-career families lies in the fact that most often the wife assumes — probably due to the socialization of both spouses — the greater burden for keeping the family unit running smoothly. Increas-ingly, men with career wives will have to realize that a home does not run smoothly without a manager. And women will have to accept the fact that even if husbands are willing to share tasks, their standards for performance may differ from those of their wives.

Home economics educators should stress the importance of helping men, women, and children to cope with both work and family roles. Cooperative work arrangements which allow for delegation of household tasks among all family members provide a more equitable approach to home responsibilities.

Flexible Schedules

Employers have been slow to recognize that jobs need to be restructured to meet the needs of the two-earner family. Although progress has been made in this area, few jobs have the flexibility which allows working parents to give adequate attention to family responsibilities.

Although the interest in more flexible work patterns has come primarily from women, an increasing number of men are experiencing the advantages of job and work sharing, flextime, and the four-day week. Such creative approaches to work schedules help ease the tensions caused by role overload.

Stress Management

Balancing work and family can cause extra stress for family members. A list of tips for managing stress follows:

- **Make minor changes.** Major changes tend to cause turmoil. Don't try to tackle everything at once. Success comes with small adjustments which result in an immediate difference.
- **Work off stress.** When pressures become intolerable, blow off steam with physical activities such as running, taking a brisk walk, or gardening.
- **Balance work with recreation.** Schedule time for relaxation — a little loafing can ease stress. This should not be a constant escape, but occasionally you deserve a break.
- **Talk out concerns.** Communicate your feelings to someone you trust who will listen without criticizing. This may be a friend, a family member, or a helping professional.
- **Learn to say "no."** If you cannot reasonably handle a request, learn to say so and not feel guilty or uncomfortable about it.
- **Lower expectations and accept what cannot be changed.** Set realistic goals. Do not let activities intended to reduce stress increase stress. Quit worrying about where the future will lead.

- **Make short lists of what should be accomplished each day.** Prioritize tasks and forget the items at the bottom of the list if they don't get done.
- **Develop a variety of interests, activities and relationships.** This will keep you from becoming bored from too few or too monotonous activities. And preventing boredom can prevent stress.
- **Pamper yourself.** Get enough sleep and rest. Take time to have fun. Cut back on excessive work hours.
- **Relax and reward yourself when you accomplish tasks.** Weekend vacations, afternoon visits with friends, or hobbies will reduce concentration on work-related stress.
- **Start each day slowly.** Get up a half hour earlier so there's time for breakfast and the morning newspaper.
- **Get involved with others and the community.** Stressed people often concentrate too much on themselves.
- **Like yourself.** Forgive yourself for your mistakes. Respect your abilities. Recognize your needs.

Positive Effects on Families

The impact of women's employment on families can be positive. Certainly, the wife's earnings provide an economic asset; for many families the wife's income means the difference between poverty and an adequate standard of living.

Additionally, some studies indicate that children of working mothers may actually have advantages over children of at-home mothers. The research seems to indicate increased self-esteem, maturity, and sense of responsibility among children of working mothers. Working mothers seem to encourage independence more than mothers who are not gainfully employed. This is good for children of both sexes, but it is especially good for daughters to have such a role model in their mothers.

Career Choices

A person's career choice can have a significant impact on family life. Jobs that offer autonomy and flexibility are easier to manage, particularly for dual-career families, than jobs that require lots of overtime work or out-of-town travel. Even where you work and how you commute to work can influence how much time and flexibility you have in balancing family and career.

Some examples of career areas that interface well with family life follow:

- Anthropology
- Architecture
- Art
- Clergy
- Cooperative Extension/4-H
- Cosmetology
- Counseling
- Dietetics
- Engineering
- Fashion Design
- Food Styling
- Gerontology
- Health Care
- Home Economics
- Interior Design
- Library Science
- Merchandising
- Product Testing
- Psychology
- Publishing
- Recipe Testing
- Recreation
- Social Work
- Sociology
- Teaching
- Technology
- Tutoring

Career Education

Career education may take two basic forms:
- Training for gainful employment in a specific occupation or cluster of occupations, such as is acquired in a vocationally oriented wage-earning program; or
- A general orientation to the world of work, which can be integrated into every course, and which helps students learn about many career choices related to the field of study.

Since many states have developed materials for teaching in cooperative and vocational preemployment programs, emphasis upon career education in this chapter will be for those teachers who work primarily in regular home economics classes. The type of career education in these programs does not focus upon a limited number of career goals, but instead covers a wide range of occupational opportunities at all levels and helps students develop positive attitudes toward work as a very important domain of life.

The Need for Career Education

The world of work is changing rapidly and constantly. Job requirements are being altered; careers that never existed before are now becoming realities; more women are employed in fields that were held by men in the past and vice versa; and there is a greater need for retraining because of changes in employment patterns. Therefore, students need to be aware of and to examine many alternatives in light of their own strengths, weaknesses, interests, goals, and values.

There are several reasons for young people to become acquainted with possibilities for work before the last two years of high school. For one thing, interest in a career often begins during early adolescence. It is during the middle-childhood and teen years that students learn to cooperate and compete with peers, to build positive or negative attitudes toward achievement, to build patterns of response to authority, and to establish a set of values concerning work. Finally, students who do not yet have career goals or even ideas will have time to explore, think, and plan before they graduate.

The ability to work well with others cannot be promoted by the development of appropriate work skills alone. Qualities of an effective worker also include a positive attitude and self-concept and a measure of self-understanding. In other words, the ability to adapt to working involves being able to make many personal adjustments successfully.

Teaching Career Education

Career education can be incorporated into the home economics curriculum in two ways: as a separate unit, or integrated into subject matter units.

■ Career Education as a Separate Unit

The separate-unit approach to career education could be used at the beginning of the school term to give students a different perspective of the concepts included in home economics or it could be used at the end of the term to show how all areas of subject matter relate to employment. When career education is covered separately, a general orientation to the world of work is usually given. Under the separate-unit approach, concepts related to selecting a career, getting and holding a job, and viewing the overall employment picture are more likely to be included than when career education is mentioned throughout the term as each content area is covered.

The learning experiences that follow could be integrated into a variety of subject areas or incorporated into a cooperative wage-earning program, but they are particularly suitable for a separate unit because of the general and broad approach to career education.

- Divide into seven groups to investigate occupational opportunities in these areas of home economics: child development, food and nutrition, housing and interior design, family relations, management, clothing and textiles, and consumer education. Ask the class as a whole to suggest additional opportunities in each of the fields. After interviewing people engaged in the occupations suggested, develop a list of qualifications desirable for each position.
- Develop a slide presentation and script featuring people in the local community at work in a variety of home economics-related occupations.
- Make a bulletin board entitled, "Graze in the Fields of

Home Economics." Around a picture, cutout, or silhouette of a giraffe or other appropriate animal, list occupations suggested by the class. Change these periodically.

- Make a bulletin board entitled, "Star-studded Careers in Home Economics." On large stars cut from construction paper, write the name of an occupation in the field of home economics. Change these as additional careers are suggested and studied by the class.
- Plan a career day in which people employed in home economics-related occupations discuss job qualifications and opportunities.
- Tell of one new idea gained or a skill developed in a home economics class that could lead eventually to a career or would help make a person more employable.
- Interview women to find out what was done and what was studied in home economics when they were in school. Discuss reasons for the changes in the curriculum today.
- Take a survey to discover how many mothers work outside the home. Compile a list of the types of work they do. Interview working mothers to find out the reasons they give for working. Compile a list to discover what reasons are given most frequently.
- List occupations in which women are more likely to be engaged than men. List occupations in which men are more frequently employed than women. Cite some of the reasons for these differences. Discuss which of these reasons are most valid and why. Suggest reasons that might cause an employer to prefer having a man, or a woman, in a particular job.
- Relate an experience of seeing a woman who is employed in a "man's job." Tell about a man who works in a position that is usually held by a woman. Discuss the following: What were your reactions to finding these employees in these situations? How did you react and why did you react this way? What special problems may these employees face? Offer solutions that may be helpful to these employees in solving their problems.
- Collect articles about experiments involving a longer workday and shorter workweek. Discuss the types of plans being tried or proposed and the advantages and disadvantages of each. Discuss the effects of current employment trends on the use of leisure time and on family life.
- Investigate and read about job sharing as a new approach to employment. Point out how job sharing is different from an arrangement whereby two persons have two part-time jobs.
- Define "moonlighting" and give examples to illustrate an understanding of the term. Discuss the reasons that lead some people to moonlight and what the possible effects might be on family relationships, standard of living, health, and personal satisfaction.

- Investigate school and community resources that are available for both personal and vocational guidance and counseling. Prepare a report on the services offered through various offices and agencies. Discuss how school and community organizations provide opportunities and experiences that could influence one's choice of an occupation or career.
- Invite someone from the local branch of the state employment commission to talk to the group about the community employment situation and about local employment problems. Discuss the effects of the situation on teenagers and their families.
- List skills that may be acquired and trades that may be learned in the armed forces, both of which could later open up occupational opportunities for the individual. Tell about a person who was able to capitalize on skills learned in the armed service by using these in a vocation or hobby after being discharged.
- Define "fringe benefits" and give examples that illustrate an understanding of the term. Analyze the actual cost to the employee and to the employer of some of the fringe benefits suggested. Give examples of fringe benefits that would appeal to some individuals more than they would to others. Discuss the reasons for such a difference in preferences.
- Discuss opportunities in the local community for teenagers to make money. List possible part-time jobs associated with the seasons of the year, special holidays, harvest time, sports, tourist attractions, and local celebrations or special events.
- Discuss occupations that exist today that were unheard of ten, twenty, or thirty years ago. List occupations for which there was a demand in the past and for which there is little need today. Discuss the factors that brought about these changes.
- Research and discuss current demographic trends and technological developments that will influence the job market ten to fifteen years from now. Identify fields that should be strong then. What fields might have declining opportunities?
- Analyze your own personality traits, aptitudes, and interests. According to this analysis, select several occupations for which you might be suited. For each of these occupations, investigate the amount of education or training required, the advantages and disadvantages of each, the chances for advancement, and beginning and potential salaries. If possible, interview people engaged in one of these occupations to find out what they like and dislike about the work. Present these findings to the class in an oral report.
- Collect and display a variety of job-application forms. Discuss the importance of completing these accurately and neatly. Discuss how the application can create either a favorable or an unfavorable first impression. Practice filling out some typical job-application forms.
- Bring to class photographs that are appropriate and inappropriate for use with job-application forms. Analyze the reasons that make each picture suitable or unsuitable. Compile a list of do's and don'ts for having pictures made for such a purpose.
- Write letters of application. One student may apply for a college scholarship. Another student may apply for a student assistantship at a college. Still another may apply for a part-time job while enrolled in college, or during the Christmas vacation, or during the summer. Other students may apply for full-time jobs following graduation or answer want ads found in the local newspaper. Prepare a résumé to enclose with letters of application or to use in interviews.
- Identify the mistakes purposely planted in a skit about a person who is applying for a job through a personal interview. Have an "instant replay" that corrects the mistakes made in the first performance. Discuss the appearance, manners, and attitudes of the person being interviewed. Discuss why you would or would not employ this person.

■ Integrating Career Education into Subject-Matter Units

In both comprehensive and specialized courses, the teacher has an opportunity to help students compare and contrast various home economics careers. Students need to look at clusters of jobs and employment opportunities in order to increase their alternatives. For example, there is a cluster of occupations in the area of services to children, and a family of careers related to food and nutrition, of which many students are unaware. When career education is incorporated into each subject-matter unit, it is often placed last so that the relationships among subconcepts can be viewed and linked in a different context. Career education is an effective closure for a unit because it substantiates the importance of that content area.

Following are examples of learning experiences that can be used when incorporating career education into two subject areas, child-development and food and nutrition. Additional content-related activities in career education are available in many state curriculum guides. A career education program should be adapted to the needs of the students and their community.

Child Development
- Role-play situations in which parents are interviewing people to care for their children. Discuss the following in relation to the scenes:
  1. Which of the applicants would you employ? Why?
  2. What other questions might the prospective employers have asked?

3. Why is each of these considerations important?
4. What would prospective employees want to know about the family?
5. Why would employees want to know these things?
- Divide a piece of paper or the chalkboard into two columns. Label one "parents" and the other "child-care employees." List competencies and attitudes desirable for each. Discuss the reasons for the similarities and differences in the lists.
- Observe a person working with children or a film showing a child-care situation. Point out the importance of a knowledge of child development and a positive attitude toward children in the situations viewed. Discuss which actions of the child-care employees reflect a concern for children and other qualities that should contribute to success in working with them.

Food and Nutrition
- List types of jobs in food services for which there is on-the-job training in the local community. Discuss the skills that people in these occupations need to develop.
- Take a field trip to a food-service establishment to observe the types of work performed at all levels from unskilled to highly skilled. Note the levels with the greatest variety of tasks. Discuss possible reasons for these findings.
- Suggest ways an individual could use competencies related to food preparation in part-time self-employment at home, such as in catering special parties, making and decorating wedding cakes, or preparing canapés and hors d'oeuvres for selected clients.

Developing Attitudes Toward Work

In any course in home economics, it is possible to incorporate a wide variety of learning experiences to help students prepare for employment of any type. A sense of responsibility, the ability to follow direction, a willingness to cooperate with others, punctuality, and the ability to accept constructive criticism are just a few traits that are assets in all endeavors. The learning experiences suggested here are designed to help students develop a broad understanding of factors contributing to success in all occupations.
- List personal characteristics that would be assets in all types of employment situations. List traits that would be liabilities in all occupations.
- Invite a school counselor to discuss the questions that employers most frequently ask about students and former students who are being considered for employment.

- Ask employers to participate in a panel to discuss qualities desired in employees, or interview employers to determine qualities they look for in prospective employees. Use the employers' ideas to develop a checklist and evaluate your own employability.
- List suggestions for good employee relationships with one's employer, customers, and other employees. Discuss reasons for similarities in the lists.
- Role-play situations in which personality conflicts affects job performance. Suggest ways of improving the relationships depicted.
- Fold a piece of paper in half. On one side list the traits and qualities desired in a friend. On the other side list the traits and qualities you would look for in an employee if you were in the position of hiring a person for a job. Unfold the paper and compare the lists.
- Explain the meaning of the expression "Let George do it." How is the attitude reflected in this statement a handicap to success at home, in school, and on the job?
- List a dozen ways to lose a job. For each way listed suggest a means for improving the situation.
- Describe people who are considered responsible. Choose one way in which to become a more responsible individual. Develop a plan of action and keep a diary for a week, showing progress toward that goal.
- Discuss your responsibility as an employee in situations such as these:
  1. You break a piece of equipment.
  2. You are sick and cannot go to work.
  3. Your car will not start when it is time to leave for work.
  4. You see one of your friends taking something from the establishment.
  5. You are offered a similar job for more money.
  6. The employer goes away for a few days.
- Develop a checklist or rating scale that could be used by any employer in any field to decide which employees should get merit raises.
- Ask guest speakers — perhaps people who have risen from disadvantaged backgrounds to become successful and respected members of the community — to talk about the factors that aided them in succeeding.
- Make a bulletin board entitled "Are You on the Beam?" On one side of the display, use a silhouette of a flashlight, lantern, or pole lamp. List qualities desired in all employees, and label light beams with these characteristics.

Professional Ethics

Chapter 25

Selling ability is the key to success in all professions, but true professionals emphasize the services they have to offer. The doctor, lawyer, and home economist are all salespeople in a sense, but they serve in a primarily advisory capacity. Reference is often made to the bedside manner of the physician and the courtroom finesse of the attorney. The home economist's ability to make consulting, writing, educating, and/or advising relevant, exciting, and challenging is equally important to her or his success as a professional.

Professional Commitment

Frequent reference is made to a "professional attitude" or "professional commitment." It is not easy to explain professional commitment because it encompasses involvement and integration of certain goals and attitudes into an individual's total personality. How-

ever, there are a dozen identifiable characteristics that are associated with professionalism and professional conduct.

1. **The professional renders service and shows concern for people.** As a professional, you really want to help and to serve others. You are concerned with *what* you can do for others and *how* you can do it best. Attaining a high quality of life and improving home and family living are goals toward which the professional home economist works.

2. **The professional does not require close supervision or direction.** You direct yourself and can be depended upon to finish any task that you undertake. Self-discipline is a key factor in your success. The professional does not have to be prodded by others and reminded of deadlines. Although you can plan your own activities and work independently, you do not hesitate to seek advice and help from others or to work cooperatively with them. The professional person does not use supplies for personal business; charge long distance calls to the business, agency, organization, or school; and pays for personal mail and photocopying.

   Teaching materials bought or made with school money are the property of the school and should be left there if you leave. Many teachers use their own funds for some teaching materials so the aids are their personal property and can be taken with them when they change positions.

3. The professional assumes responsibility for personal behavior. You are accountable for your mistakes and errors in judgment. You may seek counsel from others, but you do not transfer all your responsibilities to them. You do not make excuses for yourself or get defensive.

   As a professional, you make your grievances known through the proper channels. You discuss them directly and privately with those in authority. In the case of the home economics teacher, this may mean going to the head of the department or the appropriate school administrator. It does not mean complaining and grumbling to students, parents, or other teachers.

4. **The professional does not work by the hour or expect to be paid by the hour.** You work to get the job done. In fact, you may not regard yourself

as an employee at all. You probably consider your administrators and supervisors as professional associates who have objectives and goals very similar to your own.

Certainly, as a home economics teacher, you adjust your working hours to get the job done well without regard to the standard workweek or compensation for overtime. Professional service cannot be measured in hours. It is a fact, though, that those professional persons who demonstrate this principle are often those who advance to positions where remunerative compensation is highest.

5. **The professional maintains good physical, emotional, and mental health.** This necessitates maintaining a sense of humor and managing time efficiently.

All professional persons need to achieve a sense of balance between their family, personal, and professional lives. In fact, much professional literature focuses on balancing work and family. All professionals face, at some time, the problem of living with their work so much of the time that their social and family lives and own personal business affairs may be neglected. The professional home economist who concentrates only on work could be a boring person. Sometimes getting a good night's sleep will help a teacher more than staying up until 3:00 a.m. to plan lessons or to make visuals. If nonscheduled time at school is used efficiently and productively, there should be little need to do schoolwork every night. If, on the other hand, free classes or conference periods are spent visiting in the teachers' room, at least a commensurate amount of time will have to be spent outside of school hours in planning lessons, evaluating student achievement, and collecting materials.

6. **The professional continually seeks to improve.** You take advantage of opportunities to increase your knowledge and understanding of your field and to keep well informed on recent developments. You seek to improve yourself through reading and attending professional meetings. You are aware of local, national, and worldwide concerns.

A professional seeks and accepts advice and criticism objectively. Self-evaluation is also an important aspect of improving your professional competency. To evaluate yourself, you might list your strengths and your weaknesses as objectively as possible. You can then establish priorities and develop a plan of action for self-improvement.

Teachers may also find it helpful to have students evaluate the courses they teach. If this is done sometime near the middle of the course, some of the suggestions made by students can be used. In this way, a teacher can demonstrate the sincerity

of the request for evaluation. A brief, one-page questionnaire with items related to aspects of the course that are of particular concern to the teacher can be distributed to be answered anonymously. Another possibility would be to use two simple questions such as the following: "What parts of this course have been most helpful to you? What parts have been least helpful?" It is best to ask questions about the quality of the course rather than about you as the teacher. Writing about the course may be easier for the students.

The professional home economist contributes to the field by developing new ideas, plans, and materials to keep pace with changes in society and by sharing these with others.

The home economist has an obligation to keep informed about legislation affecting the profession. Your commitment to your profession may be evidenced in part by writing to public figures about your concerns. Personal letters sent to senators, congresspeople, and to state and local representatives help keep them informed about home economics issues and programs and about public reaction to legislation affecting all home economists.

7. **The professional is loyal to colleagues.** You avoid rumor and hearsay and do not gossip about fellow workers or those you serve. You refrain from repeating information received through the grapevine. Instead, you secure information by going directly to those who are authorized to release it.

As a home economics teacher, you respect the confidence of others. The welfare of your students often requires that information concerning them remains confidential. However, there also may be instances when you will have to use great tact and delicate persuasiveness in convincing a student to share problems with others. For instance, if an unmarried student should confide that she is pregnant, you may help her decide how she will tell her parents or encourage her to see her family doctor or a counselor. A different kind of professional may be needed. Do not attempt to assume responsibilities for which you are not qualified.

8. **The professional does not attempt to advance at the expense of others.** You strive for merit raises, promotions, and advancement on the basis of outstanding performance. Above all, you do not run others down to build yourself up.

Although as a professional you may find it ego building to hear students' complaints and derogatory comments about a co-worker, you realize that nothing positive can be gained by listening to such talk. To engage in similar behavior yourself is highly unethical. The professional is considerate of the welfare of others.

9. **The professional possesses good communication and public relations skills.** This requires expressing ideas objectively, clearly, and concisely.

   If professionals have to say "no," they explain why. If home economics teachers have to say "no" to specific learning experiences or covering certain subjects suggested by the students, they give reasons for their decisions. See Chapter 29 for information about public relations techniques.

10. **The professional gives others credit for their ideas and work.** You mention in an oral presentation the source of your information and ideas. On a written communique, the source of information is always acknowledged.

11. **The professional meets commitments and obligations fully and on time.** You fulfill all agreements entered into with co-workers and those you serve, whether they are legal contracts or not. You also meet your obligation to use constructive criticisms and helpful suggestions offered to you by your administrators.

12. **The professional is proud of home economics.** You reflect to those outside home economics a pride and satisfaction in your work. This may involve teaching others about the breadth of the field and that the family is the primary focus of home economics.

    Teachers often have to work consistently, politely, and nondefensively with their administrators to interpret home economics programs. Advisory committees, at both the local and state levels, offer unparalleled opportunities to publicize home economics. Parents can be involved through extended home experiences, advisory committees, and Future Homemakers of America/Home Economics Related Occupations programs. Asking parents and community leaders to serve as resource people and guest speakers helps keep them informed.

Improving the Image of Home Economics

Unfortunately, the picture many people have of the professional home economist is that of a homemaker with special training in the areas of cooking and sewing. While this image may be true in part, it certainly does not present the full picture of the professional. There are many discrepancies in such a limited image. First of all, the home economist may be a single homemaker, who may or may not like to cook and sew. Secondly, the home economist may be a man instead of a woman.

Furthermore, there are numerous fields in home economics that are not directly connected with cooking or sewing. Home economists, then, must be concerned with the image of the profession. It is necessary to communicate to the public that there is a home economics profession made up of men and women who hold bachelor and advanced degrees in the field and who are dedicated to seeking high-quality lives for all individuals and families.

The place to begin a concentrated program for improving the image of the profession is with you, the individual home economist. Each of you must make an effort to think through your professional commitment as a home economist. You must make a special effort to present a professional image to the public. This means not only knowing facts, but putting those facts into practice. Personal appearance and actions are two means of interpreting the values of home economics to others. Your grooming and attire may say to others that, as a home economist, you take pride in yourself and your profession. Smiling, conversing sincerely and enthusiastically, and laughing communicate a different self-concept than do frowning, slouching, and whining.

When the professional image of individual home economists is in order, the next phase is a wider interpretation of the total profession for the community. No matter how this is done, the home economist can initiate action that will create interest and build a positive image for the profession. Getting involved in the local community, professional organizations, and legislative matters helps others to get to know you. As people get to know you, they will learn more about home economics as a profession.

Consider the following means of interpreting the total home economics program: a weekly or monthly newsletter containing items about all areas of the profession, as well as items of local interest, distributed to school administrators, business personnel, civic clubs, and other interested groups; programs for community organizations that emphasize all aspects of the profession; and a newspaper column with questions and answers about home economics-related problems. The home economics teacher has additional channels of communication available: library displays, bulletin boards, showcases, assemblies, programs for parent-teacher associations, radio and television, and newspapers.

The task of expanding and improving the image of home economics needs to be a responsibility assumed by each individual in the profession.

PART 5

Contemporary Issues

Cultural Diversity and Gender Equity

Chapter 26

The aim of legislation in the areas of civil rights and gender equity is to encourage people to reappraise their basic assumptions and practices regarding different cultural groups and the roles of males and females. When biases and stereotyped ideas about others are carried to extremes, the life experiences of individuals who have these prejudices are severely limited. Some forms of bias and some stereotyped ideas are blatantly obvious; some are subtle. Many are the result of long-standing misconceptions.

Cultural Diversity

Many people see cultural diversity as relating only to people of color and national minorities, failing to understand that females, elders, and others who join nontraditional fronts bring diversity into the predominant culture of the workplace, school, community, or other unit. Cultural diversity is sometimes referred to as the ism — sexism, racism, classicism. It is important that home economists be aware of the many different forms of oppression and have an appreciation for all people regardless of religion, creed, socioeconomic, status, and other variations from the so-called "mainstream society."

Generally, the longer families are a part of American life, the more they acquire the characteristics of the so-called "typical family" and the less likely they are to identify with, and be identified by, the specific characteristics of their origins. When people are not characterized as coming from the mainstream or when they are new members of that society, they are often treated as being different. Unfortunately, being different frequently carries the false connotation of being inferior.

Martinez has pointed out that bicultural individuals, on the other hand, retain their culture of origin and are able to function effectively in mainstream society by accommodating to imposed traditional standards. For example, people who refer to themselves as Mexican-American are making a bicultural statement about being American while simultaneously acknowledging their cultural heritage. To help individuals become bicultural, it is important for home economists to have knowledge about cultures in areas such as language, values, history, architecture, home furnishings, clothing, health and hygiene practices, and foods and their preparation. You have basic knowledge in these and many other areas that relate to cultural diversity. Some of these basic facts and implications for teaching strategies are presented in the chart on pages 218-221.

As a home economist you are concerned with quality of life for all individuals and families. Thus you will want to take advantage of your opportunities to search out and disseminate knowledge about different peoples through discussions and other learning activities in all the courses you teach and the programs that you sponsor.

Guidelines for Working with People from Different Cultures

Because of the increasing mobility of our world today, teachers in all parts of our country find themselves working with students from different cultural backgrounds. If this is a new experience for you, or one that has not been satisfactorily resolved, here are some guidelines that may be helpful in promoting positive relationships with people from other cultural groups.

- Teachers who can communicate successfully with students from all cultural and socioeconomic groups are often characterized as being self-accepting individuals, aware of both their strengths and their weaknesses. When people can accept themselves, they are likely to be able to accept others who are different. Nothing can replace a sincere interest in all students — a belief that all of them have worth and the potential for success in their own individual ways.

- Calling each student by his or her name or by the name the student prefers, and pronouncing each name correctly, are aids to communication. When names from other ethnic or cultural groups are difficult to pronounce, it may be helpful to write the names phonetically (for your own use) or to get students' voices on a recorder as they give their names and tell a little about themselves and their interests.

- In talking to students, it is important to be careful about using unintended "put-downs." These are often meant to "break the ice" or to be merely friendly remarks. However, they may not be interpreted that way by the people hearing them. Some comments may be considered racist; others may be regarded as patronizing — too solicitous or artificial. These remarks can inhibit communication rather than enhance it. Examples of well-intended remarks that can easily "turn off" other people are:

  "You people are such good athletes (cooks, entertainers, and so on)." (You people always has a negative connotation.)

  "My friend Juan is also Mexican-American."

  "I know what it's like to be discriminated against, too."

  "The people on your side of town ought to go together."

  "Do you know Mary Wu in San Francisco?" (The mistaken assumption is that all people in an ethnic group know one another.)

- The best way to know how to refer to a person by cultural background is to ask that person what term is preferred. Because cultural groups are diverse, there are no terms or labels that are pleasing or appropriate for all members. Some terms may be offensive to individuals who consider them inaccurate or disparaging. For example, Hispanics are a diverse group. Latino refers to people of Latin American origin. Spanish, Spanish-Americana, and Hispano refer to people who either immigrated to the United States from Spain or to descendants of Hispanic or Indo-Hispanic forebears who resided in today's Southwest when it was under Spanish and later Mexican rule. Chicano, Mexican, and Mexican-American are often used interchangeably; however, the terms have different connotations for persons who identify themselves as such. Similarly the term "Native American" is often used to refer to a very heterogeneous group of people. Tribal diversity is recognized when you refer to individuals as Seminoles, Abnaki, or Sioux.

- If you are accused of prejudice by a member of another ethnic group, avoid appearing defensive by denying the accusation. Since you probably are not sure exactly what the student is referring to, try to get more information. For example, you might ask, "What have I done that seem prejudiced?" Or, "I am not aware I have been. When did you see me do or say something that appears to be prejudiced? Please point it out to me." This approach will encourage dialogue. If the student has specifics to point out, you will have learned something new about the way others perceive your actions. On the other hand, the student may have no concrete evidence of prejudicial actions on your part but may simply make the remark to see how you will react.

- If members of an ethnic group segregate themselves by sitting together all the time, avoid making an issue of it. It is likely that the students are apprehensive about mixing with others. Plan some activities in which students have to move around and mix with each other. When people get to know others on a one-to-one basis, the unknown becomes less threatening.

Gender Equity

Although the school is not totally responsible for the problems created by gender-role stereotyping, it is one of the major socializing agencies in our society and must assume some responsibility. Professional educators shape the milieu in which adolescents may or may not be free to develop to their full potential, without restrictions based on their gender or cultural backgrounds. Teachers also have the responsibility to help students learn to accept and deal with a wide range of human differences. Teachers' values, perceptions, and attitudes are continually reflected in the curriculum planning and classroom interaction that influence learning and individual development.

Expectations Regarding Gender Roles

Students often have a very limited perspective of what life will be like five, ten, fifteen, or more years in the future. Teachers have a responsibility to help students explore the many options open to them. Lifestyles are changing, and people are gradually becoming more objective about current-day realities. For example, it is obsolete to view the husband as the primary wage earner and the wife as a wage earner only in times of crises, such as divorce or widowhood. The options of pursuing a lifelong career, marrying later, having a small family or not having children at all, having two incomes, remaining single, and deciding on single parenthood are being considered and taken by more and more women and men today.

The traditional roles should not be discarded. Individuals who select traditional lifestyles should be respected for their preferences just as people who choose other lifestyles should be respected for their choices. However, the advantages and disadvantages of the traditional roles and the new emerging roles for both males and females need to be explored objectively to enable students to make rational choices.

It is self-defeating to educate for changing role patterns if traditional gender-role expectations are perpetuated in the classroom. The questions shown below should help you think about your professional practices with respect to gender stereotyping and gender bias.

■ *Developing Sensitivity Through Class Activities*

A variety of learning activities can be used to help students think through the effect gender-role stereotyp-

ing has had on their lives and the impact more equitable roles will have in the future. The following suggestions may help you generate other ideas:

- Brainstorm to give verbal examples of ways stereotypical behaviors are perpetuated in children such as by saying:
  "Big boys don't cry."
  "Boys don't play with dolls" or "Girls don't play with trucks."
  "Do you want to grow up to be a sissy?"
  "She's a Tom-boy?"
- Give students a fact sheet on women's issues. Include facts similar to these:
  - After divorce the husband's standard of living increases 42 percent while that of the wife and children decreases 73 percent.
  - Most teen mothers, 50 to 80 percent, do not finish high school.
  - Numerous studies have shown that women still do most of the household work even when they are employed outside the home. Some studies show that women do as much as 75 to 80 percent of the "housework" in a home.
  - "Super Moms" say their children suffer the most from the multiple roles assumed by their mothers.
  - Women are marrying later and having children at older ages than in the past. In 1950, the average age of first marriages of women was 20.1 years; in 1988 it was 23.6.
  - One in two homes in the United States experiences violence. People are at greater risk of physical vio-

---

Gender Stereotyping Questionnaire

- Do you avoid using such biased language as *the doctor ... he; mankind; the lady lawyer; mothering; John Smith and Mrs. Alex Brown; Amanda, a pretty brunette, and José, a skilled mechanic*? Instead, do you use bias-free language, such as *doctors ... they; humankind; the lawyer ... she; parenting; John Smith and Sara Brown; Amanda, an excellent athlete, and José, a skillful mechanic*?
- When you discuss career choices, do you provide nontraditional examples, such as administrative-level positions for females and clerical or nursing positions for males?
- In a class of males and females, do only male students pass out books and operate film projectors? Do only female students water plants and dust?
- If students were writing letters to business people, would you have them begin their letters *Dear Sir*?
- Do you encourage females to be more concerned about their grooming than males?
- Would you be as concerned about a senior female student as you would about a senior male student who was unable to make career plans?

- If a student made the statement that follows, would you ask the student to examine it? "Mothers pick up their children at day-care centers."
- Do you expect the males in class to be more boisterous than the females?
- Do you provide a variety of traditional and nontraditional role models of both genders for your students?
- Do you have the same work standards for males and females?
- Do you recruit both males and females for your classes?
- Do you evaluate your teaching materials and curriculum for gender stereotyping and gender bias?
- Do you work with youth groups to ensure that teenagers, themselves, do not discriminate against members of either gender?
- If members of the administration or faculty make remarks that are gender-biased, do you draw their attention to this? Do you explain tactfully why such remarks are harmful?

lence in their own homes than they are on the so-called crime-ridden city streets. Spousal murders account for 25 percent of all murders.

 - Of people over 65 years of age, there are five times more widows than widowers. In fact, half of all older women are widowed. Most older men are married and/or live in families; more older women live alone.

Using these facts, discuss the implications of women's increasing participation in the work force and changing lifestyles as they relate to educational preparation. Predict changes that will occur in interpersonal relations and the family structure.

• Divide the class in half. Have half the students prepare a list of gift items for a man and the other half, gift items for a woman. List the items on the board. Discuss any obvious stereotypes involved. Are perfume and beauty items emphasized for women, reinforcing concerns about physical attractiveness? Is sports equipment mentioned for men, reinforcing the image of athletic prowess?

• Duplicate and distribute or write on the board a list of ways in which teachers treat or react to male and female students stereotypically. For example, teachers often ask girls to put up bulletin boards and boys to repair equipment. Other examples might include: girls don't like math or science; boys have more difficulty learning to read; boys are disruptive and present behavior problems; girls prefer home economics and boys prefer industrial arts; girls have no mechanical aptitude. Students can add to this list. Discuss the impact these behaviors and assumptions have on young people.

• Use role-playing to focus on role conflicts. For example, role-play a husband telephoning his wife. A VIP is in town and wants to take them out to dinner tonight. The husband feels that this meeting is a prelude to an important promotion for him. The wife has been asked by her boss to represent their department at an important company social function taking place at the same time. She feels it is essential to her career that she attend the meeting. Encourage the students to think of and act out other role-conflict situations.

Nonsexist Treatment of Women and Men

Men and women should be treated as people, and not primarily as members of different genders. Their shared humanity and common attributes should be stressed, not their gender difference. Neither gender should be stereotyped or arbitrarily assigned to a leading or secondary role.

■ Occupations

Though some women will continue to choose traditional occupations such as homemaker or secretary, women should not be typecast in these roles but shown in a wide variety of professions and trades: as doctors and dentists, not always as nurses; as principals and professors, not always as teachers; as lawyers and judges, not always as social workers; as bank presidents, not always as tellers; as members of Congress, not always as members of the League of Women Voters.

Similarly, men should not be shown as constantly subject to the "masculine mystique" in their interests, attitudes, or careers. They should not be made to feel that their self-worth depends entirely upon their income level or the status level of their jobs. They should not be conditioned to believe that a man ought to earn more than a woman or that he ought to be the sole support of a family.

An attempt should be made to break job stereotypes for both women and men. No job should be considered gender-typed, and it should never be implied that certain jobs are incompatible with a woman's femininity or a man's masculinity. Thus, women as well as men should be shown as accountants, engineers, pilots, plumbers, bridge-builders, computer operators, TV repairers, and astronauts. Likewise, men as well as women should be shown as nurses, grade-school teachers, secretaries, typists, librarians, file clerks, switchboard operators, and babysitters.

Women within a profession should be shown at all professional levels, including the top levels. Women should be portrayed in positions of authority over men and over other women. There should be no implication that a man loses face or that a woman faces difficulty if the employer or supervisor is a woman. All work should be treated as honorable and worthy of respect; no job or job choices should be downgraded. Instead, women and men should be offered more options than were available to them when work was stereotyped by gender.

■ Marital Status and Parenthood

Books designed for children at the preschool, elementary, and secondary levels should show married women who work outside the home and should treat them favorably. Teaching materials should not assume or imply that most women are wives, but instead should emphasize the fact that women have choices about their marital status, just as men do. Teaching materials need to convey that some women choose to stay permanently single and some are in no hurry to marry; some women marry but do not have children, while others marry, have children, and continue to work outside the home.

Sexist and Non-Sexist Language

Sexist	Non-sexist	Sexist	Non-sexist
the fairer sex, the weaker sex	women	career girl or career woman	name the woman's profession: attorney Ellen Smith; Maria Sanchez, a journalist (editor, business executive, doctor, lawyer, or agent)
the distaff side	the female side or female line		
the girls or the ladies (when adult females are meant)	the women		
girl as in: "I'll have my girl check that."	"I'll have my secretary (assistant) check that." (Or use the person's name.)	Pioneers moved West, taking their wives and children with them	Pioneer families (Pioneer men and women, or Pioneer couples) moved West, taking their children with them.
lady used as a modifier, such as lady lawyer	Lawyer (A woman may be identified simply through the choice of pronouns, as in: "The lawyer made her summation to the jury." Avoid gender modifiers altogether. When you must modify use woman or female, such as a course on women writers, the airline's first female pilot.)	Jim Weiss allows his wife to work part-time.	Judy Weiss works part-time.
		mankind	humanity, human beings, human race, people
		primitive man	primitive people or peoples, primitive human beings, primitive men and women
		man's achievement	human achievements
the little woman, the better half, the ball and chain	wife	If a man drove 50 miles at 60 mph …	If a person (driver) drove 50 miles at 60 mph …
female-gender work forms, such as authoress, poetess, Jewess	author, poet, Jew	the best man for the job	the best person (candidate) for the job
female-gender diminutive forms, such as suffragette, usherette, aviatrix	suffragist, usher, aviator or pilot	manmade	artificial, synthetic, manufactured, constructed, of human origin
libber (a put down)	feminist, liberationist	manpower	human power, human energy, workers, workforce
sweet young thing	young woman, girl		
coed used as a noun (Coed should refer to any student at a coeducational college or university; since it does not, it is a sexist term.)	student	insurance man	insurance agent
		statesman	leader, public servant
		chairman	the person presiding at (chairing) a meeting, the presiding officer, the chair, head, leader, coordinator, or moderator
housewife as in: "The sound of the drilling disturbed the housewives in the neighborhood," and "Housewives are feeling the pinch of higher prices."	homemaker for a person who works at home, or rephrase with a more precise or more inclusive term, as in: "The sound of drilling disturbed everyone in the neighborhood," and "Consumers (customers or shoppers) are feeling the pinch of higher prices."		
		cameraman	camera operator
		foreman	supervisor
		you and your wife	you and your spouse
		when you shave in the morning	when you brush your teeth (wash up) in the morning
		the men and the ladies	the men and the women, the ladies and the gentlemen, the girls and the boys
cleaning woman or maid	housekeeper, house or office cleaner	man and wife	husband and wife

Thus, a text might say that some married people have children, and some do not, and that sometimes one or both parents work outside the home.

Instructional materials should never imply that all women have a "mother instinct" or that the emotional life of a family suffers because a woman works. Instead, they might state that when both parents work outside the home there is usually either greater sharing of the child-rearing activities or reliance on day-care centers, nursery schools, or other help.

■ Generic Language

Women should be treated as part of the rule, not as the exception. Generic terms, such as doctor and nurse, should be assumed to include both men and women, and modified titles, such as *woman doctor* or *male nurse*, should be avoided. Work should never be stereotyped as *woman's work* or as *a man-sized job*. Writers should avoid showing a "gee-whiz" attitude toward women who perform competently: "Though a woman, she ran the business as well as any man" or "Though a woman, she ran the business efficiently."

Women should be spoken of as participants in the action, not as possessions of men. Terms such as *pioneer, farmer,* and *settler* should not be used as though they applied only to adult males.

In references to humanity at large, language should be used that includes women and girls. Terms that tend to exclude females should be avoided whenever possible. The word *man* has long been used not only to denote a person of male gender, but also generically to denote humanity at large. To many people, however, the word *man* has become so closely associated with the first meaning (a male human being) that they consider it no longer broad enough to be applied to any person or to human beings as a whole. In deference to this position, alternative expressions should be used in place of *man* whenever such substitutions can be made without producing an awkward or artificial sentence. In cases where words containing *man* must be used, special efforts should be made to ensure that pictures and other devices make explicit that such references include women.

The English language lacks a generic singular pronoun signifying he or she. Therefore, it has been customary and grammatically sanctioned to use masculine pronouns in expressions such as "one ... he," "anyone ... he," and "each child opens his book." Nevertheless, when possible avoid the pronouns *he, him,* and *his* in reference to the hypothetical person or humanity in general.

Note that *lady* and *gentleman, wife* and *husband,* and *mother* and *father* are role words. Ladies should be used for women only when men are being referred to as gentlemen. Similarly, women should be called wives and mothers only when men are referred to as husbands and fathers. Like a male shopper, a woman in a grocery store should be called a customer or consumer, not a housewife.

■ Names

Women should be identified by their own names (e.g., Margaret Thatcher, Indira Gandhi, Pat Schroeder, Geraldine Ferraro). They should not be referred to in terms of their roles as wife, mother, sister, or daughter unless it is in these roles that they are significant in context. Nor should they be identified in terms of their marital relationship, such as *Mrs. Thatcher*, unless this brief form is stylistically more convenient than *Prime Minister Thatcher* or is paired up with similar references to men. A woman should be referred to by name in the same way that a man is. Both should be called by their full names, by first or last name only, or by title.

Males should not always be first in order of mention. Instead, alternate the order, sometimes using: women and men, gentlemen and ladies, she or he, her or his.

■ Characterizations

In descriptions of men, especially in the home, references to general ineptness should be avoided. Men should not be characterized as dependent on women for meals, clumsy in household maintenance, or foolish in self-care. Avoid characterizations that stress men's dependence on women for advice on what to wear and what to eat; men's inability to care for themselves in time of illness; and men as objects of fun, such as the henpecked husband.

Women should not be portrayed as needing male permission in order to act or to exercise rights — except for historical or factual accuracy. Women should be recognized for their own achievements. Intelligent, daring, and innovative women, both in history and in fiction, should be provided as role models for girls. Leaders in the fight for women's rights should be honored and respected, not mocked or ignored.

See the chart on page 216 for examples of sexist and non-sexist references, expressions, and words.

Strategies for Action

Walker has suggested the following approaches for helping students develop an understanding of and an appreciation for all people:

- Infuse multicultural, non-sexist, and non-racist concepts in all content areas of the home economics curriculum.
- Incorporate the study of the aging process into the home economics curriculum. Place emphasis on such topics as nutrition and aging; clothing needs of the aged; aging and family relationships; economics of aging; psychological, biological, and social aspects of aging. Invite elders and those working in the field of aging to the classroom as resources.
- Provide opportunities for students to be exposed to people of various cultures and lower socioeconomic status via person-to-person contacts or through media techniques. Plan opportunities for students to become involved with the older population. Establish Youth Volunteer Groups to provide a variety of services including reading, letter writing, doing chores, and providing transportation. Allow students to earn credit toward grades for these community services.

In addition, Mays and Fuller have suggested the following:
- Develop education programs for minority students, both college and non-college bound. Students can benefit from an integrated academic education and vocational education program where marketable skills, as well as critical and analytical thinking abilities, are developed. This helps individuals adapt to changing economic environments.
- Provide opportunities to instill self-esteem in both adults and children. As adults, people need to be helped to see that they can and need to be contributing members of society. Hopefully, if children develop a strong sense of self-esteem early, they may escape all or part of the negative economic cycle of earlier minority generations.
- Establish mentoring programs for teens and adults. Having a fellow minority member as a positive role model can be instrumental in the creation of values, behaviors, and skills necessary to psychosocial as well as socioeconomic health and well-being.

References

Martínez, Estella A. "Mexican American/Chicano Families: Challenging the Stereotypes." *Empowerment Through Difference: Multicultural Awareness in Education*, Yearbook 8, Teacher Education Section, American Home Economics Association. Peoria, IL: Glencoe Publishing Company, 1988.

Mays, Mary Helen and Jane Cripps Fuller. "Linking Work and Family Life: A Minority Women's Perspective." *Work and Family: Educational Implications*, Yearbook 11, Teacher Education Section, American Home Economics Association. Peoria, IL: Glencoe Publishing Company, 1991.

Walker, Retia Scott. "The Longevity Revolution: Improving The Quality of Life for Black Elders." *Empowerment Through Difference: Multicultural Awareness in Education*, Yearbook 8, Teacher Education Section, American Home Economics Association. Peoria, IL: Glencoe Publishing Company, 1988.

Linking Cultural Diversity and Home Economics Education Strategies

FACTS	EDUCATIONAL STRATEGIES
Food and Nutrition	
Approximately two-thirds of the world's population is lactase-deficient after early childhood. 70-80% of African-Americans, 80-100% of Asian-Americans, and large proportions of American Indians, Jews, and Middle Easterners are lactase-deficient.	Emphasize the use of fermented milk products such as yogurt and buttermilk which many lactase-deficient people can tolerate. Display commercial products such as acidophilus milk, Lact-Aid, and low-lactose milk powder (LLM) which some can use. Have students use U.S. RDA charts to plan meals without milk that provide adequate amounts of calcium. Encourage use of nondairy milks such as soy milk that is popular with Chinese and Japanese people.
In Japan the incidence of heart disease is much lower than in the U.S., but when Japanese families emigrate to Hawaii and begin eating the typical American high-fat diet, their incidence of heart disease increases.	Have students interview Japanese immigrants or invite a person of Japanese descent to class to point out what the typical Japanese diet is like. Discuss how it differs from the typical American diet. What changes in lifestyle might also affect Japanese emigrants moving to the U.S. that would contribute to increases in heart disease?

(Continued on next page)

FACTS	EDUCATIONAL STRATEGIES

Food and Nutrition (cont'd)

Many vegetarians, such as Seventh Day Adventists, have less coronary heart disease than other people.

Point out other lifestyle habits of Seventh Day Adventists that probably reduce the incidence of heart disease such as not smoking, not drinking coffee or alcohol, and living in closer knit and less stressful communities than most other people. Have students do library research to learn more about linkages between diet, health, and lifestyle among groups such as Mexicans, Finns, Swedes, and Italians.

Strokes, diabetes, and hypertension are major health risk factors among blacks. Cardiovascular diseases are greater among black than white women.

Have students plan and prepare low-fat and low-sodium meals. Explain terms associated with fats such as unsaturated, polyunsaturated, saturated, cholesterol, vegetable oils, and tropical oils. Ask students to bring food labels to class for a variety of food products. Evaluate food labels for fat content and type of fat.

There is no single dominant dietary pattern among African-Americans. Dietary patterns can be subdivided into southern vs. non-southern, urban vs. rural, native-born vs. foreign-born, and Christian vs. Muslim.

Illustrate how unique dietary patterns among blacks are influenced by historical and regional food availability and food preparation practices. Examples might include grits, chitterlings, mustard greens, and blackeyed peas.

In Latin America, a "siesta" is a two-hour break enjoyed after the largest meal of the day, lunch. Breakfast is also a large meal and dinner, eaten at night, is a small meal.

Have students report on cultural groups that do not follow a three-meal-a-day pattern. In many European societies, four meals a day is standard. People in some cultures eat only once or twice a day, while some hunters and gatherers snack all day.

Family Studies

Kinship, family ties, and the church are strong sources of emotional support for many African-Americans.

Give examples from literature, movies, television, and music to illustrate the importance of the family and religion in the development of black heritage. Ask students to give additional examples.

Familistic and *familism* are concepts associated with all Hispanic groups. Both terms mean that the bonded unit of individuals known as the family takes precedence over any one individual.

Discuss the association between familism and materialism, competitiveness, mobility, and goals often valued in mainstream society in the U.S. Point out the benefits derived from a strong familistic cultural background.

Although Hispanic women's participation in the labor force has increased much more in recent years than for other women, cultural differences in gender-role attitudes mean that Hispanic women still are less likely to be employed.

Emphasize home-based business opportunities for women. List the advantages and disadvantages of involvement in a home-based business vs. employment outside the home. Stress ways to save money in the home related to energy conservation, meal preparation, and household management that will help compensate for outside income from only one adult family member.

Families maintained by women with no husband present have considerably lower incomes than other families. In the mid '80s, 44% of black families were headed by women with no husband present. This compares to 13% for white families.

Help prepare women for single parenthood by identifying and building strengths and developing positive coping strategies. Provide assertiveness training to deal with home and job-related problems. Emphasize the development of marketable skills and desirable work habits.

Life expectancy for whites was 75.6 in 1988, while it was 69.2 for blacks. There is a reverse trend in life expectancy for blacks due to early deaths caused by homicides, car accidents, drug abuse, and AIDS — factors directly related to living in poor and violent neighborhoods.

Have students locate and use population statistics to make graphs showing the following:

- Differences in life expectancy for various cultural groups.
- Trends in life expectancy for various cultural groups.

(Continued on next page)

FACTS	EDUCATIONAL STRATEGIES

Child Development

Teen pregnancy is a national problem among all cultural groups, but it is an especially serious problem among African-Americans.

Provide teen parenting programs through FHA/HERO and other peer groups. Make an effort to include teenage males who need help in addressing issues associated with fathering.

Infant mortality among blacks is twice as high as among whites due to low birth weights, inadequate insurance and inadequate medical care, transportation and child care problems, stressful work environments, disrupted families, and other detrimental factors.

Emphasize the importance of prenatal care and proper diet by having a physician, nurse, midwife, and/or registered dietitian talk to classes about preventive care and early medical supervision, healthy food choices, and being drug free. Provide information about sources of medical help in the community.

Although family environments for Hispanic children are diverse, generally children are highly valued and child nurturing is regarded as an important family function.

Have students prepare reports about traditional family values and lifestyles among various Hispanic groups. Discuss how these traditional patterns of family life have carried over into present-day positive child rearing practices.

Breast feeding is less common among black women than among non-minority women, except for women from Caribbean countries.

Ask a health professional to point out advantages and disadvantages of breast feeding. Guide students in making a chart showing advantages and disadvantages of both breast and bottle feeding.

Approximately 70% of women in the U.S. with school age children work outside the home. The labor force participation rate is higher for black than white women, but the gap is narrowing. The result of a high proportion of mothers in the labor force means that many children are in latchkey situations.

Help the FHA/HERO chapter prepare programs for latchkey children including topics such as:
- Preparing simple, nutritious snacks safely and cleaning up afterwards.
- Handling emergencies such as accidents, fires, and robberies.
- Developing positive relationships with friends, siblings, parents, and other adults.
- Managing time efficiently for doing homework and performing homemaking tasks.

Housing

In some societies, housing style is a symbol of cultural diversity.

Point out that the term Native American is inappropriate because American Indians are not a homogeneous group. There is great tribal diversity reflected in housing, family customs, religions, and rituals. Have students prepare reports on typical housing in the past of various Indian tribes.

Blockbusting occurs when realtors sell a home in a predominantly white neighborhood to a minority buyer. This causes alarm, and realtors encourage home owners to put their houses on the market. *Redlining* refers to marking certain areas with boundaries within which lenders are discouraged from making mortgages available. *Steering* refers to the practice of showing real estate to minorities only in areas where other minorities live.

Have students role-play or write skits depicting the illegal practices of blockbusting, redlining, and steering. Discuss the business and moral issues involved.

Accessory apartments are increasing in number to meet the needs of elderly family members, to make use of under-utilized living space, and/or to produce additional income. An accessory apartment is a separate, independent living unit developed within an existing single-family home that can be identified by a separate kitchen. The two units may share an exterior entrance, yard, and parking area.

Have students — individually, in small groups, or as a class — make a chart that shows advantages and disadvantages of accessory apartments for each of these people:
- Home owner
- Older family member living in the accessory apartment.
- Non-family renter.

(Continued on next page)

FACTS	EDUCATIONAL STRATEGIES

Housing (cont'd)

There are two forms of community sponsored home sharing: match-up programs and shared living residences.	Have students interview people who are involved in match-up programs, such as disabled individuals, senior citizens, and college students, to determine the pluses and minuses of such arrangements. Have students share their interview findings with the class. Brainstorm to think of groups that might benefit from home sharing. Visit some community sponsored home sharing projects.

Clothing and Textiles

Cultural groups living in hot, humid climates dress differently from people living in frigid climates.	Show pictures of Arabs, Samoans, Eskimos, and other people who live in different parts of the world. Point out clothing characteristics appropriate for the types of climate in which the individuals live.
Clothing of the past in this country was a reflection of culture, lifestyle, and status.	Have students pretend they are designers making clothing for a movie in which the characters move from the city to the frontier in the late 1800s. How will their clothing reflect their changes in lifestyle? How will changes in clothing reflect the culture of the people with whom they live on the frontier?
	Have students bring in historical textiles from their family and share with the group the background of the fabrics and why they are so important to the family.
Body shapes and sizes are different for different cultural groups, and body shapes and sizes are changing. Blacks have different shapes from people of Asian descent and from those of Scandinavian descent. Research has shown that whites in the U.S. have different body shapes from blacks. In studies it has been found that black youths have shorter trunks, longer lower and upper extremities, wider shoulders, and narrower pelvises and hips than white youths. Even within the melting pot of the U.S., sizes are different and people are getting larger.	Point out how suits of armor, wedding dresses displayed in museums, and the size of furniture used in colonial times reflect changes in body size.
	Have students trace height and size through their parents and grandparents to see how they differ and to determine trends.
	Point out how standard size patterns can be adjusted to accommodate differences in body shapes associated with race and ethnicity.
The population is aging. By the year 2030, 20% of the population will be over 65 years of age.	Have students brainstorm to answer this question: If you were opening a specialty clothing store for older people, how would the clothing differ from that sold in a store catering to younger consumers? Discuss: How did hippies, punk rock, and other youthful cultural groups of the past influence clothing styles in their time?
	Have students conduct oral interviews with grandparents or neighbors to find out what types of clothing they wore when young and how their clothing differed from what the students wear today.
	Have students discuss with some elders concerns they have with their clothing. Have the students work in groups to redesign clothing for elders.
More clothing sold in the U.S. today than ever before is produced in industrial developing countries with low labor costs. The U.S. is struggling to keep its clothing production industry healthy.	Have students find pictures of clothing and furnishings or bring actual examples to class that are labor intensive to produce, such as hand-embroidered shirts and dresses from Mexico, hand-knit sweaters from South America, and oriental rugs from Asia. Discuss why these are not produced in the U.S.

Specific Audiences: Middle School, Special Needs, and Adult Learners

Chapter 27

Mary Hellen Mays, Ph.D., R.D.
Chair, Coordinated Program in Dietetics
The University of Texas — Pan American

Within the context of our teaching lies the purpose of our existence — the students. Without an audience, our role in the education drama would be unnecessary. Yet, even within our audiences exist subgroups with special characteristics such as middle school students, special needs students, and adult learners. One of the many challenges for home economics teachers is to identify these groups and facilitate their learning.

Middle School Students

The trip from childhood to adulthood is marked by many challenges and periods of transition. Up until about the age of 10 or 11, most children are not overly concerned with "life." Authority figures still command a healthy level of respect, and information is accepted pretty much at face value.

As children enter the middle school years, they tend to become more critical, doubtful, thoughtful, and thought-provoking. The task facing educators is to challenge the students while adapting to the normal transitions of young teens.

Curricula must be reexamined as to its approach to education as well as the validity of its content. If we fail to structure the learning experiences and environment to meet the unique needs of our audience, they will slowly but surely close their minds to us.

The future faced by today's youth promises to be dramatically different from that experienced by previous generations. For many young people, the adolescent years mark a dramatic point in their lives. Choices abound and decisions sometimes result in negative outcomes: unwanted pregnancies, sexually transmitted diseases, AIDS, drug abuse, and other physical and emotional demands. The next century may see youth at a greater risk than ever before. As home economics programs continue to gain popularity in middle schools, teachers will have an increasingly key role in recapturing those adolescents who may be at risk. See Chapter 28 for information about meeting the needs of at-risk youth.

Meeting Students' Needs

Middle school students evolve in primarily four developmental areas: intellectual, emotional, physical, and social. The chart on pages 224-225 identifies the major changes that occur in these areas and how the curriculum can be designed to meet these needs.

A few strategies that may be helpful in increasing teacher effectiveness at the middle school level are:
• Make your expectations clear to the students at the outset of the course.

- Apply the rules and guidelines for the class firmly and consistently.
- Take part in classroom activities, when appropriate, allowing students to see the "human side" of the teacher.
- Allow students to create their own learning activities.
- Create a learning environment that is supportive and fair, energetic, and recognizes each student's unique ability and contribution.

Creating Environments for Success

In a 1989 report, *Turning Point: Preparing American Youth for the 21st Century*, the Carnegie Council on Adolescent Development made eight specific recommendations for educators and administrators. Designed to improve the academic experiences of all middle school students, these points are particularly helpful in preventing those children at risk from becoming lost to the educational system.

1. **Create small communities for learning.**
   Here students may develop close, team-like relationships with teachers and fellow students. This structure will assure that every student is well-known by at least one adult, a mentor who can promote academic and personal development.
2. **Teach a core academic program.**
   This core should be designed to promote values for citizenship, critical thinking, and academic excellence.
3. **Ensure success for all students.**
   The foundation of this principle is the promotion of cooperative learning, flexibility in arranging instructional time, and adequate resources for teachers.
4. **Empower teachers and administrators.**
   Thus, these key decision-makers will have the needed creative control to create learning environments that support academic and psychological development.
5. **Staff school with expert teachers.**
   Expert here means teachers prepared for and experienced in teaching middle school-aged students.
6. **Improve academic performance by promoting health and fitness.**
   Each school must become a wellness-based community with a qualified health coordinator and access to health care and counseling services.
7. **Reengage families in the educational process.**
   Schools and families must create and actively promote channels of communication with one another. Schools can begin by giving families meaningful roles in school administration, involvement in classroom activities, and specific ways to support and enhance the learning process at home.
8. **Connect schools with communities.**
   The private sector can be an individual partner in supporting both the success of the school and the students. The community can help schools identify and utilize resources and enhance academic and after-school activities.

Team-Teaching and Interdisciplinary Teaching

Among many middle school educators, the core curriculum approach is considered basic to helping students attain critical knowledge and skills. Typically, a core academic program for middle school students includes English, literature and grammar, science, social studies, fine arts, history, mathematics, and foreign languages. The actual teaching techniques used to present this core may vary widely among schools.

Traditionally, instructional techniques at the elementary school and high school levels are, in some manner, "self-contained." Students in lower grades are basically housed in one room where the teacher is responsible for the majority of instruction — a one-teacher model. At the high school level, teachers become subject-matter experts, responsible for a limited content area.

At the middle school level, an interdisciplinary or team-teaching approach is the predominant instructional method. This method has long been considered a useful and practical bridge between the elementary and high school levels, allowing an easier transition from childhood to young adulthood.

The team-teaching/interdisciplinary structure provides home economics teachers with many unique opportunities. It offers an excellent avenue for establishing positive two-way communication with fellow educators. Home economists sometimes have a limited view of how their course content is related to other disciplines. More often, however, other colleagues have a limited understanding of home economics and how diverse the discipline is. As a member of a teaching team, you can make significant inroads for your particular course offerings while promoting the profession of home economics.

Being a member of a teaching team involves time and planning. To facilitate the success of interdisciplinary or team-teaching approaches, the following points should be considered:

- *Organization.* You and your administration must realize that team-teaching requires greater amounts of coordination, organization, and planning than other types of instructional methods. Adequate time for these processes must be allowed within a teacher's day.

Curriculum Design to Meet Middle School Students Needs

INTELLECTUALLY:

Middle School Students Tend To:

Be curious, inquisitive.

Prefer active learning activities.

Relate intellectual activities with immediate short-range goals.

Prefer interaction with peers.

Prefer to express originality.

Be interested in concrete and abstract concepts, growing in ability to deal with abstract.

Wish practical problem-solving situations.

Be interested in different races/cultures.

Challenge idealistic teachings.

Be interested in using basic skills used in elementary school.

Show strong, intense interest (not always sustained) in various pursuits.

THE CURRICULUM CAN BE DESIGNED TO:

Be activity oriented.

Be *now* oriented, dealing with where the student is now.

Have multiple opportunities for interaction.

Include both concrete and abstract concepts — concrete examples are used to illustrate abstract examples.

Utilize case studies, role-playing, and other tech-niques to encourage problem solving of situations drawn from practical problems students face.

Encourage integrations with other subject matter.

Integrate basic skills into teaching of subject matter.

Offer mini, exploration courses to provide for and encourage a wide range of interest.

EMOTIONALLY:

Middle School Students Tend To:

Be frequently impulsive with words and actions, impatient.

Want freedoms, but fear loss of securities.

Become more independent, but still feel a need for direction and regulation.

Exhibit a wide range of overt behavior and mood instability.

Need to experience frequent success, and desire attention and recognition for personal efforts and achievements.

Seek approval and acceptance of adults.

Be sensitive to criticism, often easily offended.

Be anxious, doubtful and confused about their physical and intellectual development, social relationships, and adult authority.

THE CURRICULUM CAN BE DESIGNED TO:

Provide a variety of activities within a class period.

Encourage open discussion of concerns common to this age group.

Provide opportunities for expression of thoughts and feelings.

Encourage an environment with a tolerance for a wide variety of emotional reactions.

Provide a wide variety of evaluation opportunities to cover wide abilities.

Provide success experience.

PHYSICALLY:

Middle School Students Tend To Show:

Increased interest in physical changes in the body.

Rapid, irregular physical development.

Differences between boys and girls, with girls maturing sooner than boys.

Concern about physical appearance and irregularities such as blemishes, scars, obesity.

Conformity with "in" styles (clothing, hair, etc.).

Restlessness — need to release energy.

THE CURRICULUM CAN BE DESIGNED TO:

Provide instruction in physical traits, hereditary, and environmental influences.

Explore physical changes typical of preadolescents.

Encourage accepting and/or changing self.

Explore factors related to self-concept.

Explore values, roles, and consumer aspects related to clothing selection, grooming, etc.

Provide activity-oriented learning opportunities.

(Continued on next page)

Curriculum Design to Meet Middle School Students Needs (continued)

SOCIALLY:

Middle School Students Tend To:	**THE CURRICULUM CAN BE DESIGNED TO EMPHASIZE:**
Seek peer conformity, but with a desire to be different.	Sorting out values, setting own goals.
Seek opportunities to make own decisions about food, clothing, activities with friends, etc.	Decision-making strategies.
Change close friends often.	Knowledge and skills for making sound decisions about what to eat, wear, buy, etc.
Have a strong need to belong to a group.	Adapting to social changes.
Adhere to peer standards, but are aware of acceptable behavior.	Understanding family and peer relationships.
Be concerned with right, wrong, and social justice — what is fair.	Influence of peers on choices of food, clothing, consumer purchases, behavior.
Be concerned for others less fortunate.	Critical thinking skills.

Developed by Home Economics Educators of West Virginia through a project with
Division of Specialized Allied Studies, The Department of Home Economics,
Marshall University, Huntington, West Virginia

- **Communication.** Team members must develop strong communication links. This means not only speaking skills, but being a good listener and having mutual respect for other people's ideas.
- **Planning Skills.** As a member of an interdisciplinary team, your instructional plans will need to be coordinated with those of other team members, both in content and in a timely manner. If a team member has poor planning skills, this process becomes more time consuming. Therefore, the task of planning becomes more efficient and effective when members understand their roles and can coordinate their efforts.

Planning for Understanding

As the number of home economics programs in middle schools increases, so does the diversity. Some programs range from less than six weeks in length to year-long programs. Still, when asked, students primarily expect traditional activities from home economics. In their minds, we may still be a "stitch and stir" profession.

For your home economics program to be successful, a great many concepts must be presented. These need to be appropriate to the developmental needs of students, address changing social needs, meet school administrators' emphasis on academics, and update and strengthen the image of home economics to our students and colleagues.

The following are a few characteristics of successful middle school home economics programs:
- Provide experiences in all areas of home economics.
- Use short units to accommodate attention spans.
- Frequently use activity-oriented lessons.
- Provide culminating activities for each unit that integrate all related learning.
- Encourage students to be responsible for learning.
- Provide community-based learning experiences.

The use of hands-on learning experiences for middle school students cannot be over emphasized. This type of teaching strategy supports the development of critical thinking skills, values, cooperation, and communication skills.

Middle school students are by nature curious, critical, insecure, experimental, and judgmental. They want and need to test information and value systems for themselves. Hands-on learning activities offer middle school students a personal "acid test" for life. Following are examples of hands-on learning experiences in various subject areas of home economics.

■ Family Life

- Role-play critical incidents in people's lives, such as job changes, marriage, and pregnancy.
- Develop a personal development plan outlining the person's goals, objectives, and desires for the next five and ten years.

225

- Explore reasons behind poor communication within families, and outline ways to improve communication skills.
- Discuss how family beliefs and values influence the values and beliefs of individuals.

■ Child Development

- Be a caregiver for a developmentally disabled child. Report on how the child's development and growth differs with that of a nondisabled child.
- Develop a business plan for a babysitting service.
- Interview people who became parents at various ages, such as teens, 20 year olds, 30 year olds, and 40 year olds. Report on how each perceives parenthood.
- Survey a home and childproof it for toddlers.

■ Food and Nutrition

- Contrast the cost, nutritional, and ecological differences between organically and nonorganically grown fruits and vegetables.
- Organize a food drive benefiting low-income families.
- Conduct a nutrition survey of students' attitudes towards school lunch and breakfast programs.
- Interview professionals working in food, nutrition, and dietetics-related careers.

■ Clothing and Textiles

- Explore ways to adapt clothing to meet the physical needs of disabled and older people.
- Discuss clothing used by various cultures.
- Contrast the ecological advantages and disadvantages of using natural fibers and synthetic fibers in apparel.
- Outline a plan for a neighborhood clothing recycling program benefiting the homeless.

Special Needs Students

Unless you have some personal or professional experience with physically disabled and learning disabled individuals, your first encounters with these students may be filled with anxiety and false expectations. It may help to remember that each person is an individual, each with his or her unique needs and talents. Whatever the disability, you will soon find a divine ability waiting to be discovered and nurtured.

Concept of Mainstreaming

Prior to 1973, physically and mentally disabled students were segregated to special schools or, at best, special classrooms within public schools. The passage of PL 94-142, the Education for All Handicapped Children Act, changed the education system forever.

The intent of this act is to provide each handicapped individual, up to the age of 21, with free public education in a setting that is most appropriate for the student's unique needs, in the least restrictive environment. This is most commonly referred to as *mainstreaming*. The act introduced the concept of mainstreaming, but it did not create a universally agreed upon definition of mainstreaming.

Least restrictive is usually defined as structuring the environment so that the student has the greatest access to needed resources. For example, a wheelchair-bound student would have difficulty getting up a flight of stairs leading into a building. The addition of ramps makes the building accessible. Other examples of providing a least restrictive environment include Braille textbooks, special writing devices for quadraplegics, and hearing aids for hearing-impaired students.

Team Approach to Teaching and Caring

You may encounter students with a variety of learning disabilities or handicapping conditions who have been mainstreamed. Federal legislation focusing on the disabled includes the following categories: mentally retarded, hearing impaired, deaf, deaf-blind, speech impaired, visually handicapped, seriously emotionally disturbed, orthopedically impaired, other health impaired (cystic fibrosis, epilepsy), specific learning disability (brain injury, dyslexia, aphasia), and multihandicapped.

Before a student is mainstreamed or placed in your classroom, the handicapping condition will be diagnosed. Once the student is assigned, you will become an important member of the student's team. Other members of this team include a representative of the local education agency, a special education teacher/counselor, parents/guardians, and, if appropriate, the student. Together, this team is responsible for making an individual assessment of the student's limitations and abilities and developing an Individual Education Plan (IEP) specifically for the student. This plan may also be known as an Individual Development Plan (IDP) or an Individual Service Plan (ISP). See an example of an IEP on page 228.

Whatever the name, the assessment process is meant to identify and make provisions for the needs of

Accommodations for Special Needs Students
(and Tips That Are Helpful for Working with All Other Students, Too)

- Establish a daily routine in your classroom.
- Be sure students are seated close to you, the board, and/or the work area.
- Seat students in a location where sound will be clear. Avoid seating them near distracting sounds or noises.
- Make sure students' work areas are clear of any unnecessary materials that may distract them.
- Allow time at the beginning of the class period to go over previous knowledge in relationship to the present lesson.
- Balance your oral presentations with visual or motor activities.
- Give verbal information or explanations along with visual presentations.
- Ask students to use assignment books or calendars or to set aside a special page of their notebooks for recording homework.
- Have students keep individual notebooks of words misspelled on assignments.
- Present new information to students in small sequential steps.
- Display samples of finished products along with the directions and materials needed to complete assigned projects.
- Begin worksheets with the easiest problems and add the harder problems in progressive order.
- Divide worksheets by cutting, folding, drawing lines, or blocking out with a large index card the portion of the sheet not being used at the moment.
- Write directions in a different color when making worksheets, charts, and learning center activities.
- Minimize copying activities by providing information on worksheets or handouts.
- Turn lined paper vertically to help students organize math problems.
- Give students worksheets that have few distracting diagrams or designs and that have few problems or questions to complete. Be sure there is plenty of free space so students do not feel overwhelmed.

- Condense lengthy written directions by writing them in brief steps. Use pictures and diagrams when possible to provide clarity.
- Permit students to use pictures and diagrams as part of their written assignments.
- Divide hard words by syllables on worksheets to help students decode phonetic words on their own or substitute an easier word for the difficult word.
- Assign follow-up activities that reduce the students' writing requirements.
- Give students an outline, chart, or blank web to fill in during your class presentation.
- Write key points on the board for students to copy during your oral presentation.
- Allow students to use computational aids such as number lines, counters, calculators, and operational computation charts.
- Provide a reference chart of letter formations that can be taped to the students' desks.
- Encourage students to verbalize the steps involved in solving problems as they work through them on paper.
- Pair students together for reading assignments. Have them take turns reading aloud to each other.
- Let students do a project instead of giving an oral report, or let students give an oral report instead of completing a written report.
- Allow some students more time than others to complete written assignments.
- Reduce the number of questions or problems on a test requiring written statements.
- Provide alternative methods of conveying test information to poor readers.
- Allow students to take oral exams instead of written ones.

---

the student. It may include a personal interview with the student, background information derived from records and reports, behavioral observations, and results of psychometric and basic skill tests. While each state may require additional information, PL 94-142 requires that each IEP contain:

- Level of present educational performance.
- Annual goals and short-term instructional objectives.
- List of services to be provided and statement of how much education the student will receive in the regular classroom.
- Date when supportive services are due to begin and the expected length of services.

The final plan developed must have parental approval.

Creating a Supportive Learning Environment

It is natural to have some concerns about working with disabled persons. This is especially true if you have limited experience with the disabled or if you have had no specific training in this area. New experiences are often awkward.

■ Personal Interactions

Begin by identifying your personal feelings about people with disabilities. How comfortable or uncomfort-

Individual Education Plan

Student	I.E.P. COMMITTEE

Student

Name: _____

Parent's Name: _____

Address: _____ Phone: _____

DOB: _____ Age: _____

Date of Conference: _____

I.E.P. COMMITTEE

Name   *Required:*

_____   Teacher

_____   Parent

_____   Chairperson

              Optional:

_____ Health/Nutrition Coordinator

_____ Parent Involvement Coordinator

_____ Social Services Coordinator

_____ Mental Health Coordinator

_____ Others

Current Level of Functioning:

Education — Prioritized Long-Term Goals:

1. _____
2. _____
3. _____
4. _____
5. _____

Health/Nutrition, Social Services, Parent Involvement:

1. _____
2. _____
3. _____
4. _____

Short-Term Objectives:

Short-Term Objectives	Special Materials and Methods	Person(s) Responsible	Evaluation Criteria	Time Line		
				Begin	Review	Achieved

Special Services To Be Provided:

Services Required	Date Initiated	Duration of Service	Provider

I have had the opportunity to participate in the development of this Individual Education Plan.

I agree with this Individual Education Plan. ☐   I disagree with this Individual Education Plan. ☐

_____   _____

Date   Parent's Signature

able are you? Any discomfort or sense of embarrassment is obvious to disabled persons — people who are uncomfortable often become too helpful or too solicitous. Disabled people want to be as self-sufficient as possible. They will tell you when they need assistance, or you can simply say, "Let me know when and how I can help you."

There is a certain amount of risk in communicating openly and freely with disabled persons — the risk of saying the wrong thing or being turned down if you offer to help. Remember, it's natural to use the words *walk* and *see*. Learn to feel comfortable with commonly used expressions even when they are not always literally accurate. If your offer of assistance is rejected by a disabled person, don't take it personally or be embarrassed. You have little to lose when you receive a no response and you have something to gain when someone says yes.

You need not feel guilty if you encounter disabled persons you do not like. The important point is that you dislike them for any of the reasons that would lead you to dislike any other person and not because of their disability.

■ *Adjustments and Adaptations*

A number of adjustments and adaptations can be made in existing programs and facilities that provide more effective accommodations and benefit both disabled and nondisabled students. These may include rearranging the room and making physical adaptations in equipment for physically-impaired students, using large print on visuals and marking equipment with tactile labels for visually-impaired students, looking directly at students when speaking and using captioned audiovisuals for hearing-impaired students, and presenting information and materials at the appropriate level for students with learning disabilities.

When you are considering making adjustments in the learning environment, remember to ask disabled persons themselves what would be most helpful. Other helpful resources for incorporating adaptations for disabled students are occupational therapists, physical therapists, special education teachers/counselors, vocational rehabilitation counselors, the children's physicians, and, if appropriate, registered dietitians who specialize in working with disabled individuals.

The question often arises as to whether all disabled children can be mainstreamed into regular classrooms. Children with severe impairments may need special considerations. For these children, there are a variety of options: some can attend regular classes with supplementary aid; others can attend a special class part-time; still others will need to be in a special class full-time. For the most part, however, students with mild or moderate disabilities can be successfully integrated into the regular classroom with much success.

■ *Classroom Aides*

Some disabled students will have a special aide or one-to-one aide assigned to them before they are placed in the regular classroom. The level of assistance the aide provides will vary, based on the needs of the students. For example, the aide may be trained in American Sign Language and work as an interpreter for deaf students. Severely physically-impaired students may be helped with personal hygiene and feeding at mealtimes. Or the aide may simply be available to help disabled students with classroom assignments and activities.

Whatever the role of the aide, take time to make him or her a part of the education team. Brief the aide on the subject matter, what expectations you have of students, the types of activities and assignments that will be made, and so on. Then, listen to the aide's comments to find out what is appropriate for the disabled students. Let the aide assist in modifying materials and activities, set reasonable goals and expectations for students, and suggest ways to challenge students. With the right approach and good communication, the aide can become a real teaching assistant.

Adult Learners

Adult education is becoming a major force in education, especially as our nation ages. For many years, the concept of lifelong learning has gained momentum among learners as well as educators. This is due to several factors. Along with an aging population, today's adults are better educated than previous generations. Many people are retiring earlier, have greater financial stability, and have more leisure time than before. Plus, the roles of women have changed, often necessitating the need for higher levels of education and greater skill development.

With this changing nature of adult education, it is helpful to understand some basic characteristics of adult learners. Typically, adult learners:
• have a higher level of motivation than younger learners.
• have higher levels of personal and professional expectations.
• are generally in adult learning situations by personal choice.
• are able to think on higher levels and solve more complex problems.

- build on and react to situations based on previous experiences.
- have diversified attitudes on life and learning.
- prefer direct and frequent feedback.
- may have time, economic, and physical limitations.
- want to learn that which is relevant to their needs.

These characteristics are keys to the educational needs of adult learners, the creation of optimal teaching methods, and managing the learning environment.

Meeting Adult Learners' Needs

Much of the success of working with adult learners depends on your ability to facilitate the teaching processes. Some ways that you may do this for adult learners are:
- Create an informal atmosphere.
- Establish a physical environment that meets adult needs, such as tables and chairs rather than student desks.
- Be aware of nonverbal clues of confusion or lack of interest.
- Keep group remarks focused on the main topic.
- Avoid talking down to the group or being condescending.
- Provide continual and varied reinforcement.
- Present new ideas in appealing ways.
- Consider outside pressures on adult learners, such as family and financial constraints.
- Be aware of adult learners' need for help with school or academic bureaucracy.
- Emphasize your role as a facilitator.

As our population ages, you may find more older or elderly students in your classroom. These learners often have greater critical thinking skills, better reasoning abilities, and better developed oral and written communication skills than younger learners. These qualities lend a delightful clarity to teaching older learners.

However, older adult learners may have some physical limitations that affect their learning abilities. Most of these limitations are the result of normal aging process and, if managed properly, will not hinder the learning process. In general, many older learners have lessened vision and hearing, decreased motor skills, and slower speed and reaction times. You may want to use some of the following suggestions to structure the learning environment or enhance your teaching techniques to minimize the physical limitations of these learners.

Classroom Environment
- Use large type on hand-outs and visuals.
- Avoid glare on chalkboards.
- Post materials high enough so bifocal wearers can read them easily.
- Use simplified tasks with modified materials.
- Use visual media frequently.

Teacher Techniques
- Speak clearly and distinctly.
- Pace the rate of presenting material.
- Assign a reasonable amount of work for a given time period.
- Use good voice tone and volume.
- Repeat questions as they are asked.

The Role of Home Economics

For each of these special audiences — middle school students, special needs students, and adult learners — home economics has the potential of providing many worthwhile experiences and opportunities. Perhaps more than any other discipline, home economics has its origins in caring and helping individuals develop and grow to meet their potential. For example, home economics offers disabled individuals opportunities to learn daily living skills, socialization skills, and employability skills. By realizing and appreciating what home economics programs have to offer, all students can benefit.

Meeting the Needs of At-Risk Youth

Chapter 28

Susan D. McLaughlin, M.P.A.
Director, Youth Service Bureau
Wallingford, CT

The student is the most essential component in the evaluation of what and how you teach. The student as a learner is the central piece in the mosaic of objectives, learning styles, methodology, teaching skills, and school climate. This chapter examines *who* is being taught. The focus is on the students' ability to absorb knowledge and to practice and master the skills taught in school. By understanding students' learning and living environments, you can develop a clearer picture of what you need to do to ensure your students' health and fitness, not only in school, but in all aspects of their lives.

At-Risk Youth

You cringe at the high dropout rate from school of our nation's teens and shudder at the suicide rate for America's youth. The traditional cry of "things have changed since I was a kid" has never been more poignant or dramatic. The three systems of family, church, and school, once the bedrock of our culture, have been changing along with our total society and no longer provide the foundations of nurturing, support, and knowledge which were once their hallmark.

- **Family**: Fifty percent of our children come from divorced homes. Less than one-quarter of American children now live in traditional families in which fathers work for wages and mothers care for the children in the home. Estimates are that by the year 2000 only one child in ten will be living in such a traditional family. Where children used to be cared for in the home by family members, they are now cared for out of the home by strangers. The extended family no longer exists for companionship and support. With corporate America relocating families every seven years, we see less stability and connectedness within the community. Family mealtimes have been replaced with carpooling, fast food, and reminder notes posted on the refrigerator. Parents spend an average of 15 minutes a day communicating with their children, and that 15 minutes includes all discipline, reminders, and instructions as well as sharing positive feedback, values, and loving messages.

- **Church**: Organized religion has less prominence in our society today than in the past. While families continue to worship and churches remain a stable force in the community, the trend is more fragmented and the act of worship itself is less of a focal point in the culture of the family.

- **School**: In the past, children learned their lessons in the home with their parents as teachers. The one-room schoolhouse offered tremendous opportunities in communal learning, peers helping peers, and school ownership. Families joined together for building maintenance and even housing the teacher. Once education began to be industrialized following the factory model, the belongingness and connectedness of school and family were diminished. The individual as a learner faded into the choice of mainstreaming or special education. School buildings are now departmentalized and physically separated into various subject areas. Standardized testing and building safety are administrative priorities. Every month of the school year 61,333 teenagers drop out of school.

Current Trends

The change in the family structure and dynamics has resulted in a dramatic increase in children's problems which are exhibited in school. As a combined result of all the aforementioned structural changes, young people have less skill and more difficulty in dealing with their own growth and development, interpersonal relationships, problem solving, and setting and attainment of goals. Trends and statistics which illustrate the nature and extent of the problems follow.

■ Alcohol and Other Drugs

- One out of four children come from a chemically dependent family.
- Alcohol and cigarettes are the substances most frequently used by students in grades 6-12.
- Nearly eight out of ten eighth graders have tried alcohol; of these, more than half have tried it by sixth grade.
- Although the number of times a high school senior drinks alcohol in a month has declined slightly in the past five years, the *amount* of alcohol consumed on those occasions has increased dramatically.
- While the use of marijuana and cocaine by high school seniors has declined in the past five years, the number of girls smoking cigarettes and boys using smokeless tobacco has increased.

■ Sexual Activity

- Almost 50% of girls have had sex by high school graduation.
- The average age of first intercourse in the United States is 15 for boys and 16 for girls.
- One out of ten girls, ages 15 to 19, gets pregnant every year.
- Per year, the chance of a girl 14 or under getting pregnant is nine out of 1,000 for whites and 51 out of 1,000 for nonwhites.
- Teen pregnancy rates are much higher in the United States than in many other developed countries.

- Although teenage AIDS cases account for only 1% of the nation's total, the number of cases doubles every 14 months.
- The syphilis rate for teens ages 15-19 has jumped 67% since 1985.

■ Living Conditions

- Every month 821 American children die from poverty.
- Every month an average of at least 56,000 children are abused, neglected, or both.
- One in every four girls is sexually abused; one in every seven boys is sexually abused.
- Every night of every month an estimated 100,000 American children go to sleep homeless.

Certainly the use of alcohol and other drugs, the rates of sexual activity and the resulting complications of pregnancy and disease, and the living conditions of abuse and poverty combine to form a distressing picture. Virtually none of these issues exists in a vacuum in that they tend to overlap with each other.

Characteristics of the At-Risk Youth

There exists an array of definitions and characteristics of the at-risk youth. Criteria include the following:
- **School Factors** — poor attendance, lack of basic skills, disruptive behavior, feelings of alienation and rejection by school and peers.
- **Home Condition Factors** — exclusively stressful and unhappy home life, below average economic status of family, minimal family solidarity.
- **Personal Factors** — low emotional and social maturity, low self-esteem, and substance use.

Certainly you conjure up personal definitions and develop your own list of students when you define at-risk. The chart on page 233 is a compilation of several studies of at-risk students conducted during the 1980s.

The key in understanding and making the best use of this chapter is to look at each student on an at-risk continuum; you know students on the eminent risk end, the low risk end, and a number in the middle. Many students tend to vasilate one way or the other in their placement on this continuum.

In reality, any youngster can exist on any part of the continuum over time, depending upon a multitude of external and internal circumstances. The prescription

Characteristics of At-Risk Students

Students who have *school-related problems* because they:

- are learning disabled.
- are below grade level.
- have repeated grades.
- have low intelligence test scores.
- have experienced school failures.
- have poor reading/math basic skills.
- have limited English proficiency.
- are underachievers.
- are gifted.
- are bored.
- have been expelled/suspended.
- are frequently tardy/truant.
- move frequently.
- create safety problems.
- are disciplinary problems.
- are hostile, passive, or apathetic.

Students who have a history of *anti-social behaviors* such as:

- criminal acts.
- acts of vandalism.
- acts of violence.
- being generally disruptive.
- a low level of social maturity.

Students from *families* with:

- a history of dropouts.
- low parental/sibling educational attainment.
- second and third generations of anti-school attitudes.
- low-aspirations.
- low expectations for student performance in school.
- no rewards for student for performing well in school.
- unstable living conditions.
- migrant-worker jobs.
- no shelter.
- a single parent.
- two working parents.
- foster parents.
- young sibling child care needs.

- criminal histories.
- substance abuse activities.
- physical abuse activities.

Students with *economic needs* because of:

- unemployed parents.
- a low family income level.
- a recent transition to a lower income.
- a need to support themselves.

Students with *physical health problems* such as:

- a chronic illness.
- a communicable disease.
- a pregnancy.
- a physically disabling condition.
- malnutrition.
- substance abuse problems.
- addictions.

Students with *mental health problems* such as:

- depression.
- a diagnosed mentally disabling condition.
- suicidal, personally destructive behaviors.
- low self-esteem/self-concept.
- no goals or direction for life.
- having been a victim of physical and/or sexual abuse.
- being under stress.
- having no stable support system.
- feelings of alienation.

Students who have *other characteristics* such as being:

- members of racial or ethnic minorities.
- members of language minority groups.
- immigrants.
- from inner city/urban areas.
- teenage mothers/fathers.
- unwed mothers/fathers.
- in need of child care support.
- in planning stages for marriage before completing high school.
- students with multiple needs.

necessary to help the eminent risk students can be debated, but the fact remains that all youngsters require a loving, nurturing atmosphere from birth through adolescence into adulthood. This comes from adults who need to be present and skilled. The extent to which children grow up with these prerequisites predetermines and continually colors their ability to function and thrive in this world. The extent to which you, as an educator, are able to provide skills and appropriate nurturing depends upon your knowledge of the problem and your willingness to adapt wherever possible to meet these needs.

Youthful Suicide

Paramount in the array of social ills are the youngsters who choose to end their own lives. Youthful suicides have increased 300% in the past 30 years, and it is reported that at least 5,000 young people between the ages of 14 and 24 take their own lives each year. Noted suicidologist Dr. Alan Berman cautions on the numbers, explaining that the stigma and disgrace associated with suicide circumvent accurate reporting. Berman has suggested that there are in actuality upwards of 50,000 suicides a year, with known suicide attempts as many as 100 times this number: 5,000,000.

Suicide is the second leading cause of death for young people. The leading cause of death is unintentional injury. The majority of deaths in this category are car accidents, many of which involve alcohol or other drugs. It is not fully known what percentage of these deaths are connected with suicidal intent. The suicide of concern here is not the altruistic suicide or last definitive act by a terminally ill patient. Teen suicide cuts a path across social, economic, and cultural strata. The only common denominator is that the victims share three H's: hopeless, hapless, and helpless.

Teenagers are the only group in this country for whom life expectancy is declining. Homicides for black teen males are at an epidemic high. Other sex variables show themselves in suicide attempts and completions. Girls are three times more likely to attempt to commit suicide; boys are three times more likely to complete suicide.

Experts speculate conditioning is an important variable here. Girls will more readily make a superficial attempt in a cry for help, while boys will be more apt to hold in all pain and despair until one fatal attempt is made. Method is also a factor, although in recent years the gap is narrowing. Traditionally, boys have employed more lethal methods such as hanging and firearms, and girls have employed methods of wrist slashing and the ingesting of pills which allow for some safety valve if the victim is discovered in time. Due to dramatic increases in the availability of handguns, increasing numbers of both sexes are turning to this method. Experts at the Centers for Disease Control in Atlanta stress that if current legislation involving handguns were enforced, 5,000 young lives could be saved a year.

As educators, many of you have experienced the tragic suicide of a student and cried out in frustration at what might have been done had someone only known the student was so desperate. The "Intervention Opportunity Model" shown below demonstrates the sequential progression of suicide and the many recognizable benchmarks along the way.

Self-Esteem Theory

It all begins with the self-esteem of the individual. The California State Task Force to Promote Self-Esteem and Personal and Social Responsibility was the first official body to link self-esteem to these seven insidious social problems:
1. Crime and violence
2. Alcoholism and other drug abuse
3. Child and spousal abuse
4. Teenage pregnancy
5. Criminal recidivision
6. Chronic welfare dependency
7. Failure to learn in school

Jack Canfield, an internationally known educator and proponent of self-esteem enhancement has been an integral member of this task force. There is ample documentation and information available on self-esteem from a multitude of experts including Hanoch McCarty, Virginia Satir, Stephen Glenn, Janet Woitz, and Louise Hay.

In the 1990 *Reclaiming Youth At Risk: Our Hope for the Future*, authors Brendtro, Brokenleg, and Bockern presented fascinating concepts of self-esteem from traditional Native American child-rearing philosophies called the "Circle of Courage," refined over 15,000 years of civilization. An excerpt is repeated here:

> Native American philosophies of child management represent what is perhaps the most effective system of positive discipline

*Each asterisk represents an "Intervention Opportunity."

ever developed. These approaches emerged from cultures where the central purpose of life was the education and empowerment of children. Modern child development research is only now reaching the point where this holistic approach can be understood, validated and replicated.

Fostering self-esteem is a primary goal in socializing normal children as well as in specialized work with children and adolescents at risk. Without a sense of self-worth, a young person from any cultural or family background is vulnerable to a host of social, psychological and learning problems. In his definitive work on self-concept in childhood, Stanley Coopersmith observed that four basic components of self-esteem are significance, competence, power and virtue:

Significance is found in the acceptance, attention and affection of others. To lack significance is to be rejected, ignored and not to belong.

Competence develops as one masters the environment. Success brings innate satisfaction and a sense of efficacy while chronic failure stifles motivation.

Power is shown in the ability to control one's behavior and gain the respect of others. Those lacking power feel helpless and without influence.

Virtue is worthiness judged by values of one's culture and of significant others. Without feelings of worthiness, life is not spiritually fulfilling.

Traditional Native educational practices addressed each of the following four components of self-esteem: (1) significance was nurtured in a cultural milieu that celebrated the universal need for *belonging*, (2) competence was insured by guaranteed opportunities for *mastery*, (3) power was fostered by encouraging the expression of *independence*, and (4) virtue was reflected in the pre-eminent value of *generosity*.

The authors of this work tell us that without belonging, mastery, independence, and generosity, there can be no courage but only discouragement. Discouragement, they say, is courage denied. When the Circle of Courage is broken, the lives of youth are no longer in harmony and balance.

As you examine the behaviors of your own students, you can assess their self-esteem by referring to this model. Some youth who feel rejected are struggling to find belonging through distorted behaviors such as gang loyalty, sexual promiscuity, cults, or overly dependent behaviors. Others have abandoned the pursuit and are reluctant to form human attachments, are lonely, isolated, or distrustful. Their unmet needs can be addressed by healthy relationships of *trust and intimacy*.

Frustrated in their attempts to achieve, some youth seek to prove competence or mastery in distorted ways, such as cheating, overachieving, developing skill in delinquent activities, or becoming a workaholic. Others retreat from difficult challenges by giving up in futility, avoiding risks, or living with feelings of inadequacy. These youngsters need involvement in an environment with abundant opportunities for *meaningful achievement*.

Some youngsters fight against feelings of powerlessness by asserting themselves in rebellious and aggressive ways. Those who believe they are too weak or impotent to manage their own lives are submissive, irresponsible, undisciplined, and easily led by others. These young people need opportunities to develop the skills and confidence to assert *positive leadership and self-discipline*.

Unless there are opportunities to give and share with others, young people do not develop as caring persons. Some may become experts in playing the martyr, others slip into co-dependent relationships, and still others become locked into relationships in which they are used. There are also those who plunge into life-styles of hedonism and narcissism. To experience the true spirit of generosity, Brendtro has pointed out that youngsters must experience the joys that accrue from *helping others*.

Each of the four values which contribute to self-esteem can be exemplified in positive and negative ways. Another way of looking at self-esteem is through the concept of deposits and withdrawals.

McCarty has developed the concept of a "self-esteem bank" which undergoes a continual series of deposits and withdrawals over a person's life. Upon birth, if an infant is cuddled, fed, and kept warm and clean, that constitutes a deposit into the bank as does parental nurturing and encouragement. Thus, when the child at age five falls off the bike, that withdrawal is covered by the excess of self-esteem deposits already in the bank. In short, while we can never avoid occasional withdrawals from the bank, we must do all we can to ensure the abundance of deposits (in the forms of skills, support, and positive experiences) to avoid bankruptcy in times of stress and difficult life transitions.

Problem Behaviors

All of us undergo stresses in life; indeed, a certain amount of stress is healthy and productive. The danger, however, occurs when a negative situation such as abuse, marital discord, or financial distress remains chronic and unresolved. Thus, ongoing stresses and inadequate or overburdened coping mechanisms combine to compound the problem.

Chronic stress results in symptoms of depression, problems in school, and high-risk behavior such as chemical use, eating disorders, and sexual promiscuity. At this point in a student's life, one of three interventions usually takes place. The first is the non-intervention, or ignoring of the problem by the parents and/or school system through ignorance, denial, or the naive belief that this problem is "just a phase." The second intervention focuses on the behavior as the problem and the child as the responsible party for this behavior. The third intervention option occurs when an enlightened helper, coupled with a willing and open family unit, work together to discover the *root* cause for the negative behavior, and they focus on treatment of the system as well as the individual. This third intervention option can halt the progression of more hurtful and harmful experiences for the youth.

The following list of problem behaviors is designed only as a guide and does not necessarily include all problem behaviors.

Depression

- ongoing, unresolved melancholia
- extreme mood swings — high highs and low lows
- hopelessness, helplessness
- tunnel vision

Problems in School

- sporadic or low attendance
- fluctuation in grades
- academic failure
- cheating
- behavior problems

High-Risk Behavior

- substance use of alcohol and/or other drugs
- inappropriate sexual activity
- eating disorders
- gambling
- drinking/drugging and driving
- legal conflicts
- abusive and defiant behavior
- inflexibility and intolerance.

Warning Signs of Potential Suicide

Warning signs of potential suicide can be subtle or dramatic. It is important to note that any of the warning signs listed here is, in isolation and short duration, probably a normal function of adolescence. The key is to look for *clusters of clues* across the three realms of physical, emotional, and behavioral possibilities and to be wary of *sudden and dramatic changes in behavior*.

Physical

- multiple physical complaints
- symptoms increase; headaches, stomachaches
- insomnia/increased sleeping
- slow or agitated behavior
- fatigue, loss of energy
- decreased concentration/decision making

Emotional

- depression, self-reproach/guilt ("I'm no good.")
- recurrent death thoughts/wishes
- loss of pleasure/interests
- persuasive sadness
- chronic anger, aggression, hostility

Behavioral

- increase/decrease in drinking/eating
- social withdrawal — dropping out of things that previously gave pleasure
- increased isolation (in room alone)
- giving away prized, personal possessions
- writing a will
- writing letters to friends, relatives, significant others
- declining school performance/sudden improvement
- purchasing of pills, weapons, ropes
- violent or abusive behavior
- tunnel vision
- helpless apathy
- sudden uplifting of spirits

Suicidal ideation is the phase in which suicide begins to be considered as a conscious option. Berman coined the phrase *suicide zone* to illustrate the flexibility and changeability of suicidal intent based on the life events, coping styles, and support systems of the individual. People can be more at risk and, therefore, closer to the suicide zone at different times of their lives, just as there can be varying degrees of intent and opportunity within the zone itself. Thus, the notion that teenagers kill themselves due to a broken relationship, failed course, or dead pet is an oversimplification of the myriad of unresolved problems and losses which have festered over time. There is often a precipitating factor, the straw that broke the camel's back so to speak, but the appropriate metaphor is that of a rubber band which has been stretched, contracted, and stretched again to the breaking point.

Gestures and attempts can be deceiving in their intent and degree. Adolescents who threaten to do themselves in, make clear superficial attempts (gestures), take an overdose of pills and call a friend at the last minute, or who slash their wrists and are discovered in time to be saved (attempts) *do not want to die*. What they want is to stop living in such pain, and through their tunnel vision they can only see death as their singular option.

It is possible to engage young people who have proceeded this far and to help them to recover their hope and their resolve to live. It is necessary, however, to obtain ample professional help and an array of support for the youth. The young person is at highest risk of repeating a suicide attempt for the first three to six months following the event, and should be monitored carefully for at least a year. With proper treatment, nine out of ten attempters can rebuild their lives with the proper skills and support and proceed without further suicidal trauma. They have been helped out of the suicide zone.

Following a completed suicide, it is imperative to address the needs of the grieving school community, the teachers, and the friends of the deceased, as well as those who did not personally know the youth. The entire school has suffered a loss, and appropriate measures of sharing the facts, providing resources to comfort the students, and offering opportunity for closure are necessary to prevent other students currently at risk from increasing their own alienation and risk level.

The Ultimate Risk Factor

Each student needs to be assessed on an individual basis to determine the level of risk for low self-esteem and harmful, or suicidal behavior. This does not necessarily require indepth psychological evaluation, but rather an episodic familiarity with respect to the student's personal history and present circumstance.

The most significant indicator of risk is the issue of loss and unresolved grief. The more familiar losses are death and divorce. But loss is a global issue which permeates every aspect of life. Loss can be real or imagined, concrete or intangible, past or projected. Examples of the wide variety of losses include the loss of a person through death, divorce, serious illness; or the loss of friends and familiar settings through a move or change in school. Family conflict and dysfunction can produce the loss of childhood, security, self-esteem, trust, innocence, personal safety, or unfulfilled dreams. Any period of transition fosters loss, and people are most at risk during these times, such as into and out of adolescence, college, marriage, a move, or a job. Thus, the youth who does not get accepted into the first choice college, who undergoes an abortion, who lives with a seriously ill family member, or who loses a treasured object must be encouraged and supported to face and work through grief in a healthy way.

Unresolved loss, which leads to depression, illness, high risk behaviors, and an inability to be "present" in life, results when denial, societal pressure, or inadequate life skills circumvent or prevent the necessary process of grieving. The progression entails acceptance of the loss, experiencing the anger and pain, adjusting to life without the lost person/object/dream, and, ultimately, reinvestment into new areas and continuation of life with a higher understanding and capability of function.

Possibly the most difficult phase for the adolescent to work through is the experiencing of anger and pain. Not only is this uncomfortable and scary for the youth as well as the observer, but these are the emotions most likely to be singled out and misinterpreted by our society. It is easy for an adolescent to get stuck in this phase; often behaviors of abuse, defiance, alienation, and depression — which is, interestingly, anger turned inward — are exhibited. Therapy, support groups, talking, writing, and working closely with skilled and caring adults are all helpful and reassuring methods of easing the youth through the grieving process.

The Holistic Model

We have cautioned that it is important to look at a variety of factors in assessing the youth at risk: physical, emotional, and behavioral. To expand on this concept, the Holistic Model adapted from O'Neil has been used.

The holistic model illustrates the five spheres of our individual make-up: physical, mental, social, emotional, and spiritual. While each sphere, or realm, is an entity unto itself, the health and well-being of each impacts upon the others.

The Holistic Model

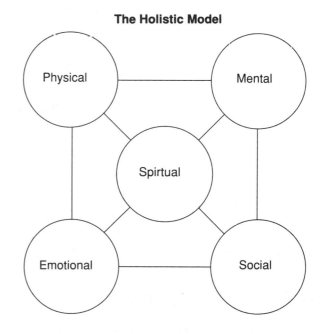

- **The physical realm** is of the body, the physical health and fitness of the individual. Nutrition and patterns of breathing have primary impact in this realm.

237

- **The mental sphere** is the cognitive realm of academic knowledge base, decision making, and problem solving. The application of healthy life skills begins here.
- **The social realm** is the seat of interpersonal and communication skills and the ability to bond in a positive way with individuals, institutions, and experiences.
- **The emotional sphere** is the base of feelings and the ability to know through personal feelings and to communicate those feelings and needs in appropriate and timely ways.
- **The spiritual realm** is the nucleus of self-esteem, self-respect, and responsibility; the personal understanding of the self in relation to higher forces, a perspective of importance and significance in the world.

The interconnectedness of this model can be demonstrated by the following example. A fourteen-year-old girl is given to outbursts of aggression and inappropriate language in class (social). She exhibits frequent mood swings, lethargy, and short attention span (mental/emotional). She complains of headaches for which she has been examined, but there is no clear diagnosis (physical). A closer look at her daily habits reveals that not only does this girl infrequently eat breakfast before school, but her diet consists mainly of sugar and dairy products. Careful coordination with a nutritionist and her doctor produces significant improvements in her physical health, thus, impacting the mental, social, and emotional realms, and ultimately creating major positive improvements in her self-esteem. Now her self-esteem bank, which was dangerously depleted due to the lack of control she was experiencing and the constant disapproval of adults and peers, has new deposits of great worth: new skills and new understanding.

It is possible to achieve good grades in school and still be at risk for unhealthy behaviors and low self-esteem. It is also possible to achieve low grades in school and still have avenues of success open to the student. We must recognize and believe that no one symptom, no one behavior tells the whole story. Therefore, each of the realms of health: physical, mental, social, emotional, and spiritual must be addressed and given opportunity to develop, grow, and achieve its fullest potential. A deficit in any particular realm will directly impact all other realms. Conversely, when a positive experience emanates from within one realm, all others will benefit.

Positive Youth Development

In addition to looking at the multi-faceted individual, it is also essential to examine the outer environments of parents, peers, school, and community. The Connecticut's Office of Policy and Management has de-veloped a model called Positive Youth Development. The PYD model was intended for and has become a primary guide for the development and implementation of youth programs.

The model is built on the premise that opportunities for skill development in themselves are not enough; there must be opportunities in the real world for the continual practice of that skill, along with positive and appropriate feedback for the young person. This, in turn, promotes and fosters the positive bonding with individuals, systems, and beliefs. This is what ultimately creates and sustains healthy, functioning, and productive citizens.

Positive Youth Development Model

Parents	Peers
School	Community

There are four major areas of opportunity, experience, and bonding for young people: the home, the school, the peer group, and the community. In order for a skill once learned within one of these areas to become habitual, the opportunity for practice and feedback must be available in each of the remaining three areas. In addition to experiences which promote skill building, practice, bonding, and positive feedback, recognition must be available within each of these areas. Ultimately, the more areas employed in the enforcement of these experiences, the stronger the skills and the healthier the self-esteem of the young learner.

For example, let's say the objective of a particular unit is to teach a stress management model in all comprehensive home economics classes. In addition to the actual lessons guided by the teacher, students practice the model in appropriate situations both in and out of school. Students team up with peer groups prior to semester exams to share and practice the skills. Parents, coaches, and school business partners in the community are taught the stress management model for themselves and how to reinforce the skills to students through a home video or workshop offered by the local mental health agency. Each group is now reinforcing the skill, providing new opportunities to practice, and is recognizing and rewarding young learners. Thus, life-long learning is fostered and celebrated.

School Based Programs

The Positive Youth Development Model requires the family, school, and community to work together to develop programs for the common good of the youth. Often simple sharing and coordination of already existing programs and opportunities are all that is needed.

But the core of effective program development can rest within the schools, and it is within this area that educators' expertise, interest, and experience are based.

■ Healthy Lifestyles Curriculum

Federal and state legislation are greatly impacting our curriculum and school climate. As mandates for drug education, human sexuality, and AIDS programs increase, we find less and less flexibility within the remaining time to teach the basics and to develop new and exciting programs. As we respond to these mandates, we are continually challenged to be creative in developing approaches which best respond to the needs of students.

Research from the National Institute of Drug Abuse, among other studies, confirms that teaching the skills of decision making, problem solving, and peer resistance lowers substance use much more effectively than "just say no." The additional benefits of imparting these skills to students include skill enhancement in other areas of their lives, and, ultimately, a significant increase in the level of self-esteem.

"Here's Looking At You 2000" is one example of a school based K through 12 curriculum which teaches substance education and decision making, along with peer resistance and the medical and legal aspects of substance use, nationwide. The D.A.R.E. program, Drug Abuse Resistance Education, is a national police sponsored program aimed at fifth graders. It is taught by uniformed officers and centered on substance information, communication skills, and self-esteem.

One way to enhance and build upon these skills that students may be learning in health or physical education classes is to offer opportunities for reinforcement of decision making, problem solving, and stress management in home economics classes. Not only are specific curriculums available, but it is also possible to adapt these concepts into existing units of instruction to further expand student skills and self-esteem.

■ Peer Programs

Many schools across the country have adopted some form of peer program, a support model of students helping other students. These peer helpers or peer advocate programs tie into school and student life in several ways. If the term *peer counseling* is used, there exists another level of skill and liability. There are extremely successful peer counseling programs, but training and supervision is much more involved.

Through a formal structure of referral, application, and orientation, a cross section of the student body is selected for the peer program. Selected students undergo training in listening, helping, and referral skills and then interface with the student body as resources. Methods vary from the very informal to structured pairing with freshmen, transfer students, students returning from treatment centers, or those experiencing life transitions such as divorce or major illness. Some programs offer peer tutoring or present educational programs to younger students. While no one will dispute the value of the work these teenagers do, the ultimate beneficiaries are the helpers themselves.

■ Guidance Groups

Due to the increasing needs of our youth, many guidance departments and support services have adapted the support group model for students. In response to overwhelming caseloads, social workers find the group concept, while not a panacea, certainly a necessary option. Groups are usually formed on the basis of a common bond: children of alcoholics/dysfunctional families; children of divorce; children in bereavement who have lost a sibling, parent, or close relation. Referral is always a sensitive issue and guidelines must be clearly defined from the outset and supported by the school administration.

The structure of the groups, be they open or closed, and the time and place of meeting are completely individual as well. Class time, study hall periods, and before and after school options each offer unique challenges. There is no ideal way to structure these groups. Willingness, flexibility, some vision, and a sense of humor are needed.

■ School Resource Teams

A suicide, the death of a teacher, a bus accident, and a space shuttle explosion are all examples of events that can hurl a school into chaos. In response to the need to be *proactive* rather than *reactive*, schools have developed an array of resource teams. Comprised of teachers, administrators, support personnel, nurses, librarians, and secretaries, each is unique to its building. Resource teams usually fall into one of three major areas, although most tend to overlap:

- **Issue focused.** This crisis resource team meets over time and develops an elaborate response to crises. It educates the students and staff about the nature of crises it will be responsible for, develops a phone tree, and develops an active plan of meetings and interventions should a crisis occur. The staff often undergoes training on issues such as crisis management or suicide prevention. Responsibility for confirming the

239

event, dealing with the press, informing the school community, and interfacing with families is pre-assigned. The group is ready for action and the school has its own insurance against panic and confusion.

- **Student focused.** Mental health or student assistance teams, which are popular at the middle school level, meet on a regular basis, usually weekly. This group is the school forum for sharing concerns about individual students, discussing the situation, and referring the case for appropriate help. Any teacher can refer a child to the team. This is a prevention approach targeting children in the early stages of problems. Student assistance teams are often coupled with peer advocate groups and advisor/advisee programs as well.

- **Prevention and education.** The true resource arm of the school, this team regularly assesses needs and gaps in services for youth, develops an assessment and referral policy, and maintains ongoing relationships and aftercare programs with those agencies and treatment centers to which they refer students. There is regular, routine dissemination of information to staff and students related to mental and emotional health offerings and activities. There are coordinated library displays and parent newsletters on relevant issues of AIDS, substances, or stress management. This team continually looks at risk factors and attempts to develop approaches to minimize them.

■ *Community Service*

Scouting, key clubs, and church youth groups all carry the rich tradition of volunteerism with community projects. Often home economics classes provide nursery care for young children or develop special relationships with senior centers and nursing homes. Community service has never been more important for young people.

Community service creates a bonding, a belonging between the student and the world at large. Whatever skill or task is performed — reading, playing games, raking leaves, or making crafts — the connection of giving of self to meet a genuine need has a tremendous impact on the giver's self-esteem. No matter how valuable and appreciated the service, the ultimate beneficiary is the young person.

Particularly now in the 90s, there is an increasing alienation of groups within our culture: the elderly, homeless, and terminally ill who are often isolated and unable to interface with the general society. Some examples of community service are:

- Plan and give a holiday party at a local school for emotionally/physically disabled children. Prepare refreshments, make decorations, sing holiday songs, play games, and perhaps dress up as Santa Claus.

- Visit a senior center or nursing home on a weekly basis to play cards, write letters, wash hair, or chat with residents.
- Tutor peers or younger students.
- Read to elementary children.
- Participate in community recycling projects.
- Offer a job bank for household chores and errands.
- Participate in a local Habitat for Humanity project.

The possibilities are limitless. You can promote the popular ecological maxim: Think Globally, Act Locally. Our youth are a tremendous untapped resource of energy, altruism, and compassion. The sophistication and cynicism of Music Television (MTV) can only penetrate that student who has no sense of worth or meaning. Many of the most successful student volunteers are the at-risk youth. They have never been aware of people less fortunate than themselves. Whatever minimal gift they can share becomes magnified, and their sense of worth and well-being makes a tremendous deposit in their bank of self-esteem, lessening the possibility of harmful behavior to themselves or others.

What Teachers Can Do

Just as we look at the total picture of the whole child in order to accurately assess need and develop appropriate programs, so it is necessary to understand and address the total environment which surrounds the learner.

The Environment

It is imperative to establish and consistently nurture an environment of safety, trust, and enthusiasm in order to foster positive learning experiences and personal growth for young people. This learning climate must build upon a common ground where interactions between, among, and around students at each level promote security, consistency, recognition, ownership, and a sense of belonging and worth on a personal, school, and community level.

The nucleus of learning is the student/teacher interaction: the exchange of positive role modeling, pertinent information, and thought-provoking questions with student presence, deductive reasoning, probing, self-discovery, and celebration. This partnership resides within the next level of interaction: student/student. Peers enable each other through bonding, support, and respect, and they work together to achieve appropriate goals and objectives on a group as well as on an individual basis. The next level of interaction is among the teach-

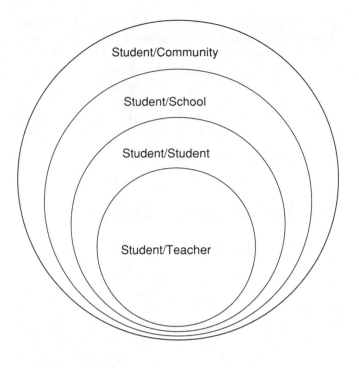

Student/Community

Student/School

Student/Student

Student/Teacher

ers and learners and the broader environment: the principal, school policies, and the physical plant. Ultimately all these exchanges take place within the rubric of the community at large.

The level of control you can exert continues to diminish the further you move from the student/teacher interaction. You can, however, set firm guidelines for peer interactions: no put-downs; one person talks at a time; respect for self, each other, and property. Students may choose their own guidelines for class interaction.

The broader environment has great impact on the student. The degree to which teacher and student input is achieved will enhance interactions at this level. As far as your program is concerned, your relationship with your principal and his or her understanding of and interest in your work will greatly color the environment.

School resource teams can play an important role in student/school interactions as well as shared decision making at the building level. This concept, long practiced in many alternative school models, promotes the involvement of teachers, parents, and students in the development of building policy, procedure, and physical environment. A certain degree of autonomy is granted to the building administration. As a result, individual schools develop a unique and client-appropriate flavor which directly reflects and caters to the truly community-based school and its members.

In the same vein, students will experience the large community to the extent in which they participate: performing community service, participating in community events, and utilizing public facilities.

Self-Esteem Building

The central and most impactful partnership is that of teacher and student. Far beyond the all-important academic knowledge the student will absorb — and, hopefully, implement — is the personal motivation for learning, and the excitement and personal rewards of achievement. In short, self-esteem.

It is possible to weave self-esteem enhancement into the existing curriculum without making major changes. Recognition of and adherence to a collection of simple guidelines may alter your methods a bit to include more group work, more discussion and sharing, or perhaps journal work, to site a few options. A highly recommended book is *100 Ways to Enhance Self Concept in the Classroom* that includes a variety of exercises and information appropriate to different ages and subject areas which can be used as is or adapted.

Self-esteem materials usually build on McCarty's theory of five conditions for enhancing self-esteem:

1. **Safety** — establishing a sense of safety and security in your environment.
2. **Identity** — creating a sense of personal uniqueness, personal contribution, and irreplaceability.
3. **Connectedness** — developing affiliation, affection, and inclusion; a network of meaningful relationships.
4. **Power** — creating a sense of one's ability, hope for success, and achievement.
5. **Models** — exploring ideals, heroes, role models, standards, and values.

In addition to these five necessary conditions, McCarty espouses five psychological needs central to the development of self-esteem and asks what you do, or can do to enhance each one:

1. **Identity** — the need to be a *unique* person, to be noticed and recognized as special. This is expressed in dress, walk, talk, word choices, hobbies, interests, and beliefs. Identity suffers when comparisons are made, feelings are rejected or minimized, judgements are voiced, and/or the person is ignored or lumped in with others.
2. **Connectedness** — the need to be accepted by others, to belong, to be part of things, and to be included or wanted. Connectedness suffers when all things are done for individuals or for the faceless mass, when all activities must revolve around the teacher, and/or when ridicule is tolerated.
3. **Power** — the need to feel potent, able to achieve something, able to succeed or pass the course, to define a desired future and be able to attain it, and to have self-control. Power suffers when teachers make all the important decisions, when the class is manipulated into rubber-stamping their ideas, and when students have no input into the choice of topics or study methods.

241

4. **Meaning** — the need to have the events in your life add up to something, to find a reason for being, to accept one's self, to have hope for your future. Meaning suffers when things seem random, when the control of your life is in other people's hands, and when you are trapped. For students, meaning is lost when lessons seem unrelated to anything of value in their lives.

5. **Variety** — the need for variety and positive changes in your daily life, to avoid ruts and sameness, and to renew the self. Variety suffers when the person is locked into the same pattern too long (patterns are comforting but can become traps), and when safety is valued over growth.

Ideally, within each course taught, you are able to develop all of these conditions to the fullest extent possible. McCarty has listed the following teachers' behavioral styles that enhance self-esteem in students:

- Really listening to students.
- Talking *with* rather than talking *to* students.
- Cutting down on advice-giving.
- Trusting students.
- Allowing a wide variety of choices.
- Allowing a wide variety of opinions.
- Consistent, regular, small praise, and positive notice.
- Positive notice for the approximation of the desired behavior.
- Sharing adult inner feelings, problems, and worries, where appropriate, and your process of coping with them and solving them.
- Taking students seriously — never laughing at or seeing them as cute.
- Sharing the tasks and responsibilities; giving students a real place in the "economy and ecology" of the classroom.
- Allowing students to have the real consequences of their choices (with moderation added for the negative ones) instead of no consequences (overprotection) or massive consequences (overwhelming).

Your effectiveness will expand in direct relation to your personal comfort level with these concepts. They are meant only to guide, not to dictate, personal style.

Teacher Education

It is no longer enough to be master of your subject area. In order to meet the needs of students in the 90s, you must continually upgrade your skills in classroom management and learning styles as well as keep abreast of new trends and developments in home economics.

The concept of professional development has expanded from the time of simple in-service days. Because of the need for teachers to accumulate continuing education units (C.E.U.s), many school systems offer real options and opportunities for personal and professional growth as a result of state mandates and built-in system-wide professional development programs. Take advantage of training on bereavement, self-esteem, and assertive discipline. If it's not available, work to make it so. Calls for increased accountability in home economics can only be answered if your skills are regularly expanded and honed.

Teachers as Human Beings

You can only provide safety, identity, connectedness, power, and positive modeling to the extent you yourself experience these things in your own life. Your ability to recognize a youth at risk and to offer the appropriate intervention is contingent upon the state of your own mental and emotional health. The amount of energy you have to help young people is directly proportionate to the support and encouragement you feel from your environment and your administration.

As an adult in the teaching profession, you exhibit risk factors: 40 to 60 percent of all teachers come from alcoholic homes, half of all teachers have experienced a divorce, and substantial numbers were abused as children. The National Association of Secondary School Principals has reported that during any given school day, eight percent of all teachers are under the influence of alcohol. You know only too well the toll that the stress of the profession can take.

In order to be fully present, to be energized and enthusiastic, you need to take inventory of your own holistic model and look at areas of strength and need. How is your level of physical fitness? Social skills? Self-esteem? Where do you find pleasure? Frustration? Success?

Take some time and design your own personal stress management plan:

- **Develop your problem-solving techniques.** Identify the source of a problem and to whom it truly belongs. Learn how to explore a problem with questions and logical steps, and how to set realistic and achievable goals.
- **Assess your personal support network.** Decide who in your network is a positive support for you and what kind of support is available: emotional, financial, child care, and/or assistance in chores. To whom do you provide support and in what ways? Who in your network causes you negative stress? Who would you like to include in or exclude from your network? Improve your skills in assertiveness and active listening, and use "I messages" and other interpersonal communication techniques.

- **Strengthen your own self-esteem.** Seek out and destroy old negative tapes ("I'm not good enough," "I'm too old/young/fat/thin") and replace them with positive affirmations. Rethink negative experiences to find the positive message for your personal growth. Unlearn irrational beliefs ("I must be liked by everyone or I'm no good," "I'm really too busy to take care of myself").

- **Learn to manage the stress.** If you can't remove the source of your stress (always the first choice) or change your appraisal of the problem ("I'm stuck here in traffic and blowing my cool won't get me there any faster"), then practice techniques that will lower your stress response, improve your health, and lessen your potential dependence upon counterproductive coping strategies such as overdrinking, over/under eating, and smoking. Deep breathing and muscle relaxation have immediate positive impact. Guided visualization and meditation emanate from the spiritual realm, quiet the chattering mind, and directly benefit your total being.

- **Enjoy natural highs.** Noted drug educator Andrew Weil promotes "natural highs," non-substances that make you feel good such as running, a beautiful sunset, sending or receiving flowers for no special reason, a favorite work of art, or an ice cream cone. Encourage yourself and your students to keep a running list of natural highs. Keep it visible, update it regularly, and enjoy them!

Ultimately, becoming familiar with your own stress management plan will enable you to impart this knowledge and related skills to your students. That is the precious gift of a life skill that has meaning and longevity. Remember that as human beings you are all in this together. School curriculum and methodology must honor each aspect of the outer and inner environment in order to foster and promote healthy students, teachers, adults, and communities. Student health and success is totally dependent upon the health and well-being of the common environment.

References

Brendtro, L., M. Brokenleg, and S. Van Bockern. *Reclaiming Youth at Risk: Our Hope for the Future.* Bloomington, IN: National Educational Service, 1990.

"Calendar of statistics." Children's Defense Fund, Washington, DC, 1990.

Canfield, J. and H. Wells. *100 Ways to Enhance Self Concept in the Classroom.* New Jersey: Prentice-Hall, Inc., 1976.

"High School Senior Drug Use: 1975-1989." National Institute of Drug Abuse, Department of Health and Human Services, Public Health Service, Alcohol, Drug Abuse and Mental Health Administration, Rockville, MD, 1989.

"Report of the Secretary's Task Force on Youth Suicide, Volumes I-V," DHHS Pub No. (ADM) 89-1621. Alcohol, Drug Abuse, and Mental Health Administration, Supt. of Docs, U.S. Govt. Printing Office, Washington, DC, 1989.

"Youth Suicide Surveillance 1970-1980." The Centers for Disease Control, Atlanta, GA, 1986.

Marketing Your Home Economics Program

Chapter 29

Effective public relations and marketing strategies are management functions that are essential for successful home economics programs. The most important strategy is to do a good job, but doing a good job is not enough. Public relations plans are designed to create a favorable environment in which a program enjoys acceptance and respect. Marketing strategies focus on selling and promoting products and services. In this case, the products are your home economics curriculum and program, and the services are home economics-related occupations and careers.

You need to be clear about what you're selling, about what home economics is today. It is much more forceful to say what home economics is than to say what it is not. The focus of home economics is the family in all its forms, and it is the only profession with this focus. Critical thinking and decision-making skills are essential for maintaining or improving the quality of life. It is essential that you have your own succinct definition of home economics right at your finger tips so you can be clear, brief, and positive when you're asked "What do you do?" or "What is home economics?"

Successful public relations and marketing campaigns are planned carefully, not left to chance. They are planned efforts to influence people to your point of view—in this case, to understand the importance, value, and benefits of home economics. You need to communicate to others the value they will receive from sharing your point of view. It has been said that public relations is doing well and getting credit for it. It is important to tell people outside of home economics about your successes.

It is just as important to plan your public relations and marketing programs in writing as it is your teaching units and lessons. Stating objectives clearly is an important component in all planning. Developing a written timetable that includes specific marketing tasks is similar to developing a scope-and-sequence chart for your curriculum. Evaluation is an important part of all planned programs to ascertain if objectives have been met. Some public relations and marketing objectives will require several months, even several years, to achieve. Few successful campaigns are short term.

Both public relations and marketing programs need to be continuous, not one-shot strategies. They need to be proactive rather than defensive. You need to communicate with a variety of strategies. Public relations and marketing cannot be left to chance.

Focusing on Your Audience

Who do you want to influence? To whom do you want to target your marketing plan? Is it sixth grade or eighth grade students in feeder schools who will be moving up to your school? Is it parents? School staff, particularly guidance personnel? School board members? Community leaders? Policy makers? Undoubtedly you want to influence all of these groups, but it is important to focus on one target audience at a time because the same approaches will not be equally effective with all groups. What may be appealing and humorous to an eighth grader may be looked upon as ridiculous by a legislator.

Students

With students, you want to point out the value of home economics courses—to show what's in it for them—how the content will benefit them now and in the future. Course titles and descriptions need to be appealing. It is important for you to be involved in the total school program so you know students and they know you. Visibility for you and your program is essential.

Parents

Parents may be interested in having their children learn more about meal preparation because they are not home to do this themselves. Parents may want their children to learn about careers, how to find a job, and how to say no.

School Staff

You will want to be cooperative with staff members, but you do not want to be exploited. If you are asked to make choir robes, use this as an opportunity to teach assembly line techniques. If you are asked to prepare refreshments, use this opportunity to the fullest. Compare home-made, convenience, and ready-to-eat products for taste, texture, and cost. When might each be most appropriate? Compare storage methods. Analyze and label the refreshments for fat, sodium, fiber, calorie, and vitamin content.

Bring teachers into your department as guest speakers and panel members. Work with guidance personnel all year, not just at sign-up time. Work to incorporate dual credit courses into the curriculum. Consider the entire school. If a particular department is overloaded, work to incorporate a cross credit course in that area.

School Board Members

Bring school board members into your department to judge contests and award prizes. Prepare a presentation to let the board know about your curriculum. Involve students in the presentation. Interact with board members on an on-going basis, not just when there are crises.

Consider your audiences' needs. Have facts and statistics at your fingertips related to this particular audience and their home economics-related concerns.

Enhancing the Image of Home Economics

You represent home economics. To people in your school and community, you *are* home economics. Do you reflect the image you're trying to sell? Before you can sell your program, you have to believe in it sincerely and deeply. You need to have established personal and professional credibility with your audiences: students, administrators, school board members, guidance counselors, and community citizens.

First, think about the image of home economics you want others to have. Plan ways to reinforce and build this image. Be sure your programs, physical environment, and the students in your classes project a favorable image.

Programs

Home economics programs that are contemporary, meaningful and relevant, well planned, motivating, and effectively taught are the best means of creating a positive image for the profession. Such programs also foster student success. Nothing will enhance your program better than successful students. They are your most effective ambassadors.

Physical Environment

Does your classroom convey the image you want to portray? An attractive, reasonably uncluttered, and clean room helps say, "Students, I care about you." Changing bulletin board displays, having plants and other decorative items, displaying student work, and having seating arrangements that foster group interaction help create a positive attitude toward your program.

People

Although your students can be your most effective promoters, it is also vitally important to have the support of your administrators, school board members, and guidance counselors. These people can make or break your program. Let them know the good things you're doing. Better yet, show them. Ask them to be guest speakers and panel discussion members in your classes, invite them to attend the Future Homemakers of America/ Home Economics Related Occupations (FHA/HERO) banquet, and encourage them to employ your students.

Your Own Image

To help you enhance your own image as a professional home economist, follow these guidelines:
- Do your job better than well.
- Practice what you preach.
- Reach out to share your expertise with others.
- Emphasize your educational and professional credentials.
- Dress professionally.
- Use effective communication skills.
- Be assertive.
- Participate in professional organizations.
- Develop your advocacy and public relations skills.

Community Visibility

Effective marketing of home economics includes the involvement of "outside" people in your program. Local business people, newspaper personnel, and other community leaders can be utilized as:
- guest speakers.
- judges for contests.
- interviewees.
- panel discussion participants.
- authorities for certain content areas.
- experts in home economics-related fields via real life experiences, such as being the parent of an adopted or special needs child.
- advisory council members.

Invite these people to the department so they gain a better idea of activities that go on there. Also, accept personal invitations to go to community meetings as a resource expert in home economics subject areas.

Visibility for your program can be gained by having posters, exhibits, displays, and activities in public places such as shopping malls, libraries, community centers, town halls, and commercial establishments. Take advantage of opportunities to use free radio and television public service announcements (PSAs), to write articles about department events for the local paper, and to publicize home economics activities through posters and on the outdoor school marquee.

Publicity Ideas

Here are some specific suggestions for activities within the community that can help sell your program by providing publicity and visibility:
- Set up displays in local grocery stores that feature "Buys of the Day." Display fresh foods and other products near the entrance. Have students give out heart healthy recipes, give customers consumer tips, and point out seasonal buys.
- Publish news articles in local papers. Feature activities focusing on consumer issues, wellness, and parenting rather than the traditional areas of home economics.
- Honor alumni of your program for their achievements. Seek endorsements from them for your program to gain greater community support. Alumni might be willing to speak to incoming groups of students, the school board, and/or the PTA.
- Use an advisory council to gain credibility in the community. Rotate people who can help you gain visibility.
- Sponsor a nutrition education poster contest. Display entries in the library, shopping mall, or other appropriate places in the community. Posters might be designed for young children and used in an elementary school. Awards may be donated by local merchants. Send your newspaper an article about the contest and winner.
- Establish a catering service to provide food for showers, picnics, and birthday parties. Use the profits for students to dine in a fine restaurant. Describe the experience in an article written for the local paper.
- Go to a community gym, exercise class, or aerobic dance group to give information on sensible weight-loss techniques and plans.
- Plan and have a party for the residents of a retirement or nursing home. With approval from the director and staff, take pets with you to visit the elders.
- Implement a telephone pal calling service in which convalescing shut-ins or elderly individuals are called daily. Call to check and be sure that the homebound person is all right. If there seems to be a problem, call the appropriate authority and request that the telephone pal's home be visited.
- Arrange furniture displays in the show windows of local furniture stores. Give your students and department credit by placing posters listing all the names in the windows. The posters could be produced in art or graphics classes.
- Implement a home cleaning business, a street number painting service for curbs or buildings, a limited plant care or rental service, or a pet-sitting business to earn money for a community-wide service project.
- Provide a Parent's Day Out Center in the Home Economics Department one morning or afternoon per week for approximately a month. Select and lead games and provide other appropriate activities for young children. Plan, prepare, and serve refreshments.
- Help sponsor a Cub Scout or Brownie troop, assist at scout troop meetings, or plan and carry out another activity for a local children's group.

- Prepare displays for a local fabric store. Illustrate pattern and fabric selections for individual school or home clothing construction projects. Rotate displays until every student's choice has been shown. This type of display could be titled "Creating an Original."
- Sponsor a display, exhibit, or demonstration contest depicting energy-saving tips, techniques, and methods.
- Have a car wash at a local store or restaurant and use the earnings to carry out a community beautification project. Use the decision-making process to select the beautification project, and develop, use, and evaluate a spending plan for implementing it. Determine how much money could be saved by substituting and exchanging various human and material resources needed to carry out the project. Suggest recycled products that could be used in place of new ones in implementing the plan, and compute the savings.

School Visibility

As you exemplify the image of a professional home economist and educator, it is important to be an integral part of the total school program. Be the adviser for the cheerleaders, director for a one-act play contest, or sponsor for a school-wide service project such as Career Day or Wellness Day. These activities give you visibility and they are enjoyable, too.

Provide exhibits and displays in the school lobby, library, and hallways that show administrators, counselors, and students the breadth and relevance of the home economics program. Ideas for reaching some of your specific audiences, such as students, parents, counselors, and other professionals in your school, follow.

Students

- Have a "Home Economics Week" when there are wellness and consumer tips given by students on the school P.A. system during morning announcements.
- Use the P.A. announcement system to play Trivial Pursuit — Home Economics Style. Have answers to the interesting questions in the Home Economics Department where teachers and students have to pass creative displays and materials to find the answers. The next day, announce the winners and give the answers.
- Have students tell about their classes and activities at a moving-up assembly for students at feeder schools. Invite these students to visit your classes, or go on a field trip to their schools to tell them about your program.
- Guide your students in working with students from lower grades through orientation meetings; teaching

home economics concepts in elementary, middle, or junior high schools; or in developing and implementing a contest related to home economics subject matter.
- Develop a video showing class activities. Be sure to show males and school leaders, and include testimonials. Also develop a slide presentation telling the home economics story to larger audiences than is usually possible with a videotape.
- Conduct a survey to find out why some students are not taking home economics. Use this information to develop recruitment plans.
- Honor a Student of the Month, or in a cooperative course an Employee of the Month. Bringing recognition to a deserving person will also bring visibility to your program.
- Use course titles that have appeal to teenagers: *Fitness for Life* instead of *Food and Nutrition*; *Creative Fashions* instead of *Clothing* (or, worse yet, *Sewing*); or *Life Skills* for *Personal and Home Management*.
- Develop brochures, leaflets, or flyers capitalizing on how home economics courses help students develop skills for a lifetime. Use words and terms such as decision making, academic content, career connection, and "high-touch living in a high-tech society" that give your courses credibility with students and parents.

Parents

- Make personal contact. Take advantage of opportunities to talk with parents about what and how their students are doing in your classes.
- Operate a "Latchkey Hotline" after school. Have students volunteer to call children when they are due to get home, or have the children call the teens so they have someone to reach out to when they are alone. This could be an FHA/HERO chapter project.
- Plan learning activities that extend class content into the home and community, such as having a child care service during ball games, visiting elders in day-care centers, and implementing clean up and beautification projects.

Counselors

- Make friends with the counselors. Friends are more likely to be supportive than acquaintances.
- Provide counselors with copies of up-to-date, attractive, and appealing home economics textbooks. Ask them to comment on those texts that focus on human development, relationships, child development, and family living.

- Ask counselors to talk to your classes about balancing work and family, developing interpersonal skills for employment, effective communication, or some other appropriate topic.
- Invite counselors to serve as judges for contests or participate in panel discussions.

Other Professionals in Your School

- Associate with other teachers. Eat lunch occasionally in the Teachers' Conference Room (don't call it the Teachers' Lounge — teachers don't lounge on tax payers' money) or the cafeteria, rather than always staying in your classroom.
- Attend ball games and other after-school activities.
- Serve on committees with a variety of teachers from other departments.
- Volunteer to go to other departments in the school as a resource expert on related topics.
- Invite the principal, counselors, and other teachers to be resource people and consultants for your program. Then they will have a better idea of what you do.
- Be a professional, in appearance and demeanor, that the principal and other teachers respect.
- Work on making home economics a required course in your school. Elective courses are being dealt less and less space in the curriculum as graduation requirements are becoming tighter. However, computer science is required in most schools because it is a management skill needed to survive in society today. That is precisely the same reason why home economics skills are needed by all students.

Effective Presentations

If you want home economics to be a required subject in your school, you will have to present your justification and rationale to your administrators and school board. It is absolutely essential to be well prepared for these meetings, as it is for all professional appearances.

Know Your Audience

Your approach, vocabulary, verbal examples, statistics, arguments, visual materials and even your attire should be chosen with your audience in mind. The size of your audience, its composition, the time of day and year, and the seating arrangement are just a few factors to consider. For example, if your audience consisted of elders you might use a reminiscing approach and a microphone. You would prefer to speak before a meal, rather than after it.

Present your material from a point of view that will be meaningful to the particular audience being addressed. Think about what will get these listeners' attention. Know their positions and attitudes. Find out who the leaders and decision-makers are.

Clarify your purpose in speaking to this group. Is it to inform? Persuade? Inspire? Motivate to action? Specifically, what action, when, and how?

Be Prepared

No presentation should be considered unimportant. Your image and the image of home economics are at stake: Here are some guidelines to follow:

- **Research your topic.** Get the latest information you can. Think about what this particular audience wants to know. Anticipate questions the audience might want answered. Be able to document your sources of information if you're asked to do so. It is usually preferable to mention facts detrimental to your cause rather than to have someone else do this and put you on the defensive.
- **Use a conversational vocabulary.** Your spoken vocabulary is different from your written vocabulary. If you write out a speech word-for-word, you are likely to use long and complex sentences that are hard to follow orally. When you write out sentences you may stumble, grasping for just the right word you had selected previously. Never use a word you had to look up in the dictionary for its meaning because it is not in your everyday vocabulary.

  Notes with only key words written down focus your thoughts without causing you to sound stilted. You want to convey that you are talking *with* your audience *not to* them. "Bifocal" notes also help you maintain eye contact with your audience.
- **Keep it short.** Very few audiences can concentrate on any topic more than 20 minutes. If you are asked to speak for 45 minutes, try to persuade the person organizing the meeting that this would be inadvisable and say why.
- **Practice.** Check your timing. Rehearse with the notes you'll use, but know your subject matter so well that you are not tied to your notes. Be so well prepared that you can deviate to react to a puzzled look or questioning glance.
- **Check out the location.** Remove detractors such as writing on a chalkboard. Refrain from passing around items while you're talking. It diverts the audience's attention away from what you're saying. If possible, do not use a podium. It puts a psychological barrier between you and the audience.

Check on the overhead projector or video player. Mark the floor with chalk or tape to indicate where the cart needs to be. Focus the slide projector so it can be used immediately. Bring an extra projector bulb.

Involve Your Audience

Effective speakers involve their audiences at the beginning of their presentations and throughout — either literally or passively. You might ask a rhetorical question which really does not require an answer. You can ask for a show of hands in affirmative response to a question. You can ask the audience to think about some lines of poetry or about a story or play. Audience members can be asked to close their eyes and imagine something you suggest.

You might put notes under some chairs so people have to get up to find them. Or people can be asked to stand up and say something to the person next to or behind them.

The Introduction

Introducing a presentation is very much like establishing set for a lesson. (See page 54.) Using *you, we,* and *our* is more effective than using *I, me,* and *my.* Limit your use of *I* unless personal self-revelation will help you establish rapport with the audience or lend credibility to your knowledge of the topic. For example, a recovering drug abuser might share this fact with listeners if that is the subject of the talk. You might tell where you're from if this helps to establish a positive atmosphere. But don't tell a joke unless it is related to the subject and leads into the presentation logically. Beginning with a gimmick is an insult to an audience.

"Today we're going to share ..." or "Today we're going to explore ..." begin positively. We like people to share and explore with us. You want to give people reasons to listen. Tell them why they want to listen — what's in it for them.

By arousing curiosity, you create interest. The unexpected grabs your attention. You want to have a memorable introduction, but not necessarily a shocking one. A well chosen question or comment can reflect concern for the audience. Within 10 seconds a person usually decides if a presentation is going to be worthwhile.

Using Visuals

Any element that adds variety, interest, or color can enhance your presentation. Here are some helpful guidelines:

- Use a visual when you think your oral explanation can be enhanced. Do not use a transparency, flip chart, poster, videotape, or other aid to stand alone.
- Prepare your audience for viewing the visual *before* seeing it by giving appropriate guidance such as:
  "Look at ..."
  "After seeing the videotape we will ..."
  "You'll notice that ..."
In other words, verbalize what it is your listeners are supposed to understand from viewing the visual.
- Use aids that contain only material directly pertinent to your topic. Eliminate whatever might divert the audience's attention to other matters.
- Keep visuals simple. Too much information on any one graphic can be overwhelming. When there is too much reading, the audience tends to read ahead rather than listen to you. A graphic should be like a visual outline with you providing the details.
- Use large visuals and bold lettering with straight lines. Be sure that your visuals can be seen and read easily from all parts of the room. Run type horizontally, even on graphs and charts. Make it as easy as possible for the audience to follow you.
- Remove a visual from sight so the audience does not dwell on it when you want attention focused on the next point.
- Pretest sight lines and sound levels from all the places in which the audience will be seated. Pretest the workings of any equipment that has to operate in any way.
- Give your attention to the audience when using visuals, not to the aids. You are the chief communicator, and your listeners need your attention. To maintain eye contact, have copies of what is being projected and glance at them rather than the screen.

The Conclusion

The end of your presentation might be a call for action. It might answer a question asked in the introduction. It should bring to mind the major points made in the presentation. It should be remembered later as people reflect on the talk. It might be memorable because it is dramatic. There is no need to say, "Now in conclusion ..." This tends to send a message like "You can stop listening now. The presentation is over."

Presenters sometimes say, "Thank you" to indicate that a talk is finished. If your conclusion is effective, it should be evident that you have finished.

Answering Questions

When an individual asks you a question, look directly at that person until the question has been asked.

If you can, take a step toward the person. Repeat the question to the entire audience, then answer the question for the entire audience. In other words, don't just answer the person who asked the question.

Don't force your audience to ask questions. If there are none, it may be because you did an excellent job of explaining your topic. If you don't know an answer, it is better to admit it than to give incorrect information. It might be appropriate to say "I'll try to find the answer for you. If you give me your phone number (or address if more appropriate), I'll get in touch with you."

Some Don'ts

- **Don't apologize.** Avoid sentences such as these:
  "I'm really not well prepared, but ..."
  "I don't know much about ..."
  "I don't want to offend anyone, but ..."
  If you don't know the subject, the audience will realize this without you mentioning it. Saying you don't want to offend anyone is sure to do just that.
- **Avoid too much repetition.** When you are told something too often, you begin to question, "Does this speaker think I'm stupid?" And you are offended.
- **Avoid giving too many statistics orally.** Statistics are hard to follow unless they are portrayed visually as well as orally.
- **Avoid the word little.** Saying I have a little handout or a little poster makes it seem unimportant.
- **Do not thank the audience for listening.** Thanking the audience for listening is like apologizing. It

lessens your impact. Can you imagine the effect if Patrick Henry had said, "Give me liberty or give me death. Thank you very much."?

Successful Writing

Effective public relations and marketing strategies usually involve writing — for news articles, newsletters, radio, and/or public service announcements.

Some ways to make your writing readable are to keep in mind these S-words:
- Simple, short, specific, and concrete words.
- Strong, action verbs.
- Short sentences, but with some variation.
- Short paragraphs, keeping in mind that there are six to eight columns per page in many newspapers.
- Spelling, grammar, and punctuation without errors.

Writing News Articles

The A, B, Cs of news writing are Accuracy, Brevity, and Clarity. Using the smallest possible words and writing with few adjectives and adverbs help you achieve these desirable characteristics.

Include the following at the beginning of your article: *Who* did *what, where, when, why,* and *how*? These italicized words are called "The Big Six" of news writing.

The *who, what, where,* and *when* are in the first paragraph of the story. *Why* usually comes after the first

---

BASIC B'S FOR PUBLICITY

1. **Be the only person** from your group to contact news media. Two members calling the same newspaper editor or program director are bound to bring conflict or confusion.
2. **Be quick** to establish personal contact with the right persons at each newspaper, radio and television station in your area.
3. **Be sure** to write everything down. Train your memory, but don't trust it.
4. **Be prompt** in meeting every deadline.
5. **Be legible.** Type or word process all news releases. If typing, erase and correct errors carefully.
6. **Be accurate.** Double check dates, names, places before you submit your copy.
7. **Be honest and impartial.** Give credit where due.

8. **Be brief.** Newspaper space and air time are costly.
9. **Be brave.** Don't be afraid to suggest something new if you honestly believe you have a workable idea. Media people welcome original ideas when they're practical and organized logically.
10. **Be business-like.** Never try to obtain publicity by pressure of friendship or business connections. Never ask when a story will appear. Never ask for clippings.
11. **Be appreciative** of all space and time given your group's publicity. The media giving it also have space and time for sale.
12. **Be professional.** Members of the press are always invited guests. Never ask them to buy tickets or pay admission. Arrange a special "Press Table" for large banquets.

paragraph. *How* is often used later as well. You will want to tell who is involved in what. Where and when it is going to take place or did take place. Where and how you can get in touch with the best person to provide more information. Why this event is of interest. How you get there.

Put the most important information in your article first. Write the rest in descending order of importance. When an article is shortened, it is cut from the end. Your less important information would be that which is eliminated. A weekly newspaper is more likely to publish your article than a daily, and a weekly is more likely to use the article just as you send it.

Write out numbers from one to ten. For 11 or more, use numerals. Exclamation marks are not used. Use Lisa Smith's full name the first time she is referred to; thereafter use Smith.

Remember that three-fourths of the word *NEWS* is *NEW*. Don't wait so long to send your article that it is no longer newsworthy.

■ *Pictures*

Black and white photographs are sent to newspapers. Some points to keep in mind when taking pictures to accompany an article follow:
- Make the picture as self-explanatory as possible.
- Be sure the picture tells your story quickly.
- Use action shots whenever possible.
- Be sure people look natural, not posed.
- Use a background that strengthens your message without distracting from it.
- Select interesting, dramatic shots that catch the reader's attention.

Writing Newsletters

Newsletters to parents, administrators, and school board and advisory council members are effective means of keeping your audience informed about your program and activities. You control and edit what goes in a newsletter, whereas a news article or public service announcement may be changed and edited by someone else. You also control the audience that receives your newsletter, whereas with mass media you are not sure of the audience at any given time.

A newsletter must pass the "refrigerator test," meaning that the perspective reader will decide whether to read the newsletter before reaching the kitchen with it. If the reader is not motivated to read it immediately and puts it aside to read later, in all probability it will not be read at all.

Free space, headings that break up the page, and some variation in print help motivate people to read. Two or three columns are effective because they can be read more quickly than wide columns. Clip art consisting of simple line drawings add interest. Of course any of these techniques can be overused and create a cluttered effect.

Keep the tone conversational and personal by using *you, we,* and *us.* Use the present tense when possible. Also be consistent in using or not using a comma at the end of a series, in using P.M. or p.m., and in capitalization. Any of these may be correct, but if you use different forms throughout the newsletter some seem wrong.

Consider what your audience *wants* to know and provide some of this. Also consider what your audience *needs* to know. Use some of what it *wants* to produce what it *needs*.

■ *The Name*

Alliteration or a play on words may be helpful in deciding on a name for your newsletter. A title such as *News to Use, Inside Information,* or *Reader's Roundup* may appeal to your audience. Consider having a contest to select the name for your newsletter. Then include an article about the contest winner and the chosen name.

■ *Types of Articles*

You want a balance of news, feature, editorial, and promotional columns. Consistency in types of feature columns gives you credibility. For example, you might consistently include letters to the editor on the second page, tips for readers on the third page, and a calendar of events on the last page.

Writing for Radio

Before writing, decide on your purpose. Do you want your listener to try a new practice, abandon an old one, consider alternatives? Send for a booklet, attend a meeting, join a campaign? You need to identify your goal precisely. Here are some guidelines:
- Make your opening as appealing as possible. Don't talk about pesticides or even insects; instead, describe the juicy apples that will be available in the fall if ... After you've pictured the possible benefits, tell your listeners how they can get them.
- Keep your sentences short, no longer than three lines. If you have a three-liner, follow it with a short sentence or even a fragment.

- Use dots to indicate breathing spots and to make reading easier:

  As she packed the car, she checked off the essentials: His sleeping bag and tent ... food for seven days ... an all-weather jacket ... insect repellent ... and stamped postcards to send home.

- Use dashes to make titles easier to handle:

  The President of the Extension Homemakers Club — Mary E. Smith — used an antique pruning fork to cut the ribbon, opening the 50th Home and Garden Show exactly at 9:00 a.m.

  Note that the name comes after the title in radio.

- Keep an informal sound by using contractions instead of complete words: "I can't go." (Not, "I cannot go.") Use *won't, wouldn't, don't.* Short, simple words are best. Speak to inform, not impress. Listeners can't ask you to repeat when they don't understand.

- Put power in your writing by using strong, active verbs. Instead of using a verb and an adverb, look for a verb that says it all:

  He walked erratically.

  He staggered.

  The coach spoke loudly.

  The coach hollered, bellowed, shouted, or screamed.

  She struck him sharply.

  She punched or slapped him.

- Avoid freight trains:

  He's going to get going in the morning.

  He leaves tomorrow.

- End your copy with a clear call to action.

Writing Public Service Announcements

A 30- or 60-second public service announcement (PSA) advocates some change of behavior or attitude. For example, you might want listeners to follow the Dietary Guidelines, to check total interest charges on installment loans, or to enroll in your new adult home economics class. Be sure listeners know what's in your recommended course of action for them.

Keep your message simple. About 30 words is average. Use short sentences, no longer than three lines. Follow a long sentence with a short one. Remember that with radio PSAs there are no visuals. People are not hanging on your every word. They may be working or driving the car, so repeat names. If you use a telephone number, try to get one that spells a word associated with your cause. Read your message aloud for timing and ease of breathing.

Type or word process your message on soft paper so the pages won't crinkle as they are turned. Triple-space the copy and use wide margins so it can be edited easily. Use caps and lower case, not all caps, unless requested. Be sure to do the little things that make your copy attractive at the stations. Of course, check that names, dates, times, and other facts are accurate. Include your name, address, and phone number in case the station wants to check the authenticity of the PSA or get more information.

Here are some other helpful guidelines:

- Use dashes (---) for pauses:

  Home economics --- focusing on the family --- is more important today than ever before.

- Use dots (...) for pauses in a series of items:

  Home economics includes child development ... consumer education ... housing and interiors ... resource management ... nutrition and foods ... family studies ... textiles and clothing.

- Keep sentences short and clear:

  Good: Linda Jones won first prize.

  Poor: Linda Jones, who attended the 4-H Youth Camp at Mt. Dora last August, won the blue ribbon.

- Use simple verbs:

  Good: She walked.

  Poor: She sauntered.

Shaping Public Policy

Most members of the Senate and House of Representatives want to try to represent their constituents. However, their perceptions of their constituents' views often depend on who they hear from, how often they are contacted, and how persuasive the people and the facts are that gain their attention.

Compile Valid Information

Collect data showing how home economics is being affected by budget cuts and tax changes. These facts are important, but it is equally important to identify how individuals are being affected personally by cuts in funding to home economics. Describe how federal money is used to benefit specific groups of citizens such as pregnant teenagers, abused children, and at-risk families.

Contact Your Legislators

Contacting legislators is the most effective way of getting support on legislation. Letters and phone calls from constituents help legislators make up their minds on how to vote. However, personal letters addressed to specific legislators are much more effective than form letters. An individual's letter need not be long to be persuasive.

Here are a few suggestions for writing an effective letter:

- Address the recipient correctly. For a U.S. representative, send it to: The Honorable (name), U.S. House of Representatives, Washington, D.C. 20515; or if a senator, The Honorable (name), U.S. Senate, Washington, D.C. 20510.
- Be specific. When writing about a particular bill, try to identify the bill by name and number. In the House, bills are listed H.R. (number) and in the Senate, S (number). If you do not know the number, then give a description.
- Write early so it will do some good.
- Be brief, but take time to give your own views. If the particular topic you are writing about directly affects your life, state this. Whether you support or oppose legislation, give reasons for your position.
- Be polite. Name-calling and other similar approaches detract from the effectiveness of letters.
- Ask for assistance. Members of Congress are happy to answer questions and provide information. Some have newsletters you may receive.

Calling or writing your legislator is good, but not as effective as arranging to meet him or her. Consider having a meeting where you invite your local legislators to learn about your programs. Send letters of invitation about two weeks in advance, and call a couple of days in advance to confirm that the legislator is coming. Talk about why you are concerned about home economics. Real life stories are good—but be careful that they are not too long. Give a few examples that are to the point. You might want to have some information to hand out.

Let your legislator know that you are a registered voter. Tell her or him that you vote, and if you represent other registered voters, convey this.

Send a thank-you note to a legislator who meets with you. Maintain contact and let that person know that you're interested in the political process and that you'll be watching the outcomes of votes.

Develop Public Support

Get all the press you can. Keep an eye on the media to determine which reporters are most likely to give you coverage. Let them know who you are and what you're doing. Feed them information and ideas for articles or, better yet, send them ready-to-use stories and photos. Invite reporters to your advisory council meetings and/or invite a media person to be a council member. This will be a good investment of time for this person because other important people are on the council. Other ways to communicate your message follow:

- Letters to the editor are more often published if you react to a recent editorial, news story, or letter to the editor. Perhaps you can point out an irony.
- Weekly question-and-answer columns in your local paper may be a forum for getting your message to the public.
- Radio and TV talk shows in less populated areas often need guests with current issues. Some of your students would be effective interviewees.
- Radio and TV call-in shows can help you make an impact. Get your students, their parents, and other supporters to call in and ask questions that give you the opportunity to communicate your message positively. You want to respond to misunderstandings and to predictions with which you disagree, but don't get caught up in a defensive mode of operation. Remember that it is much more effective to be proactive than reactive.

Index